Mixed Vegetables

Volume 8
CONTENTS

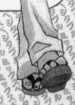

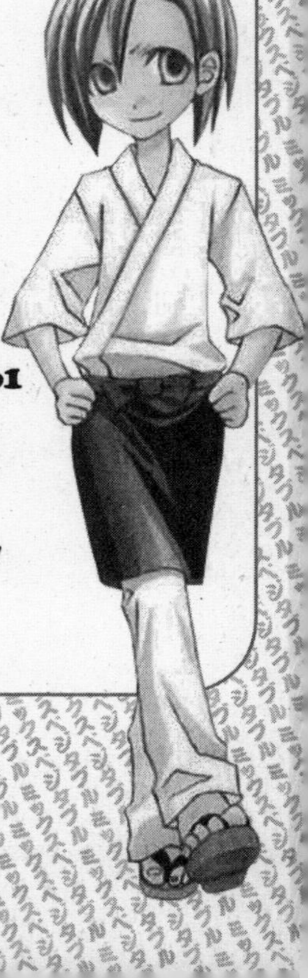

Shojo Beat

Mixed Vegetables

Vol. 8
Story & Art by
Ayumi Komura

Hanayu's classmate; his family owns a famous sushi shop called Sushidokoro Hyuga—but he dreams of being a pastry chef!

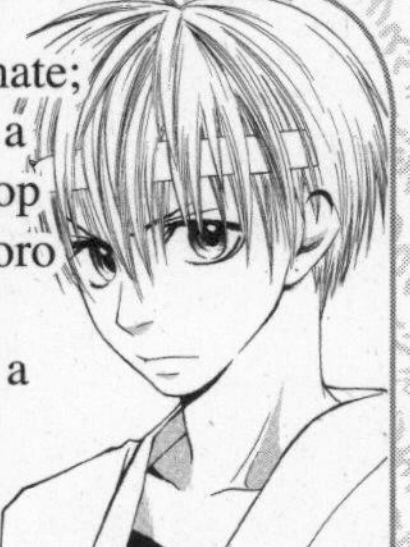

Hayato Hyuga

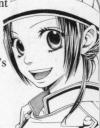

First-year student in the culinary-arts program of Oikawa High School; a baker's daughter who aspires to be a sushi chef.

Hanayu Ashitaba

What happened in Volume 7:

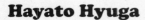

Hanayu begins apprenticing at Hayato's family restaurant, Sushi Hyuga, alongside Hayato and is finally on her way to making her dream come true.

While Hayato's dream is to make pastries, he can't forget a promise he made to his late grandfather to take over the sushi shop. When he's offered the chance to join the Ashitaba family pastry-tasting trip to France, he agrees to go so that Hanayu can stay in Japan and continue studying sushi.

Hayato's in pastry heaven until he learns some unsettling news—Hanayu's father is planning to open a pastry shop in France… and he wants Hayato to join him!

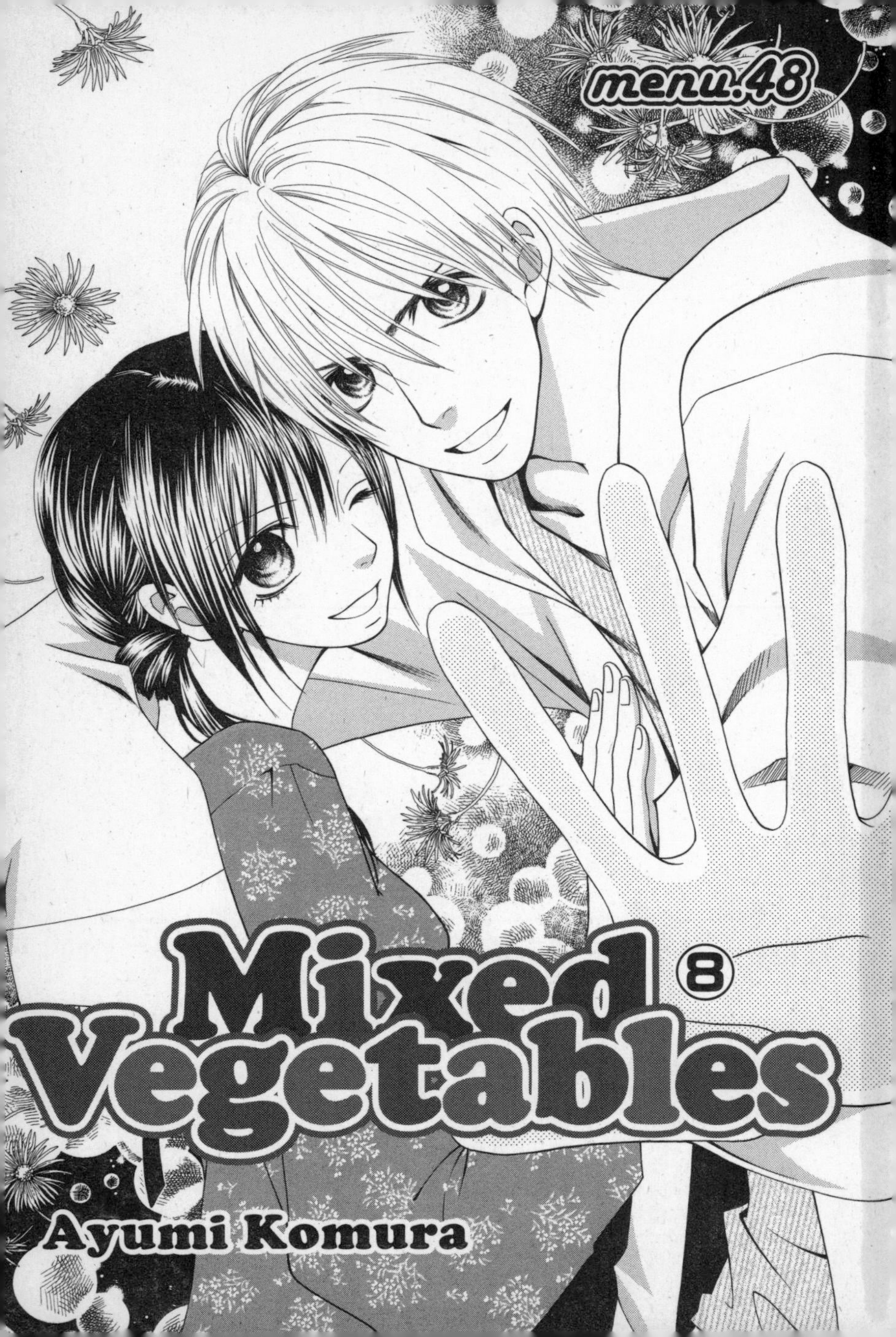
menu.48
Mixed Vegetables 8
Ayumi Komura

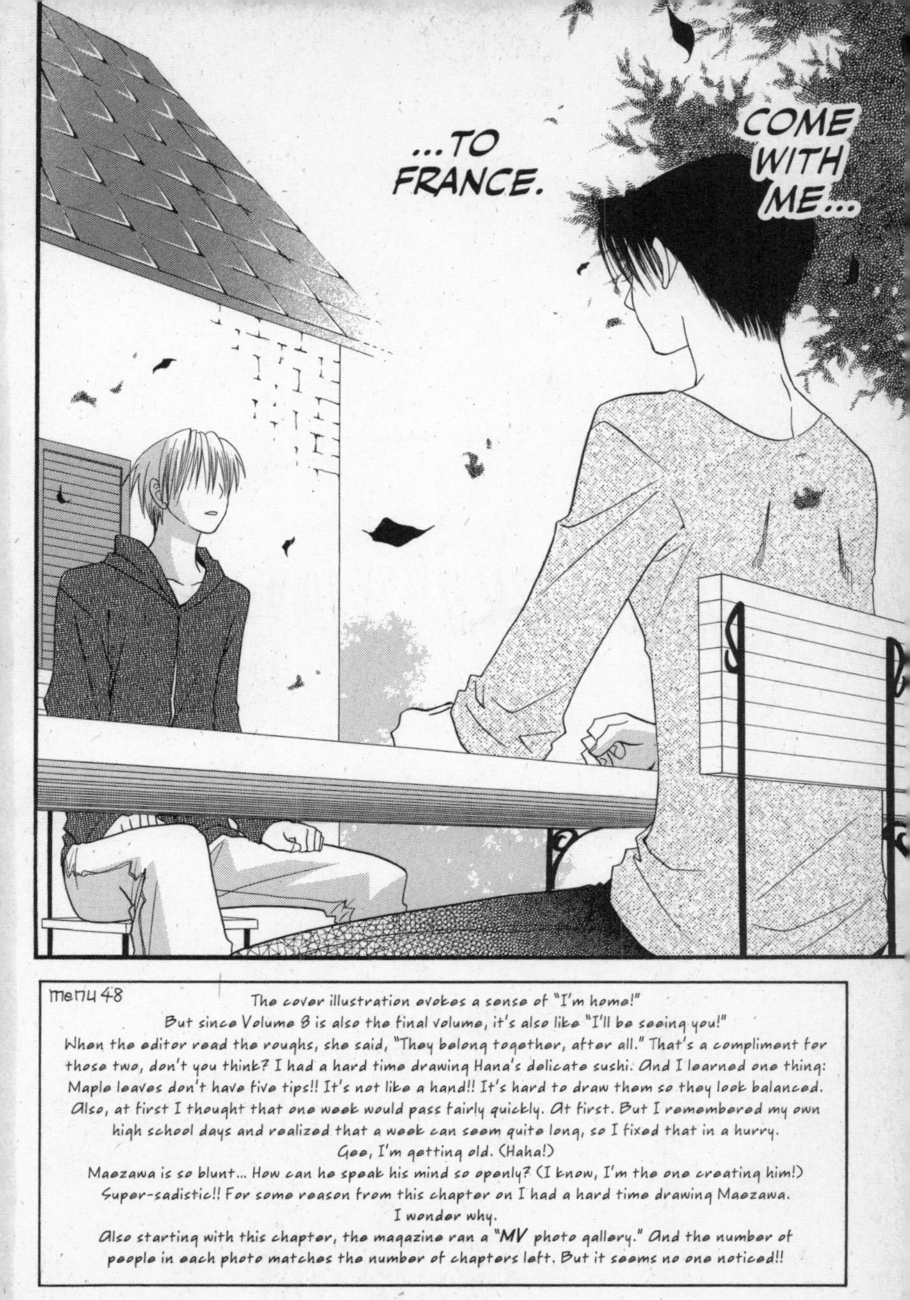
COME WITH ME...
...TO FRANCE.

menu 48

The cover illustration evokes a sense of "I'm home!"
But since Volume 8 is also the final volume, it's also like "I'll be seeing you!"
When the editor read the roughs, she said, "They belong together, after all." That's a compliment for those two, don't you think? I had a hard time drawing Hana's delicate sushi. And I learned one thing: Maple leaves don't have five tips!! It's not like a hand!! It's hard to draw them so they look balanced. Also, at first I thought that one week would pass fairly quickly. At first. But I remembered my own high school days and realized that a week can seem quite long, so I fixed that in a hurry.
Gee, I'm getting old. (Haha!)
Maezawa is so blunt... How can he speak his mind so openly? (I know, I'm the one creating him!) Super-sadistic!! For some reason from this chapter on I had a hard time drawing Maezawa.
I wonder why.
Also starting with this chapter, the magazine ran a "**MV** photo gallery." And the number of people in each photo matches the number of chapters left. But it seems no one noticed!!

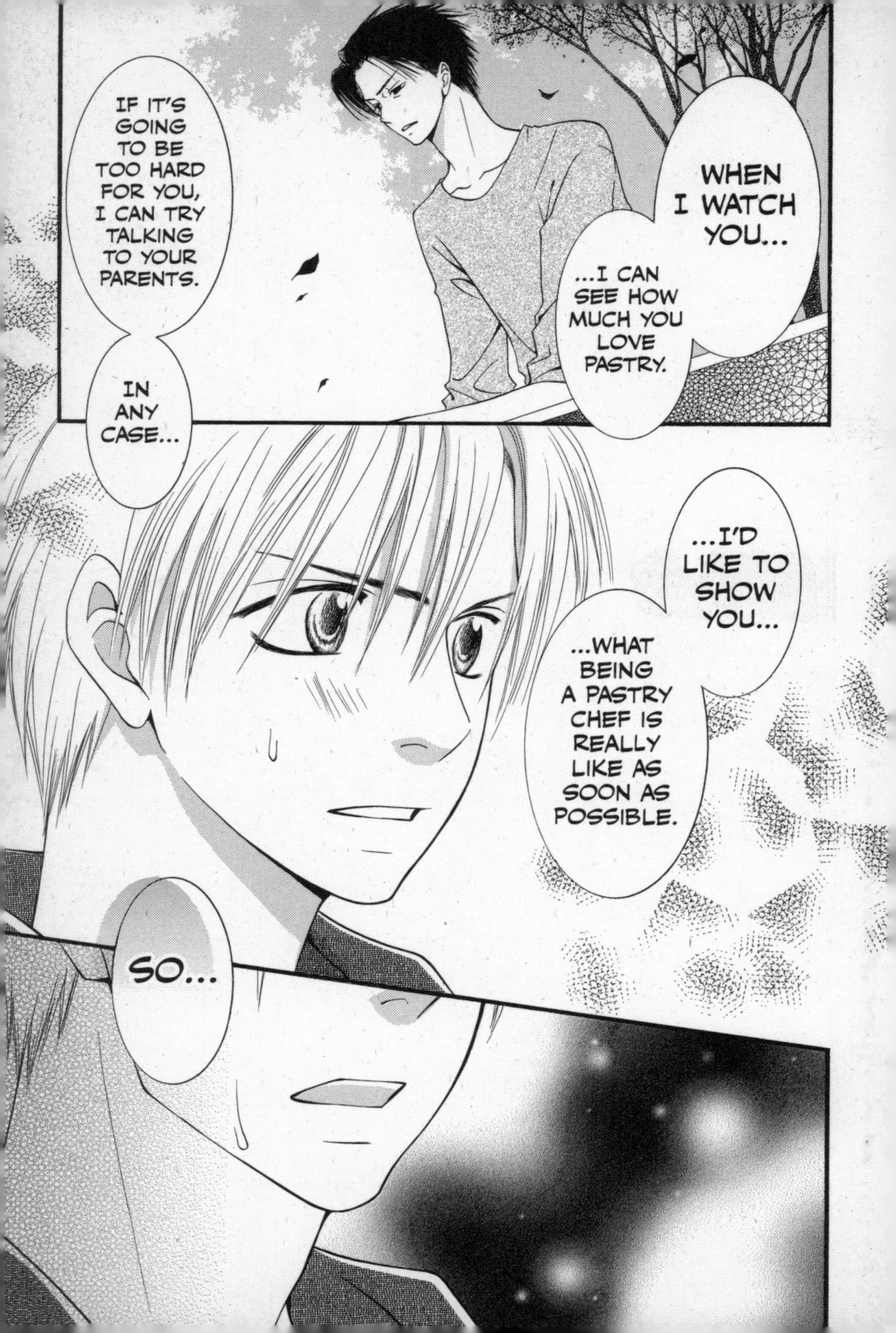
WHEN I WATCH YOU...
...I CAN SEE HOW MUCH YOU LOVE PASTRY.
IF IT'S GOING TO BE TOO HARD FOR YOU, I CAN TRY TALKING TO YOUR PARENTS.
IN ANY CASE...
...I'D LIKE TO SHOW YOU...
...WHAT BEING A PASTRY CHEF IS REALLY LIKE AS SOON AS POSSIBLE.
SO...

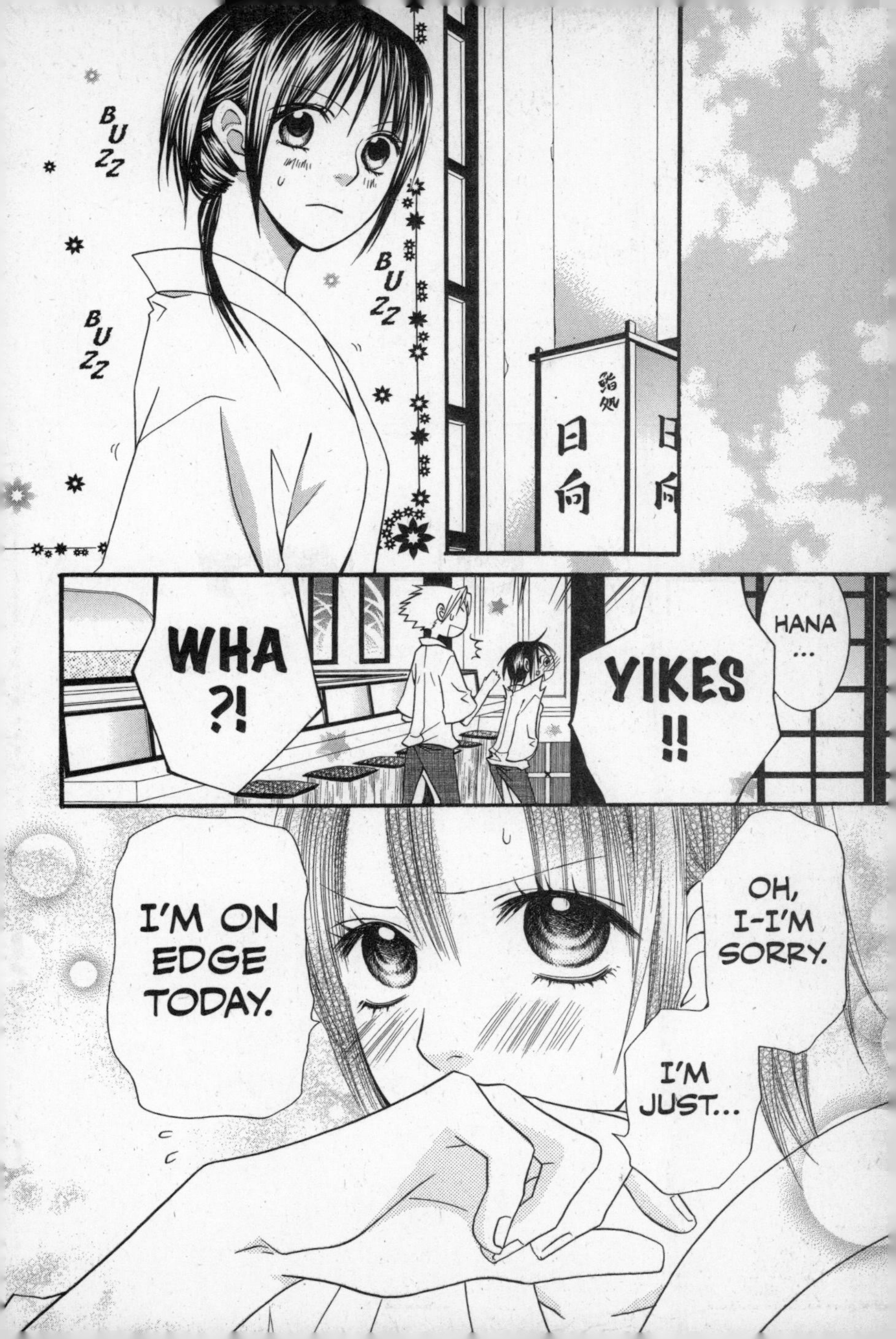
BUZZ
BUZZ
BUZZ
日向
日向
HANA...
YIKES!!
WHA?!
OH, I-I'M SORRY.
I'M JUST...
I'M ON EDGE TODAY.

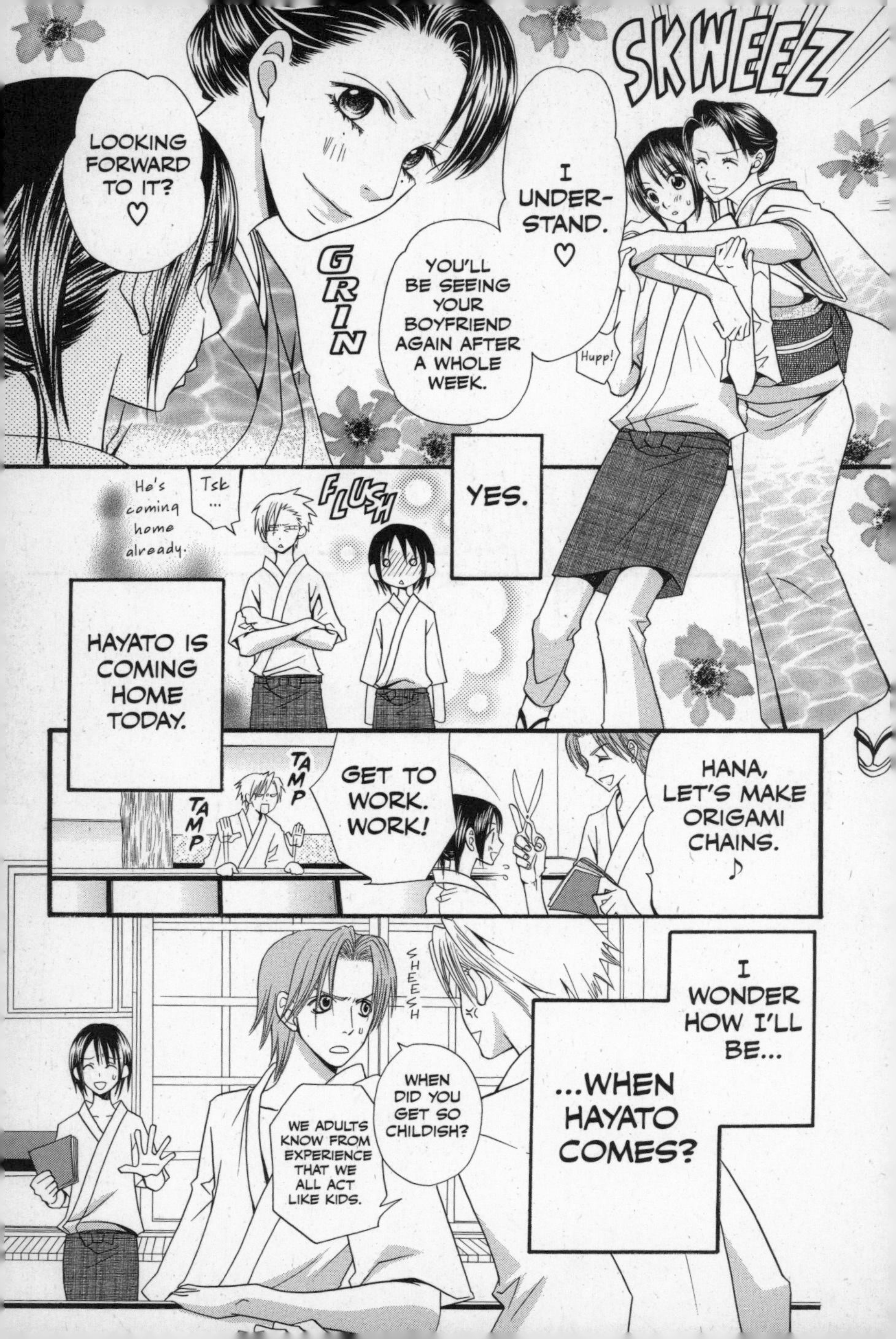
SKWEEZ
I UNDER-STAND. ♡
Hupp!
YOU'LL BE SEEING YOUR BOYFRIEND AGAIN AFTER A WHOLE WEEK.
GRIN
LOOKING FORWARD TO IT? ♡
YES.
FLUSH
Tsk ...
He's coming home already.
HAYATO IS COMING HOME TODAY.
HANA, LET'S MAKE ORIGAMI CHAINS. ♪
GET TO WORK. WORK!
TAMP
TAMP
I WONDER HOW I'LL BE...
...WHEN HAYATO COMES?
SHEESH
WHEN DID YOU GET SO CHILDISH?
WE ADULTS KNOW FROM EXPERIENCE THAT WE ALL ACT LIKE KIDS.

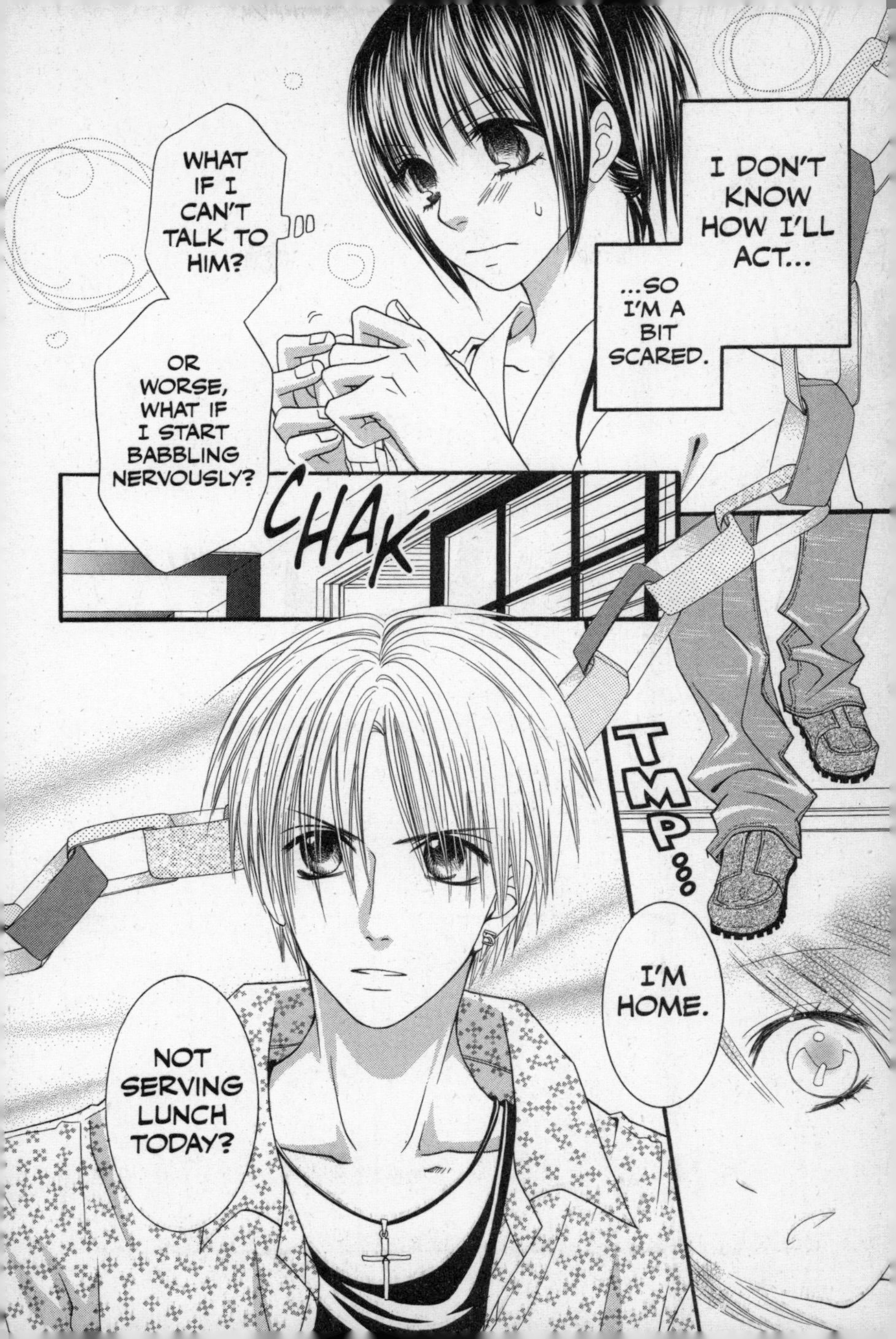
I DON'T KNOW HOW I'LL ACT...
...SO I'M A BIT SCARED.
WHAT IF I CAN'T TALK TO HIM?
OR WORSE, WHAT IF I START BABBLING NERVOUSLY?
CHAK
TMP...
I'M HOME.
NOT SERVING LUNCH TODAY?

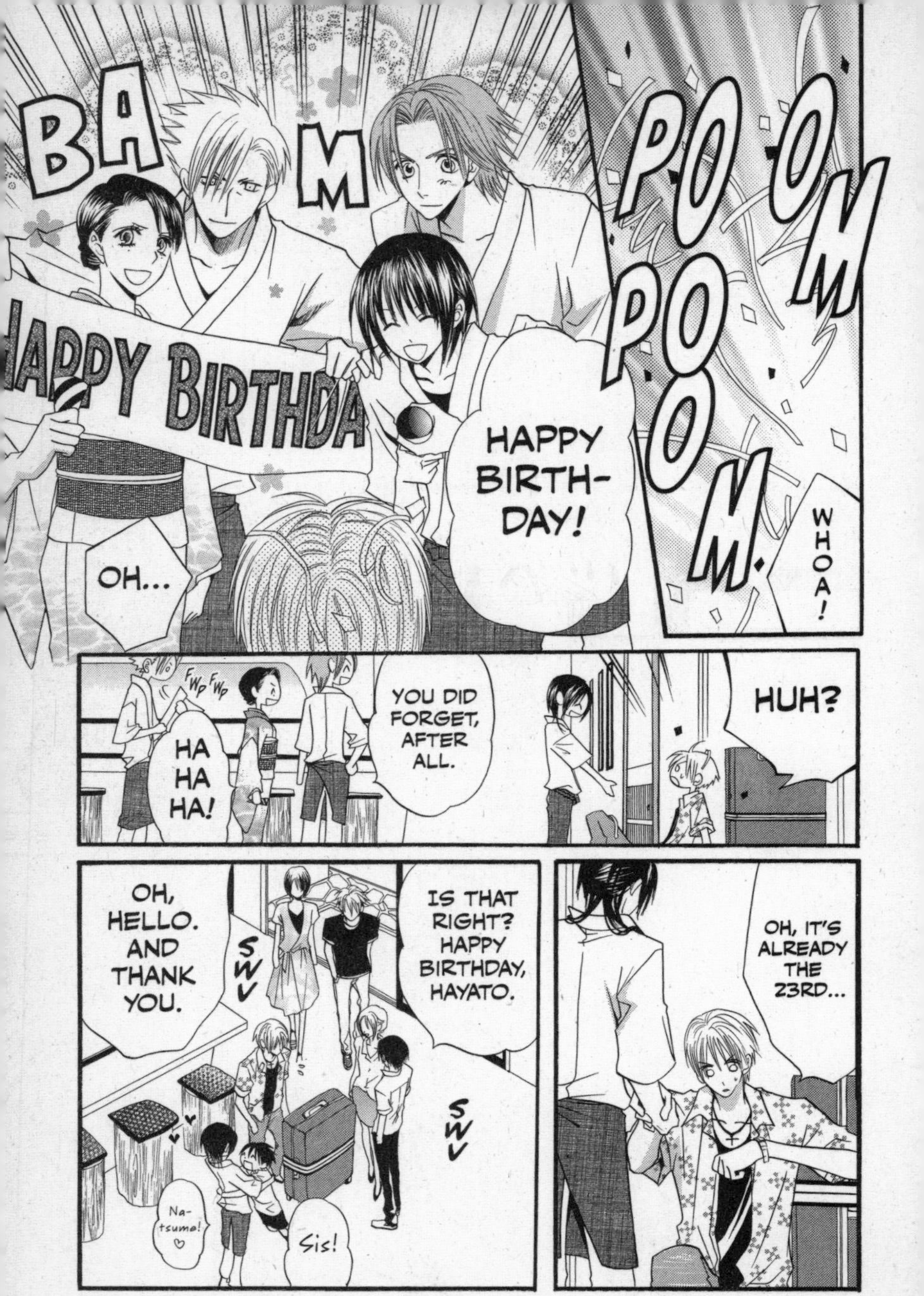
POOOM POOOM.
WHOA!
BAM
HAPPY BIRTHDAY!
HAPPY BIRTHDA
OH...
HUH?
YOU DID FORGET, AFTER ALL.
HA HA HA!
FWP FWP
OH, IT'S ALREADY THE 23RD...
IS THAT RIGHT? HAPPY BIRTHDAY, HAYATO.
SWV
OH, HELLO. AND THANK YOU.
SWV
Sis!
Na-tsume! ♡

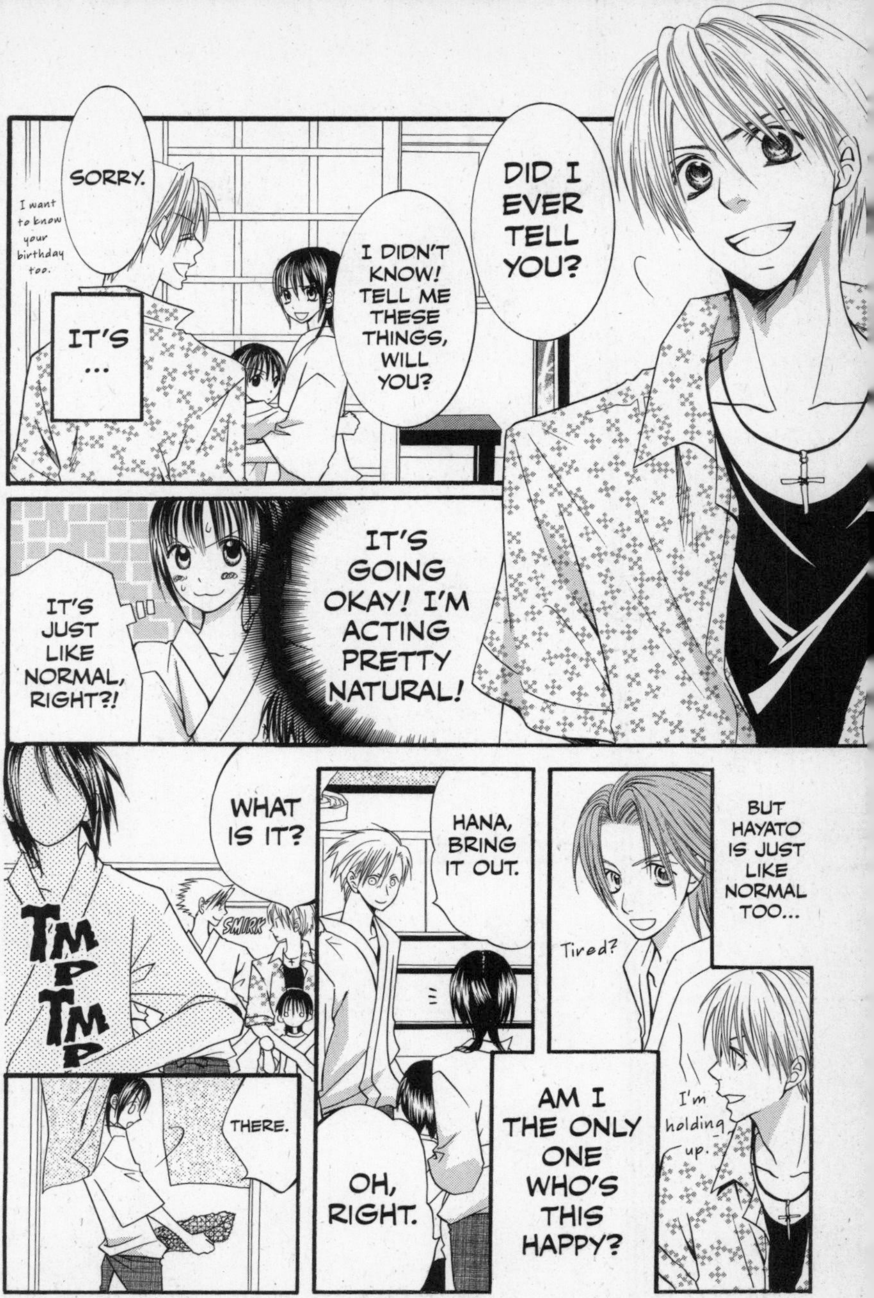
DID I EVER TELL YOU?
I DIDN'T KNOW! TELL ME THESE THINGS, WILL YOU?
SORRY.
I want to know your birthday too.
IT'S ...
IT'S GOING OKAY! I'M ACTING PRETTY NATURAL!
IT'S JUST LIKE NORMAL, RIGHT?!
BUT HAYATO IS JUST LIKE NORMAL TOO...
Tired?
AM I THE ONLY ONE WHO'S THIS HAPPY?
I'm holding up.
HANA, BRING IT OUT.
OH, RIGHT.
WHAT IS IT?
SMIRK
TMP TMP
THERE.

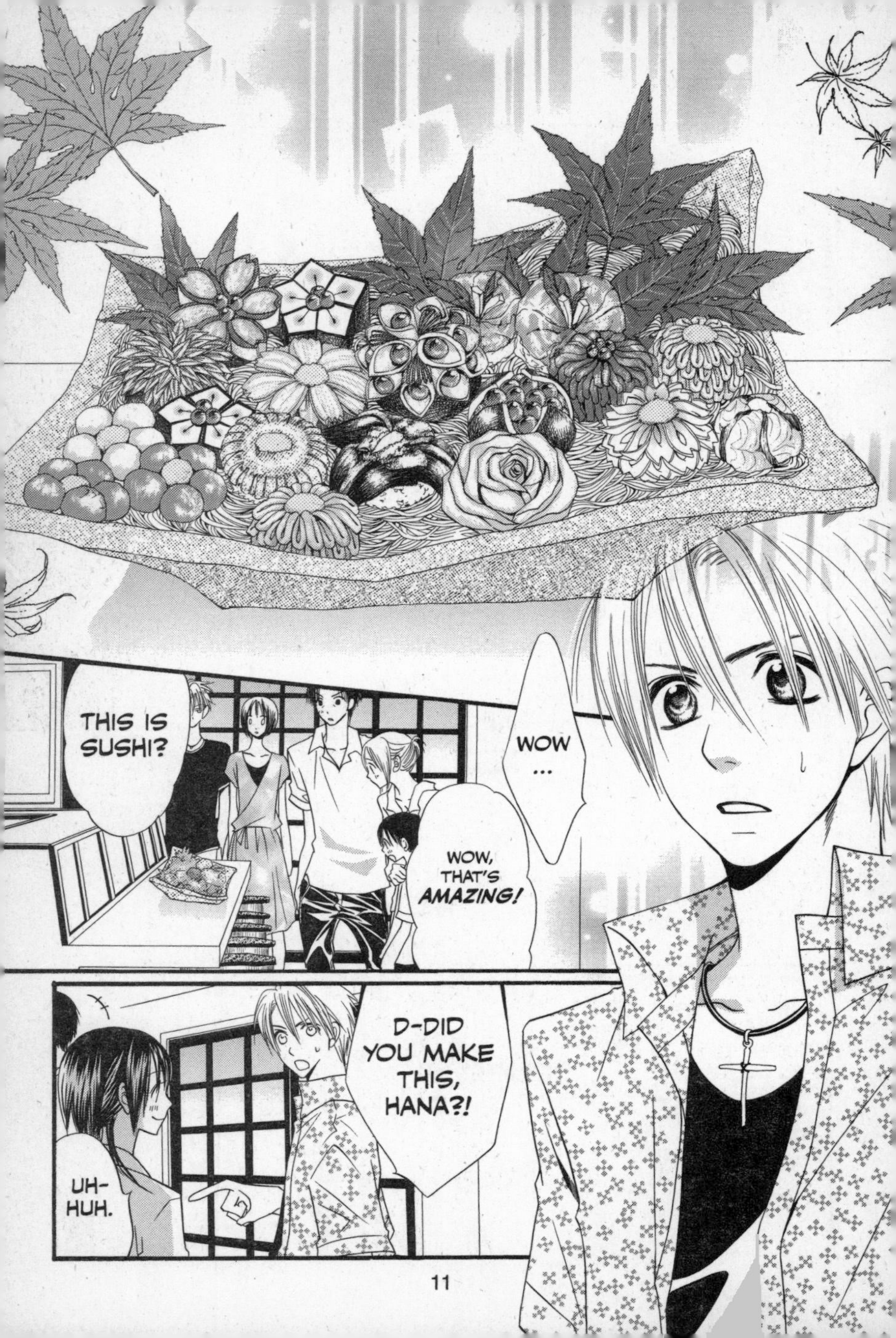
WOW ...
WOW, THAT'S AMAZING!
THIS IS SUSHI?
D-DID YOU MAKE THIS, HANA?!
UH-HUH.

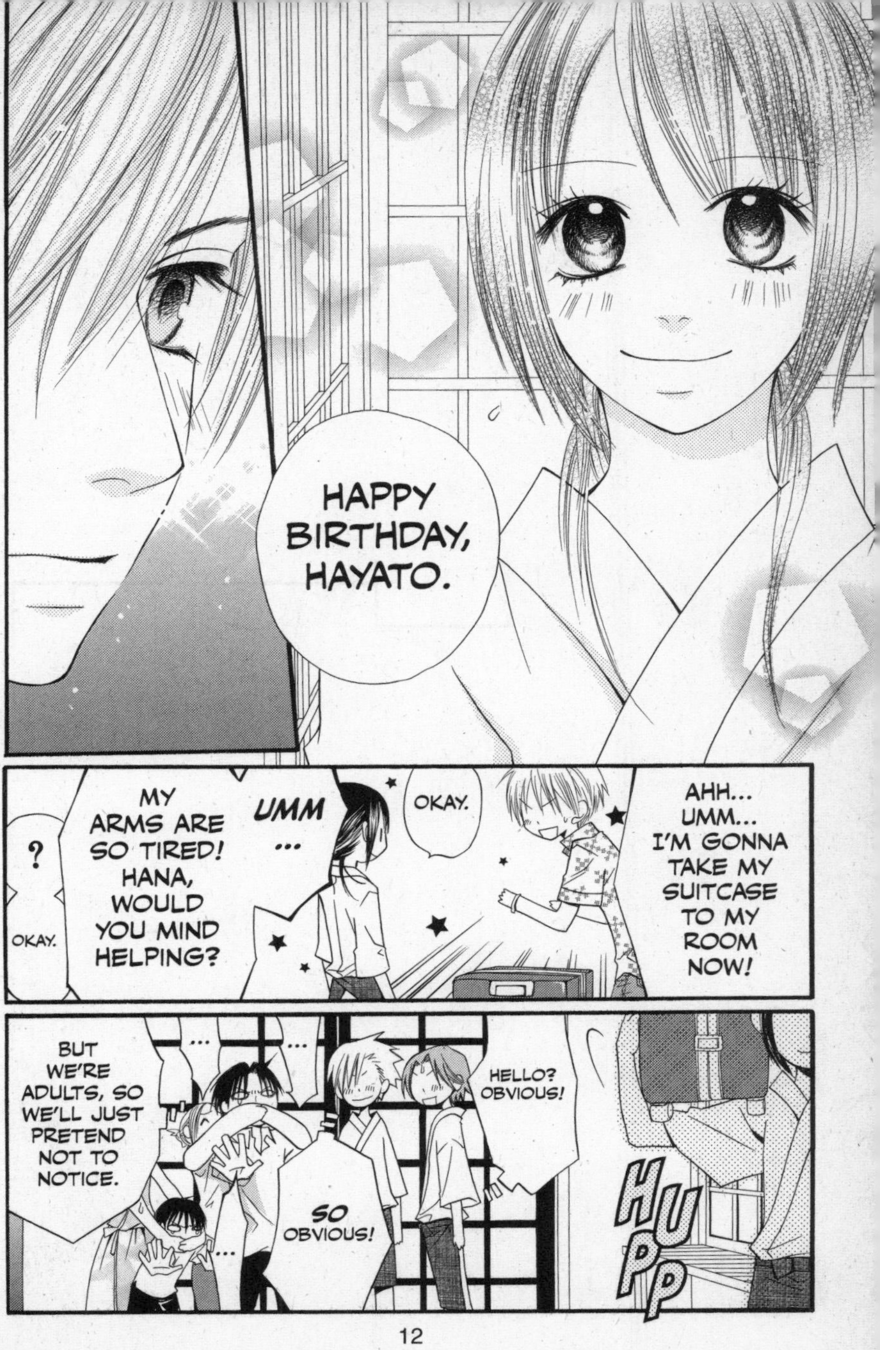
HAPPY BIRTHDAY, HAYATO.
AHH... UMM... I'M GONNA TAKE MY SUITCASE TO MY ROOM NOW!
OKAY.
UMM ...
MY ARMS ARE SO TIRED! HANA, WOULD YOU MIND HELPING?
?
OKAY.
HUPP
HELLO? OBVIOUS!
...
...
BUT WE'RE ADULTS, SO WE'LL JUST PRETEND NOT TO NOTICE.
SO OBVIOUS!
...

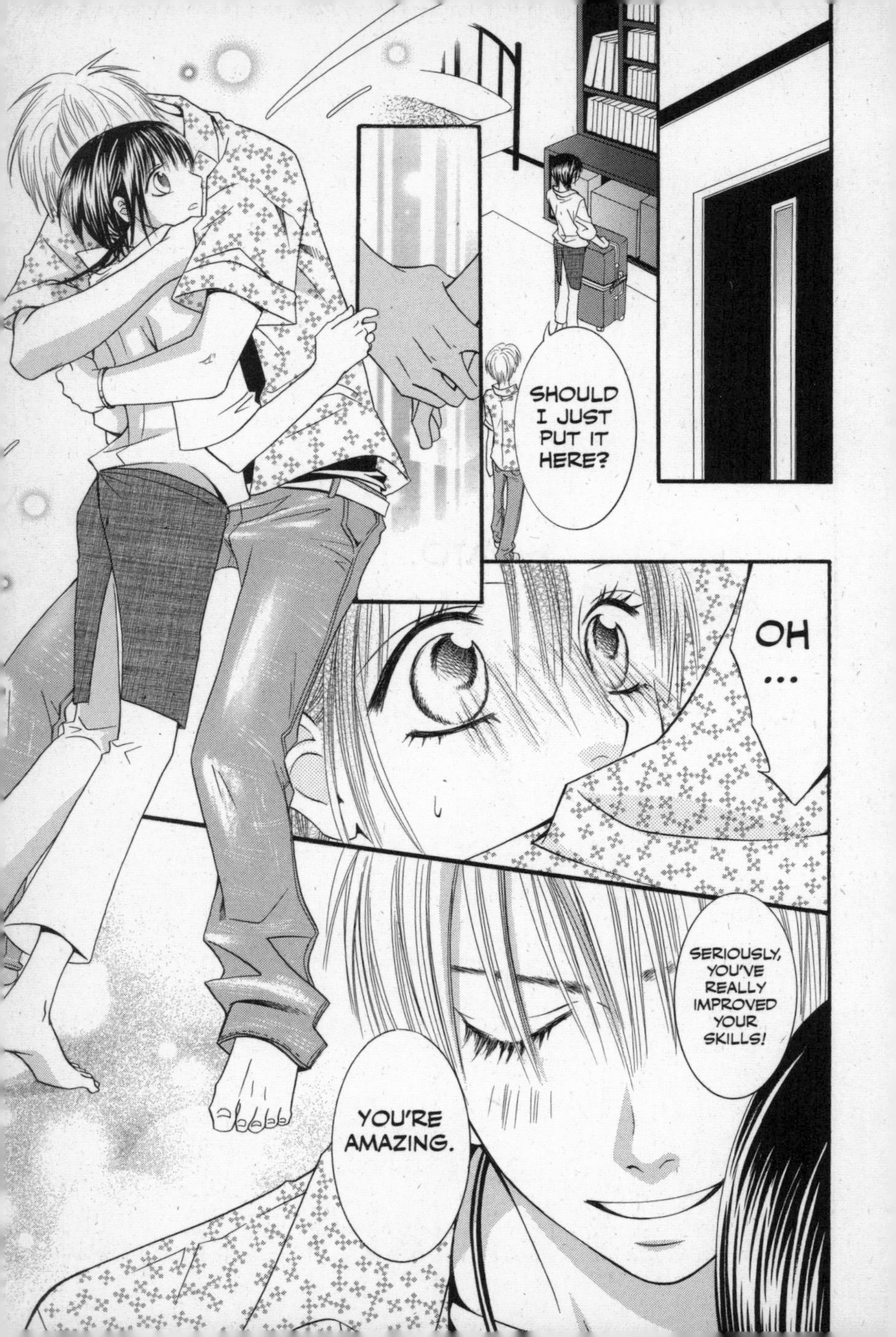
SHOULD I JUST PUT IT HERE?
OH ...
SERIOUSLY, YOU'VE REALLY IMPROVED YOUR SKILLS!
YOU'RE AMAZING.

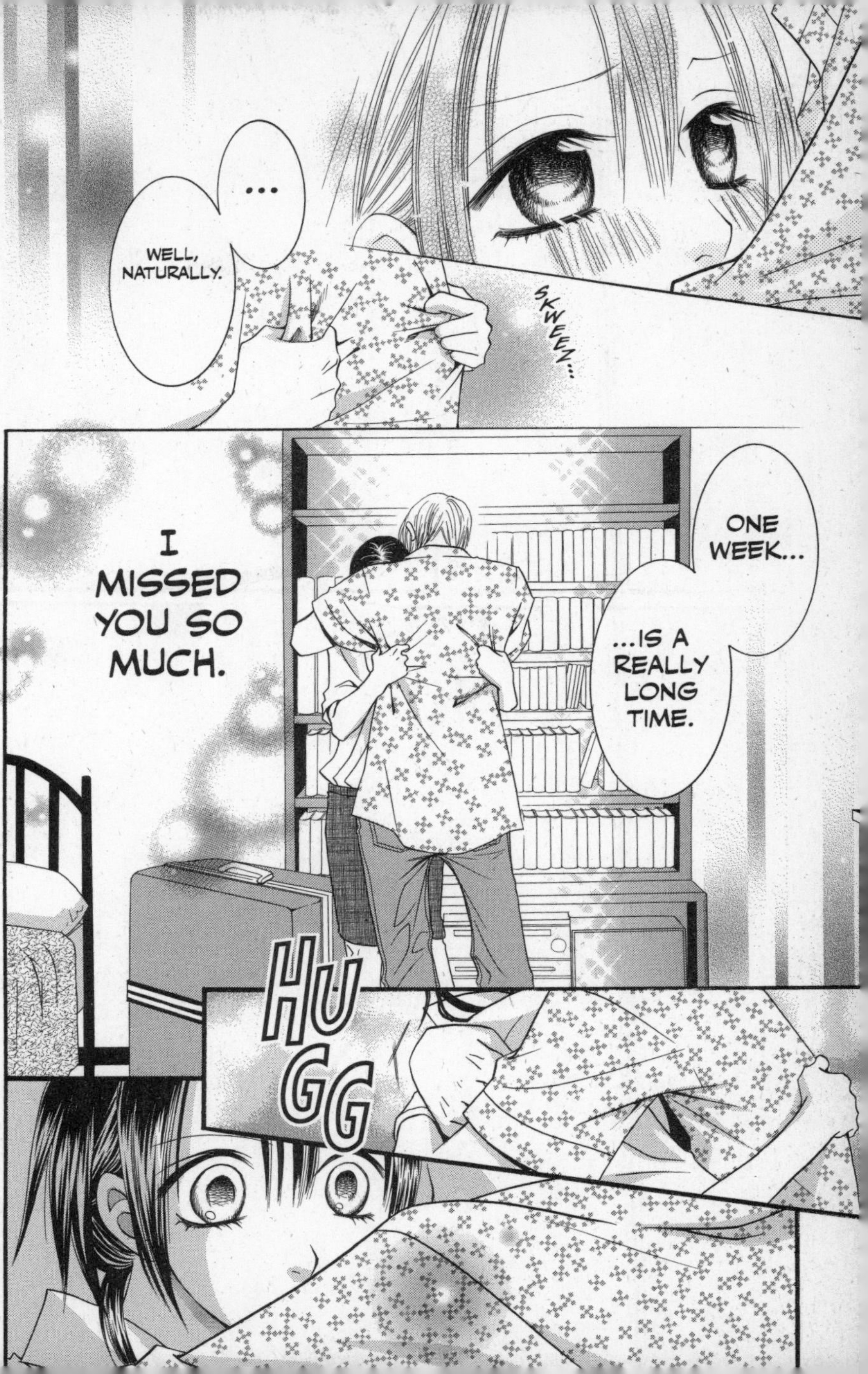
...
WELL, NATURALLY.
SKWEEZ...
ONE WEEK...
...IS A REALLY LONG TIME.
I MISSED YOU SO MUCH.
HUGG

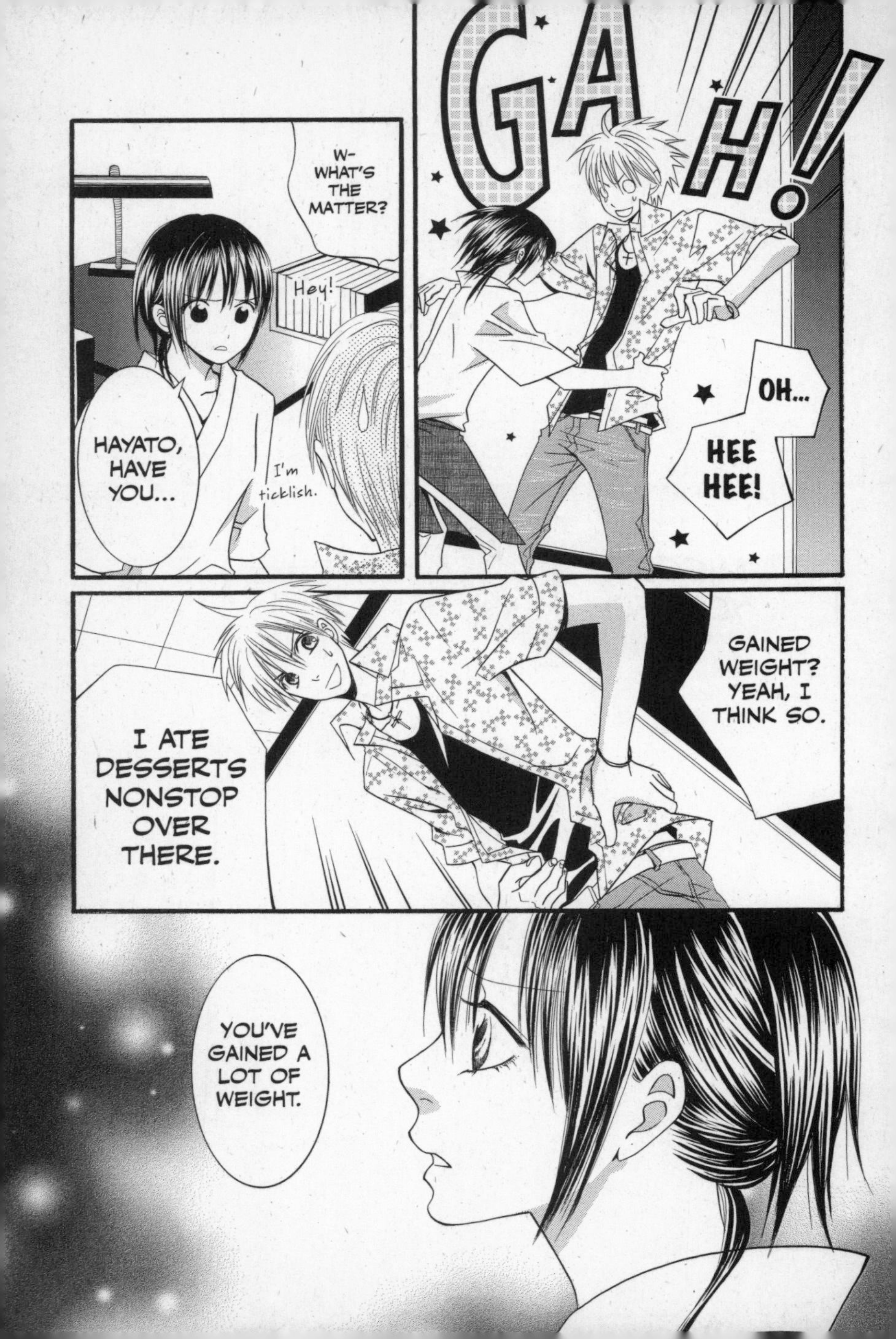
GAH!
OH... HEE HEE!
W-WHAT'S THE MATTER?
Hey!
I'm ticklish.
HAYATO, HAVE YOU...
GAINED WEIGHT? YEAH, I THINK SO.
I ATE DESSERTS NONSTOP OVER THERE.
YOU'VE GAINED A LOT OF WEIGHT.

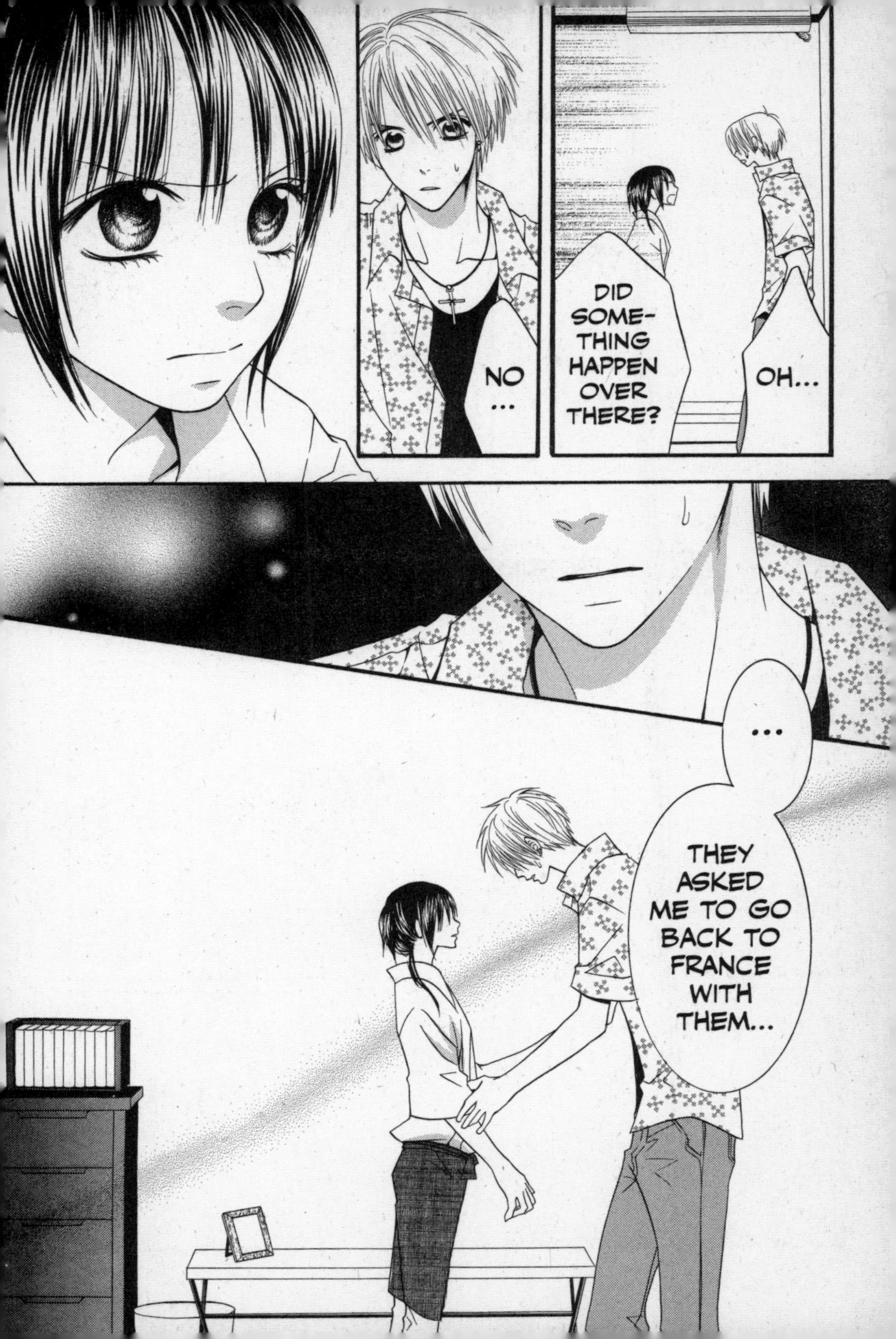
OH...
DID SOMETHING HAPPEN OVER THERE?
NO ...
...
THEY ASKED ME TO GO BACK TO FRANCE WITH THEM...

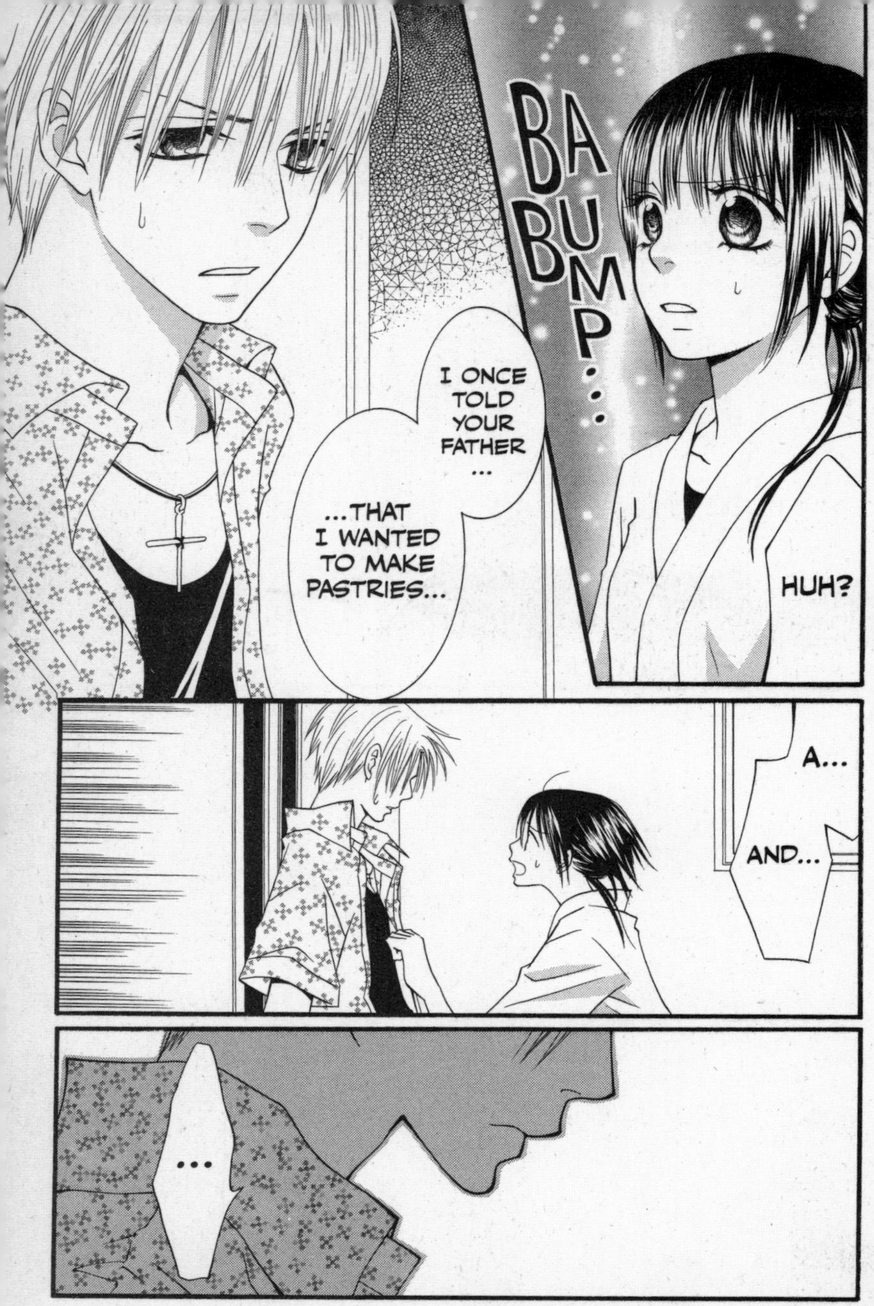
BA BUMP...
HUH?
I ONCE TOLD YOUR FATHER ...
...THAT I WANTED TO MAKE PASTRIES...
A...
AND...
...

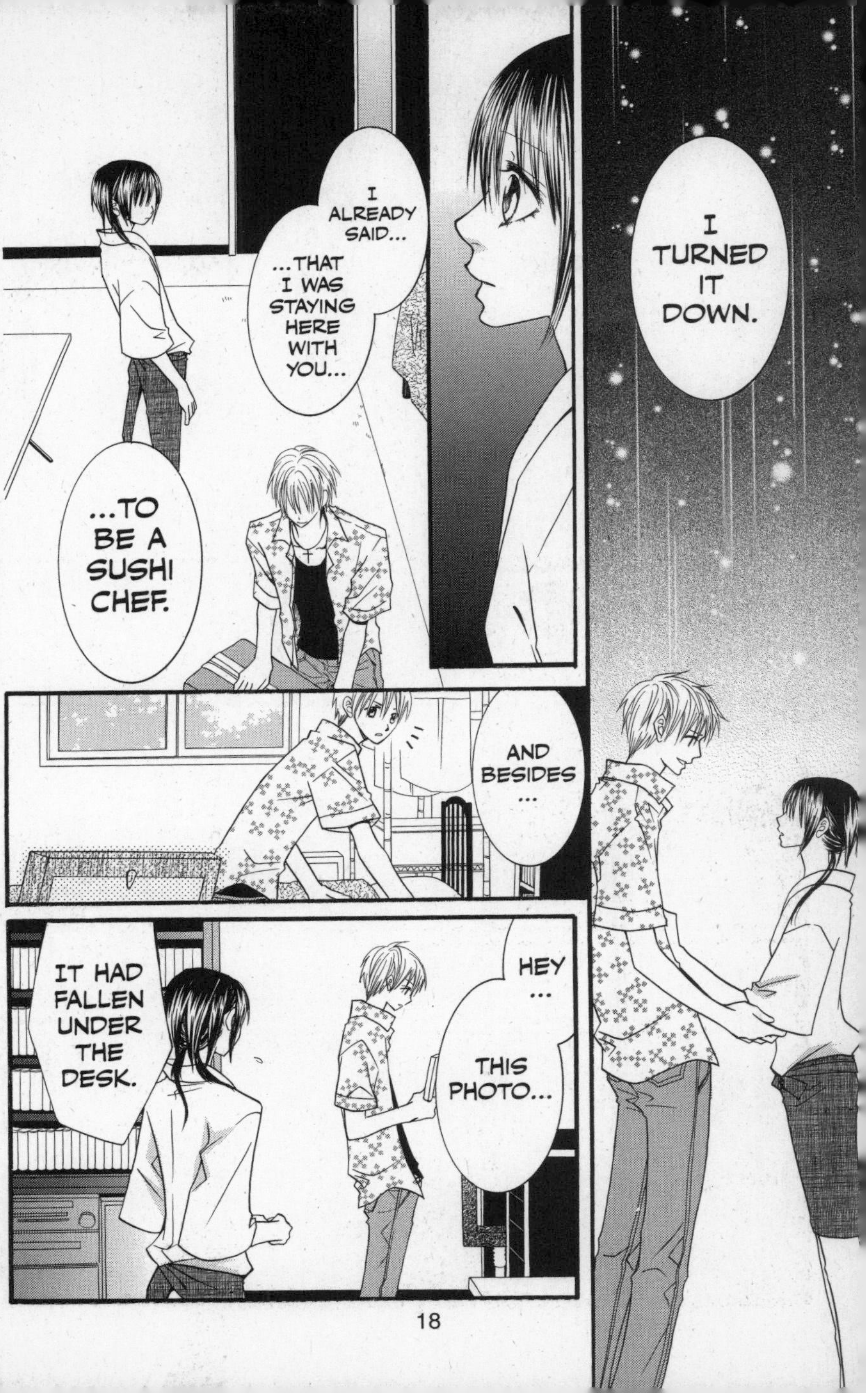
I TURNED IT DOWN.
I ALREADY SAID...
...THAT I WAS STAYING HERE WITH YOU...
...TO BE A SUSHI CHEF.
AND BESIDES...
HEY... THIS PHOTO...
IT HAD FALLEN UNDER THE DESK.

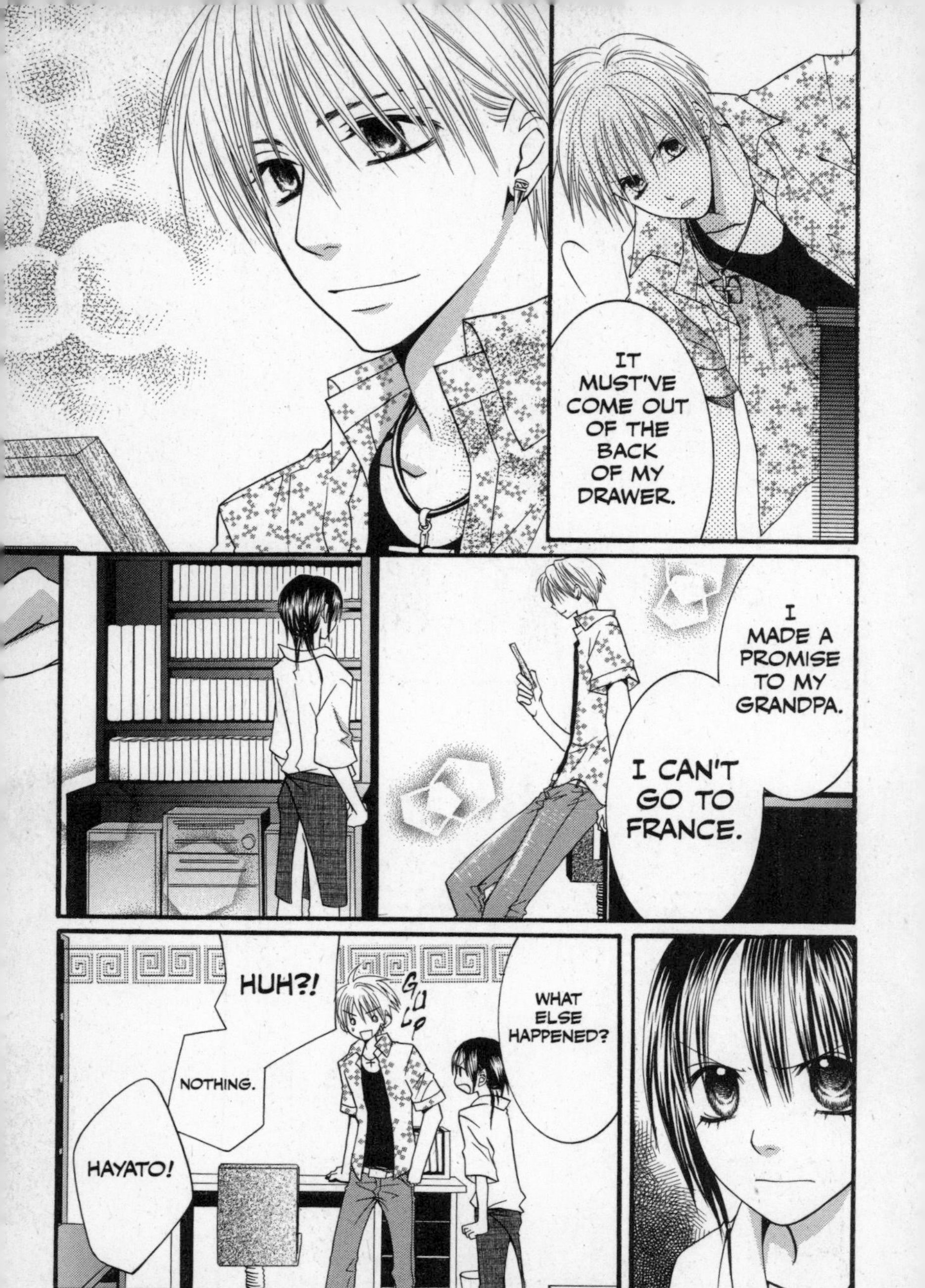
IT MUST'VE COME OUT OF THE BACK OF MY DRAWER.
I MADE A PROMISE TO MY GRANDPA.
I CAN'T GO TO FRANCE.
WHAT ELSE HAPPENED?
GULP
HUH?!
NOTHING.
HAYATO!

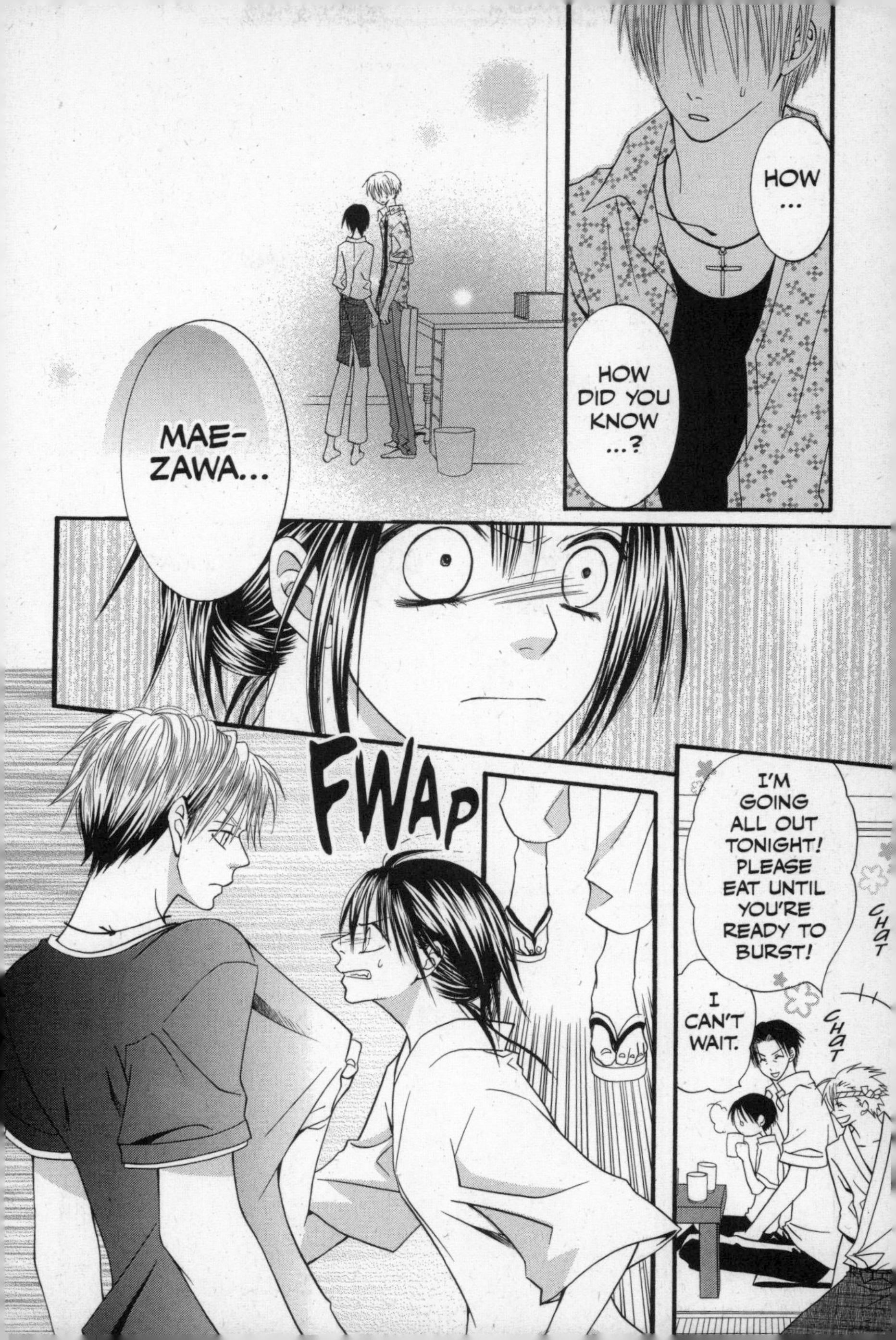
HOW ...
HOW DID YOU KNOW ...?
MAE-ZAWA...
I'M GOING ALL OUT TONIGHT! PLEASE EAT UNTIL YOU'RE READY TO BURST!
I CAN'T WAIT.
CHAT
CHAT
FWAP

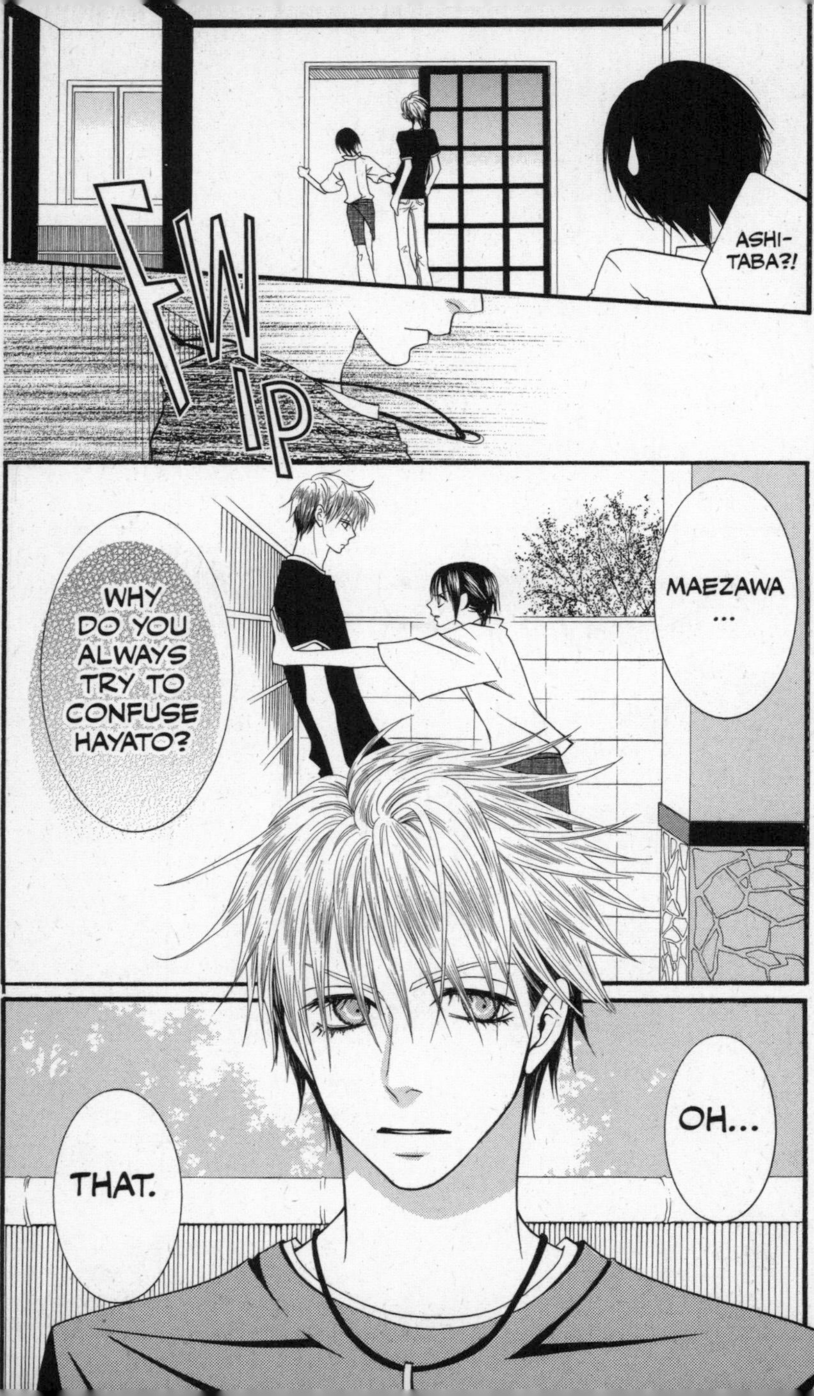
ASHI-TABA?!
FWIP
MAEZAWA...
WHY DO YOU ALWAYS TRY TO CONFUSE HAYATO?
OH...
THAT.

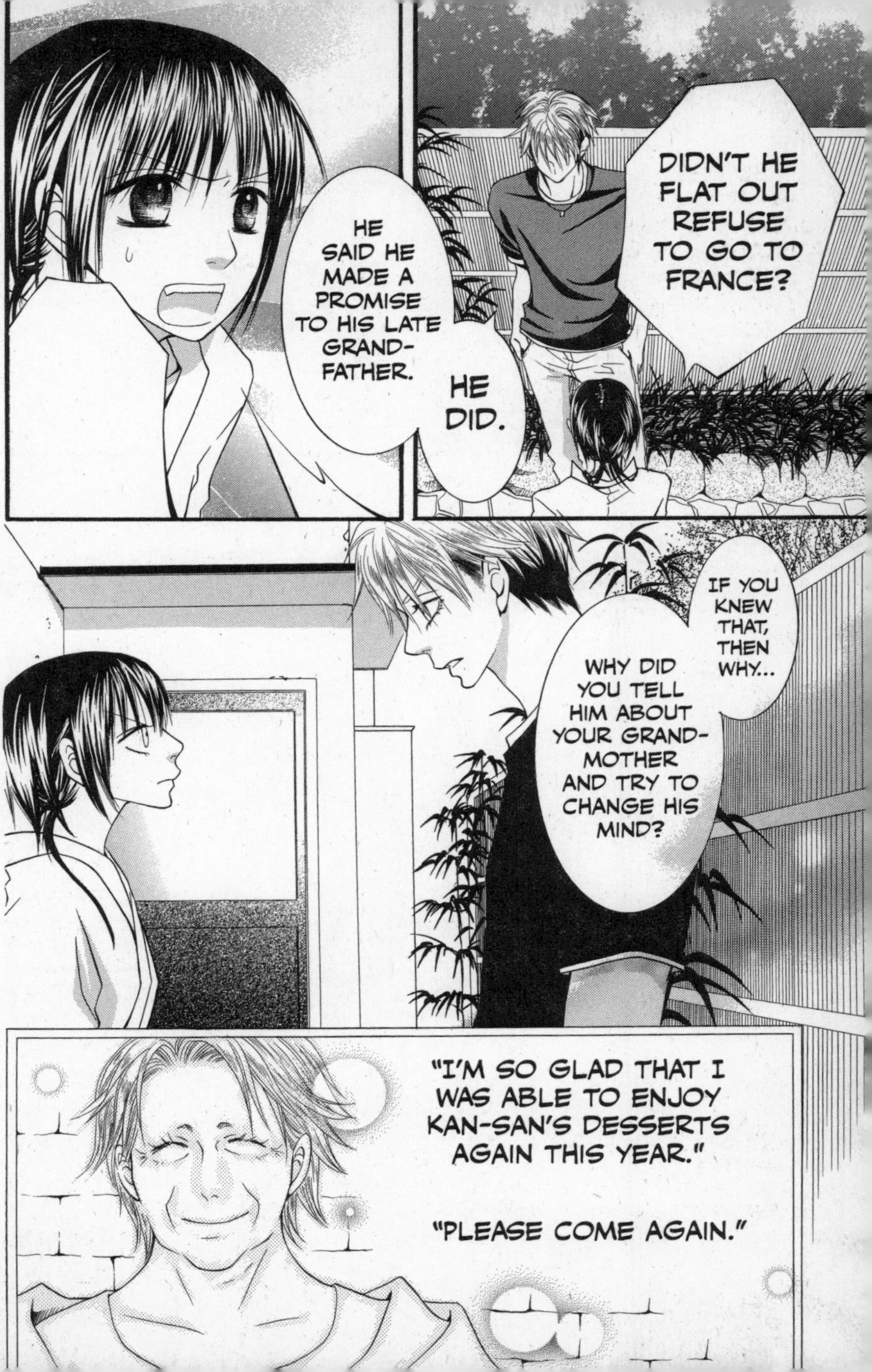

DIDN'T HE FLAT OUT REFUSE TO GO TO FRANCE?
HE DID.
HE SAID HE MADE A PROMISE TO HIS LATE GRAND-FATHER.
IF YOU KNEW THAT, THEN WHY...
WHY DID YOU TELL HIM ABOUT YOUR GRAND-MOTHER AND TRY TO CHANGE HIS MIND?
"I'M SO GLAD THAT I WAS ABLE TO ENJOY KAN-SAN'S DESSERTS AGAIN THIS YEAR."
"PLEASE COME AGAIN."

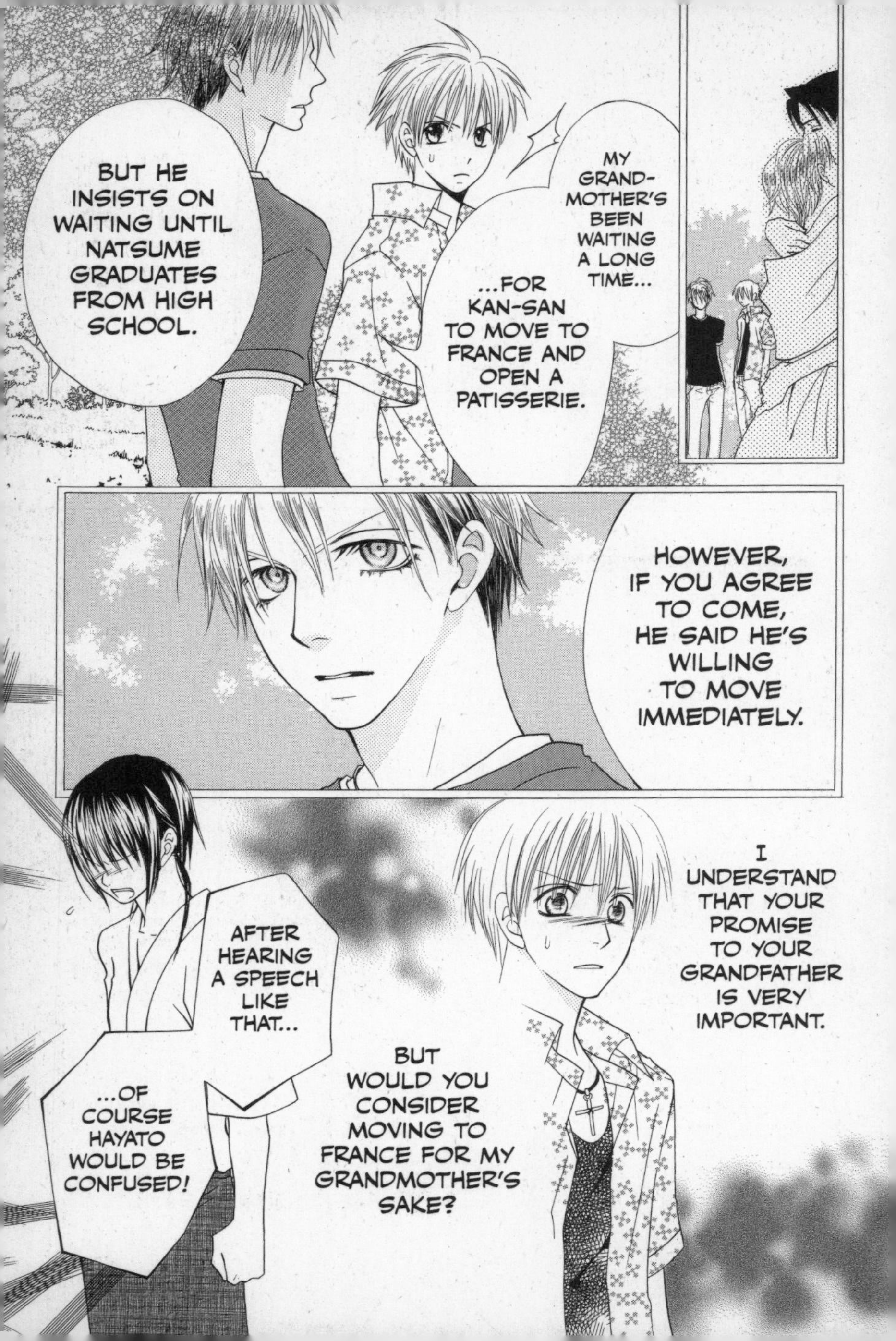
MY GRAND-MOTHER'S BEEN WAITING A LONG TIME...
...FOR KAN-SAN TO MOVE TO FRANCE AND OPEN A PATISSERIE.
BUT HE INSISTS ON WAITING UNTIL NATSUME GRADUATES FROM HIGH SCHOOL.
HOWEVER, IF YOU AGREE TO COME, HE SAID HE'S WILLING TO MOVE IMMEDIATELY.
I UNDERSTAND THAT YOUR PROMISE TO YOUR GRANDFATHER IS VERY IMPORTANT.
BUT WOULD YOU CONSIDER MOVING TO FRANCE FOR MY GRANDMOTHER'S SAKE?
AFTER HEARING A SPEECH LIKE THAT...
...OF COURSE HAYATO WOULD BE CONFUSED!

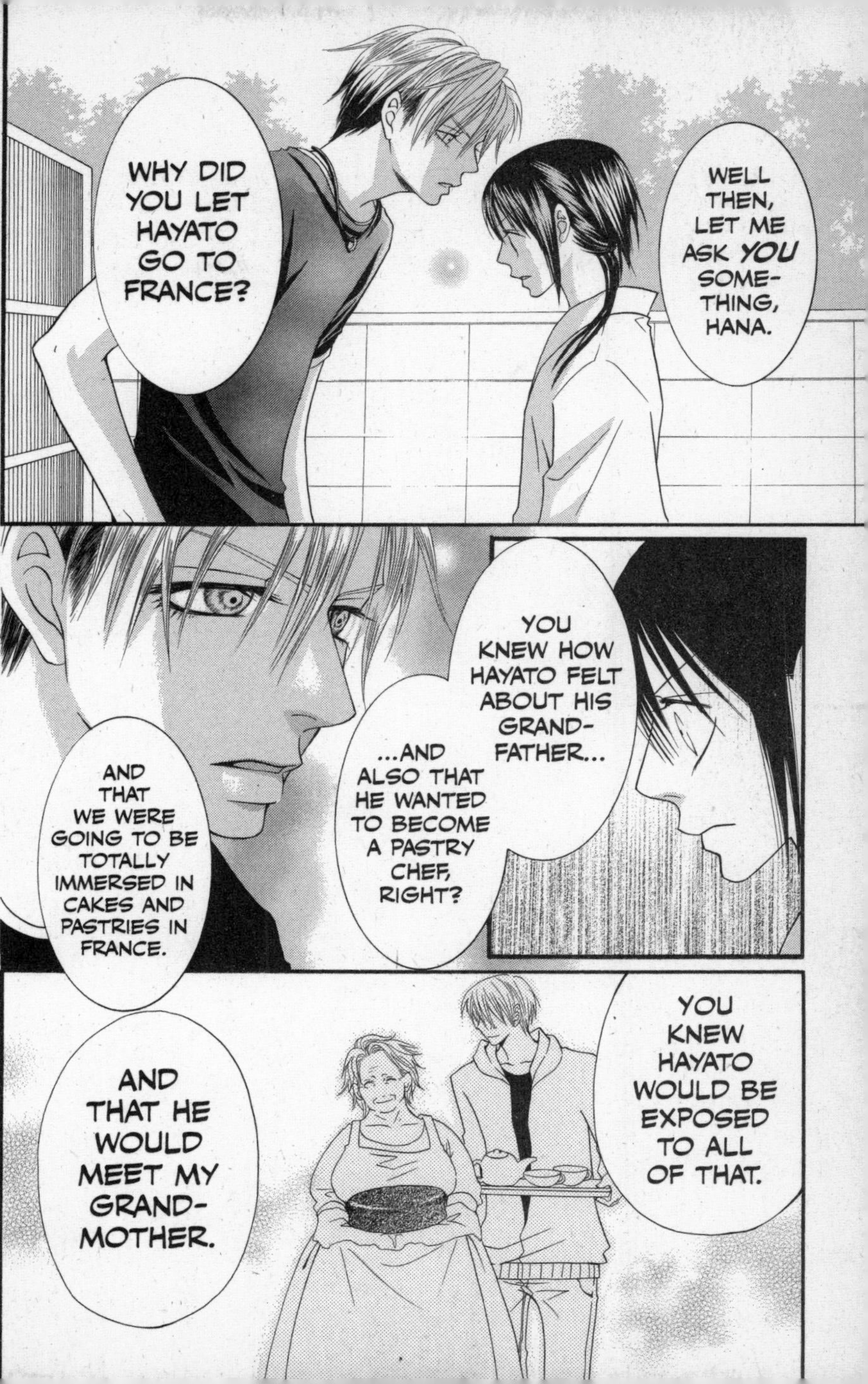
WELL THEN, LET ME ASK *YOU* SOMETHING, HANA.
WHY DID YOU LET HAYATO GO TO FRANCE?
YOU KNEW HOW HAYATO FELT ABOUT HIS GRANDFATHER...
...AND ALSO THAT HE WANTED TO BECOME A PASTRY CHEF, RIGHT?
AND THAT WE WERE GOING TO BE TOTALLY IMMERSED IN CAKES AND PASTRIES IN FRANCE.
YOU KNEW HAYATO WOULD BE EXPOSED TO ALL OF THAT.
AND THAT HE WOULD MEET MY GRANDMOTHER.

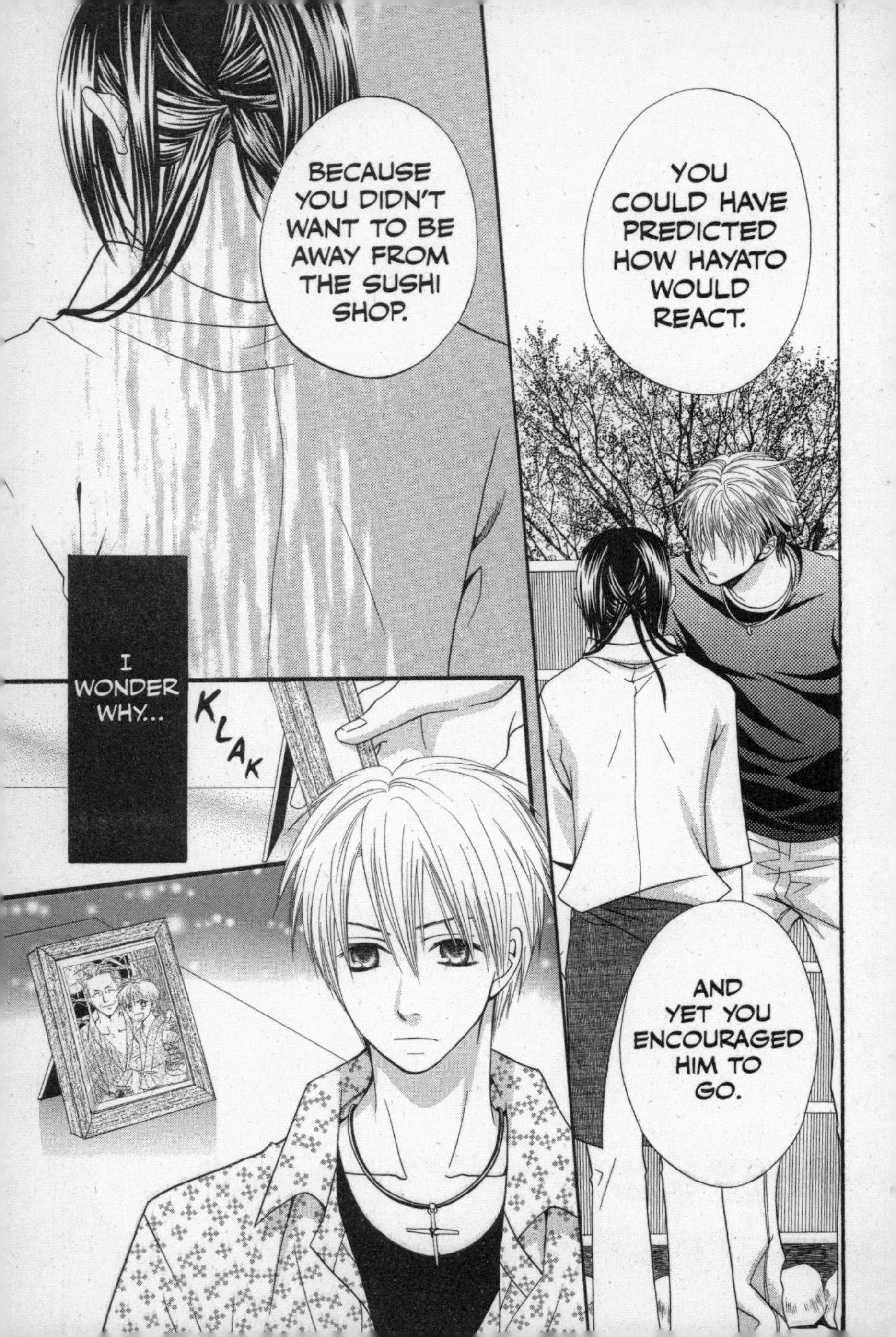
YOU COULD HAVE PREDICTED HOW HAYATO WOULD REACT.
AND YET YOU ENCOURAGED HIM TO GO.
BECAUSE YOU DIDN'T WANT TO BE AWAY FROM THE SUSHI SHOP.
I WONDER WHY...
KLAK

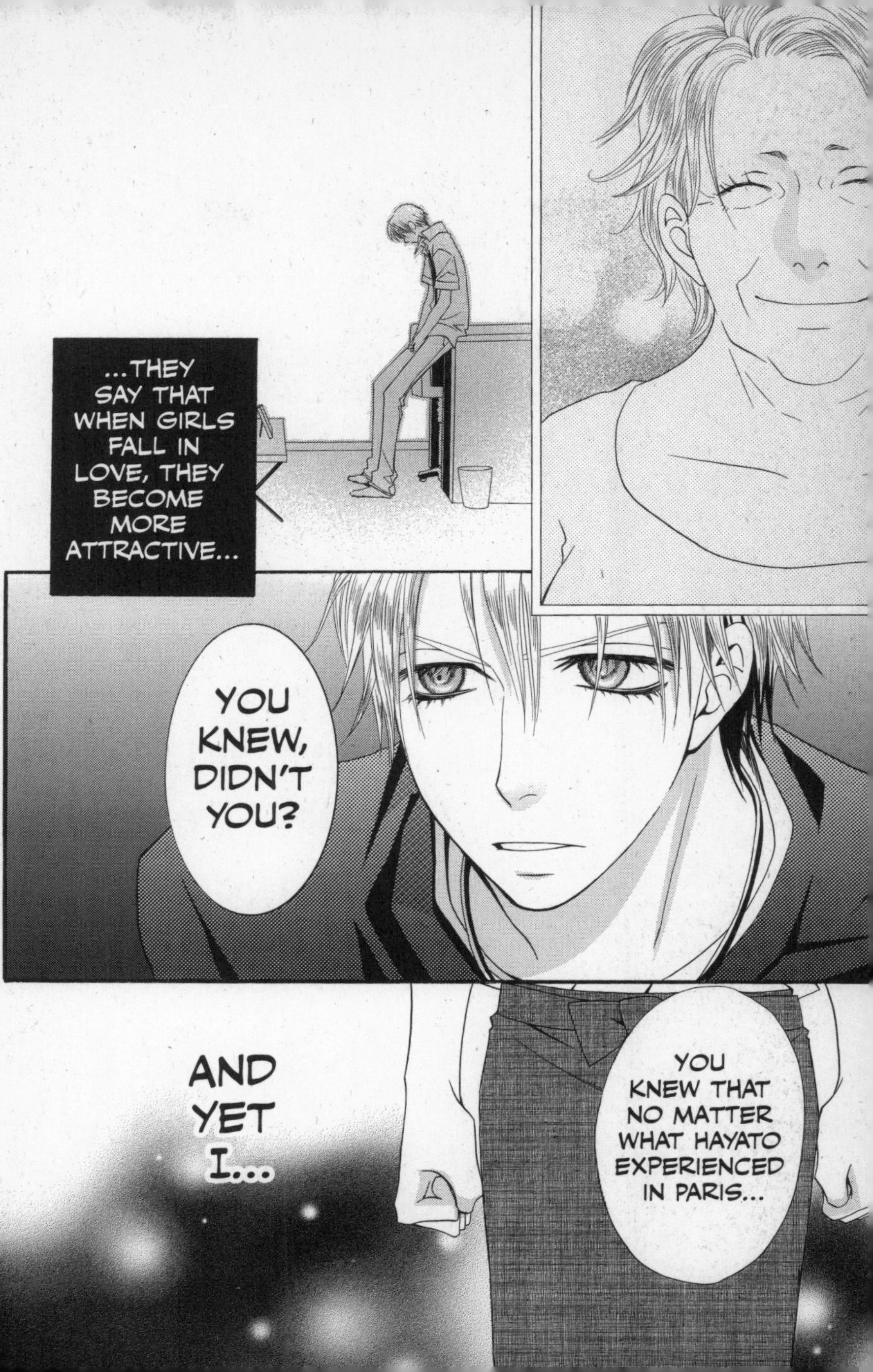
...THEY SAY THAT WHEN GIRLS FALL IN LOVE, THEY BECOME MORE ATTRACTIVE...
YOU KNEW, DIDN'T YOU?
YOU KNEW THAT NO MATTER WHAT HAYATO EXPERIENCED IN PARIS...
AND YET I...

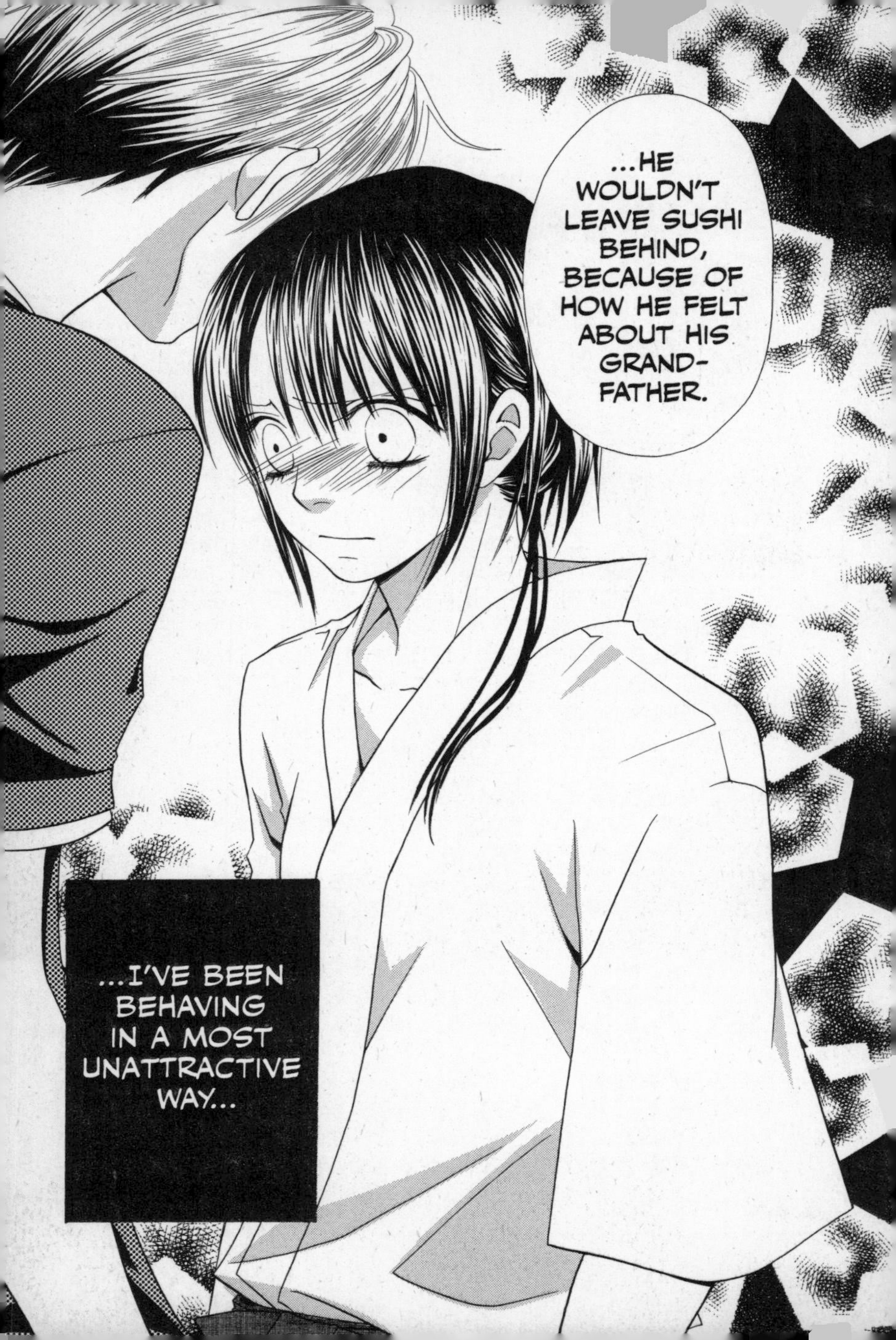
...HE WOULDN'T LEAVE SUSHI BEHIND, BECAUSE OF HOW HE FELT ABOUT HIS GRAND-FATHER.
...I'VE BEEN BEHAVING IN A MOST UNATTRACTIVE WAY...

MIXED VEGETABLES Encyclopedia of Characters

HANAYU ASHITABA

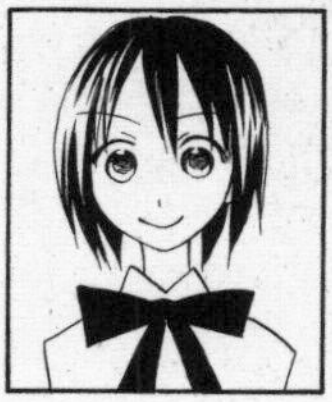

HANAYU → A CITRUS FRUIT (A SMALL YUZU)

THE CHARACTERS IN *MIXED VEGETABLES* ARE NAMED AFTER FOODS. I WAS LOOKING THROUGH A FOOD ENCYCLOPEDIA AND CAME ACROSS "HANAYU" AND THOUGHT IT SOUNDED CUTE. I WANTED THE LAST NAME TO ALSO BE THE NAME OF THEIR SHOP (LIKE SUSHI HYUGA), SO I TRIED TO THINK OF SOMETHING THAT WOULD MATCH A PASTRY SHOP. I ENDED UP WITH HANAYU ASHITABA, WHICH IS A LITTLE (?) STRANGE... OH, WELL.☆

SHE DEVELOPED INTO A STRONG-WILLED WORRIER, ONE WHO IS WILLING TO GO TO EXTREMES, BUT THAT IS TOTALLY THE CREATOR'S FAULT... I THINK SHE DID QUITE WELL. THE HEROINE IN MY PREVIOUS WORK HAD SHORT HAIR, SO I MADE HANAYU'S A BIT LONGER, BUT I PERSONALLY PREFER SHORT HAIR. I DREW THE HAIR ON A WHIM, AND I KEPT CHANGING HER AS I DREW HER.

HANA IS ALWAYS HOT. SHE WAS BORN IN DECEMBER. WHICH BIRTH DATE DO YOU THINK WOULD SUIT HER? (IT'S TOO LATE FOR ME TO ASK THAT NOW!)

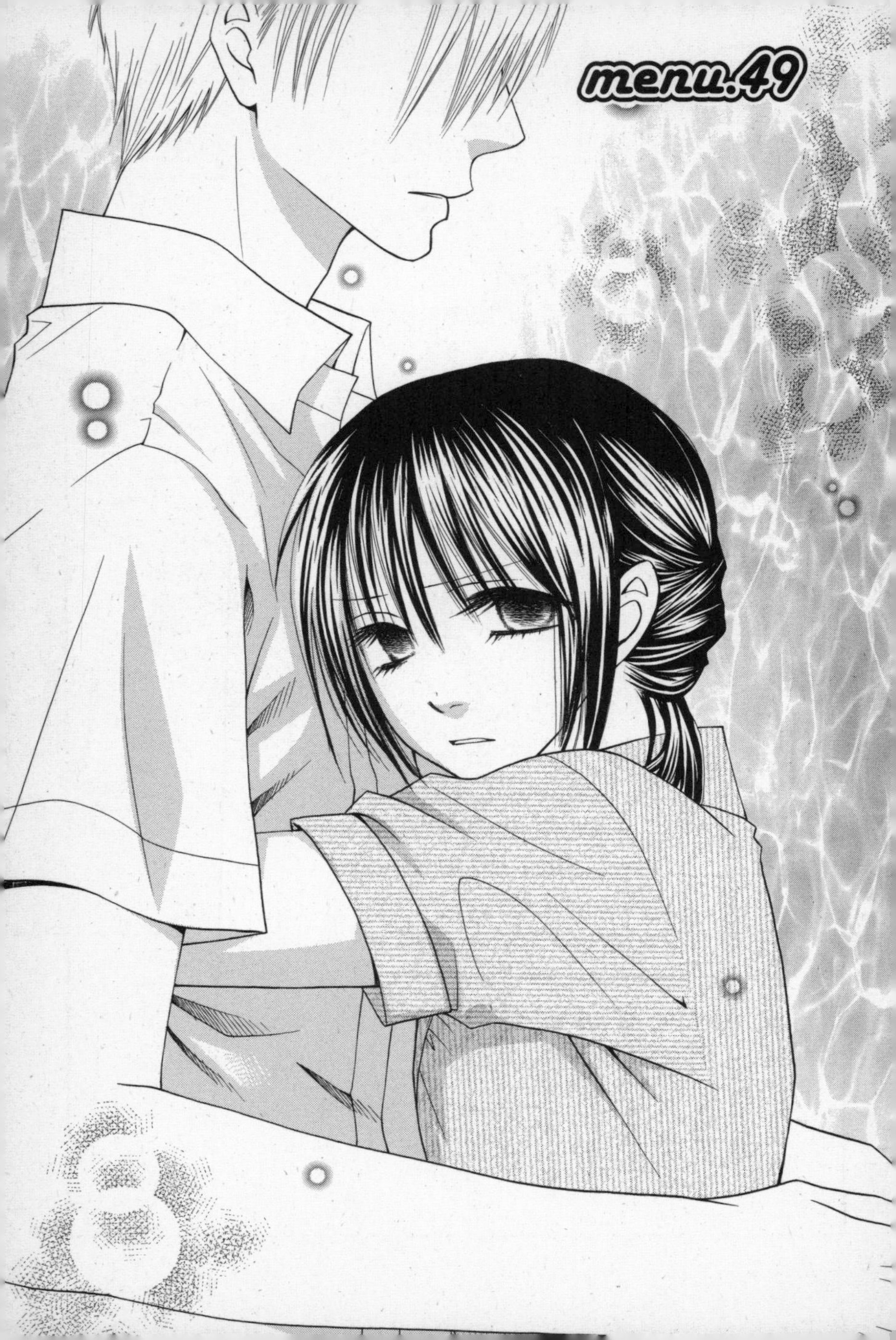
menu.49

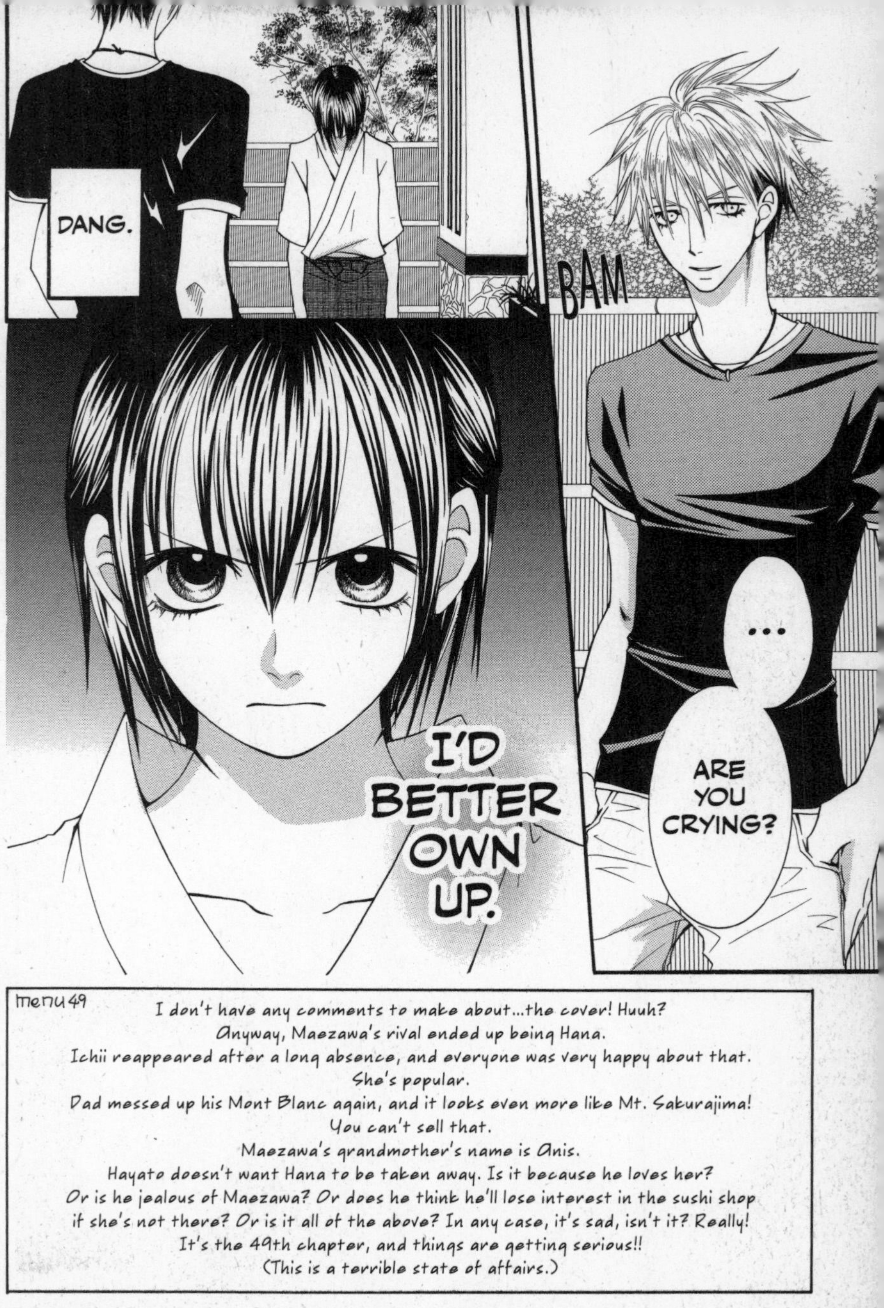
BAM
...
ARE YOU CRYING?
DANG.
I'D BETTER OWN UP.

menu 49

I don't have any comments to make about...the cover! Huuh?
Anyway, Maezawa's rival ended up being Hana.
Ichii reappeared after a long absence, and everyone was very happy about that.
She's popular.
Dad messed up his Mont Blanc again, and it looks even more like Mt. Sakurajima!
You can't sell that.
Maezawa's grandmother's name is Anis.
Hayato doesn't want Hana to be taken away. Is it because he loves her?
Or is he jealous of Maezawa? Or does he think he'll lose interest in the sushi shop if she's not there? Or is it all of the above? In any case, it's sad, isn't it? Really!
It's the 49th chapter, and things are getting serious!!
(This is a terrible state of affairs.)

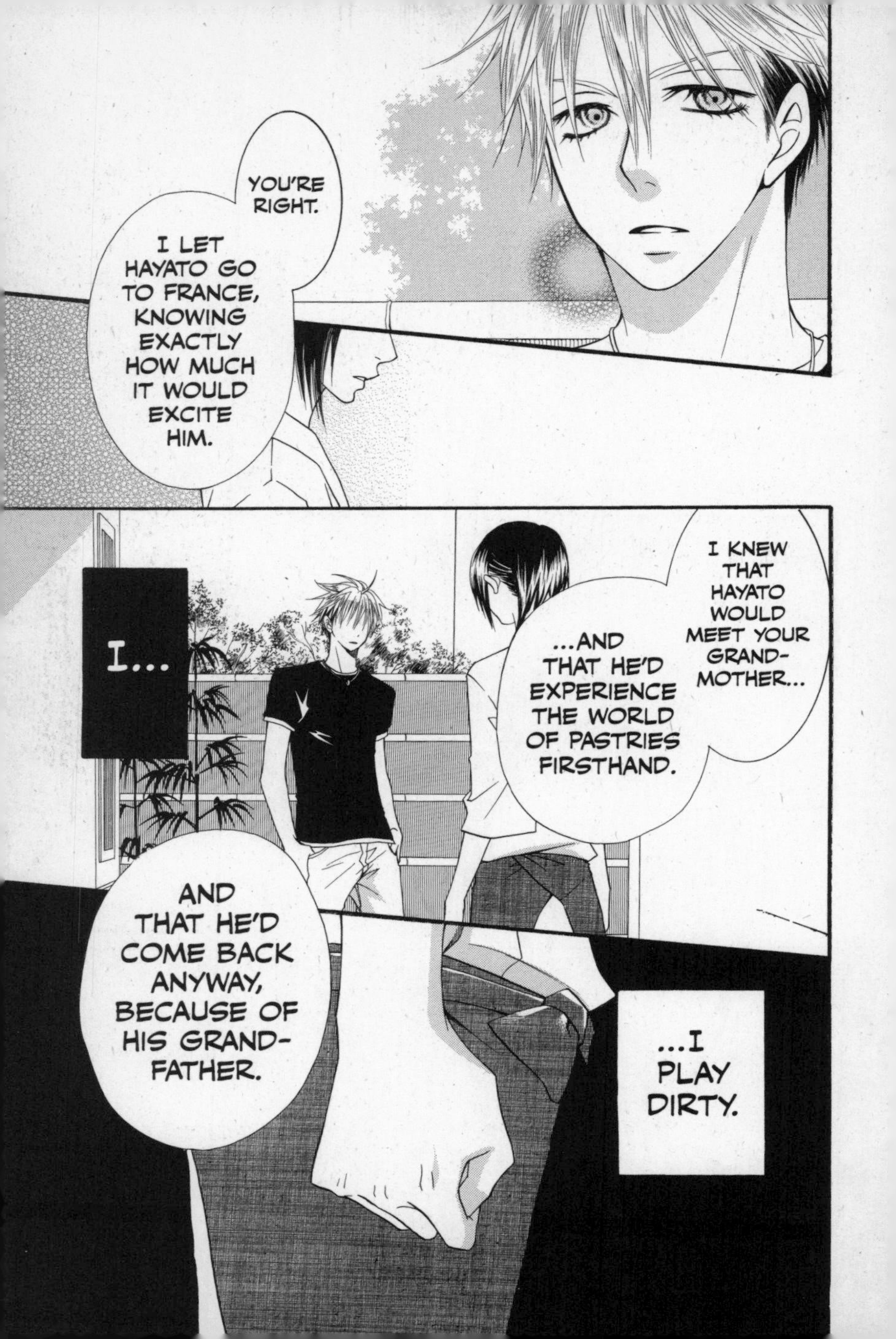
YOU'RE RIGHT.
I LET HAYATO GO TO FRANCE, KNOWING EXACTLY HOW MUCH IT WOULD EXCITE HIM.
I KNEW THAT HAYATO WOULD MEET YOUR GRAND-MOTHER...
...AND THAT HE'D EXPERIENCE THE WORLD OF PASTRIES FIRSTHAND.
I...
AND THAT HE'D COME BACK ANYWAY, BECAUSE OF HIS GRAND-FATHER.
...I PLAY DIRTY.

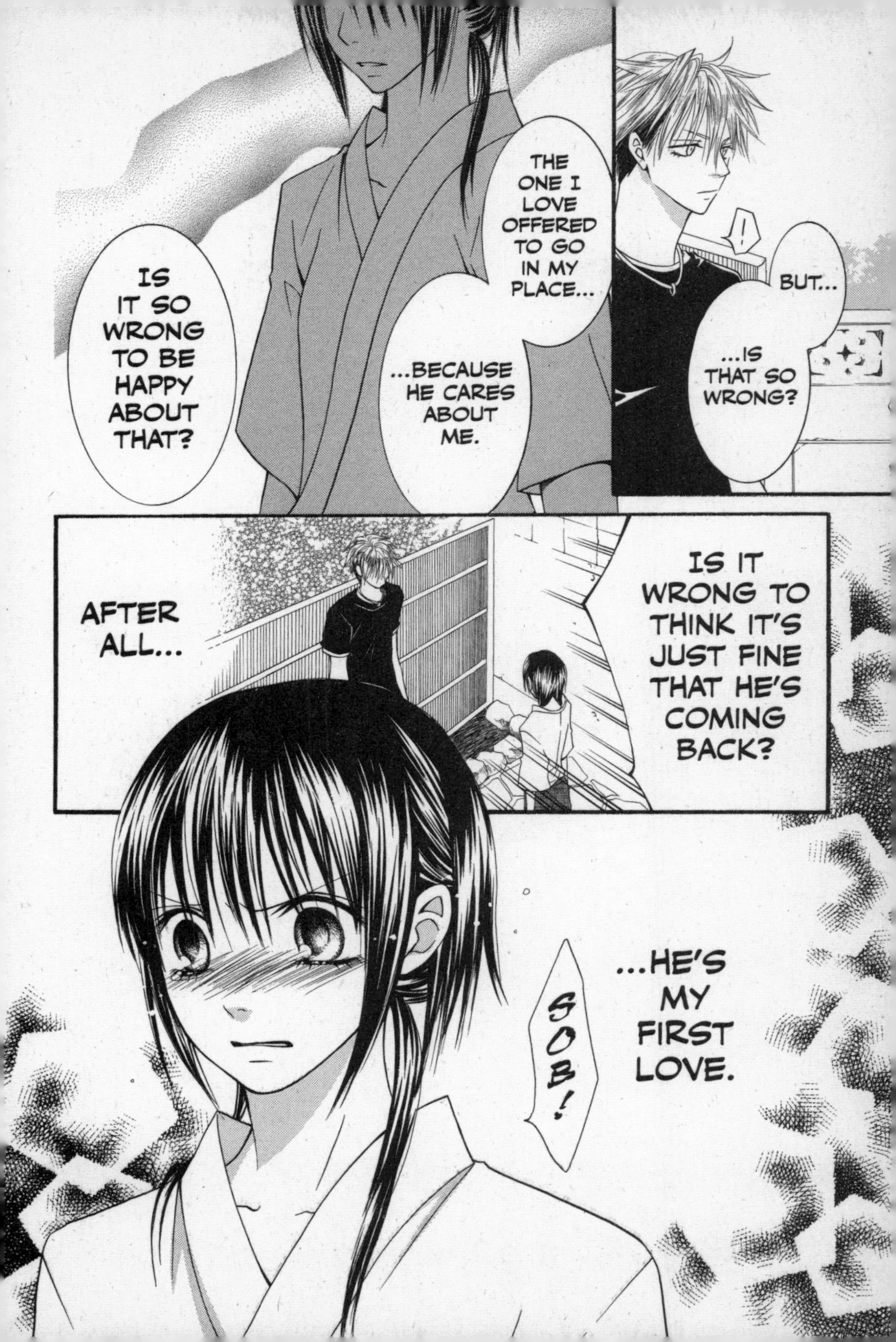
!
BUT...
...IS THAT SO WRONG?
THE ONE I LOVE OFFERED TO GO IN MY PLACE...
...BECAUSE HE CARES ABOUT ME.
IS IT SO WRONG TO BE HAPPY ABOUT THAT?
IS IT WRONG TO THINK IT'S JUST FINE THAT HE'S COMING BACK?
AFTER ALL...
...HE'S MY FIRST LOVE.
SOB!

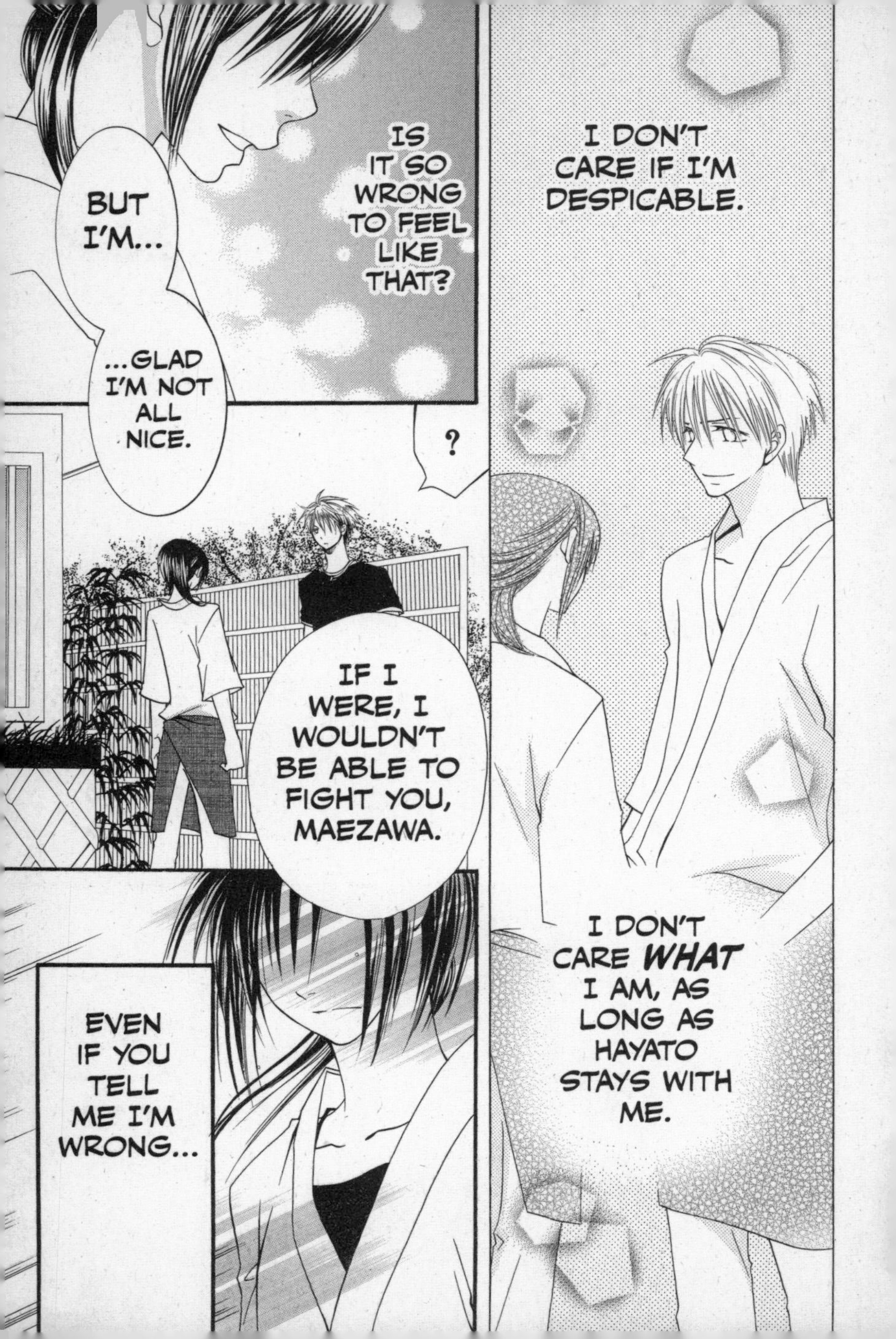
I DON'T CARE IF I'M DESPICABLE.
I DON'T CARE WHAT I AM, AS LONG AS HAYATO STAYS WITH ME.
IS IT SO WRONG TO FEEL LIKE THAT?
BUT I'M...
...GLAD I'M NOT ALL NICE.
?
IF I WERE, I WOULDN'T BE ABLE TO FIGHT YOU, MAEZAWA.
EVEN IF YOU TELL ME I'M WRONG...

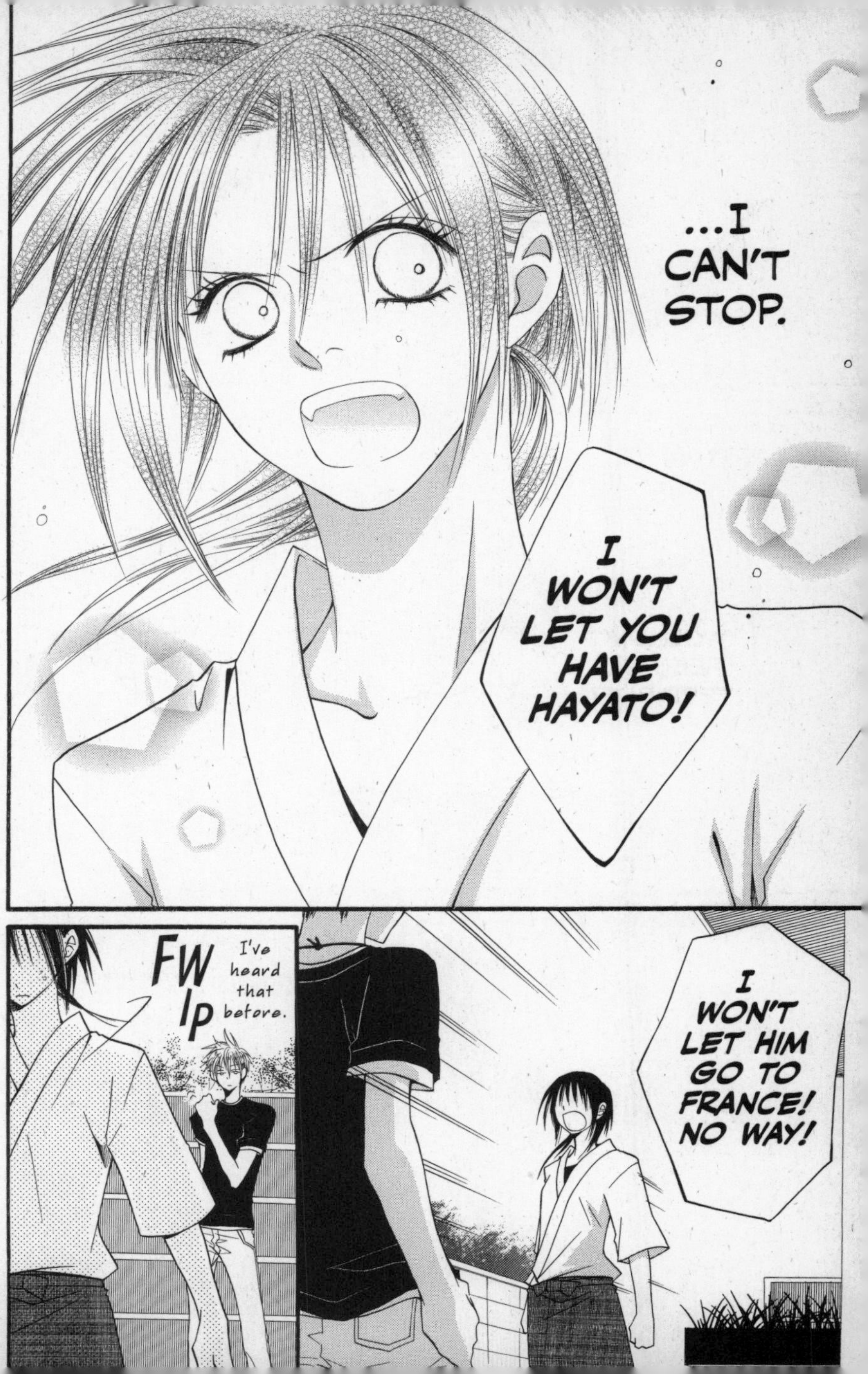
...I CAN'T STOP.
I WON'T LET YOU HAVE HAYATO!
I WON'T LET HIM GO TO FRANCE! NO WAY!
FWIP
I've heard that before.

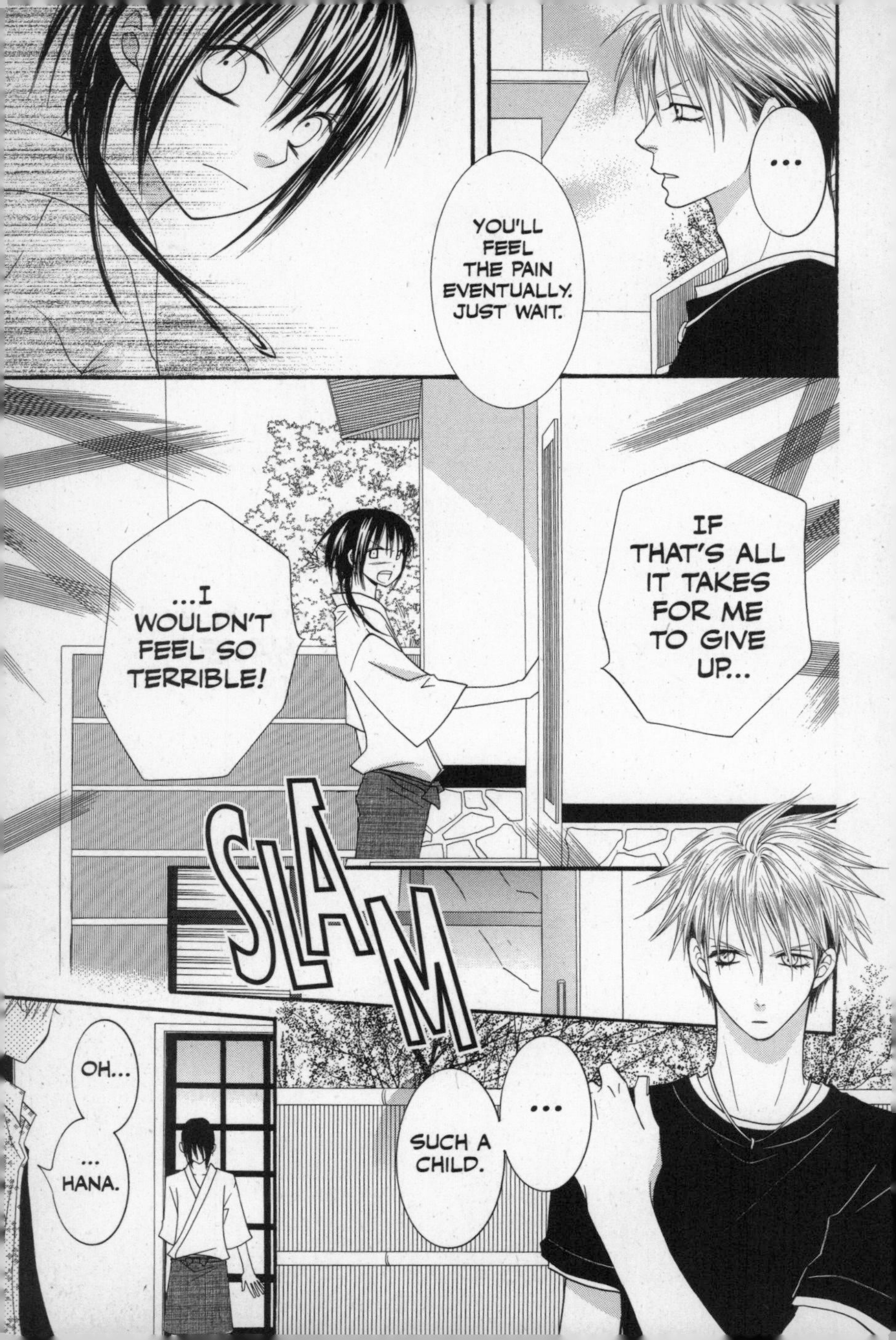
...
YOU'LL FEEL THE PAIN EVENTUALLY. JUST WAIT.
IF THAT'S ALL IT TAKES FOR ME TO GIVE UP...
...I WOULDN'T FEEL SO TERRIBLE!
SLAM
...
SUCH A CHILD.
OH...
...HANA.

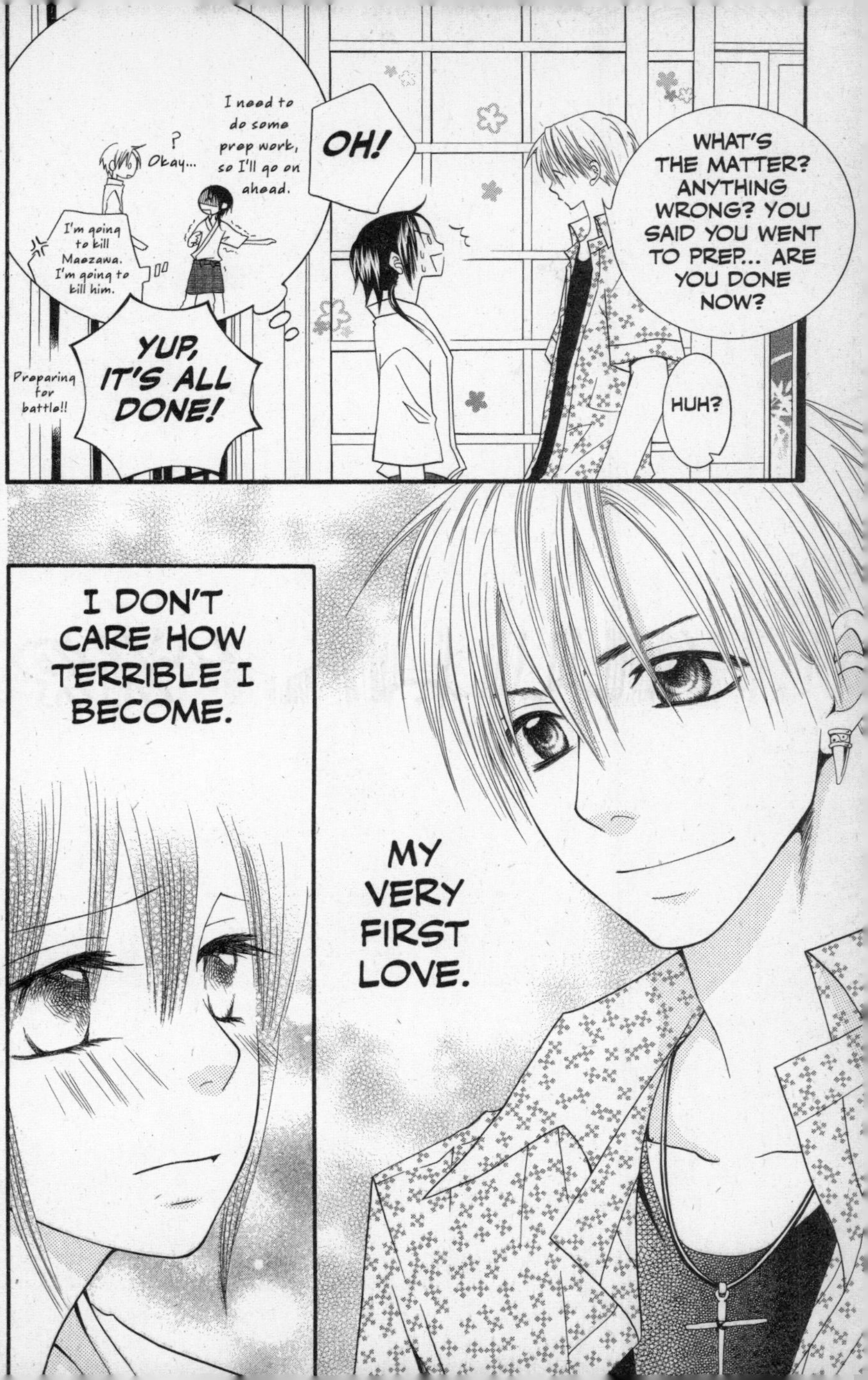
WHAT'S THE MATTER? ANYTHING WRONG? YOU SAID YOU WENT TO PREP... ARE YOU DONE NOW?
HUH?
OH!
I need to do some prep work, so I'll go on ahead.
? Okay...
I'm going to kill Maezawa. I'm going to kill him.
YUP, IT'S ALL DONE!
Preparing for battle!!
I DON'T CARE HOW TERRIBLE I BECOME.
MY VERY FIRST LOVE.

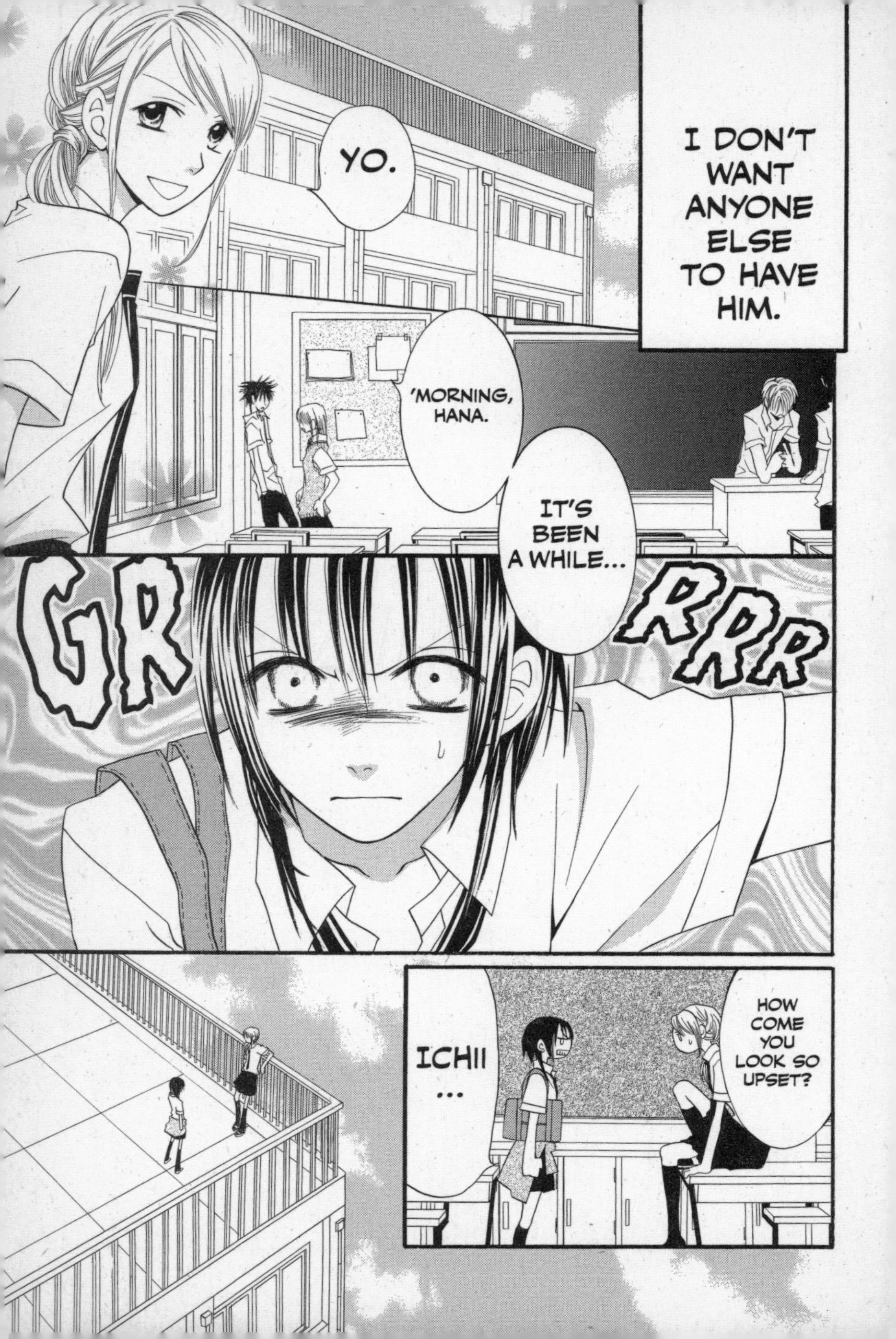
I DON'T WANT ANYONE ELSE TO HAVE HIM.
YO.
'MORNING, HANA.
IT'S BEEN A WHILE...
GR
RRR
HOW COME YOU LOOK SO UPSET?
ICHII ...

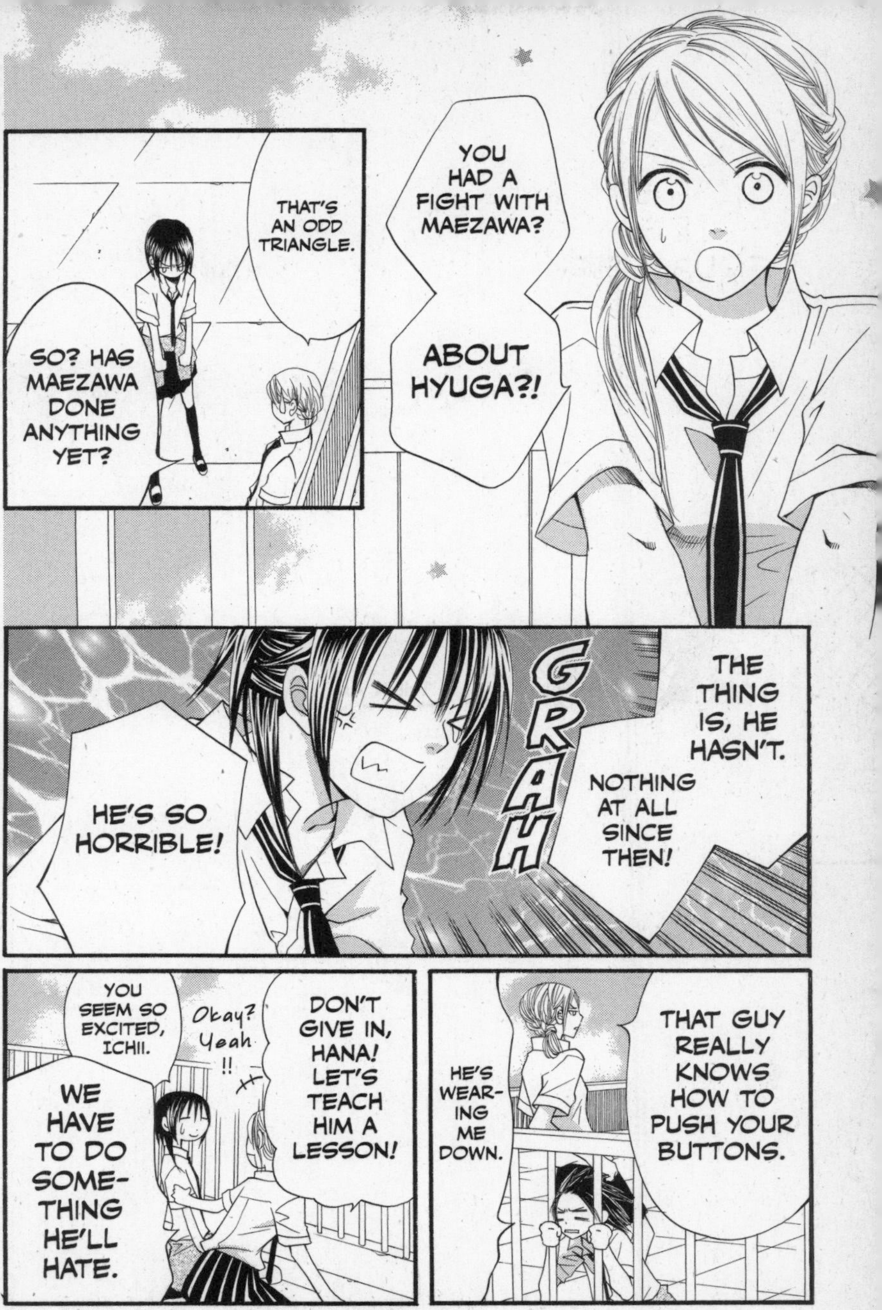
YOU HAD A FIGHT WITH MAEZAWA?
ABOUT HYUGA?!
THAT'S AN ODD TRIANGLE.
SO? HAS MAEZAWA DONE ANYTHING YET?
THE THING IS, HE HASN'T.
GRAH
NOTHING AT ALL SINCE THEN!
HE'S SO HORRIBLE!
THAT GUY REALLY KNOWS HOW TO PUSH YOUR BUTTONS.
HE'S WEARING ME DOWN.
DON'T GIVE IN, HANA! LET'S TEACH HIM A LESSON!
Okay? Yeah !!
YOU SEEM SO EXCITED, ICHII.
WE HAVE TO DO SOMETHING HE'LL HATE.

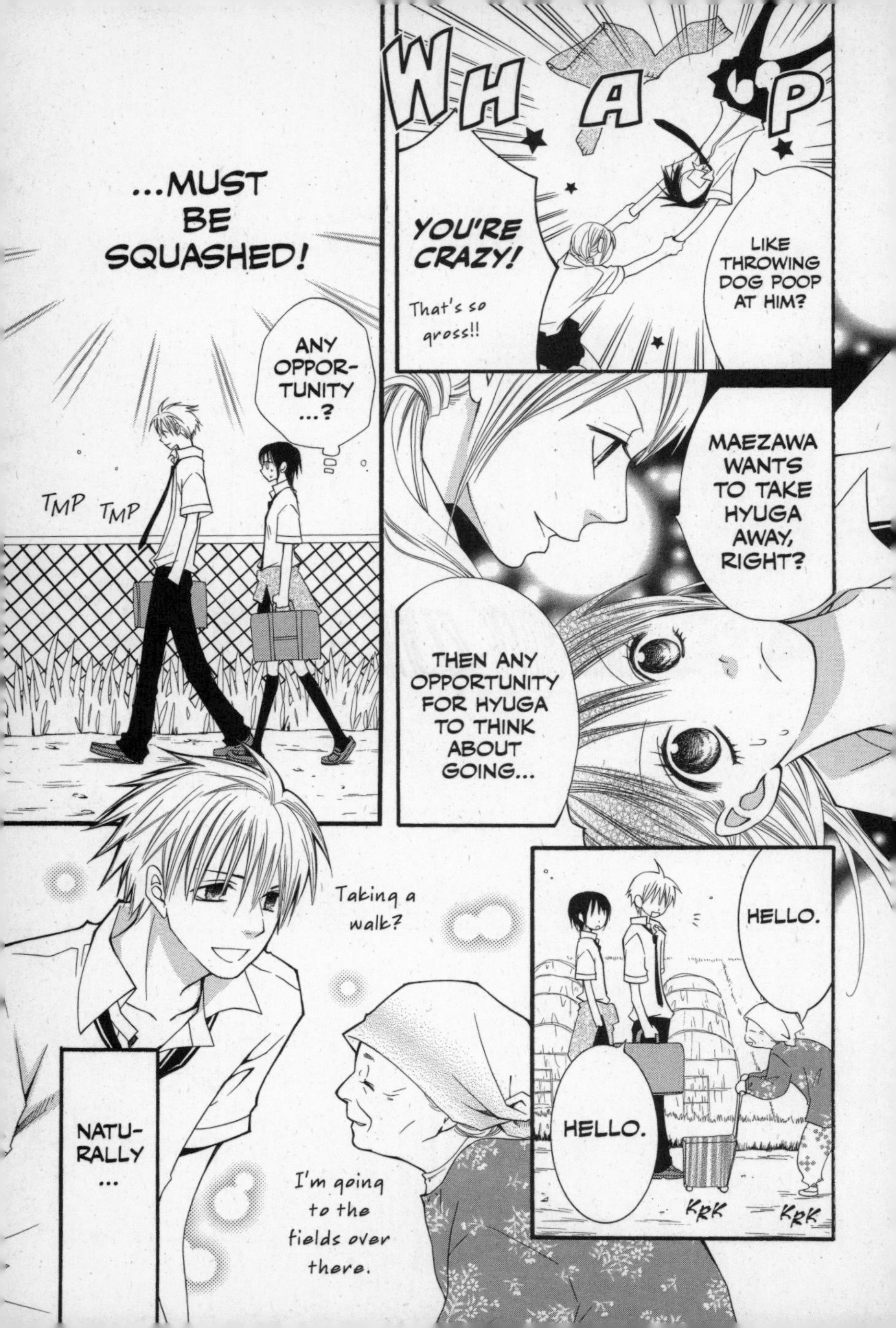
WHAP
LIKE THROWING DOG POOP AT HIM?
YOU'RE CRAZY!
That's so gross!!
MAEZAWA WANTS TO TAKE HYUGA AWAY, RIGHT?
THEN ANY OPPORTUNITY FOR HYUGA TO THINK ABOUT GOING...
...MUST BE SQUASHED!
ANY OPPORTUNITY...?
TMP TMP
HELLO.
HELLO.
KRK KRK
Taking a walk?
I'm going to the fields over there.
NATURALLY...

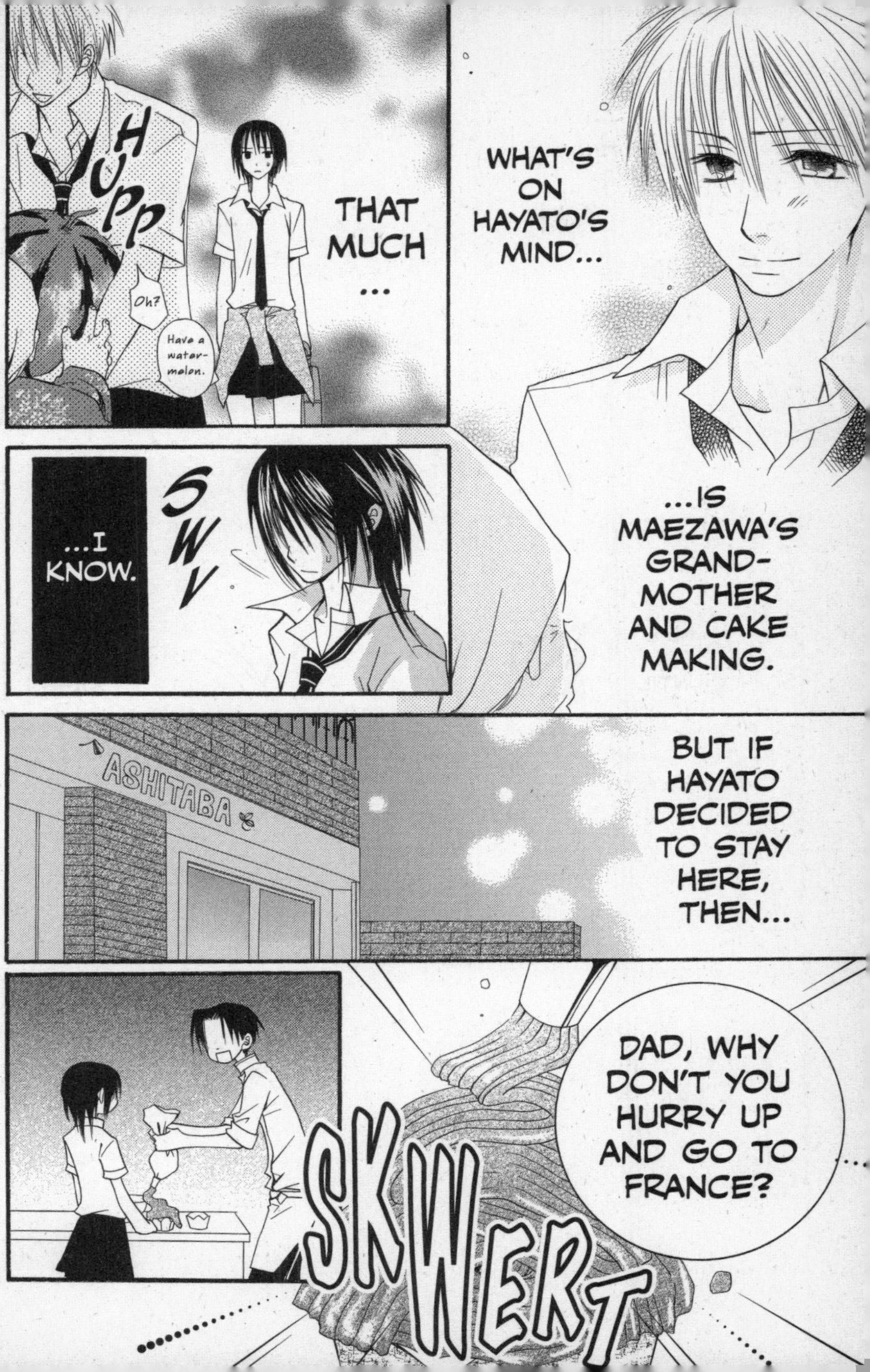
WHAT'S ON HAYATO'S MIND...
THAT MUCH ...
HUPP
Oh?
Have a water-melon.
...IS MAEZAWA'S GRAND-MOTHER AND CAKE MAKING.
SWV
...I KNOW.
BUT IF HAYATO DECIDED TO STAY HERE, THEN...
ASHITABA
DAD, WHY DON'T YOU HURRY UP AND GO TO FRANCE?
SKWERT

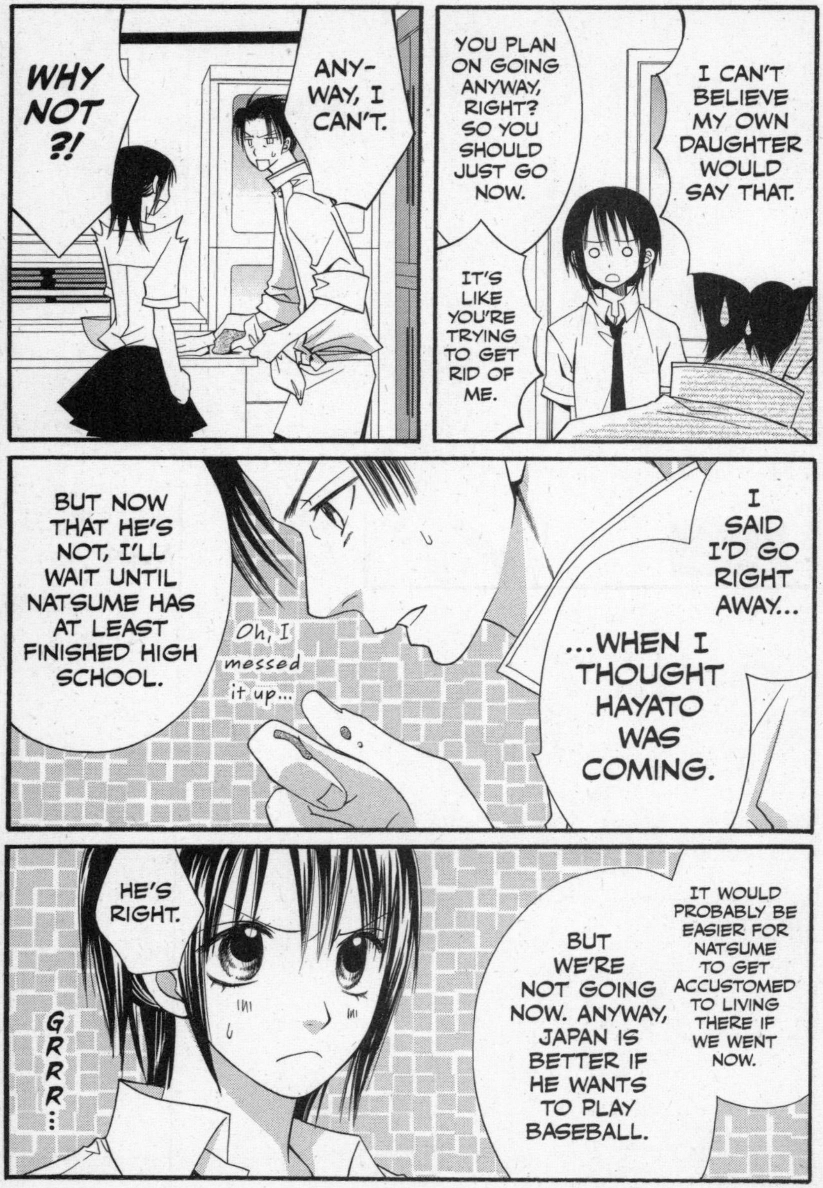
I CAN'T BELIEVE MY OWN DAUGHTER WOULD SAY THAT.
YOU PLAN ON GOING ANYWAY, RIGHT? SO YOU SHOULD JUST GO NOW.
IT'S LIKE YOU'RE TRYING TO GET RID OF ME.
ANY-WAY, I CAN'T.
WHY NOT?!
I SAID I'D GO RIGHT AWAY...
...WHEN I THOUGHT HAYATO WAS COMING.
Oh, I messed it up...
BUT NOW THAT HE'S NOT, I'LL WAIT UNTIL NATSUME HAS AT LEAST FINISHED HIGH SCHOOL.
IT WOULD PROBABLY BE EASIER FOR NATSUME TO GET ACCUSTOMED TO LIVING THERE IF WE WENT NOW.
BUT WE'RE NOT GOING NOW. ANYWAY, JAPAN IS BETTER IF HE WANTS TO PLAY BASEBALL.
HE'S RIGHT.
GRRR...

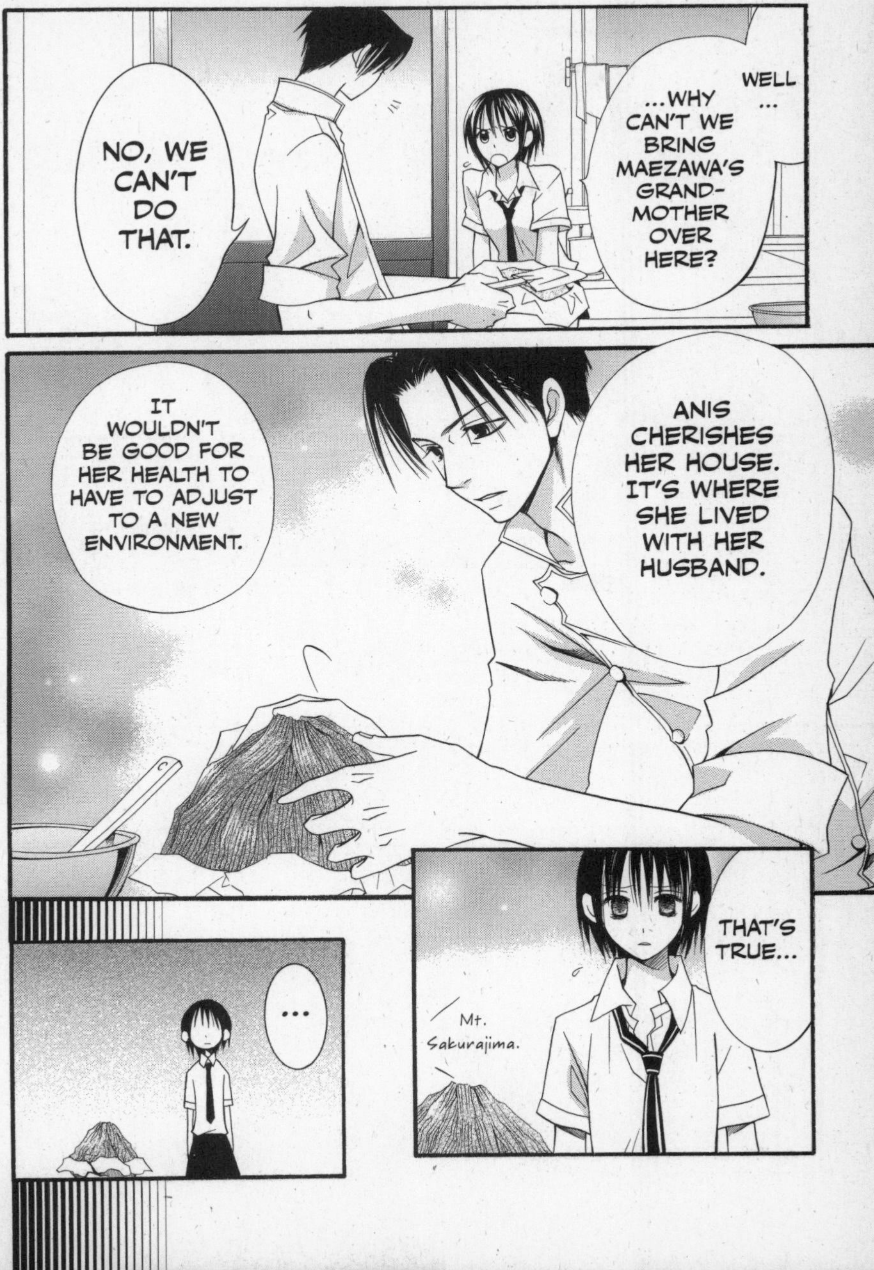
WELL ...
...WHY CAN'T WE BRING MAEZAWA'S GRAND-MOTHER OVER HERE?
NO, WE CAN'T DO THAT.
ANIS CHERISHES HER HOUSE. IT'S WHERE SHE LIVED WITH HER HUSBAND.
IT WOULDN'T BE GOOD FOR HER HEALTH TO HAVE TO ADJUST TO A NEW ENVIRONMENT.
THAT'S TRUE...
Mt. Sakurajima.
...

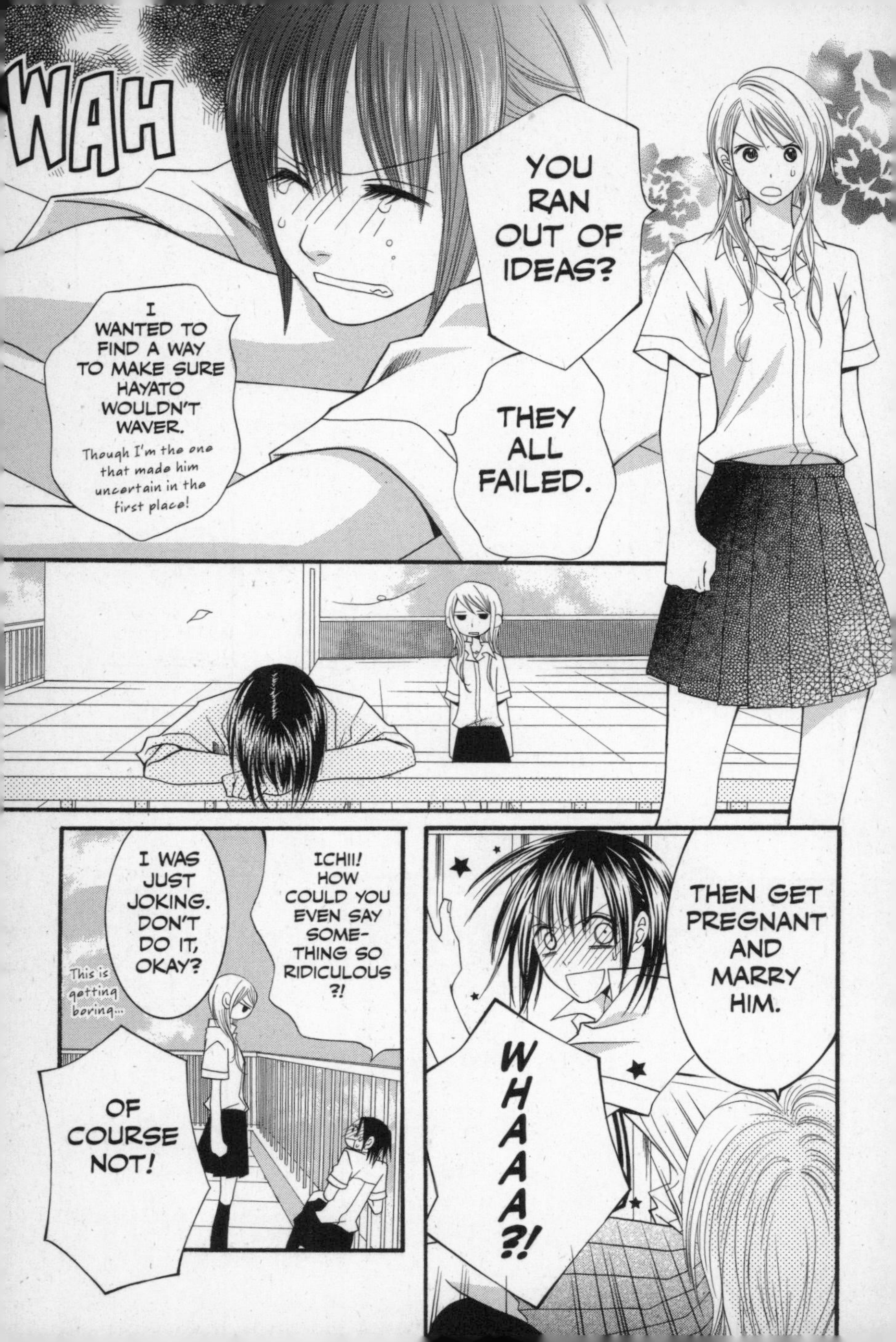
YOU RAN OUT OF IDEAS?
THEY ALL FAILED.
WAH
I WANTED TO FIND A WAY TO MAKE SURE HAYATO WOULDN'T WAVER.
Though I'm the one that made him uncertain in the first place!
THEN GET PREGNANT AND MARRY HIM.
WHAAAA?!
ICHII! HOW COULD YOU EVEN SAY SOME-THING SO RIDICULOUS?!
I WAS JUST JOKING. DON'T DO IT, OKAY?
This is getting boring...
OF COURSE NOT!

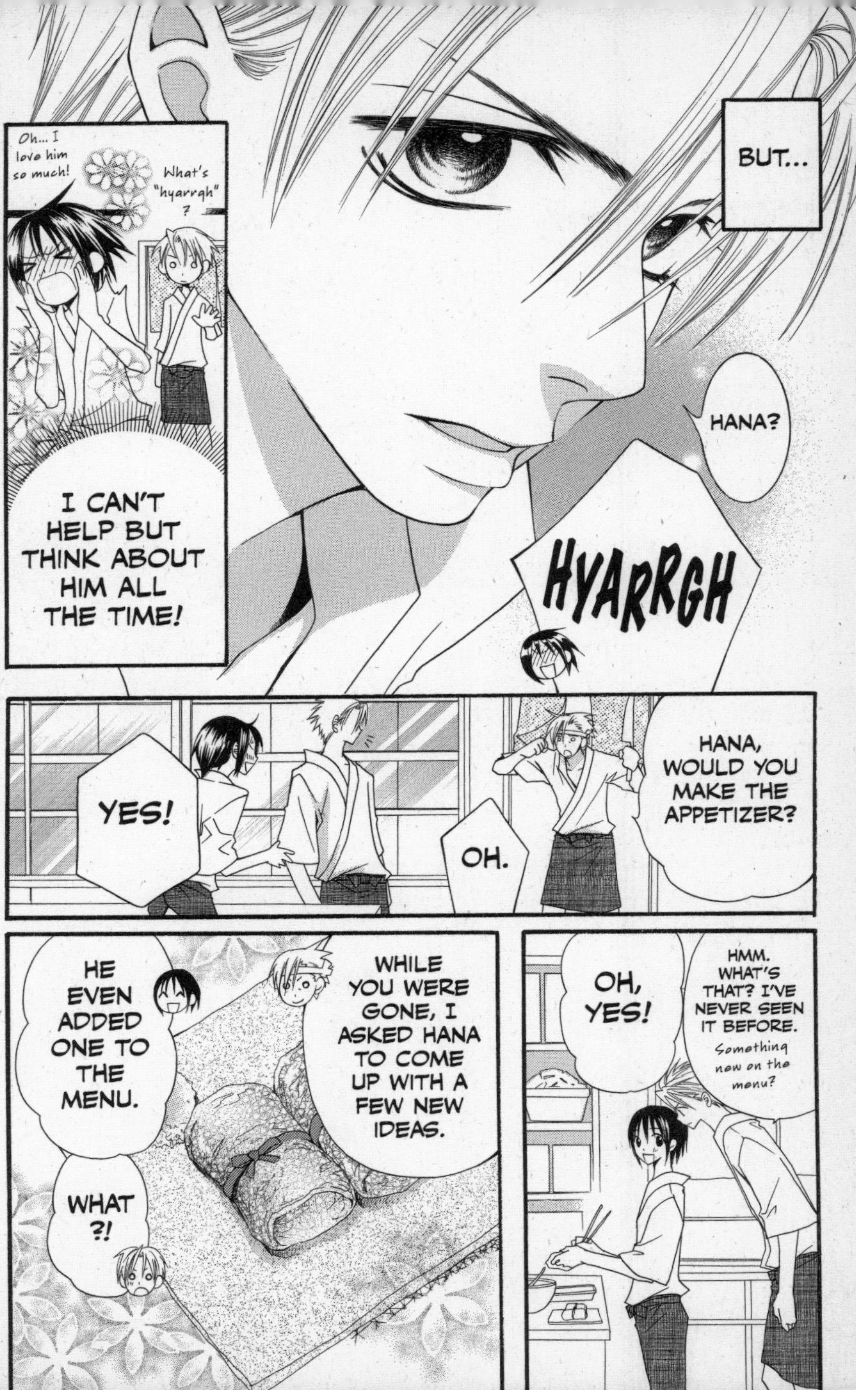
BUT...
HANA?
HYARRGH
What's "hyarrgh"?
Oh... I love him so much!
I CAN'T HELP BUT THINK ABOUT HIM ALL THE TIME!
HANA, WOULD YOU MAKE THE APPETIZER?
OH.
YES!
HMM. WHAT'S THAT? I'VE NEVER SEEN IT BEFORE.
Something new on the menu?
OH, YES!
WHILE YOU WERE GONE, I ASKED HANA TO COME UP WITH A FEW NEW IDEAS.
HE EVEN ADDED ONE TO THE MENU.
WHAT ?!

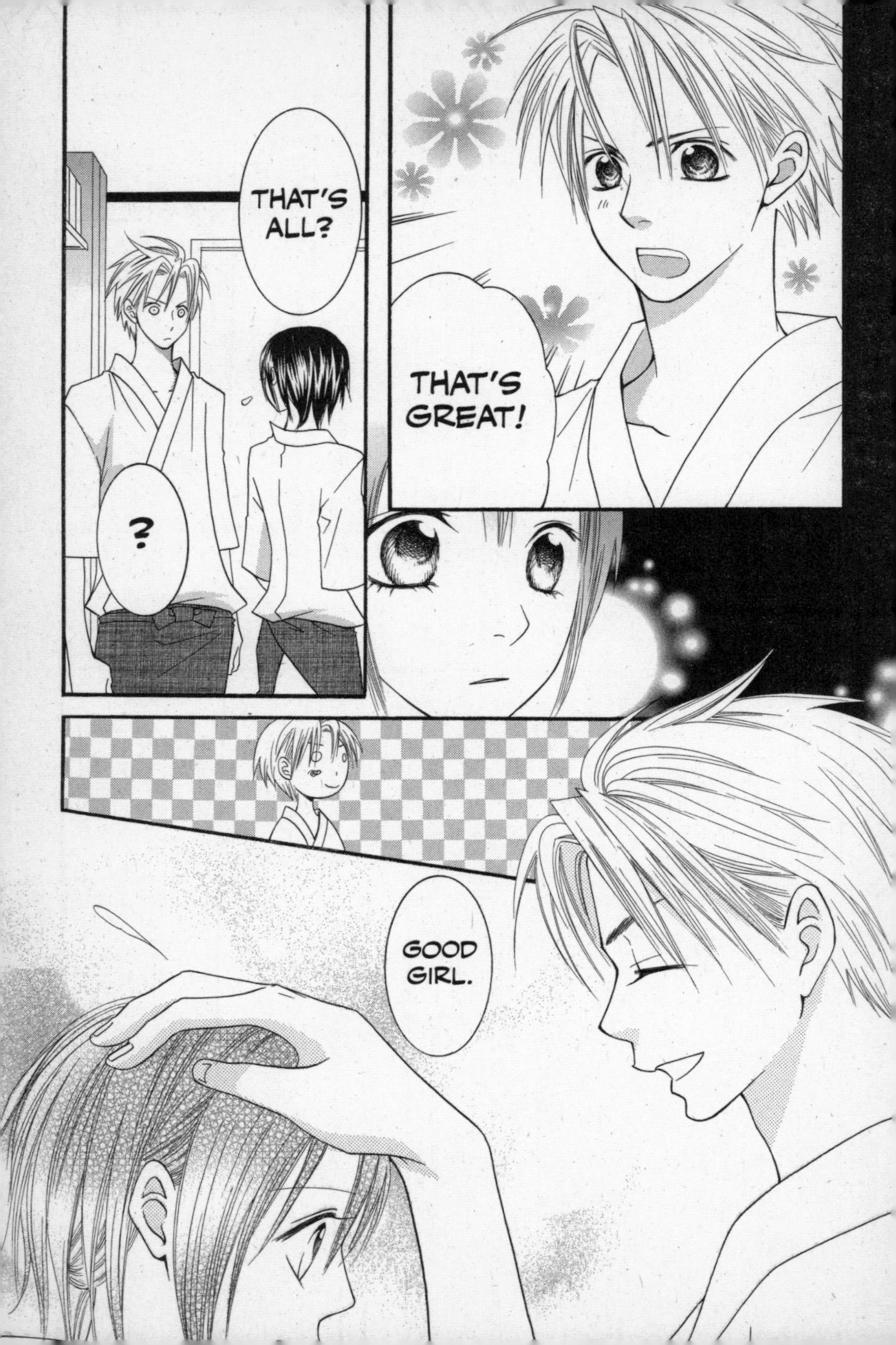
THAT'S GREAT!
THAT'S ALL?
?
GOOD GIRL.

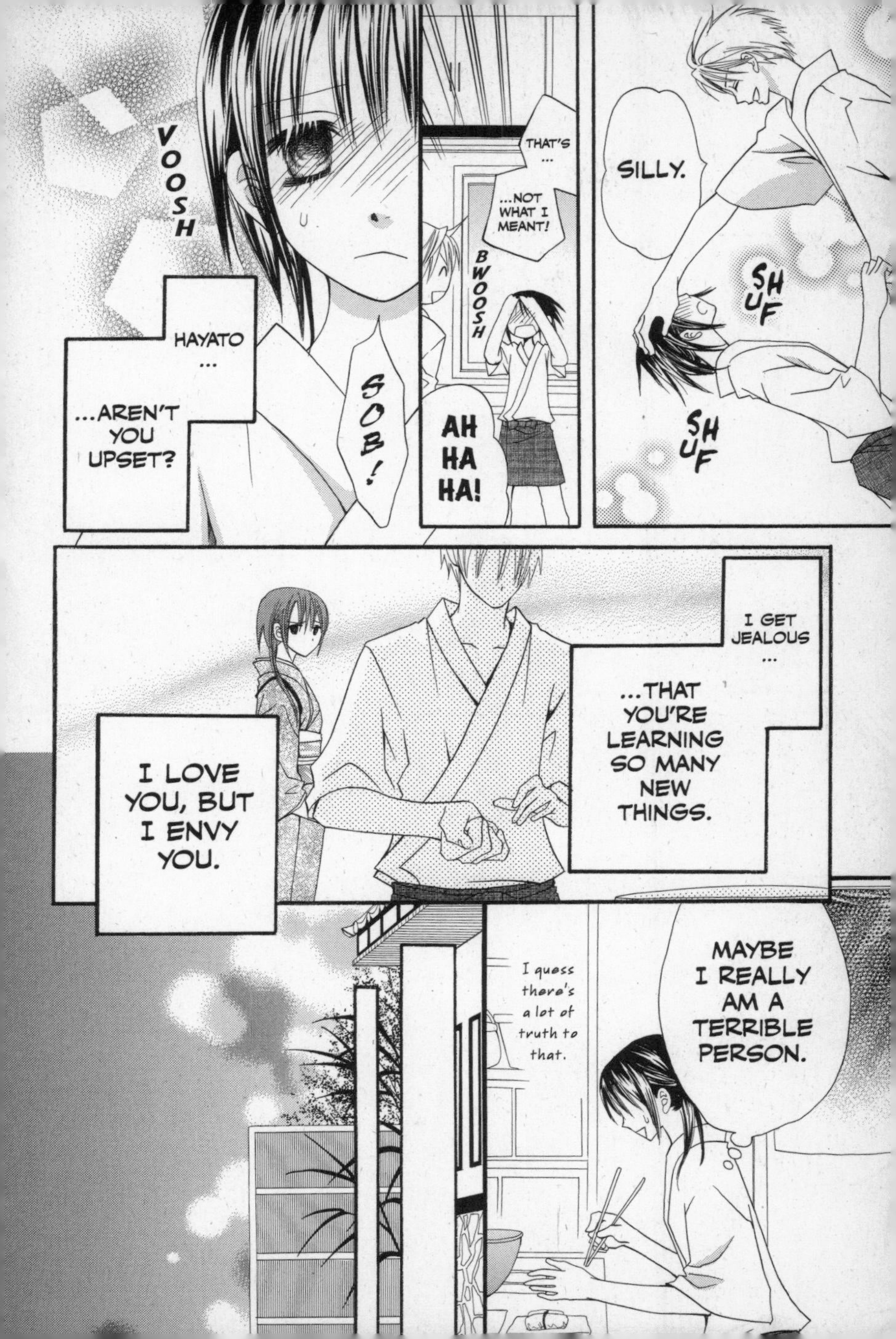
SILLY.
SHUF
SHUF
THAT'S ...
...NOT WHAT I MEANT!
BWOOSH
AH HA HA!
VOOSH
SOB!
HAYATO ...
...AREN'T YOU UPSET?
I GET JEALOUS ...
...THAT YOU'RE LEARNING SO MANY NEW THINGS.
I LOVE YOU, BUT I ENVY YOU.
MAYBE I REALLY AM A TERRIBLE PERSON.
I guess there's a lot of truth to that.

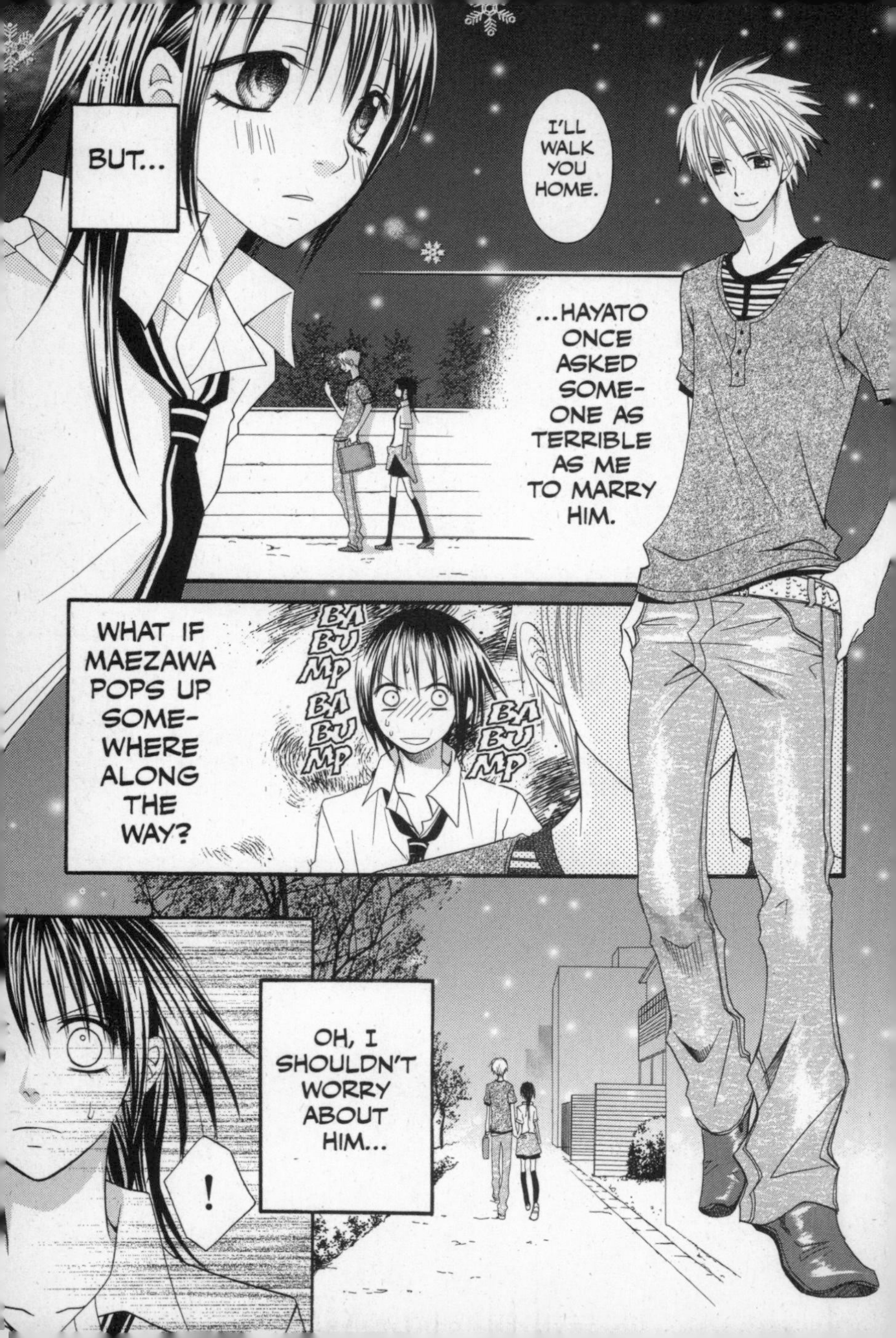
I'LL WALK YOU HOME.
BUT...
...HAYATO ONCE ASKED SOME-ONE AS TERRIBLE AS ME TO MARRY HIM.
BA BUMP
BA BUMP
BA BUMP
WHAT IF MAEZAWA POPS UP SOME-WHERE ALONG THE WAY?
OH, I SHOULDN'T WORRY ABOUT HIM...
!

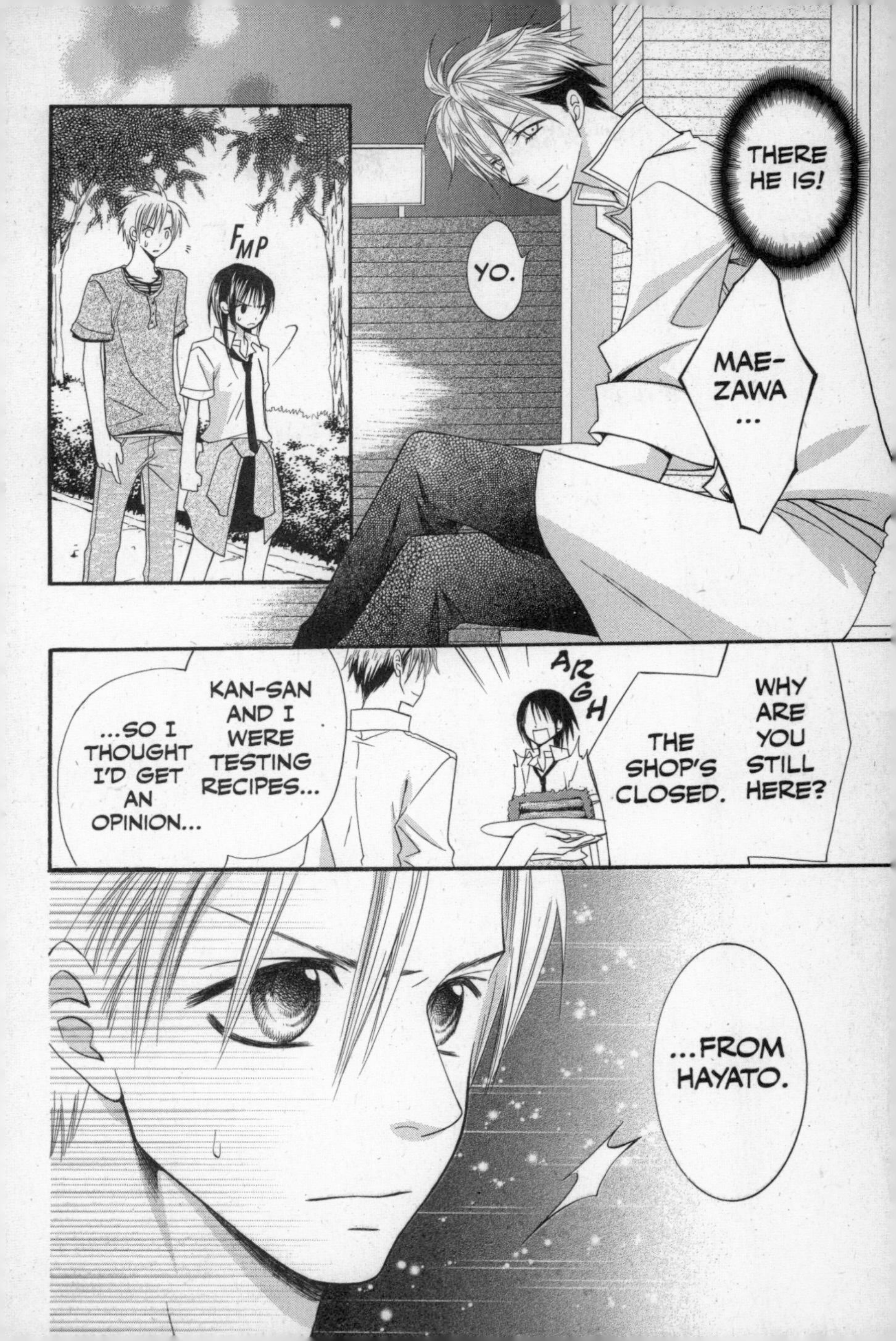
THERE HE IS!
YO.
MAE-ZAWA...
FMP
WHY ARE YOU STILL HERE?
THE SHOP'S CLOSED.
ARGH
KAN-SAN AND I WERE TESTING RECIPES...
...SO I THOUGHT I'D GET AN OPINION...
...FROM HAYATO.

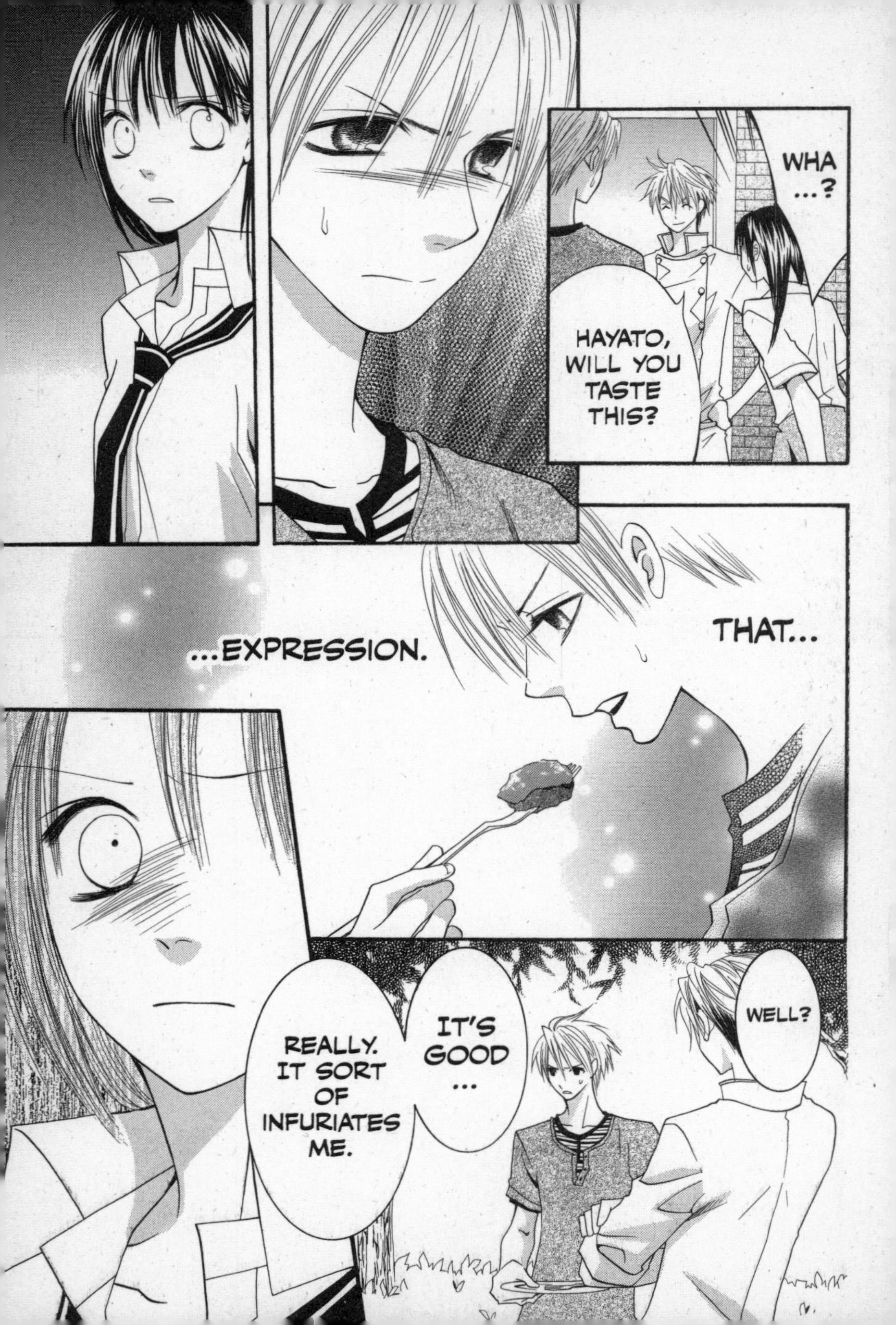
WHA ...?
HAYATO, WILL YOU TASTE THIS?
THAT...
...EXPRESSION.
WELL?
IT'S GOOD ...
REALLY. IT SORT OF INFURIATES ME.

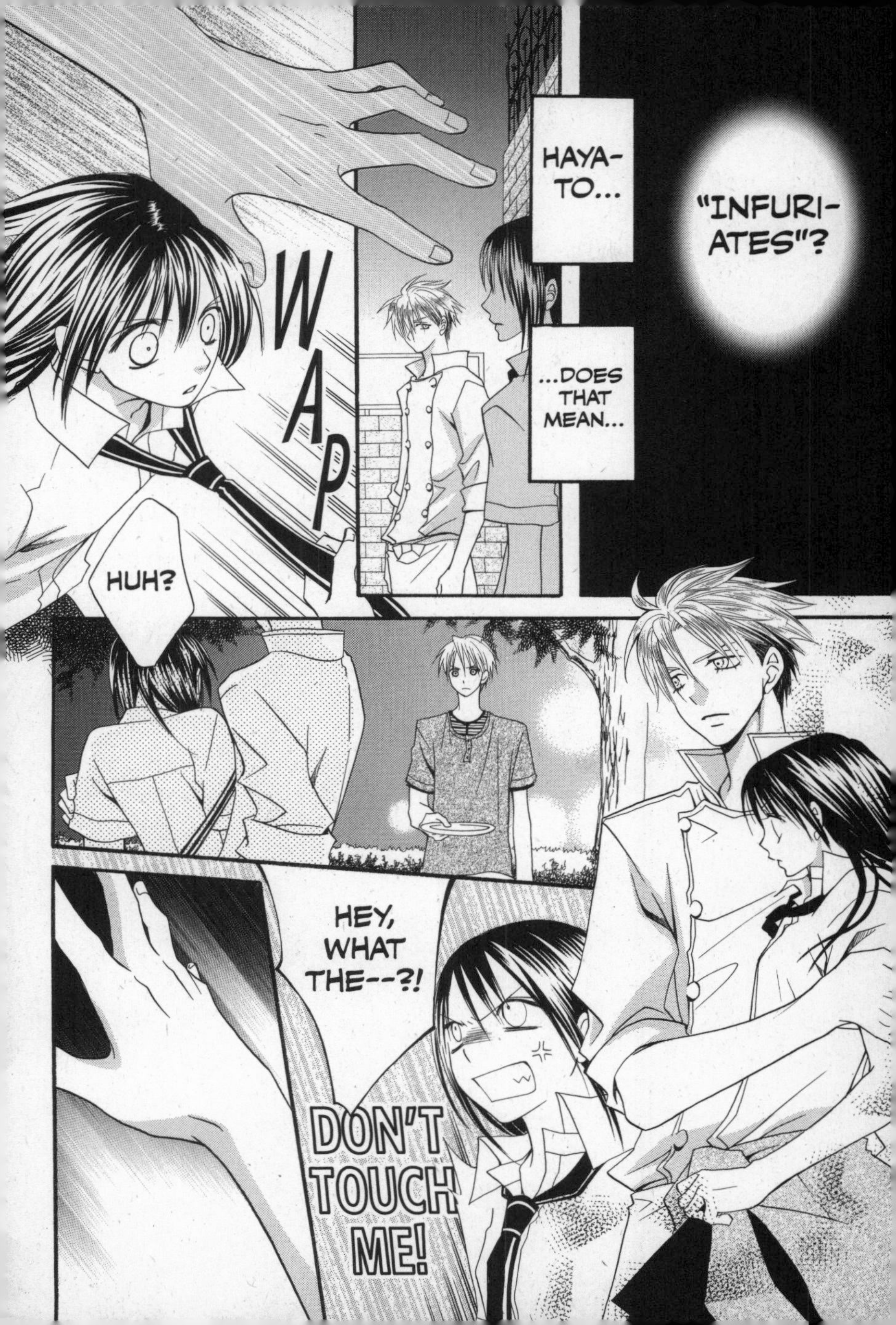
HAYA-TO...
...DOES THAT MEAN...
"INFURI-ATES"?
WAP
HUH?
HEY, WHAT THE--?!
DON'T TOUCH ME!

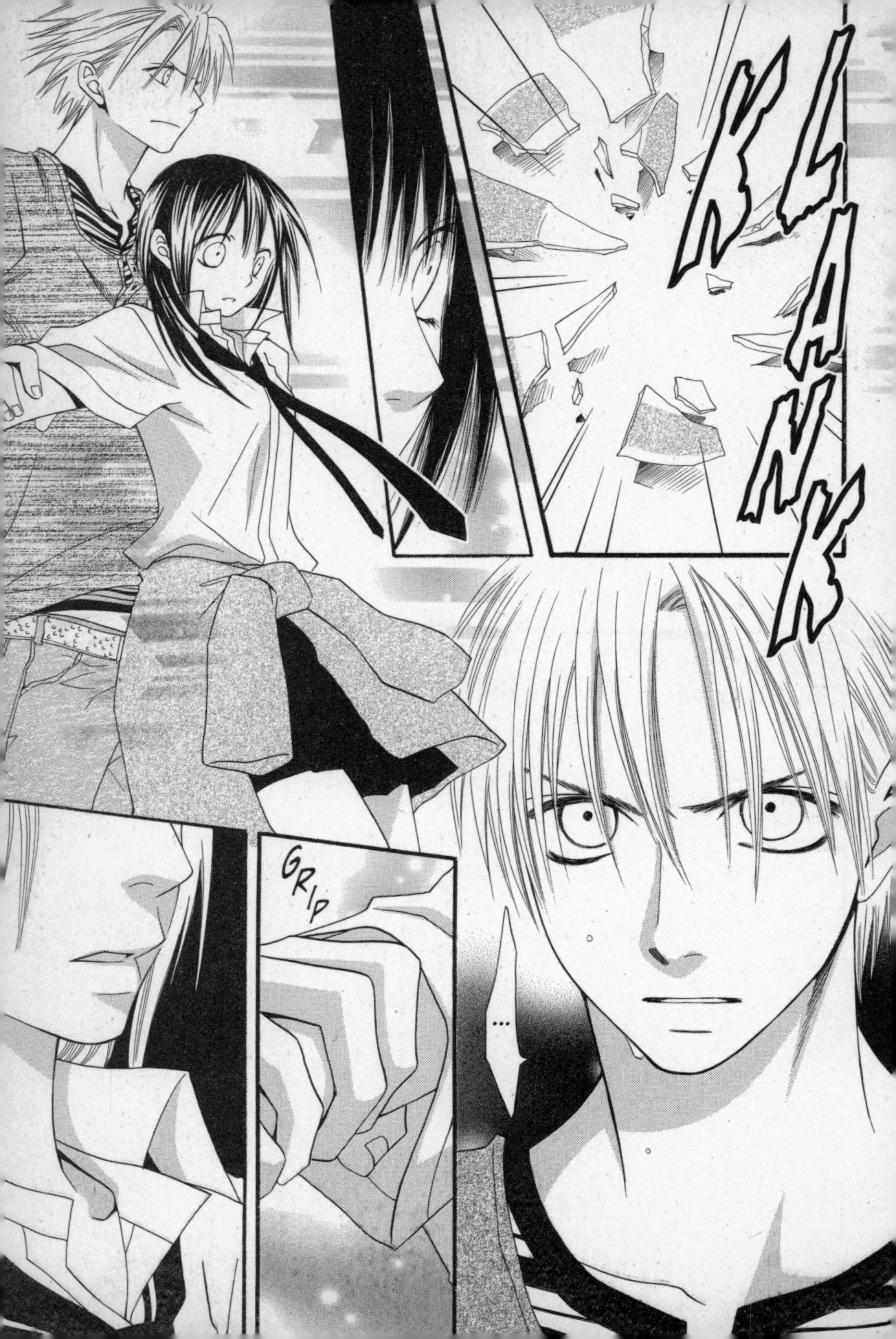
KLANK
GRIP
...

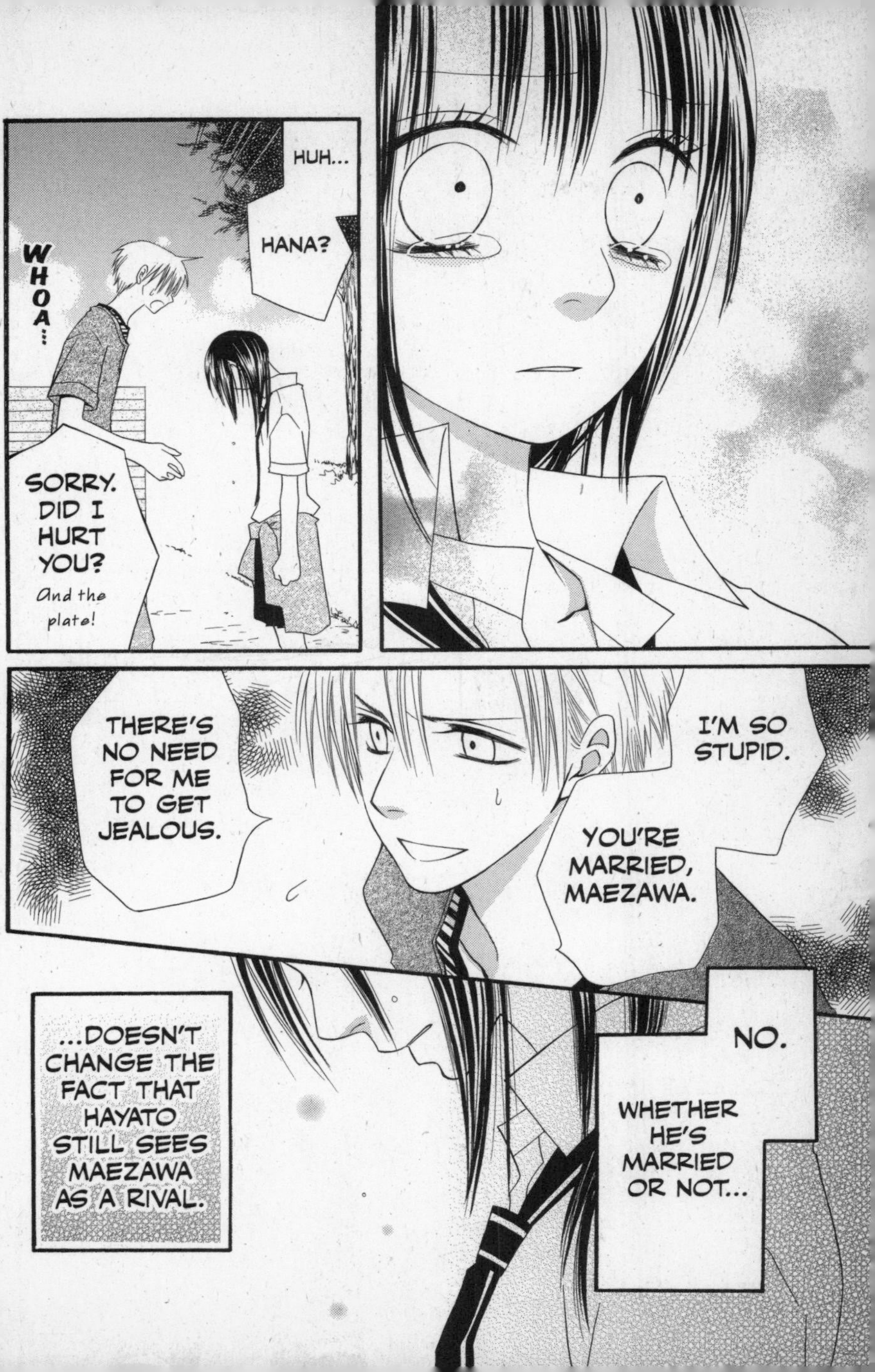
HUH...
HANA?
WHOA...
SORRY. DID I HURT YOU?
And the plate!
I'M SO STUPID.
YOU'RE MARRIED, MAEZAWA.
THERE'S NO NEED FOR ME TO GET JEALOUS.
NO.
WHETHER HE'S MARRIED OR NOT...
...DOESN'T CHANGE THE FACT THAT HAYATO STILL SEES MAEZAWA AS A RIVAL.

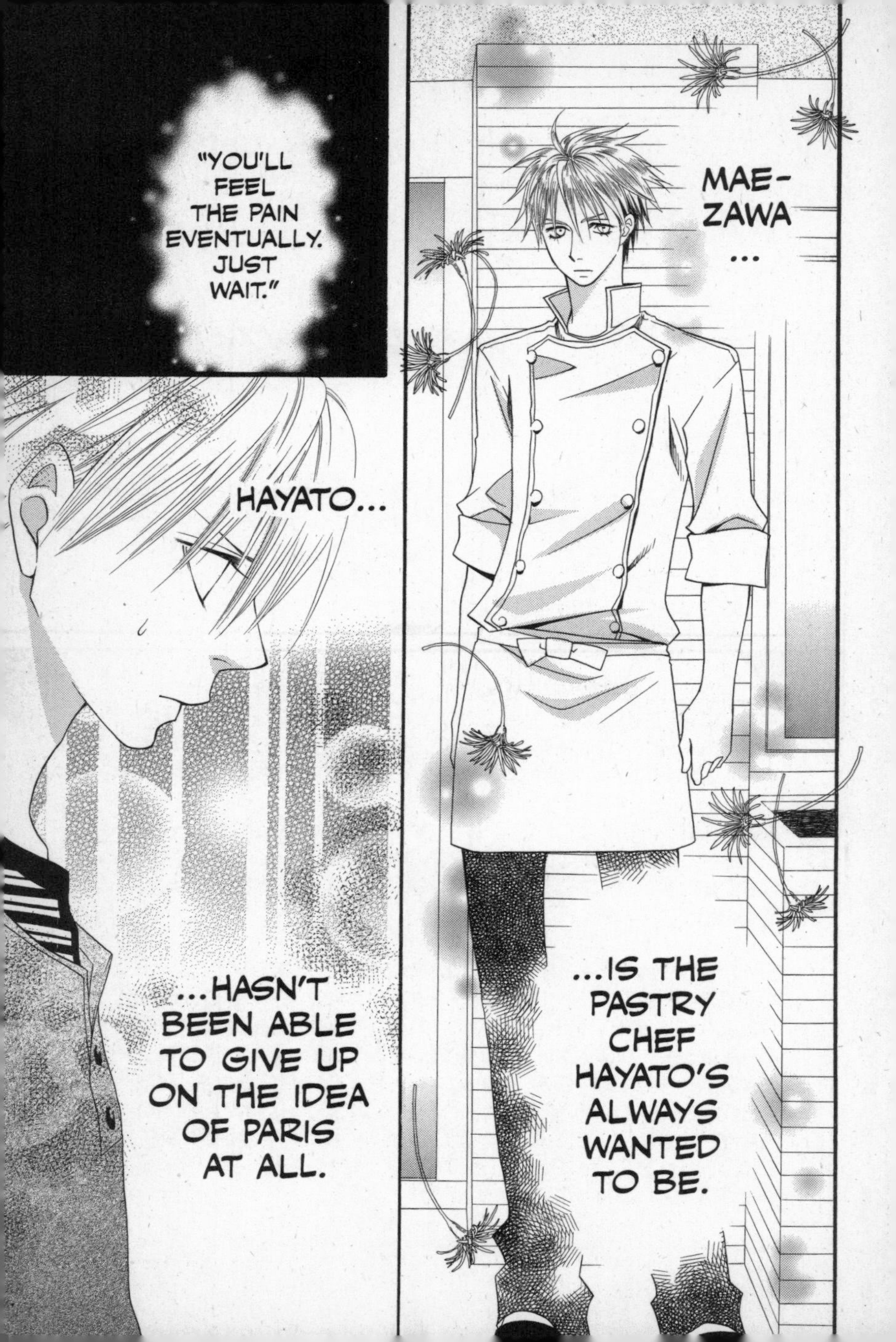
MAE-
ZAWA
...
...IS THE PASTRY CHEF HAYATO'S ALWAYS WANTED TO BE.
"YOU'LL FEEL THE PAIN EVENTUALLY. JUST WAIT."
HAYATO...
...HASN'T BEEN ABLE TO GIVE UP ON THE IDEA OF PARIS AT ALL.

MIXED VEGETABLES Encyclopedia of Characters

HAYATO HYUGA

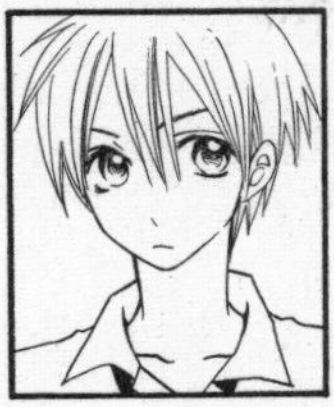

HAYATO → *HAYATO URI*

AS I WROTE IN HANA'S ENTRY, LAST NAME = SHOP NAME, SO I CHOSE SOMETHING THAT MATCHED A SUSHI SHOP. AND SINCE THERE WEREN'T MANY NAMES THAT COULD BE USED FOR A BOY, IT TURNED OUT TO BE A PRETTY FANCY NAME... EVEN THOUGH IT IS A SQUASH.

IT SOUNDS SLIGHTLY WEAK, BUT I THINK IT SUITS SOMEONE WHO IS KIND, GENEROUS AND LOVES HIS GRANDFATHER. I'M GLAD I HAD THE OPPORTUNITY TO CREATE A CHARACTER LIKE HIM.

IN A WAY, MY EDITOR SERVED AS A MODEL; HE WAS ALWAYS INTERESTED AND ENTHUSIASTIC ABOUT MY WORK, AND I HAD HIM IN MIND WHEN I CAME UP WITH HAYATO.

BUT TOWARD THE END, THE EDITOR KEPT TELLING ME THAT BOTH HANA AND HAYATO WERE "CLUMSY, CLUMSY," AND THAT THEY SEEMED TO CHANGE INTO QUITE DIFFERENT CHARACTERS. HAYATO'S BIRTHDAY IS AUGUST 23. HE WAS BORN IN SUMMER AND HATES THE COLD. HE MUST HAVE VERY LITTLE BODY FAT. WHICH MEANS HE PROBABLY DOESN'T FLOAT. A NEW BIT OF INFORMATION AT THIS LATE DATE...

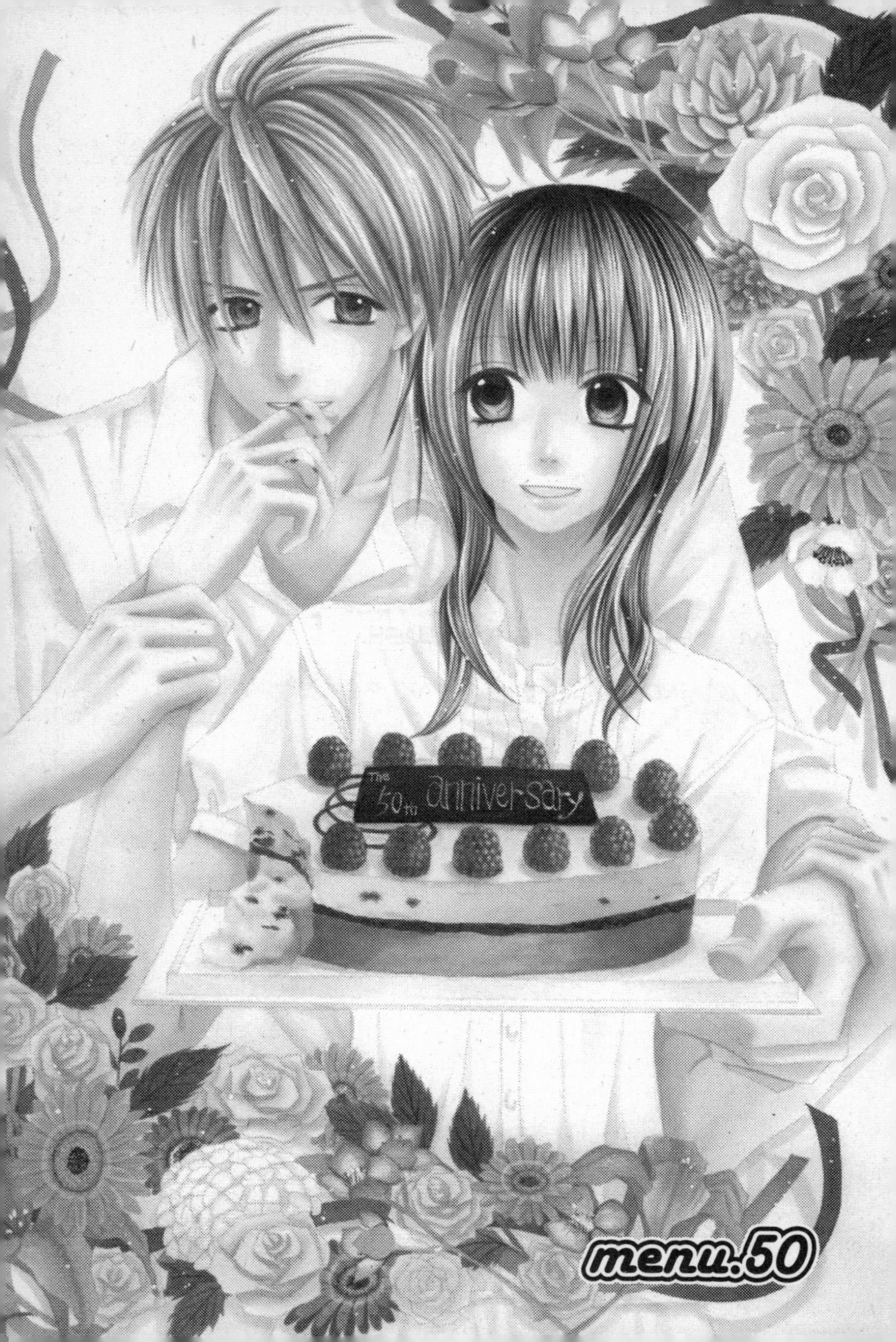
The 50th anniversary
menu.50

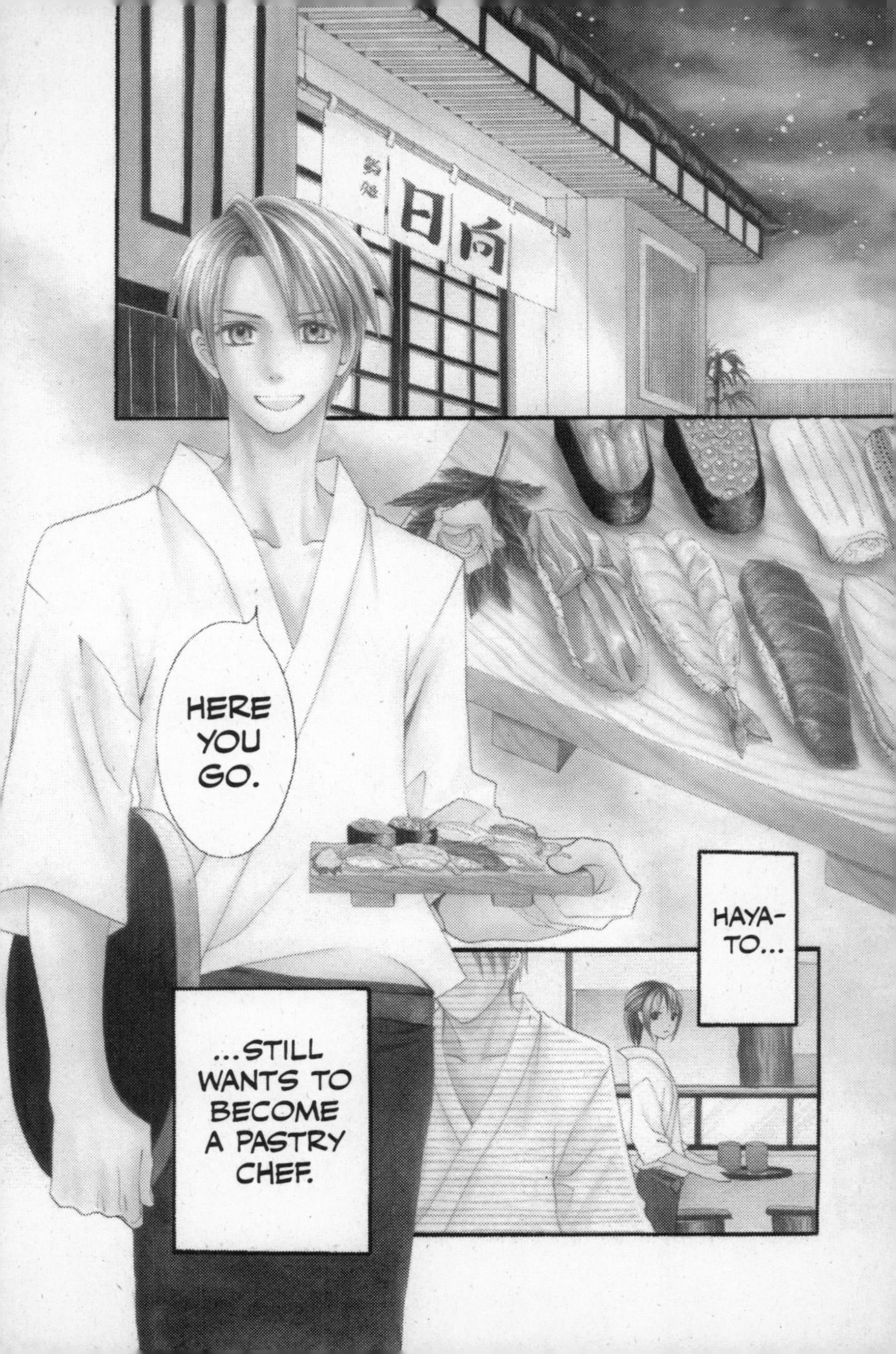
日向
HERE YOU GO.
HAYA-TO...
...STILL WANTS TO BECOME A PASTRY CHEF.

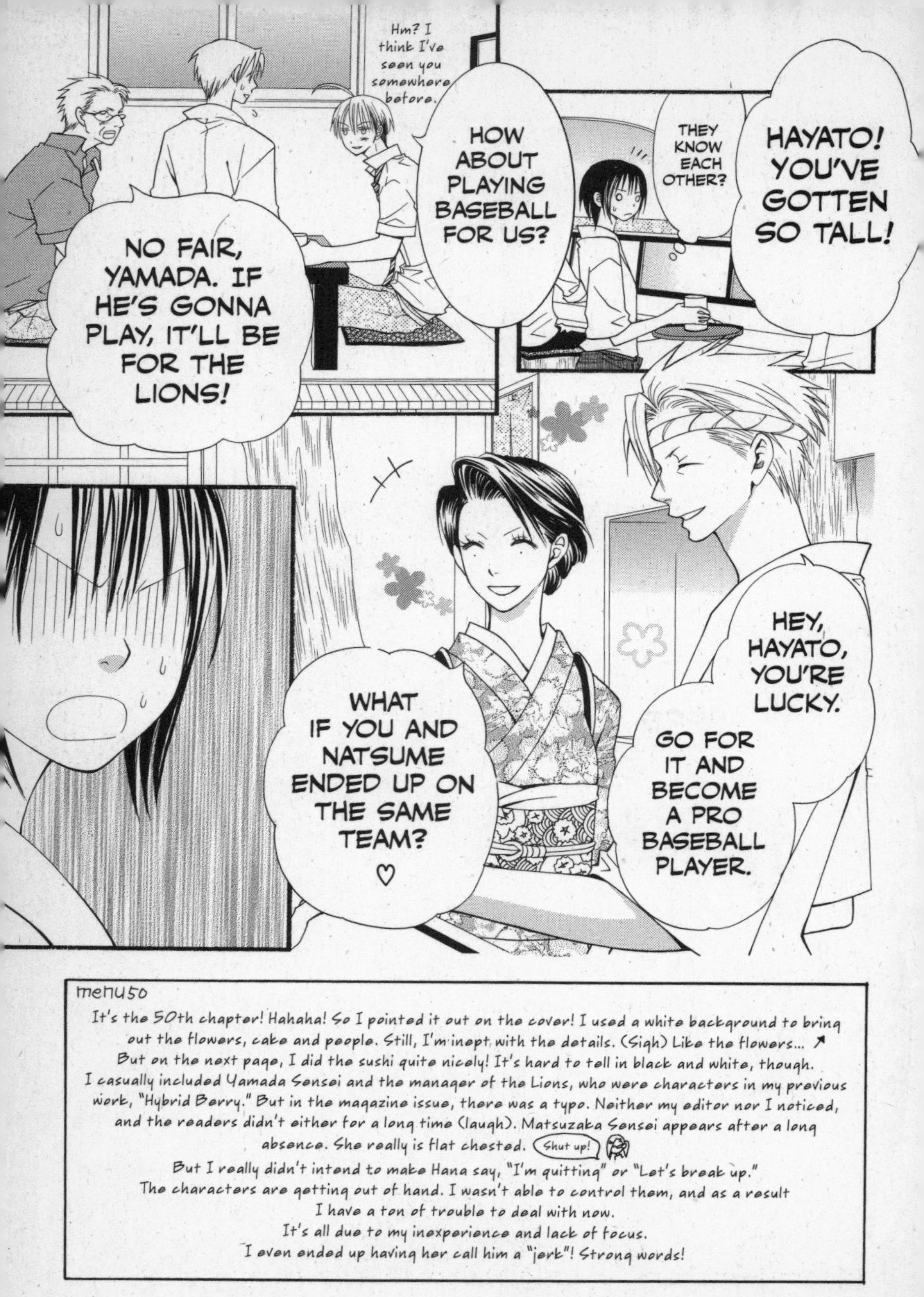
HAYATO! YOU'VE GOTTEN SO TALL!
THEY KNOW EACH OTHER?
Hm? I think I've seen you somewhere before.
HOW ABOUT PLAYING BASEBALL FOR US?
NO FAIR, YAMADA. IF HE'S GONNA PLAY, IT'LL BE FOR THE LIONS!
HEY, HAYATO, YOU'RE LUCKY.
GO FOR IT AND BECOME A PRO BASEBALL PLAYER.
WHAT IF YOU AND NATSUME ENDED UP ON THE SAME TEAM? ♡

menu50

It's the 50th chapter! Hahaha! So I pointed it out on the cover! I used a white background to bring out the flowers, cake and people. Still, I'm inept with the details. (Sigh) Like the flowers... ↗ But on the next page, I did the sushi quite nicely! It's hard to tell in black and white, though. I casually included Yamada Sensei and the manager of the Lions, who were characters in my previous work, "Hybrid Berry." But in the magazine issue, there was a typo. Neither my editor nor I noticed, and the readers didn't either for a long time (laugh). Matsuzaka Sensei appears after a long absence. She really is flat chested. (Shut up!)

But I really didn't intend to make Hana say, "I'm quitting" or "Let's break up."

The characters are getting out of hand. I wasn't able to control them, and as a result I have a ton of trouble to deal with now.

It's all due to my inexperience and lack of focus.

I even ended up having her call him a "jerk"! Strong words!

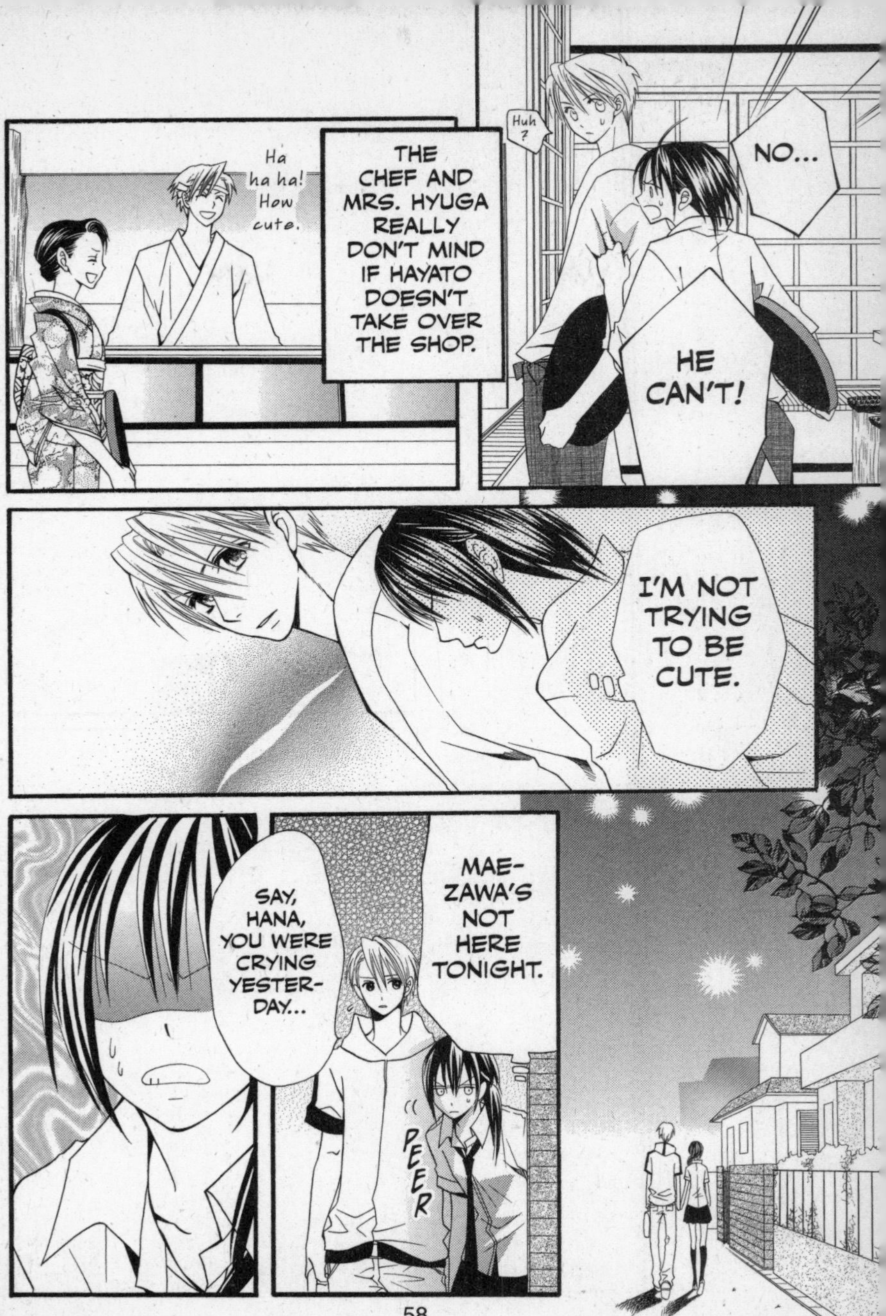
NO...
Huh ?
HE CAN'T!
THE CHEF AND MRS. HYUGA REALLY DON'T MIND IF HAYATO DOESN'T TAKE OVER THE SHOP.
Ha ha ha! How cute.
I'M NOT TRYING TO BE CUTE.
MAE-ZAWA'S NOT HERE TONIGHT.
SAY, HANA, YOU WERE CRYING YESTER-DAY...
PEER

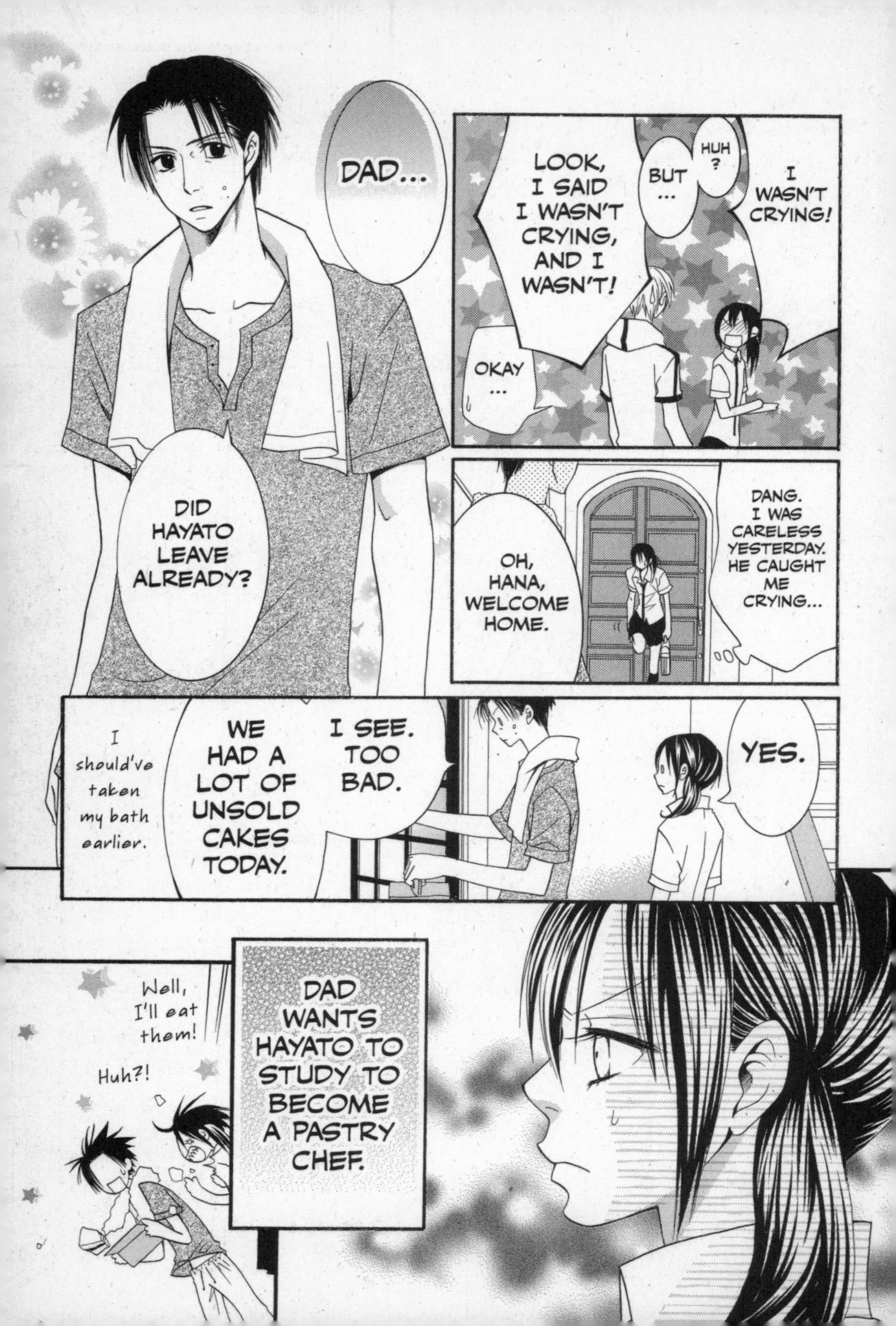
I WASN'T CRYING!
HUH?
BUT...
LOOK, I SAID I WASN'T CRYING, AND I WASN'T!
OKAY...
DANG. I WAS CARELESS YESTERDAY. HE CAUGHT ME CRYING...
OH, HANA, WELCOME HOME.
DAD...
DID HAYATO LEAVE ALREADY?
YES.
I SEE. TOO BAD.
WE HAD A LOT OF UNSOLD CAKES TODAY.
I should've taken my bath earlier.
DAD WANTS HAYATO TO STUDY TO BECOME A PASTRY CHEF.
Well, I'll eat them!
Huh?!

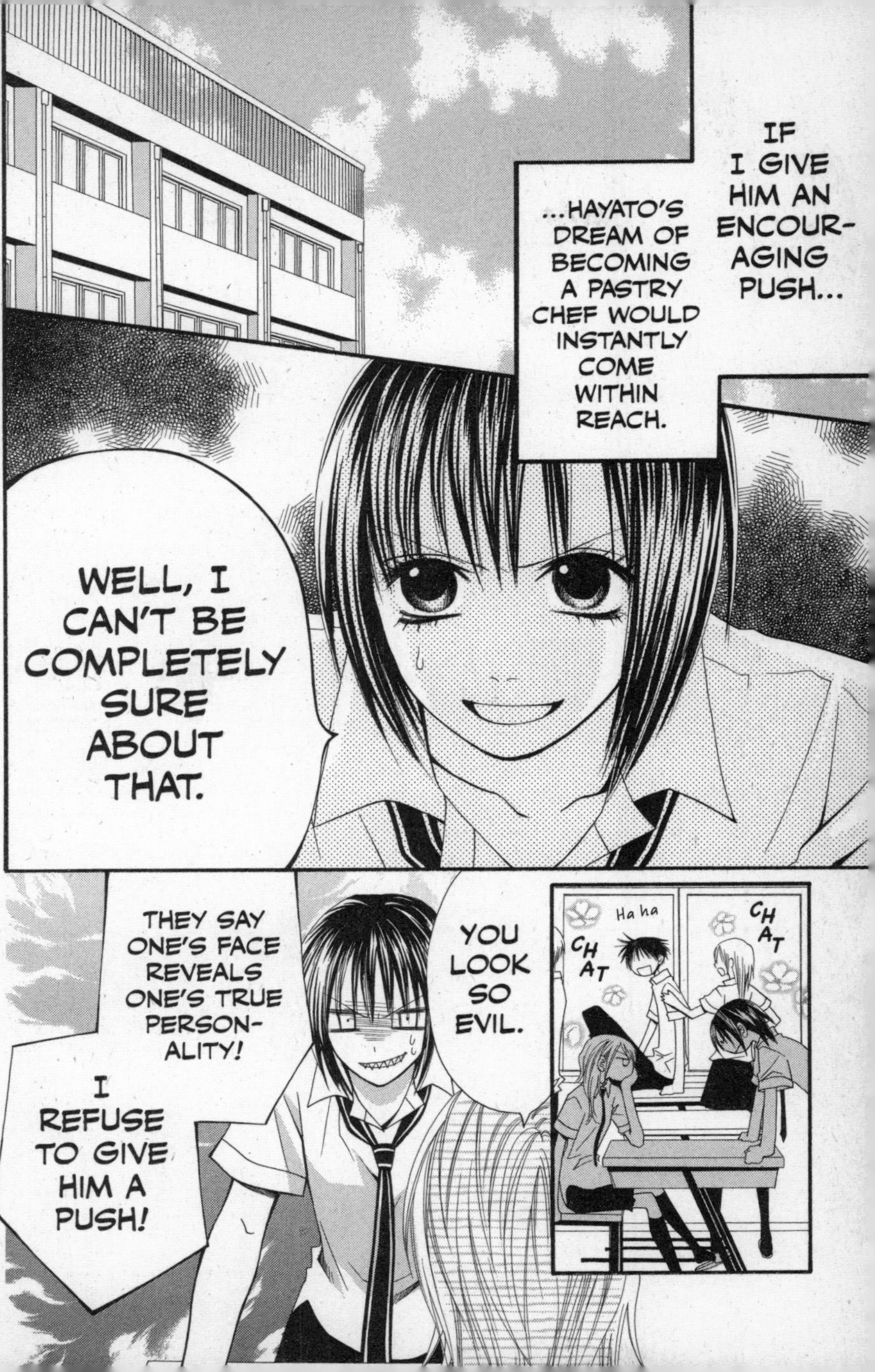
IF I GIVE HIM AN ENCOURAGING PUSH...
...HAYATO'S DREAM OF BECOMING A PASTRY CHEF WOULD INSTANTLY COME WITHIN REACH.
WELL, I CAN'T BE COMPLETELY SURE ABOUT THAT.
Ha ha
CHAT
CHAT
YOU LOOK SO EVIL.
THEY SAY ONE'S FACE REVEALS ONE'S TRUE PERSONALITY!
I REFUSE TO GIVE HIM A PUSH!

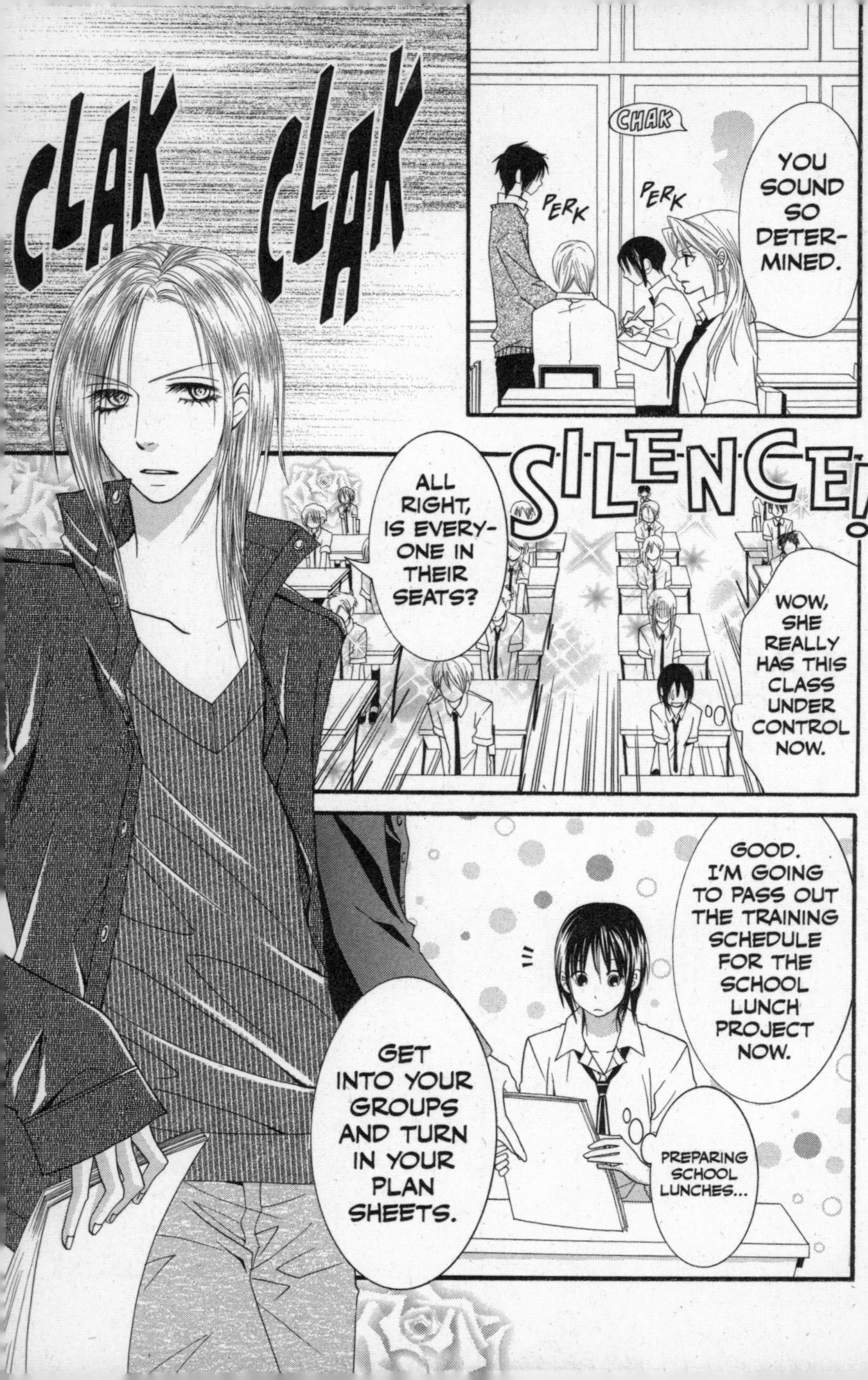
CHAK
PERK
PERK
YOU SOUND SO DETERMINED.
CLAK CLAK
SILENCE!
ALL RIGHT, IS EVERYONE IN THEIR SEATS?
WOW, SHE REALLY HAS THIS CLASS UNDER CONTROL NOW.
GOOD. I'M GOING TO PASS OUT THE TRAINING SCHEDULE FOR THE SCHOOL LUNCH PROJECT NOW.
GET INTO YOUR GROUPS AND TURN IN YOUR PLAN SHEETS.
PREPARING SCHOOL LUNCHES...

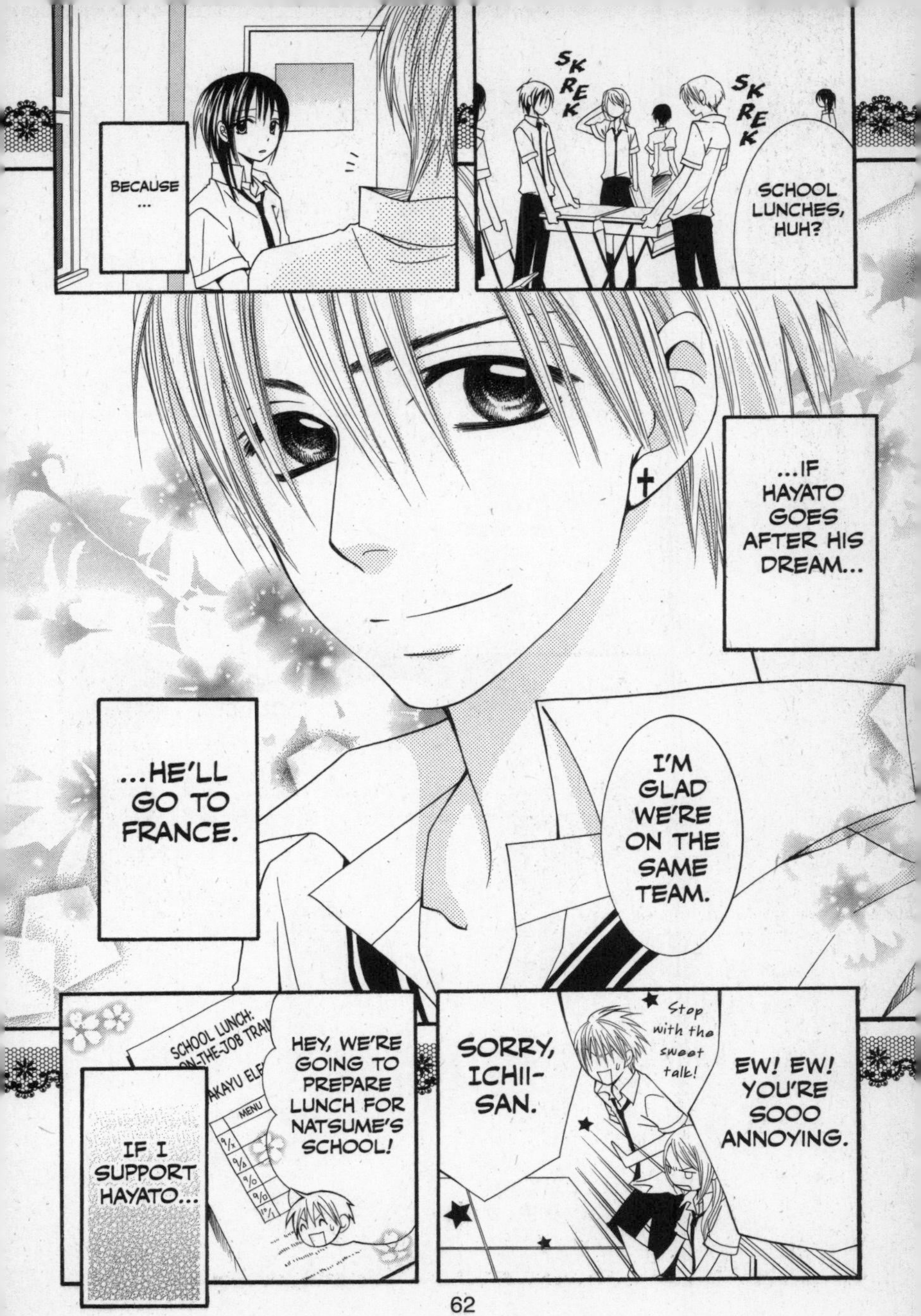
SKREK
SKREK
SCHOOL LUNCHES, HUH?
BECAUSE ...
...IF HAYATO GOES AFTER HIS DREAM...
I'M GLAD WE'RE ON THE SAME TEAM.
...HE'LL GO TO FRANCE.
EW! EW! YOU'RE SOOO ANNOYING.
Stop with the sweet talk!
SORRY, ICHII-SAN.
HEY, WE'RE GOING TO PREPARE LUNCH FOR NATSUME'S SCHOOL!
SCHOOL LUNCH:
MENU
IF I SUPPORT HAYATO...

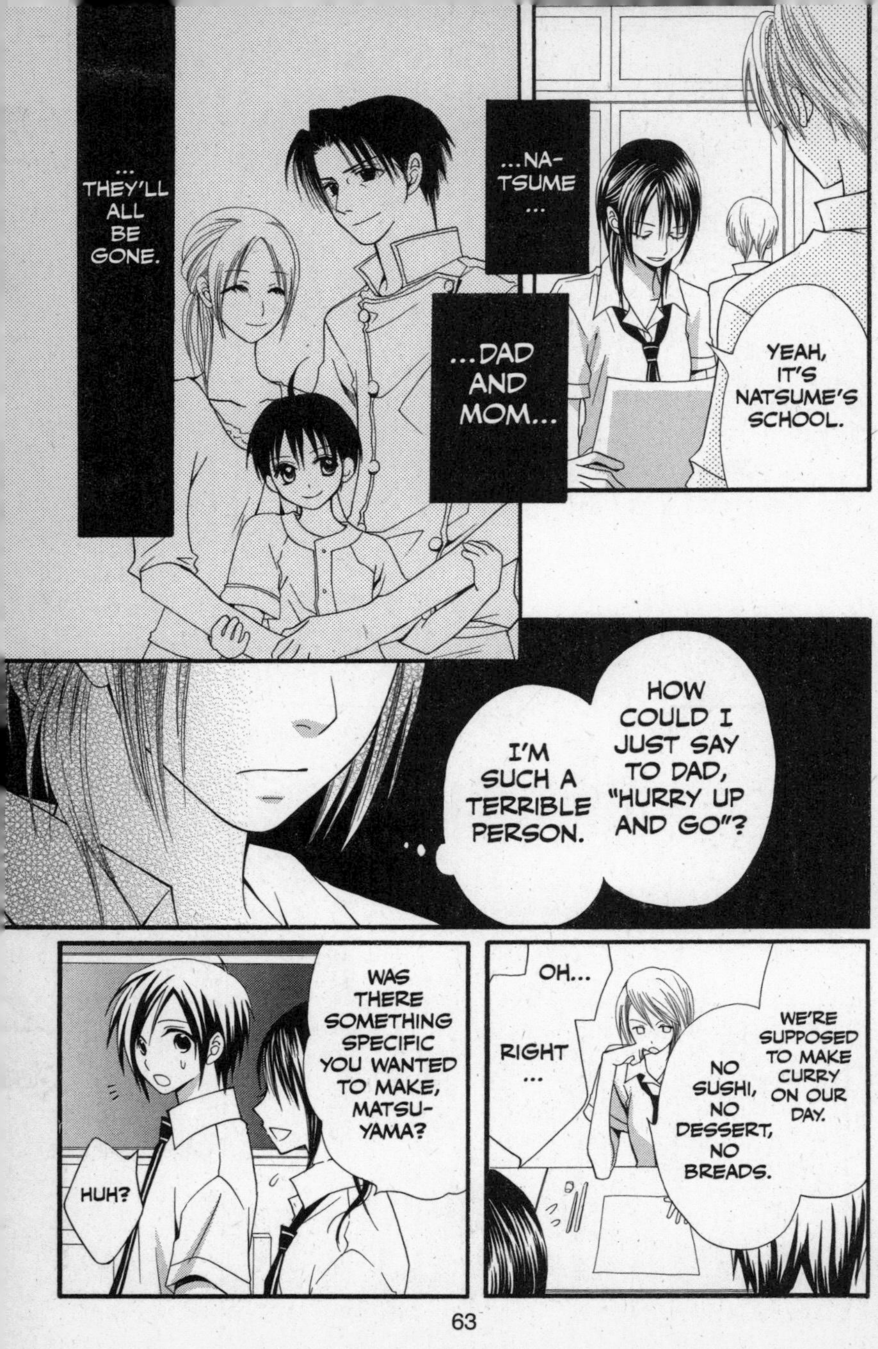
YEAH, IT'S NATSUME'S SCHOOL.
...NA-TSUME...
...DAD AND MOM...
...THEY'LL ALL BE GONE.
HOW COULD I JUST SAY TO DAD, "HURRY UP AND GO"?
I'M SUCH A TERRIBLE PERSON.
WE'RE SUPPOSED TO MAKE CURRY ON OUR DAY.
NO SUSHI, NO DESSERT, NO BREADS.
OH...
RIGHT...
WAS THERE SOMETHING SPECIFIC YOU WANTED TO MAKE, MATSU-YAMA?
HUH?

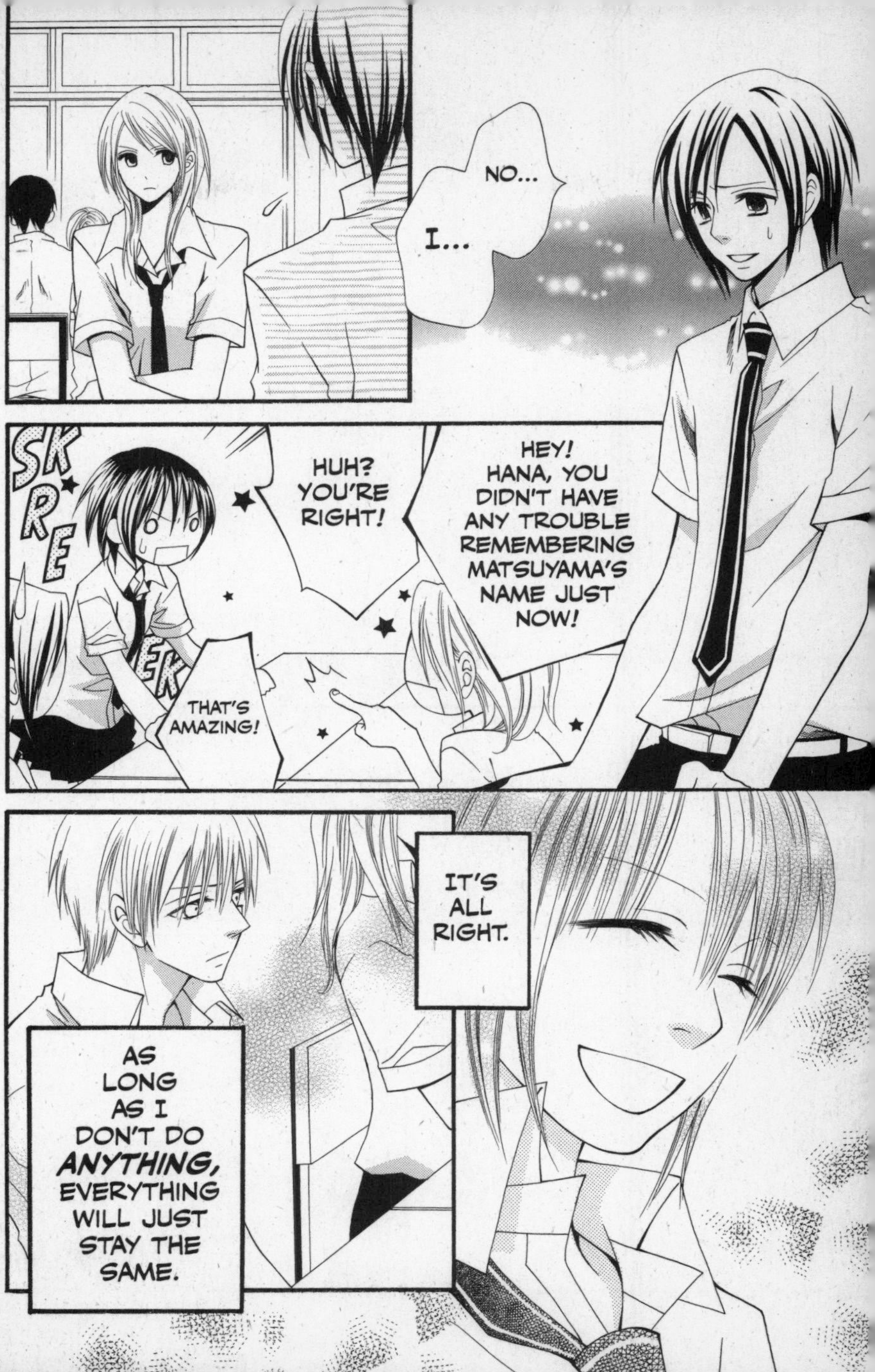
NO...
I...
HEY! HANA, YOU DIDN'T HAVE ANY TROUBLE REMEMBERING MATSUYAMA'S NAME JUST NOW!
HUH? YOU'RE RIGHT!
SKREEK
THAT'S AMAZING!
IT'S ALL RIGHT.
AS LONG AS I DON'T DO *ANYTHING*, EVERYTHING WILL JUST STAY THE SAME.

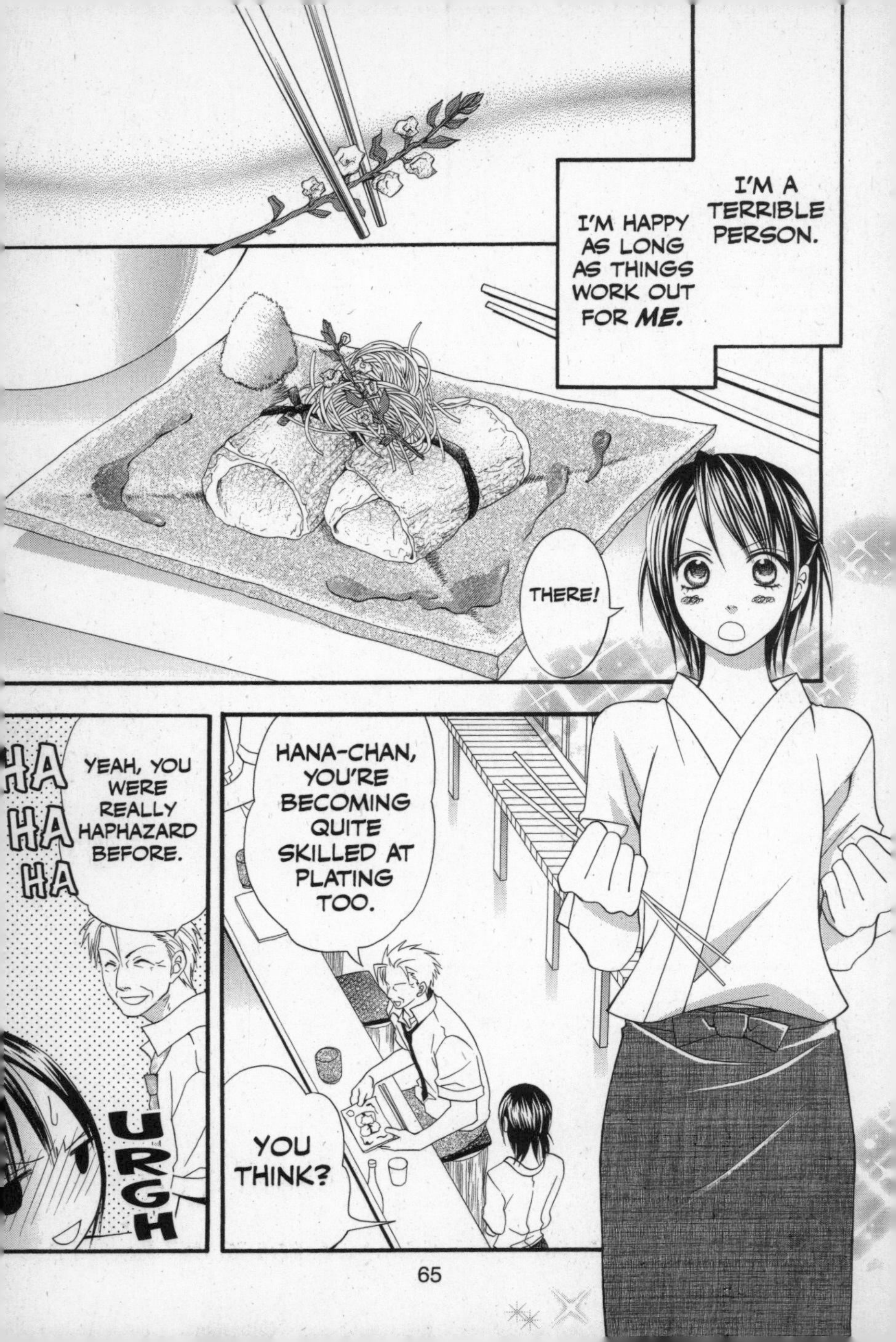
I'M A TERRIBLE PERSON.
I'M HAPPY AS LONG AS THINGS WORK OUT FOR *ME.*
THERE!
HANA-CHAN, YOU'RE BECOMING QUITE SKILLED AT PLATING TOO.
YOU THINK?
HA HA HA
YEAH, YOU WERE REALLY HAPHAZARD BEFORE.
URGH

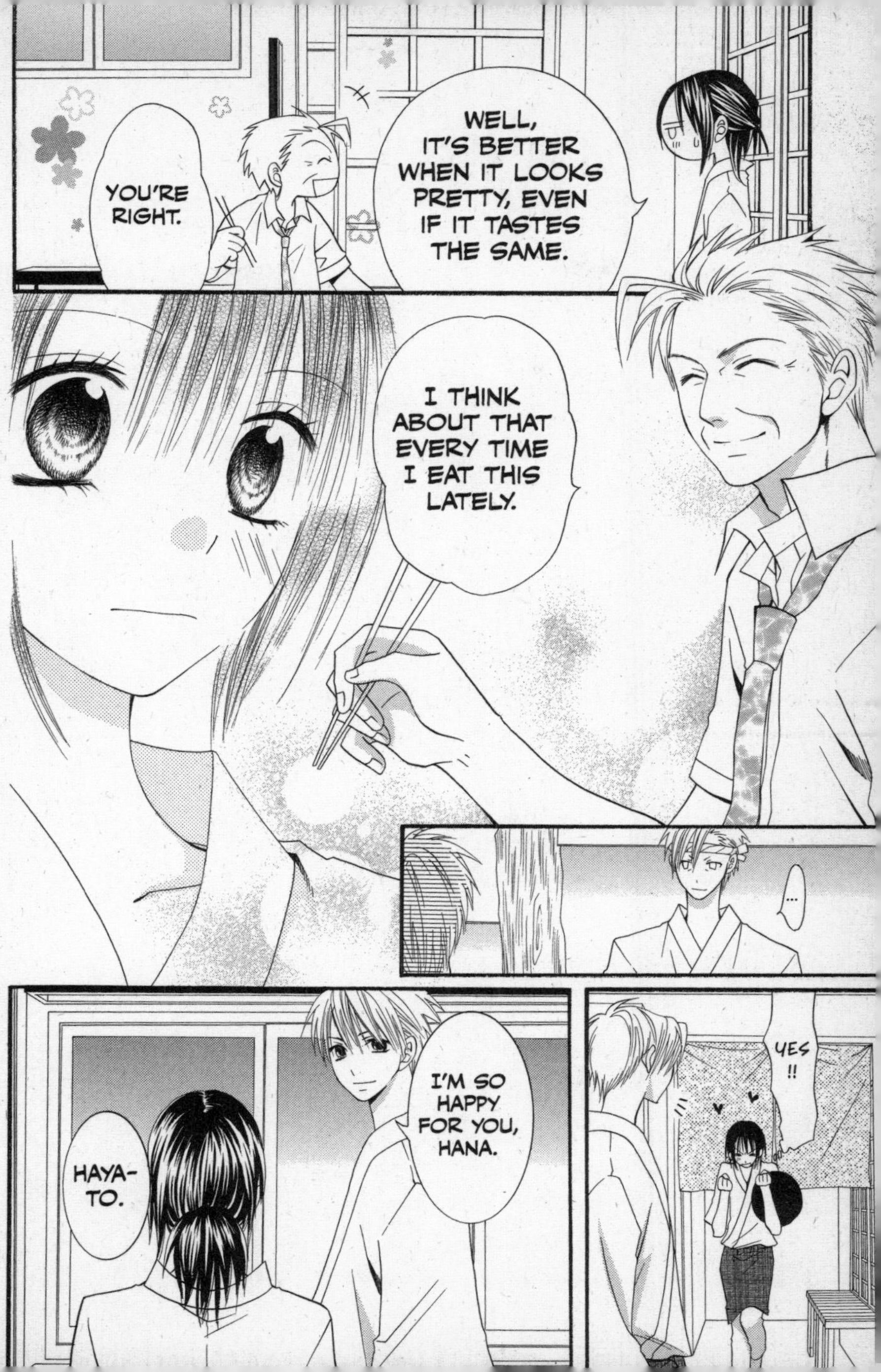
WELL, IT'S BETTER WHEN IT LOOKS PRETTY, EVEN IF IT TASTES THE SAME.
YOU'RE RIGHT.
I THINK ABOUT THAT EVERY TIME I EAT THIS LATELY.
...
YES !!
I'M SO HAPPY FOR YOU, HANA.
HAYA-TO.

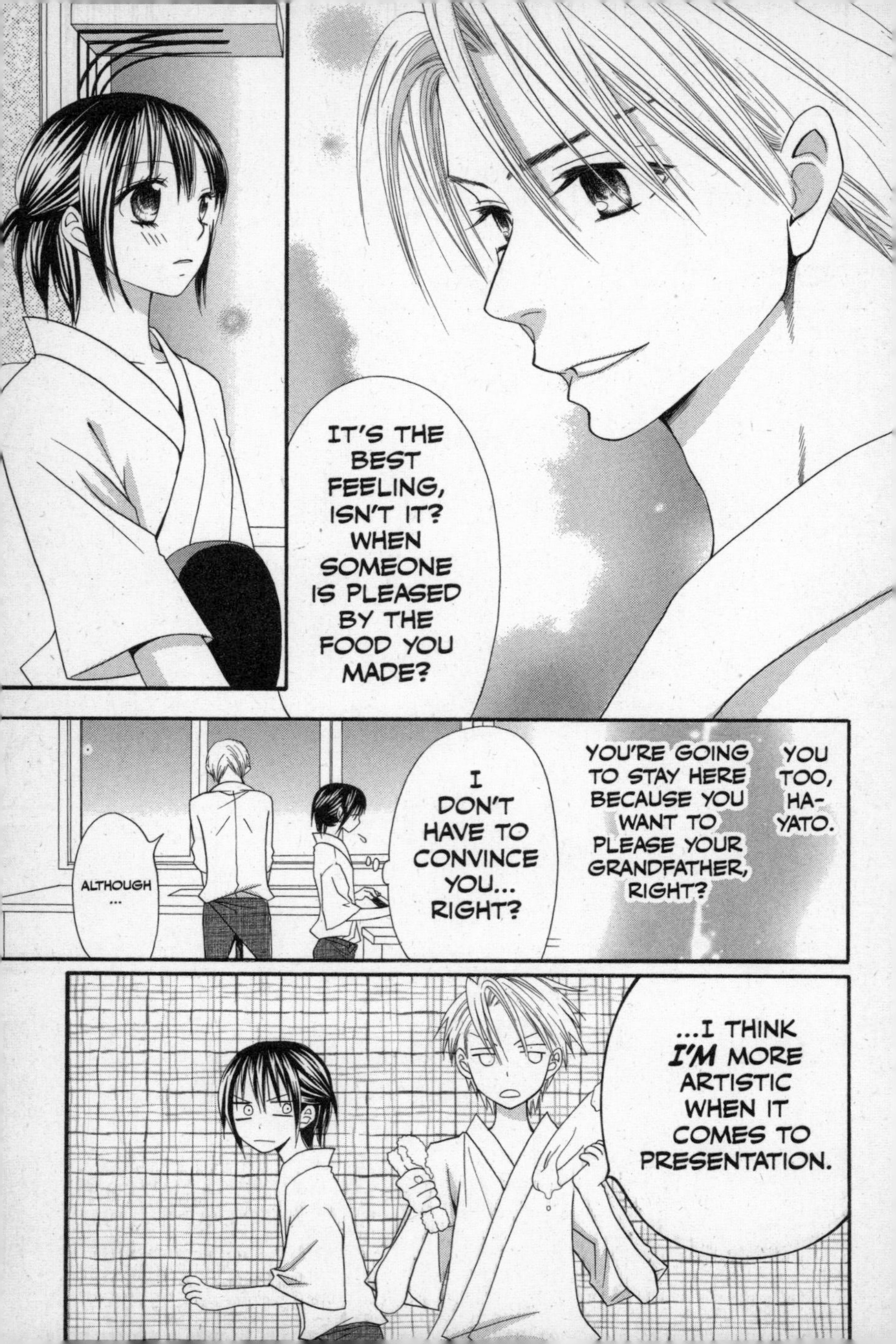
IT'S THE BEST FEELING, ISN'T IT? WHEN SOMEONE IS PLEASED BY THE FOOD YOU MADE?
YOU TOO, HA-YATO.
YOU'RE GOING TO STAY HERE BECAUSE YOU WANT TO PLEASE YOUR GRANDFATHER, RIGHT?
I DON'T HAVE TO CONVINCE YOU... RIGHT?
ALTHOUGH ...
...I THINK *I'M* MORE ARTISTIC WHEN IT COMES TO PRESENTATION.

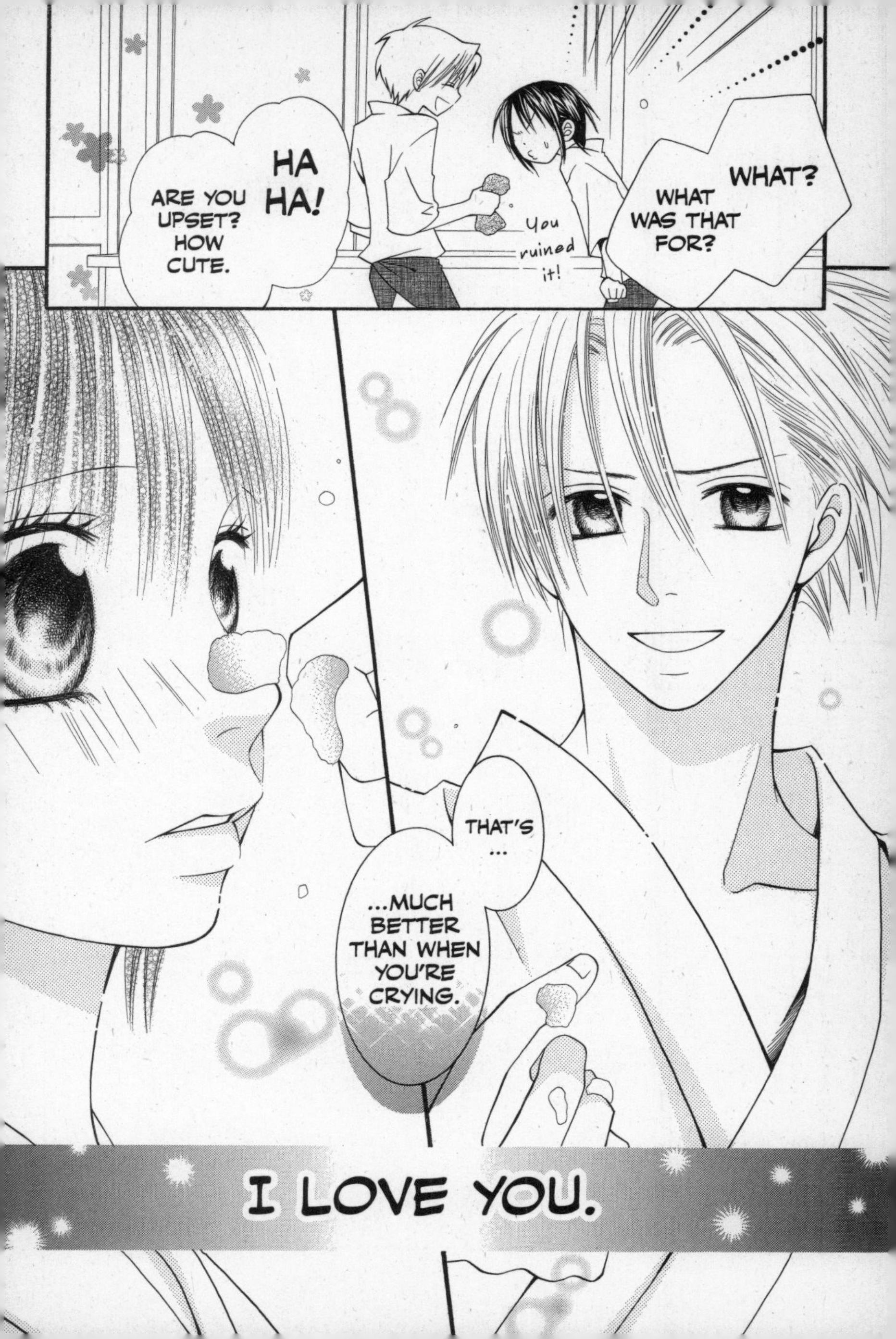
WHAT?
WHAT WAS THAT FOR?
You ruined it!
HA HA!
ARE YOU UPSET? HOW CUTE.
THAT'S ...
...MUCH BETTER THAN WHEN YOU'RE CRYING.
I LOVE YOU.

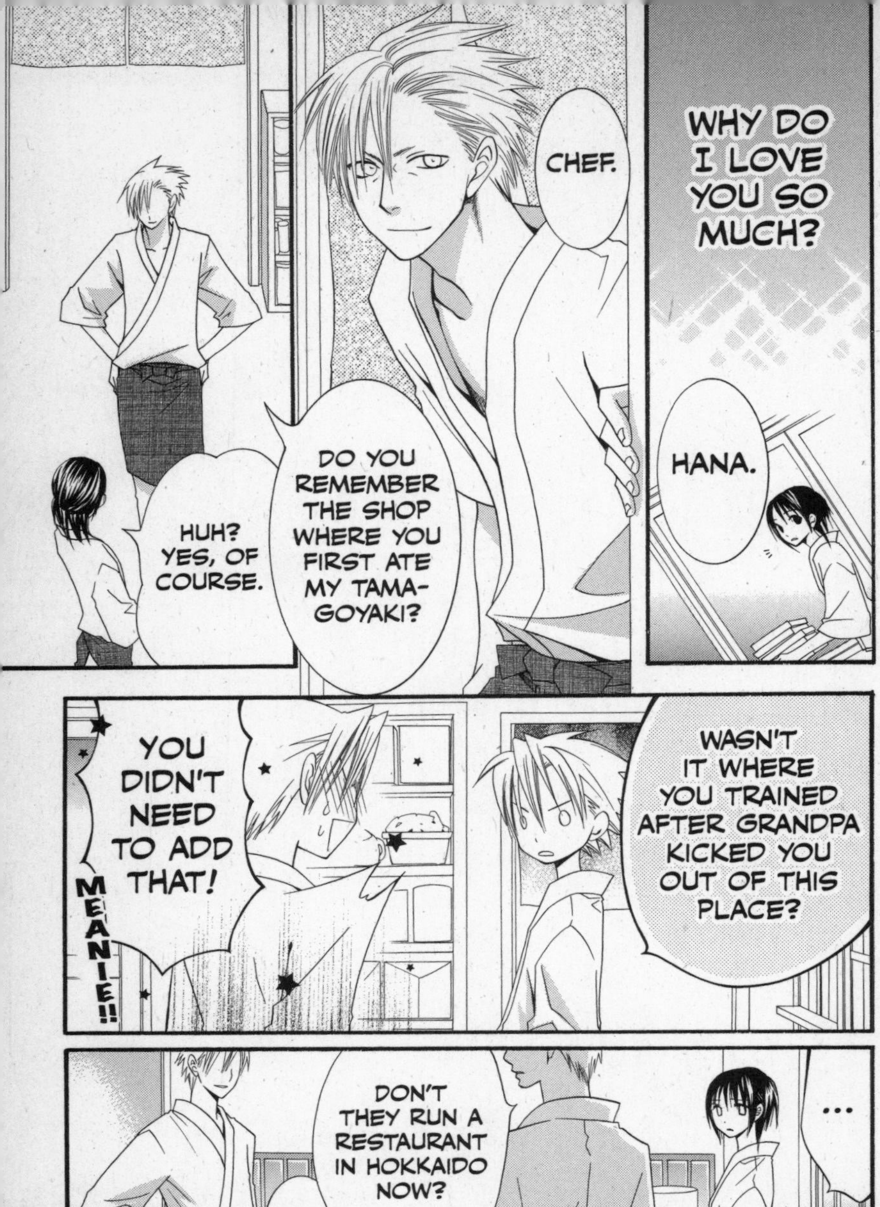
WHY DO I LOVE YOU SO MUCH?
HANA.
CHEF.
DO YOU REMEMBER THE SHOP WHERE YOU FIRST ATE MY TAMA-GOYAKI?
HUH? YES, OF COURSE.
WASN'T IT WHERE YOU TRAINED AFTER GRANDPA KICKED YOU OUT OF THIS PLACE?
YOU DIDN'T NEED TO ADD THAT!
MEANIE!!
...
DON'T THEY RUN A RESTAURANT IN HOKKAIDO NOW?
YEAH.

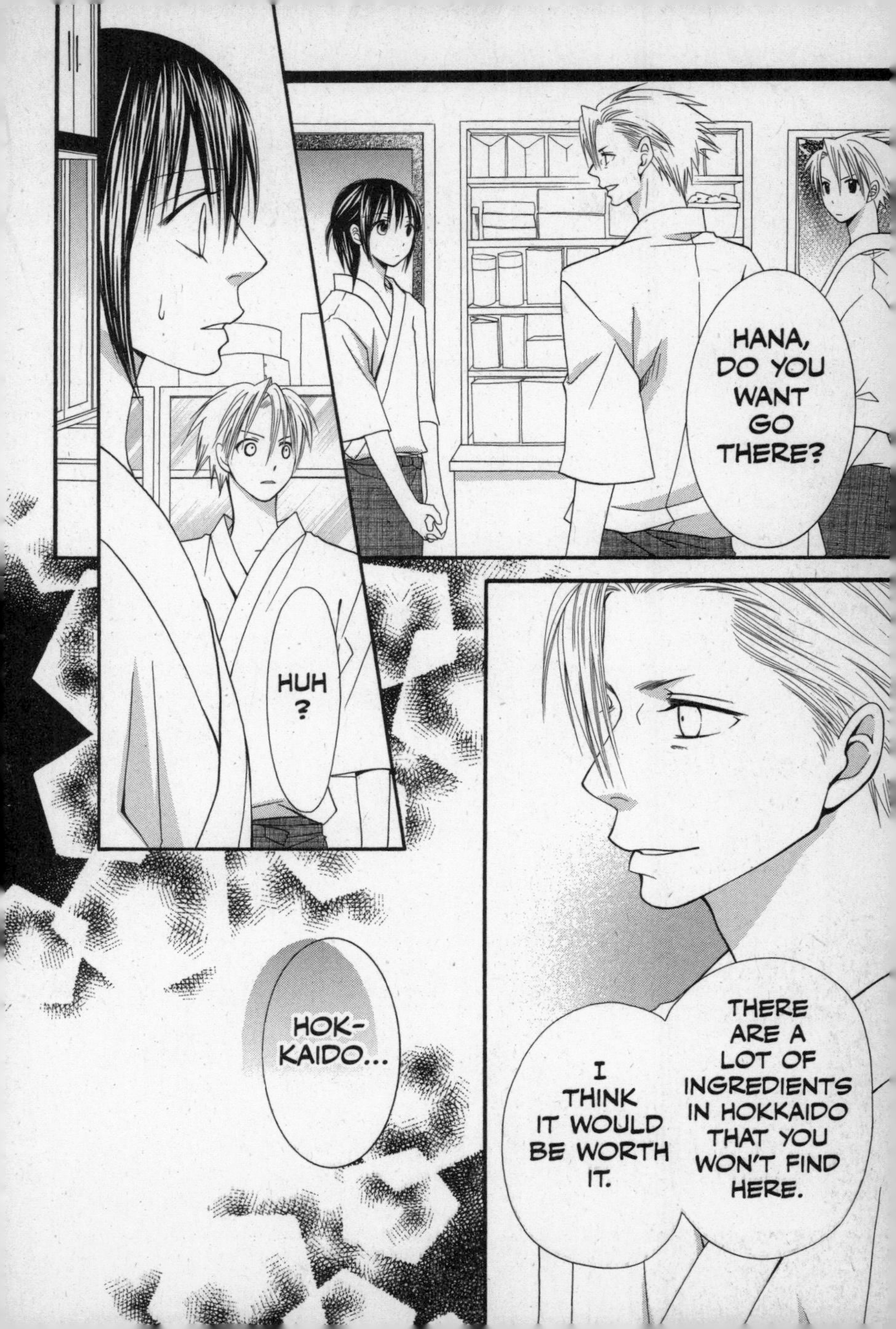
HANA, DO YOU WANT GO THERE?
HUH?
THERE ARE A LOT OF INGREDIENTS IN HOKKAIDO THAT YOU WON'T FIND HERE.
I THINK IT WOULD BE WORTH IT.
HOK-KAIDO...

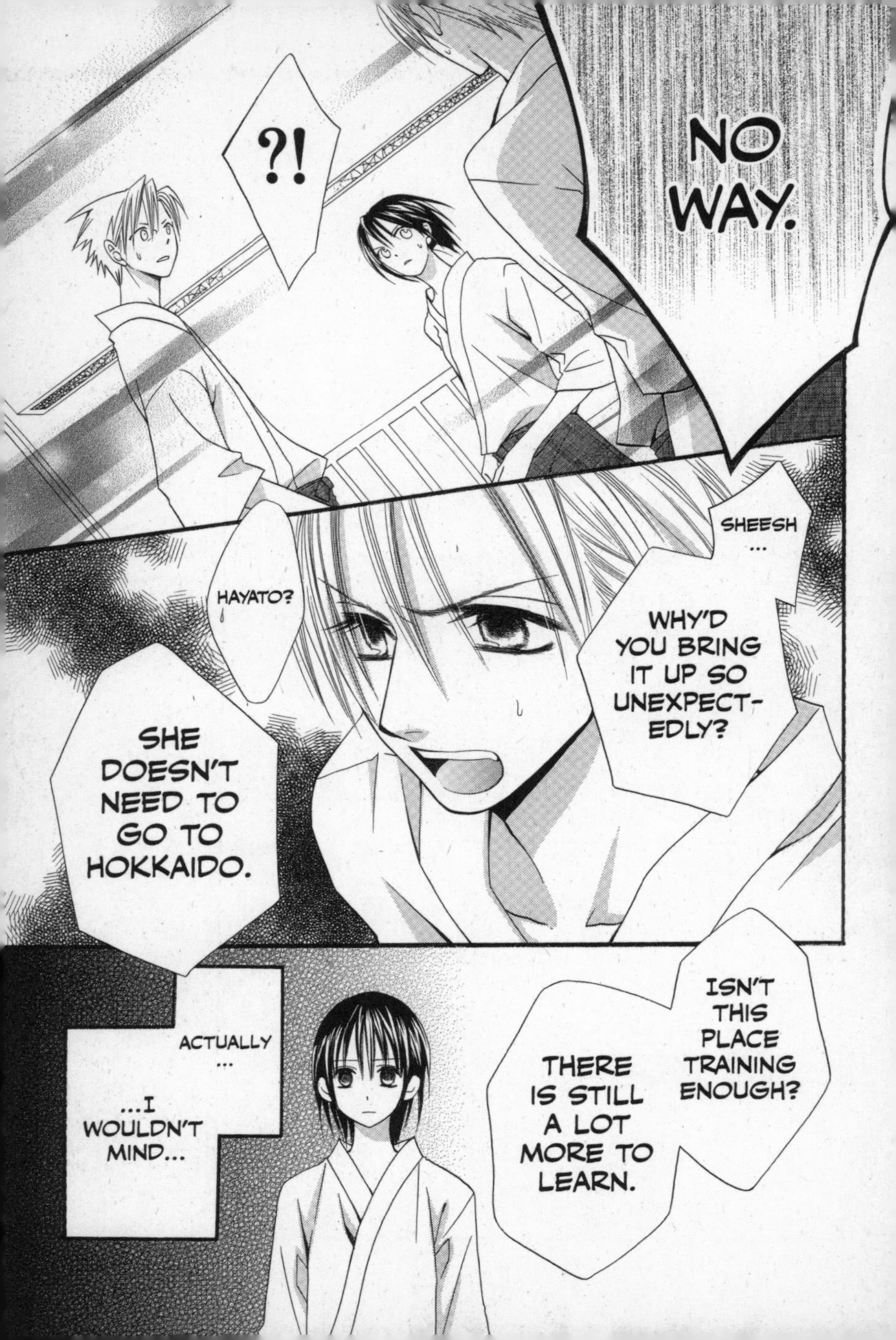
NO WAY.
?!
SHEESH ...
WHY'D YOU BRING IT UP SO UNEXPECT-EDLY?
HAYATO?
SHE DOESN'T NEED TO GO TO HOKKAIDO.
ISN'T THIS PLACE TRAINING ENOUGH?
THERE IS STILL A LOT MORE TO LEARN.
ACTUALLY ...
...I WOULDN'T MIND...

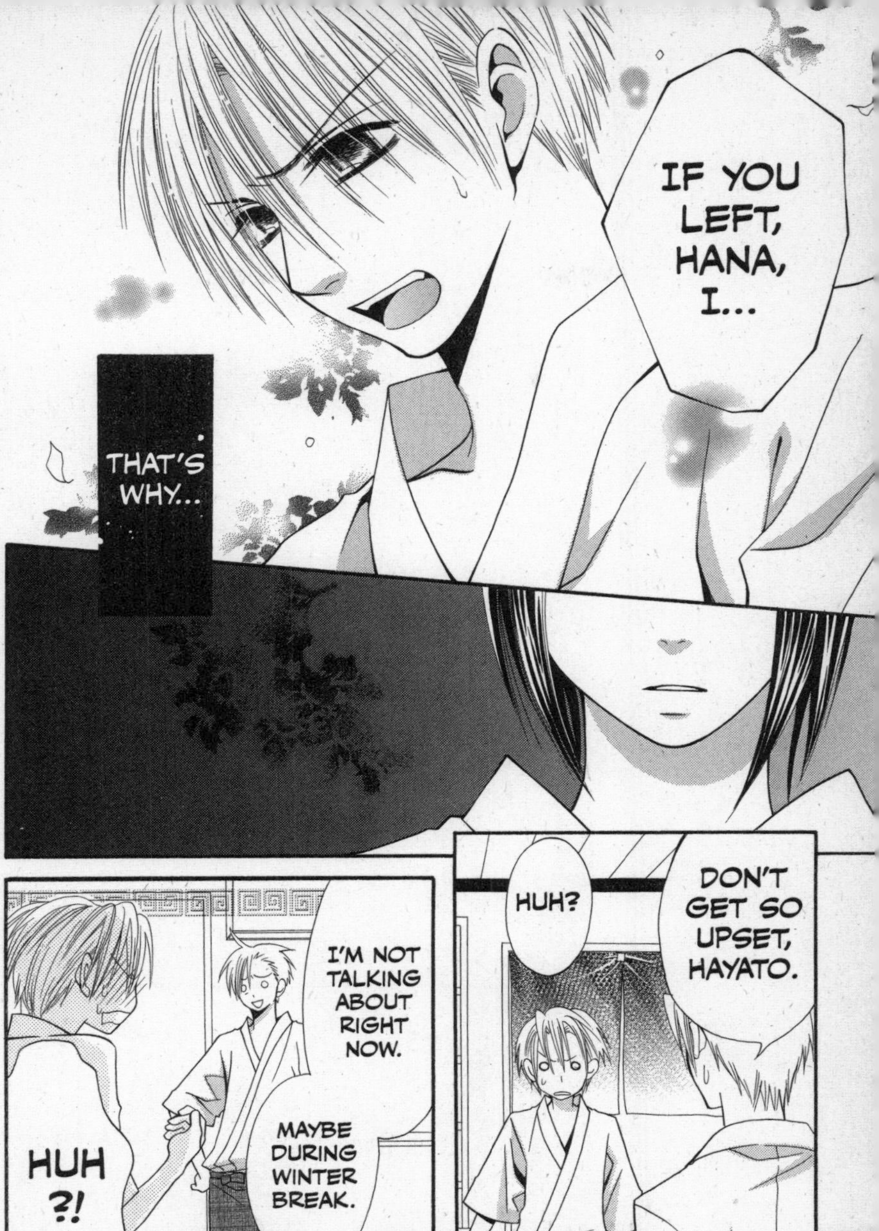

IF YOU LEFT, HANA, I...
THAT'S WHY...
DON'T GET SO UPSET, HAYATO.
HUH?
I'M NOT TALKING ABOUT RIGHT NOW.
MAYBE DURING WINTER BREAK.
HUH ?!

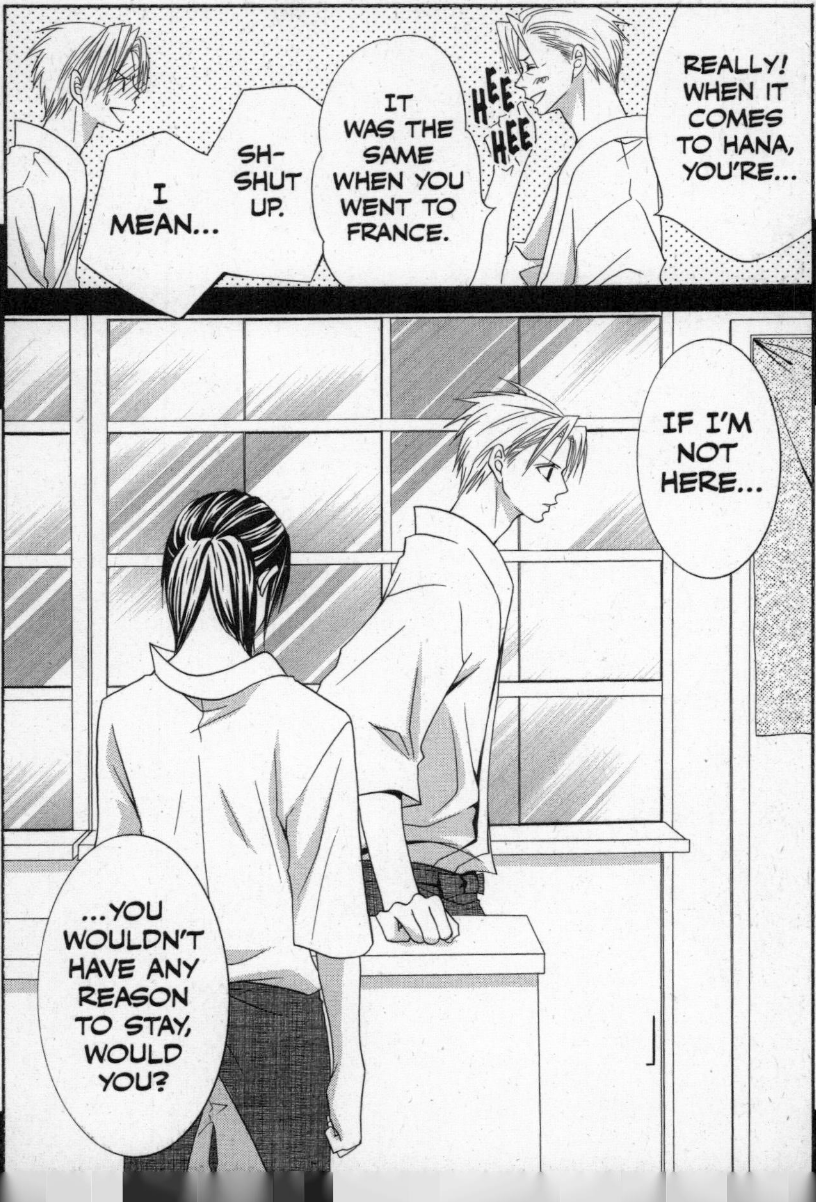
REALLY! WHEN IT COMES TO HANA, YOU'RE...
HEE HEE
IT WAS THE SAME WHEN YOU WENT TO FRANCE.
SH-SHUT UP.
I MEAN...
IF I'M NOT HERE...
...YOU WOULDN'T HAVE ANY REASON TO STAY, WOULD YOU?

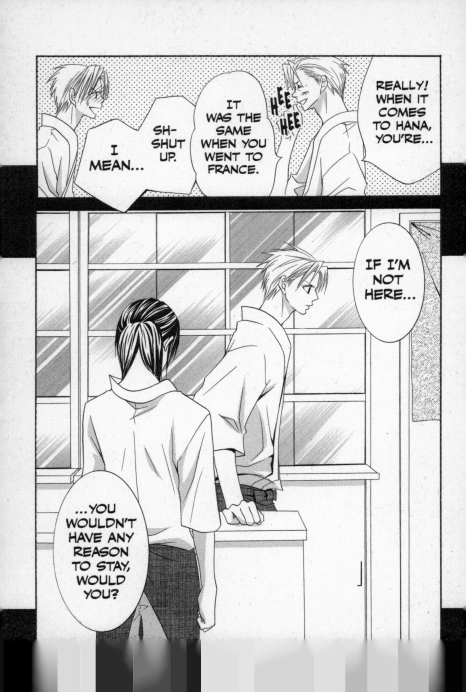

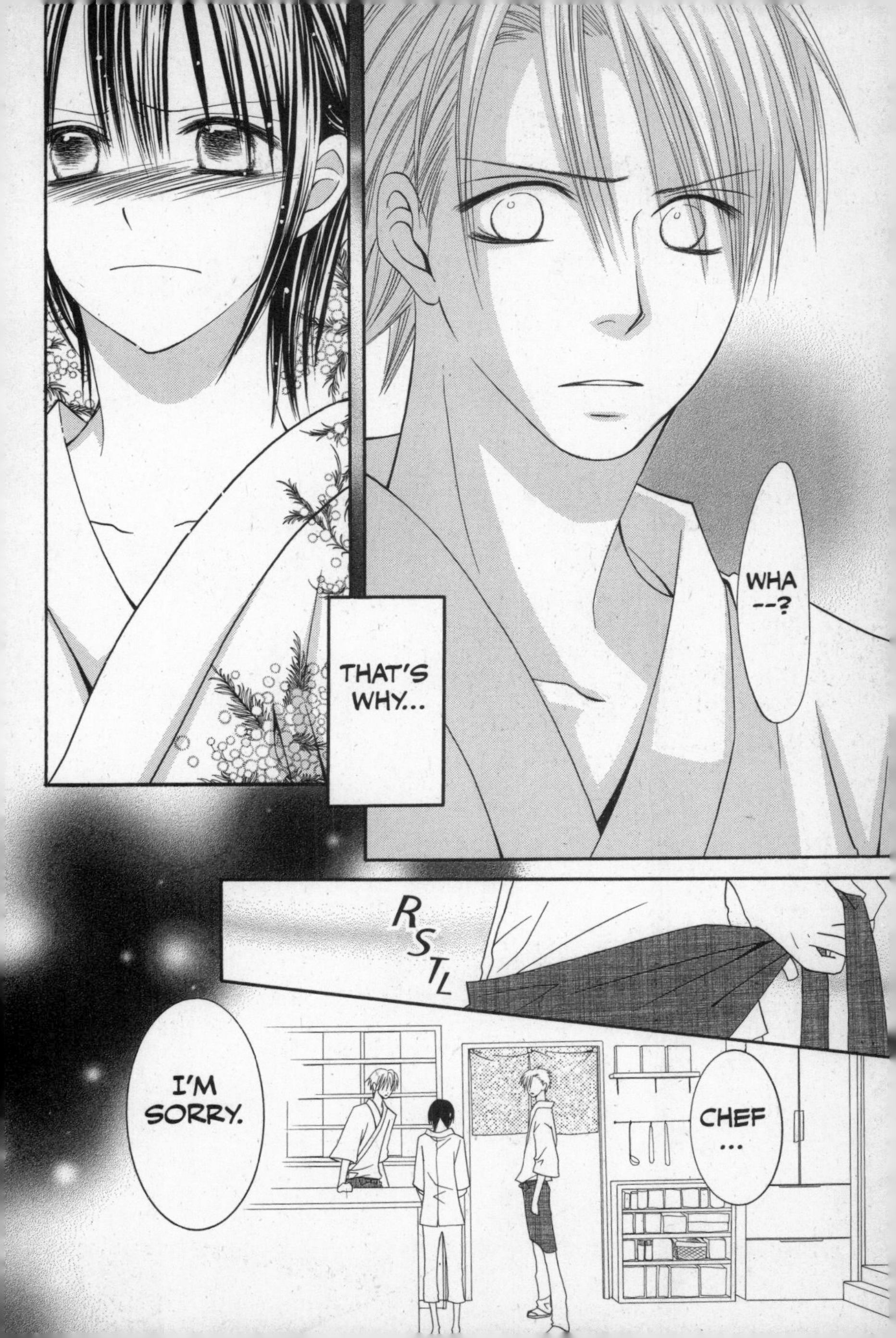
WHA --?
THAT'S WHY...
RSTL
CHEF ...
I'M SORRY.

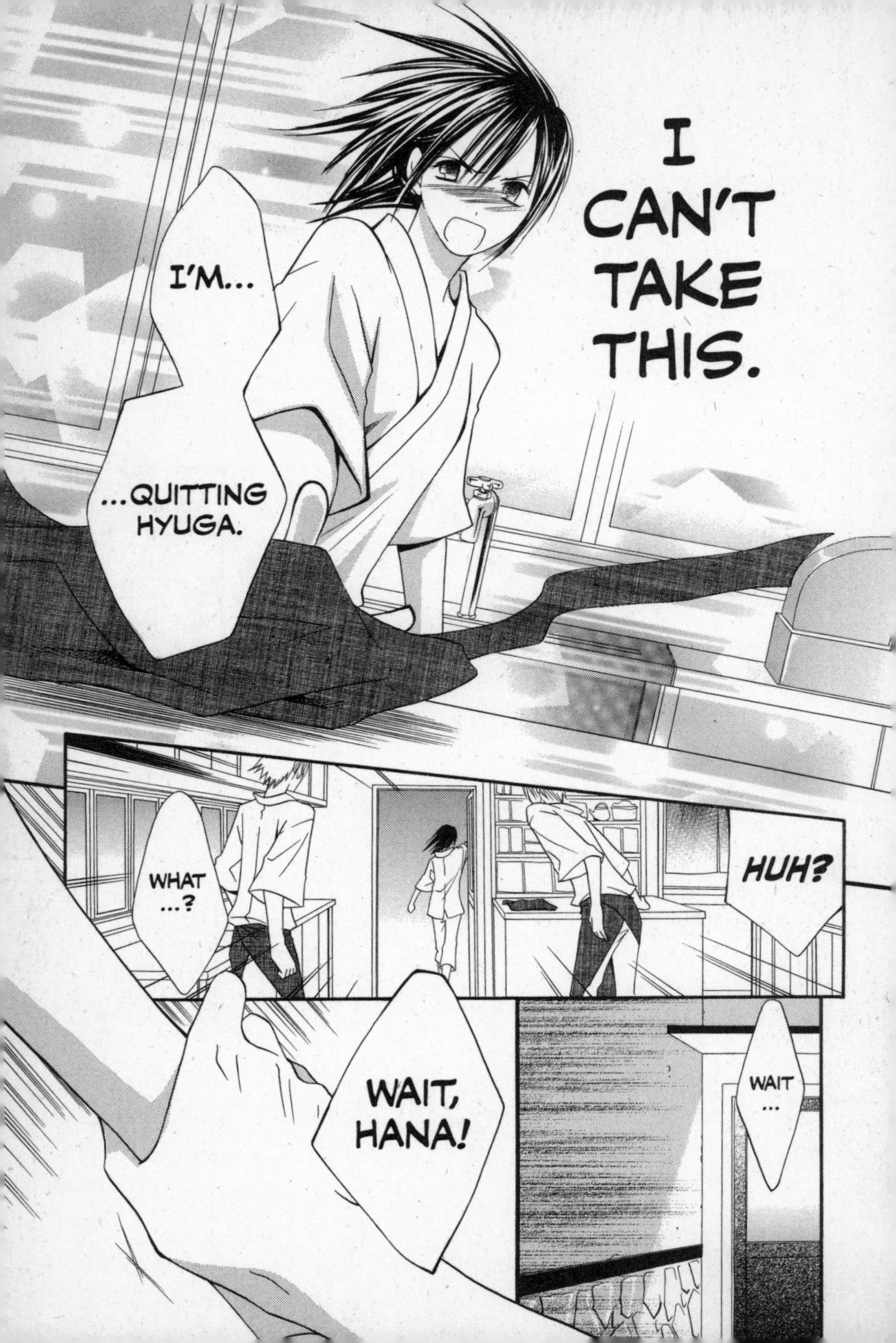
I CAN'T TAKE THIS.
I'M...
...QUITTING HYUGA.
HUH?
WHAT ...?
WAIT ...
WAIT, HANA!

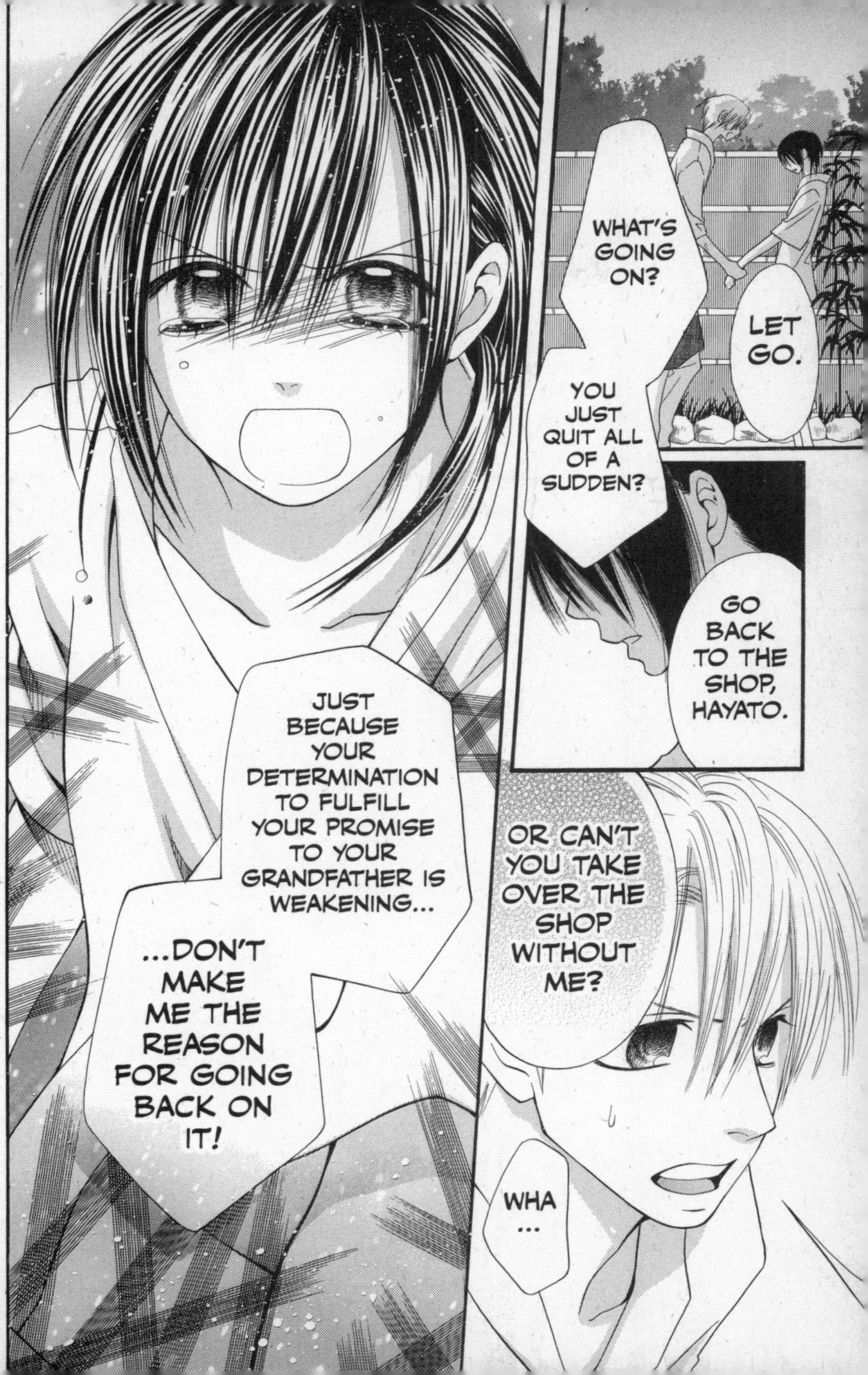
WHAT'S GOING ON?
LET GO.
YOU JUST QUIT ALL OF A SUDDEN?
GO BACK TO THE SHOP, HAYATO.
OR CAN'T YOU TAKE OVER THE SHOP WITHOUT ME?
WHA...
JUST BECAUSE YOUR DETERMINATION TO FULFILL YOUR PROMISE TO YOUR GRANDFATHER IS WEAKENING...
...DON'T MAKE ME THE REASON FOR GOING BACK ON IT!

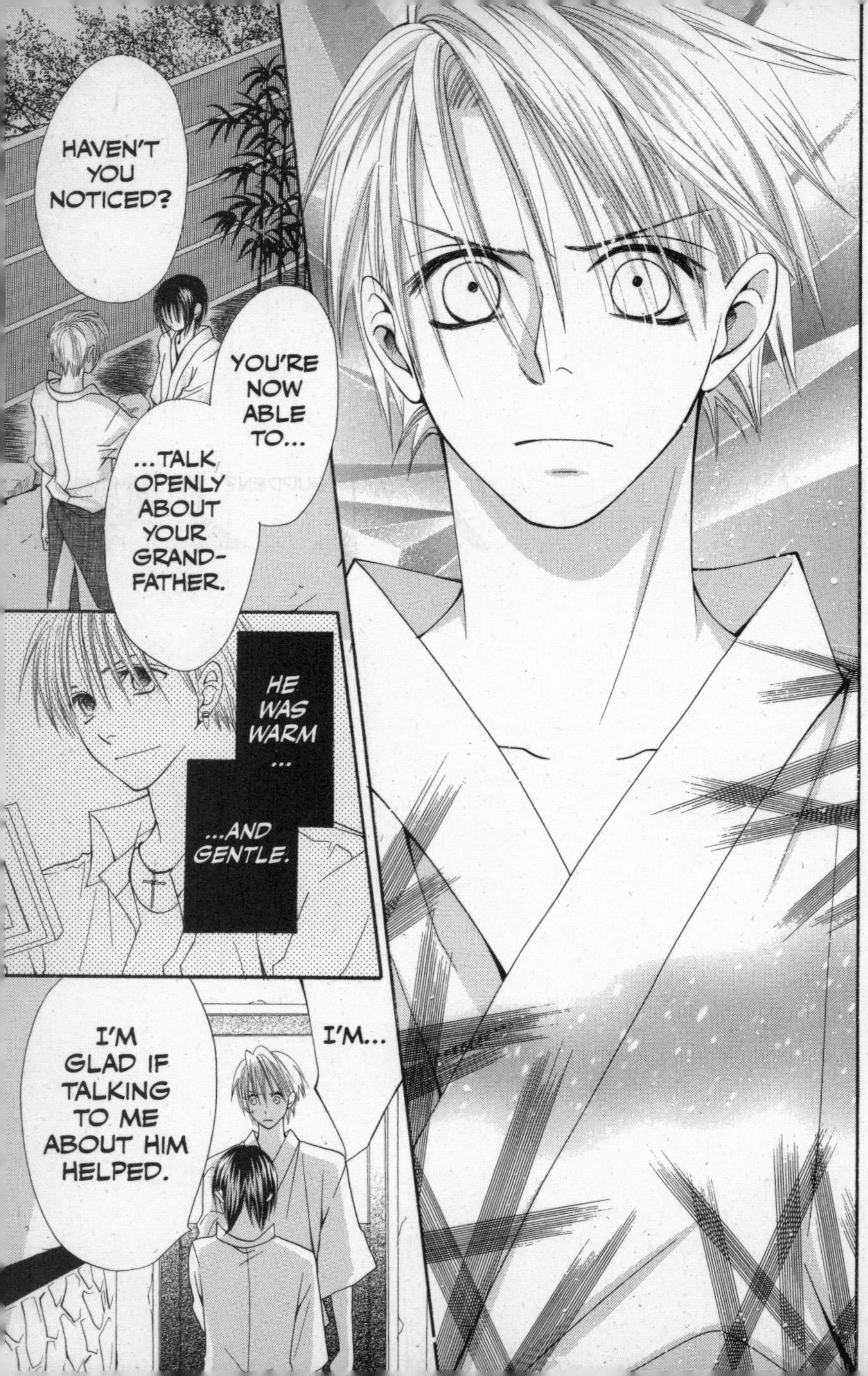
HAVEN'T YOU NOTICED?
YOU'RE NOW ABLE TO...
...TALK OPENLY ABOUT YOUR GRAND-FATHER.
HE WAS WARM...
...AND GENTLE.
I'M GLAD IF TALKING TO ME ABOUT HIM HELPED.
I'M...

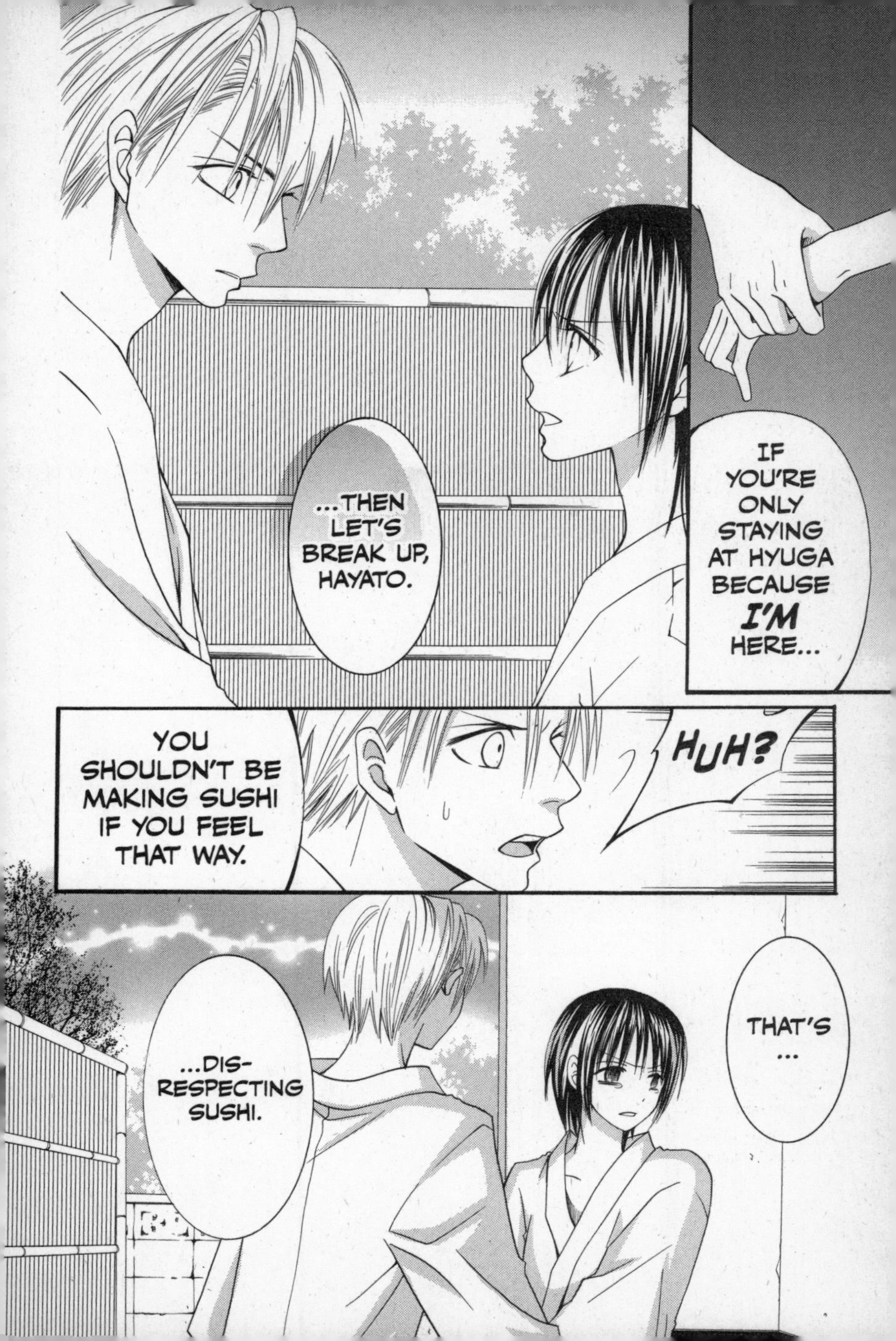
IF YOU'RE ONLY STAYING AT HYUGA BECAUSE *I'M* HERE...
...THEN LET'S BREAK UP, HAYATO.
HUH?
YOU SHOULDN'T BE MAKING SUSHI IF YOU FEEL THAT WAY.
THAT'S ...
...DIS-RESPECTING SUSHI.

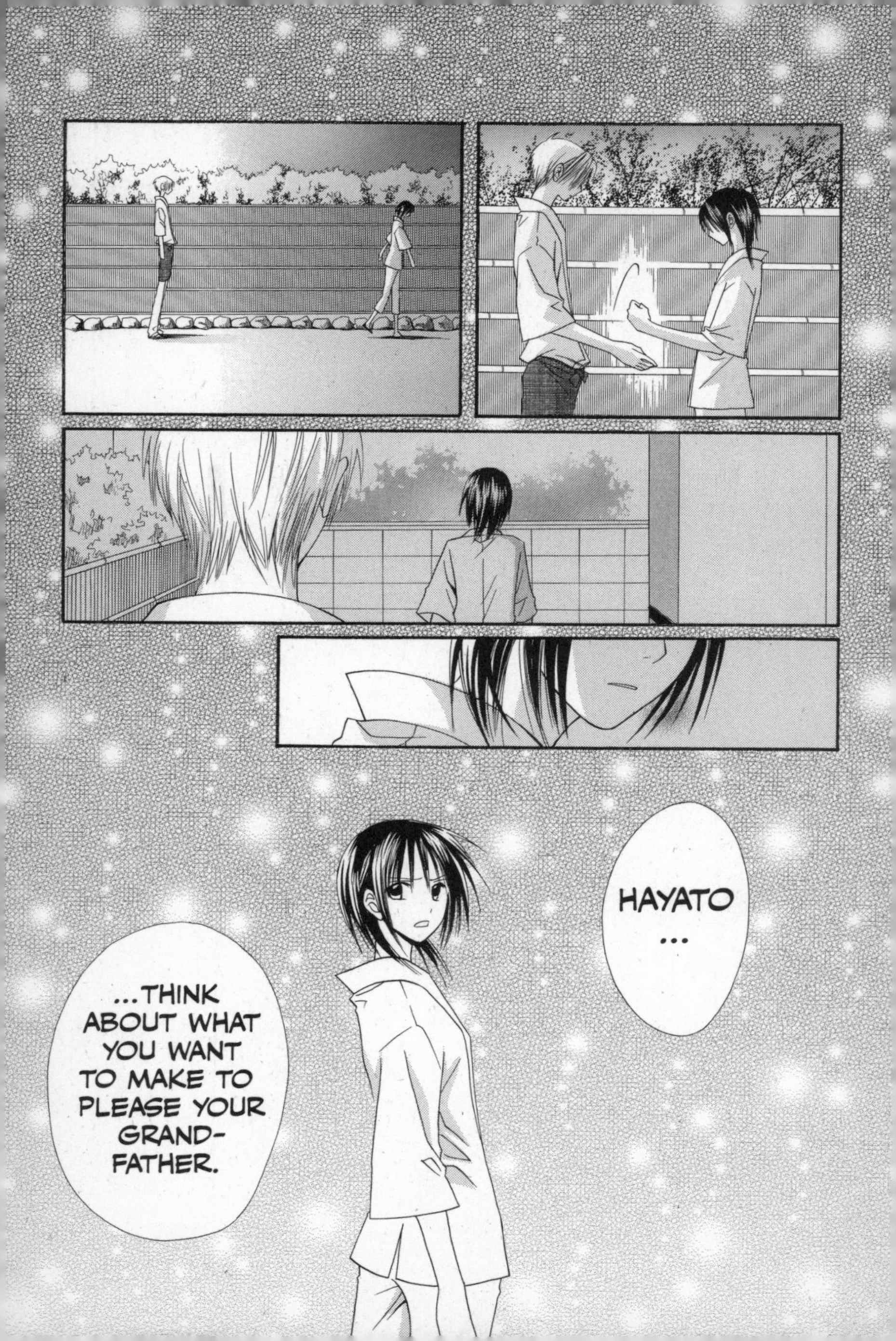
HAYATO ...
...THINK ABOUT WHAT YOU WANT TO MAKE TO PLEASE YOUR GRAND-FATHER.

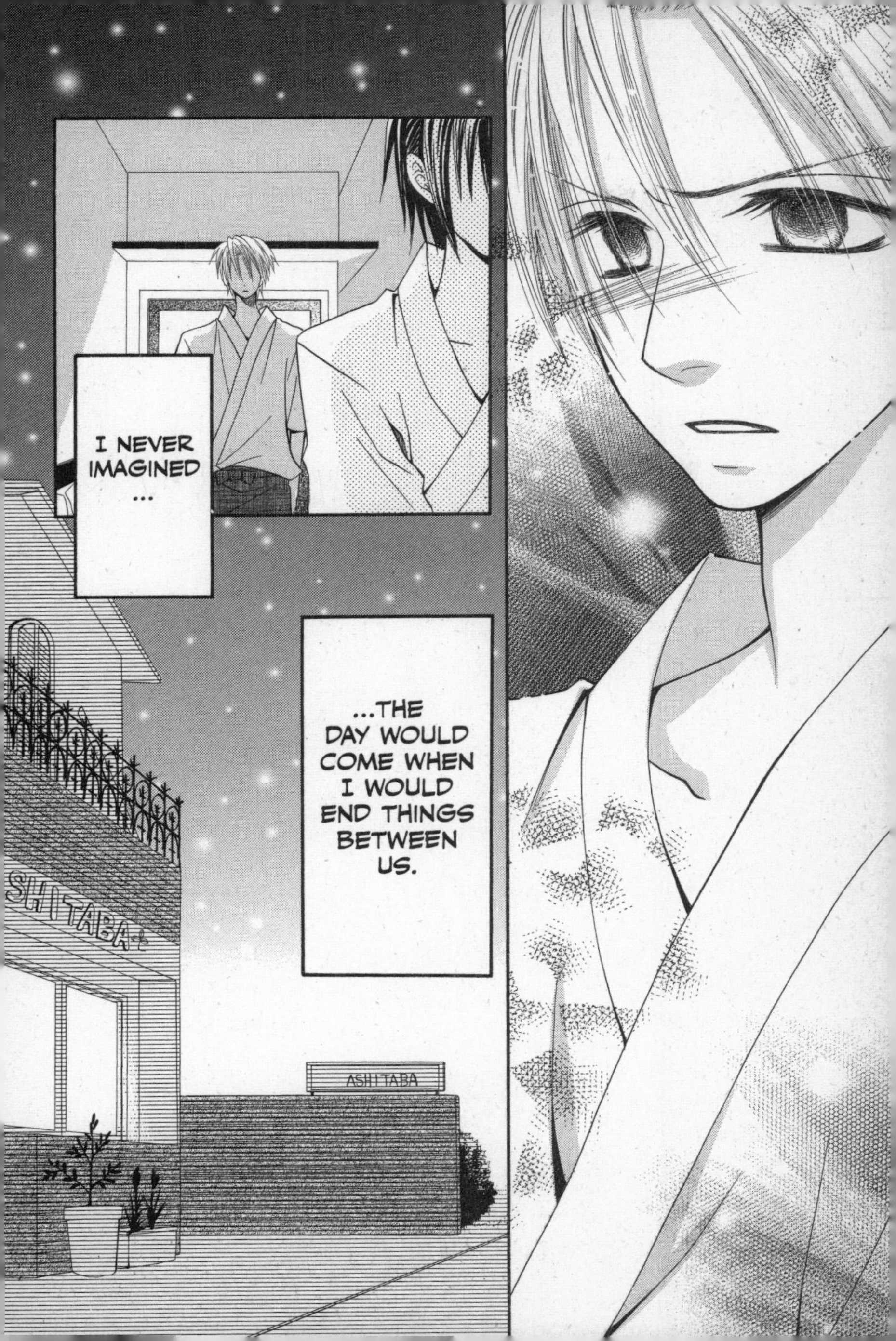
I NEVER IMAGINED ...
...THE DAY WOULD COME WHEN I WOULD END THINGS BETWEEN US.
ASHITABA

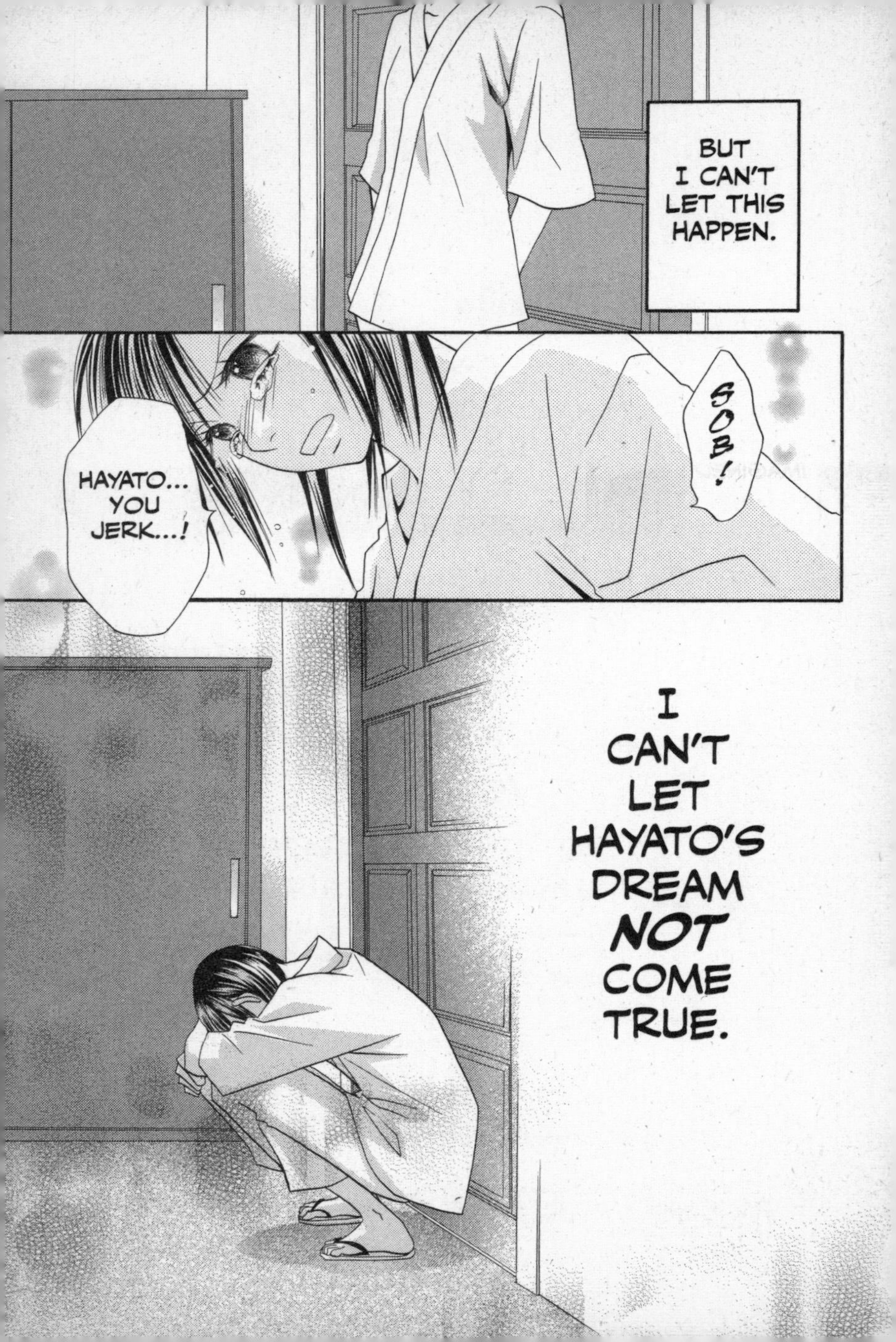
BUT I CAN'T LET THIS HAPPEN.
SOB!
HAYATO... YOU JERK...!
I CAN'T LET HAYATO'S DREAM NOT COME TRUE.

MIXED VEGETABLES Encyclopedia of Characters

KAYA ICHII

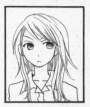

KAYA ICHII → *KAYA NO MI*

COMPARED TO WHO SHE WAS IN THE BEGINNING, THIS CHARACTER HAS CHANGED. INITIALLY JUST A FOIL TO THE HEROINE, HER CHARACTER GREW STRONGER AND STRONGER.

BUT SHE BECAME QUITE POPULAR.
SHE'S STRONG AND NO-NONSENSE AND A GOOD COOK; A REAL BIG-SISTER TYPE... YES!
ISN'T SHE COOL?! (YEAH, YEAH.)
SHE'S A BIT TALLER THAN HANA. AND SHE LOVES NECKTIES. IN AN ARM-WRESTLING COMPETITION, THOUGH, HANA WILL WIN.

AOI MATSUYAMA

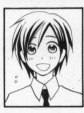

AOI → THE NAME AOI REFERS TO WASABI MATSUYAMA WAS CHOSEN AT RANDOM

FOR SOME REASON, HE'S BEEN AROUND SINCE THE FIRST CHAPTER. I HADN'T DEVELOPED HIS CHARACTER FULLY AT FIRST, SO HIS SPEECH WAS A BIT MORE MASCULINE, BUT HE'S THE ONLY ONE IN *MV* WHO SPEAKS IN THE FIRST PERSON WITH THE MORE FEMININE *BOKU*.

HE'S A BIT SHORTER THAN HAYATO AND ALWAYS WEARS HIS SCHOOL UNIFORM PROPERLY.
THERE'S A BIT OF THE CHARACTER FROM MY PREVIOUS WORK, "PUSH!" (IT HASN'T BEEN PUBLISHED AS A GRAPHIC NOVEL) IN HIM.
MATSUYAMA-KUN FOUND A GOAL. HE WANTED TO BE THE LUNCH MAN AND HAS REALIZED HIS DREAM. I'M SO GLAD!

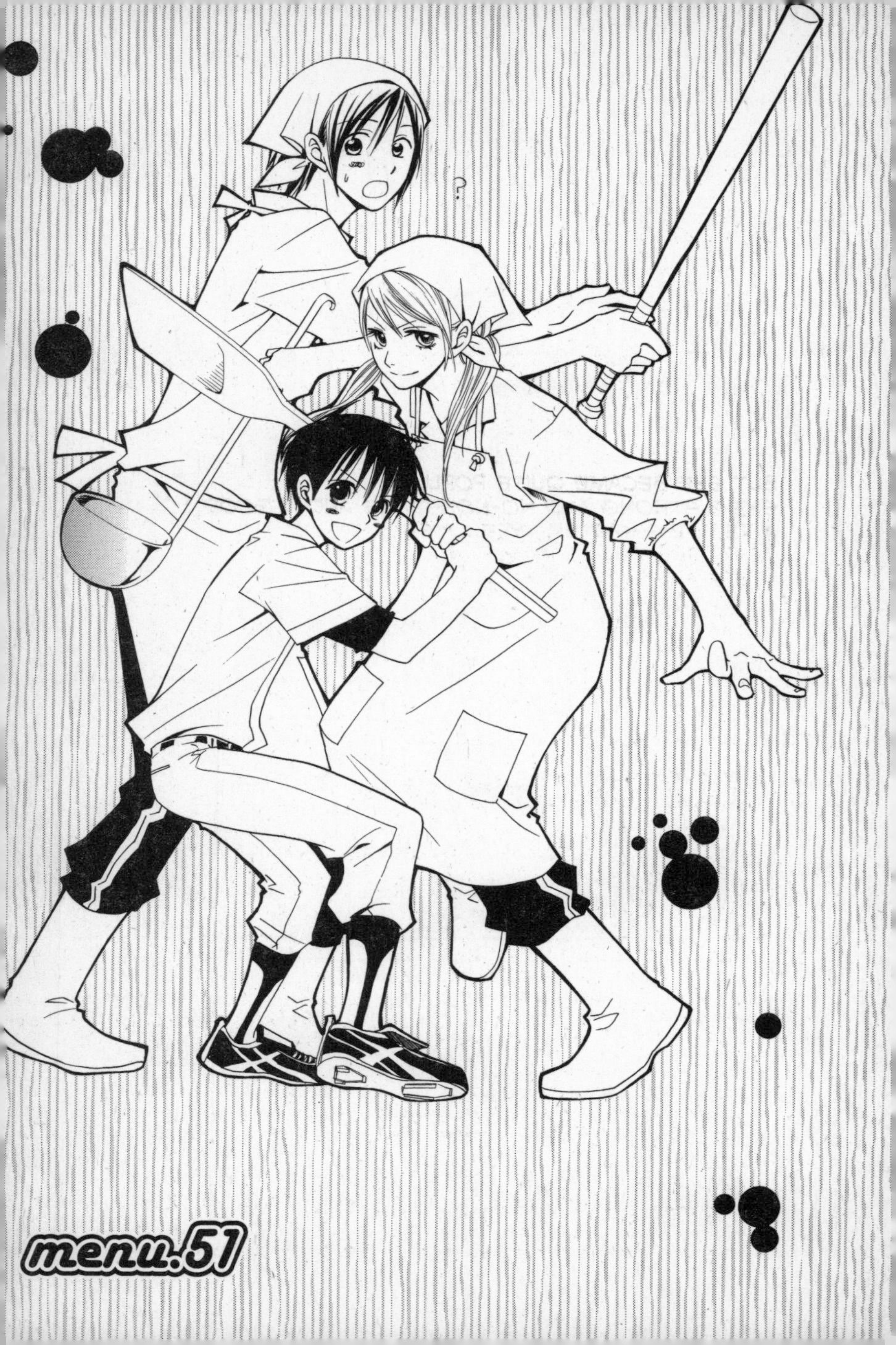
menu.51

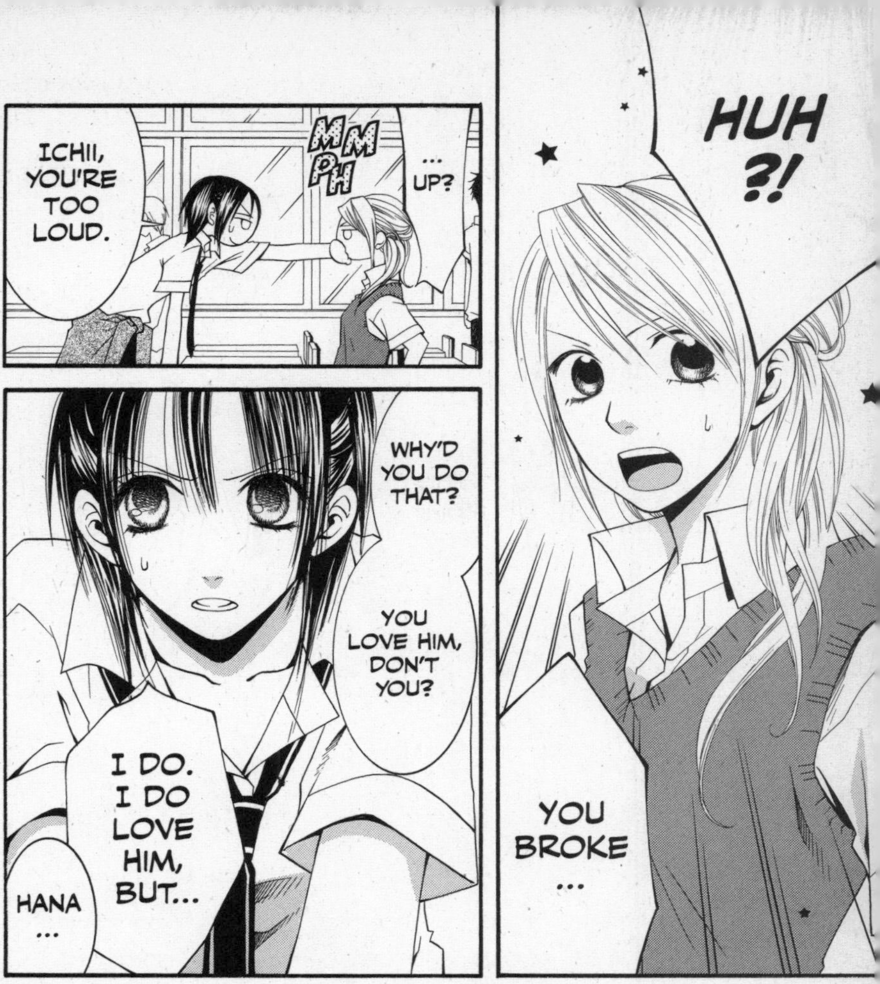
HUH ?!
YOU BROKE ...
... UP?
MMPH
ICHII, YOU'RE TOO LOUD.
WHY'D YOU DO THAT?
YOU LOVE HIM, DON'T YOU?
I DO. I DO LOVE HIM, BUT...
HANA ...

menu 51

I love the cover. It's kind of silly.
For the phone conversation, I wondered which hand to put the phone in. I drew it the way I hold it. Usually, right-handed people hold it in their right hand, don't they? When people are doing something, is it in their left hand? Also, I can't talk with the receiver between my head and shoulder. Actually, I don't like phones.
The relationship between Ichii and Matsuyama started in Volume 6, and now it's already Volume 8.
I'm sorry!
I think there are many people like Matsuyama, who are confused about what they want.
I gave it a lot of thought, but I don't think goals come easily, so I left it like this.
I think Ichii-chan's declaration of love was satisfactory, but many people wrote that they wanted to read about Ichii and Matsu, so I added the end-of-volume feature. Please read it.
This chapter was really, really difficult since my editor and I weren't able to sort through things satisfactorily.
I don't even want to look back on it.
But later, S••bata Asuka said, "It's good," and I was very relieved. I was so grateful.

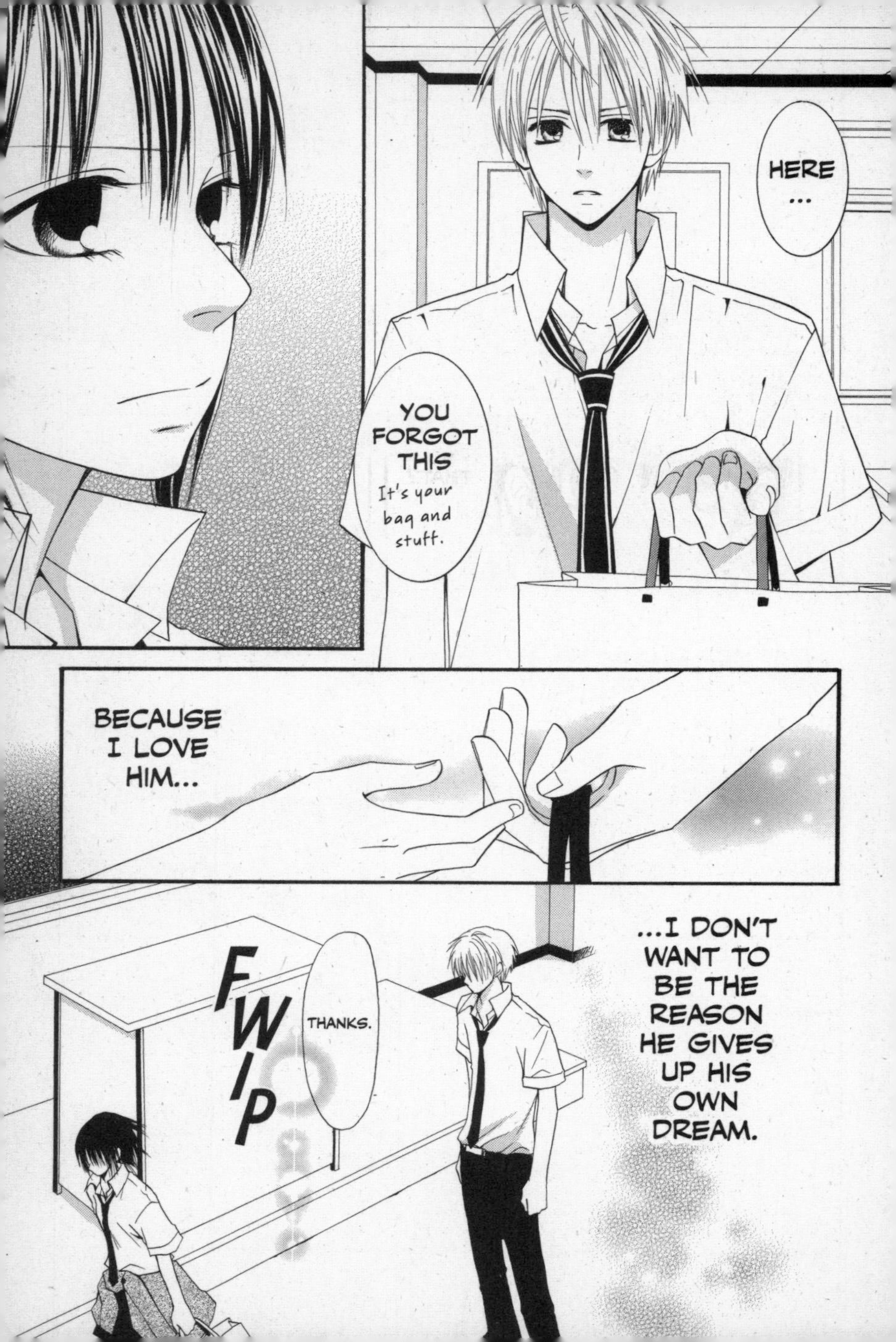
HERE ...
YOU FORGOT THIS
It's your bag and stuff.
BECAUSE I LOVE HIM...
...I DON'T WANT TO BE THE REASON HE GIVES UP HIS OWN DREAM.
THANKS.
FWIP

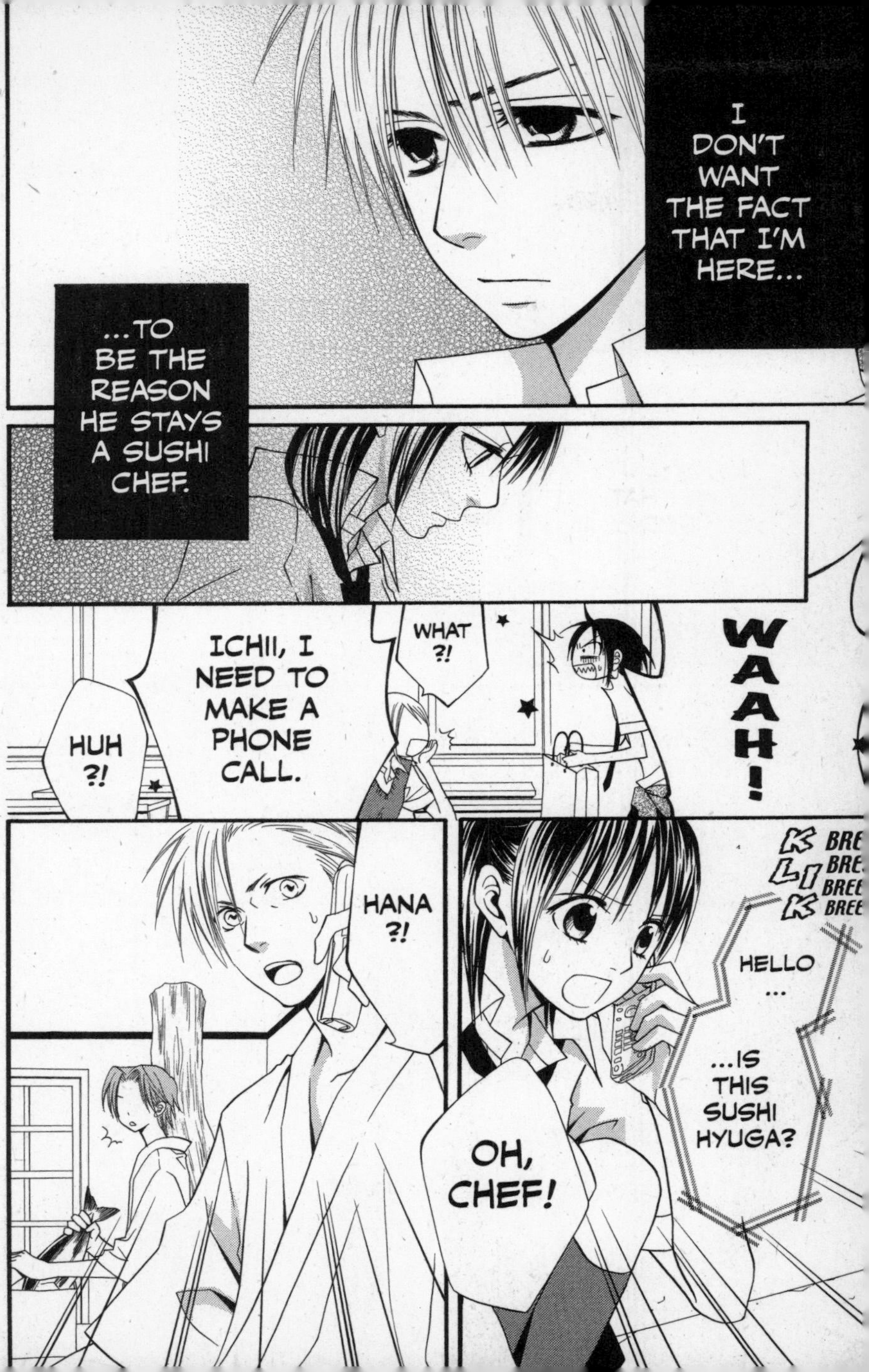
I DON'T WANT THE FACT THAT I'M HERE...
...TO BE THE REASON HE STAYS A SUSHI CHEF.
WAAH!
WHAT?!
ICHII, I NEED TO MAKE A PHONE CALL.
HUH?!
KLIK
BRE BRE BREE BREE
HELLO...
...IS THIS SUSHI HYUGA?
OH, CHEF!
HANA?!

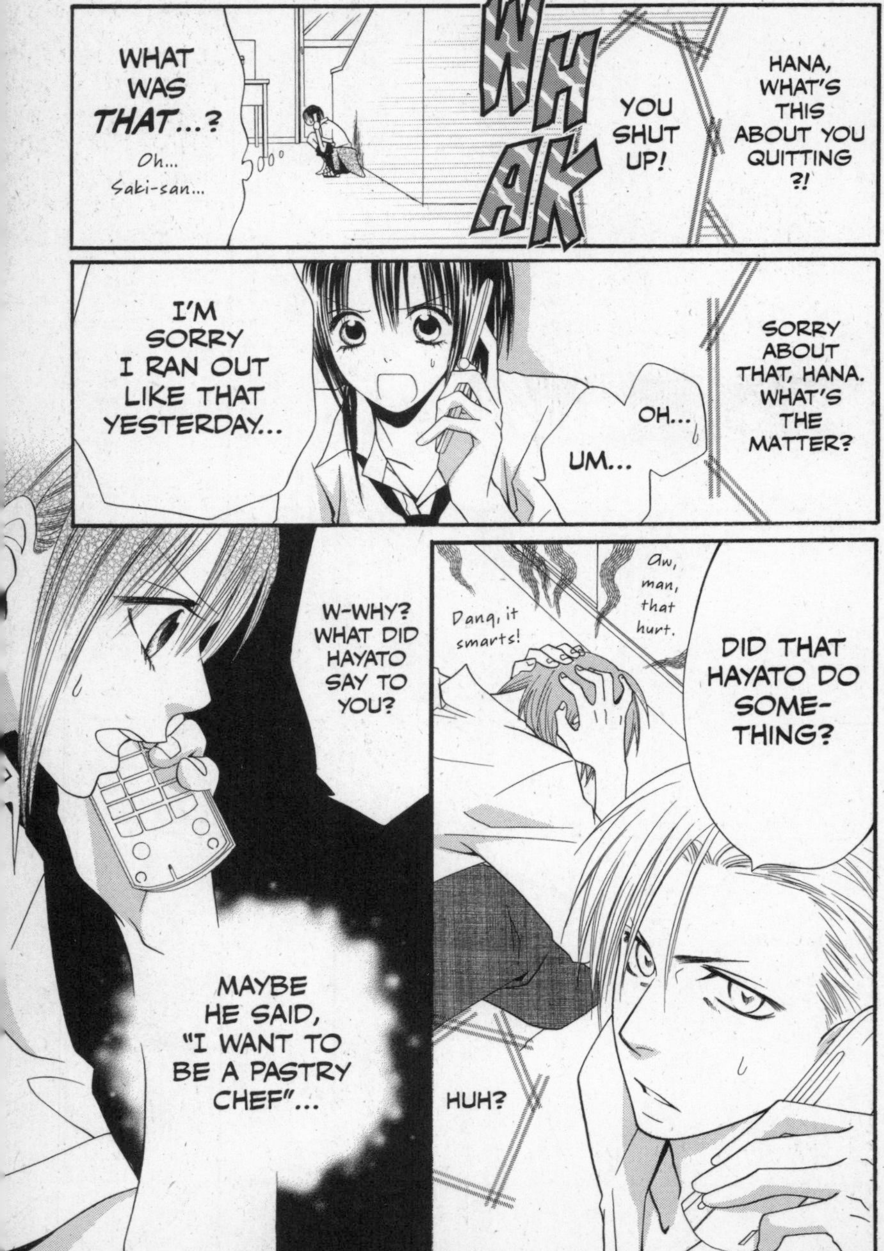
HANA, WHAT'S THIS ABOUT YOU QUITTING ?!
YOU SHUT UP!
WHAK
WHAT WAS THAT...?
Oh... Saki-san...
SORRY ABOUT THAT, HANA. WHAT'S THE MATTER?
OH...
UM...
I'M SORRY I RAN OUT LIKE THAT YESTERDAY...
Aw, man, that hurt.
DID THAT HAYATO DO SOME-THING?
Dang, it smarts!
HUH?
W-WHY? WHAT DID HAYATO SAY TO YOU?
MAYBE HE SAID, "I WANT TO BE A PASTRY CHEF"...

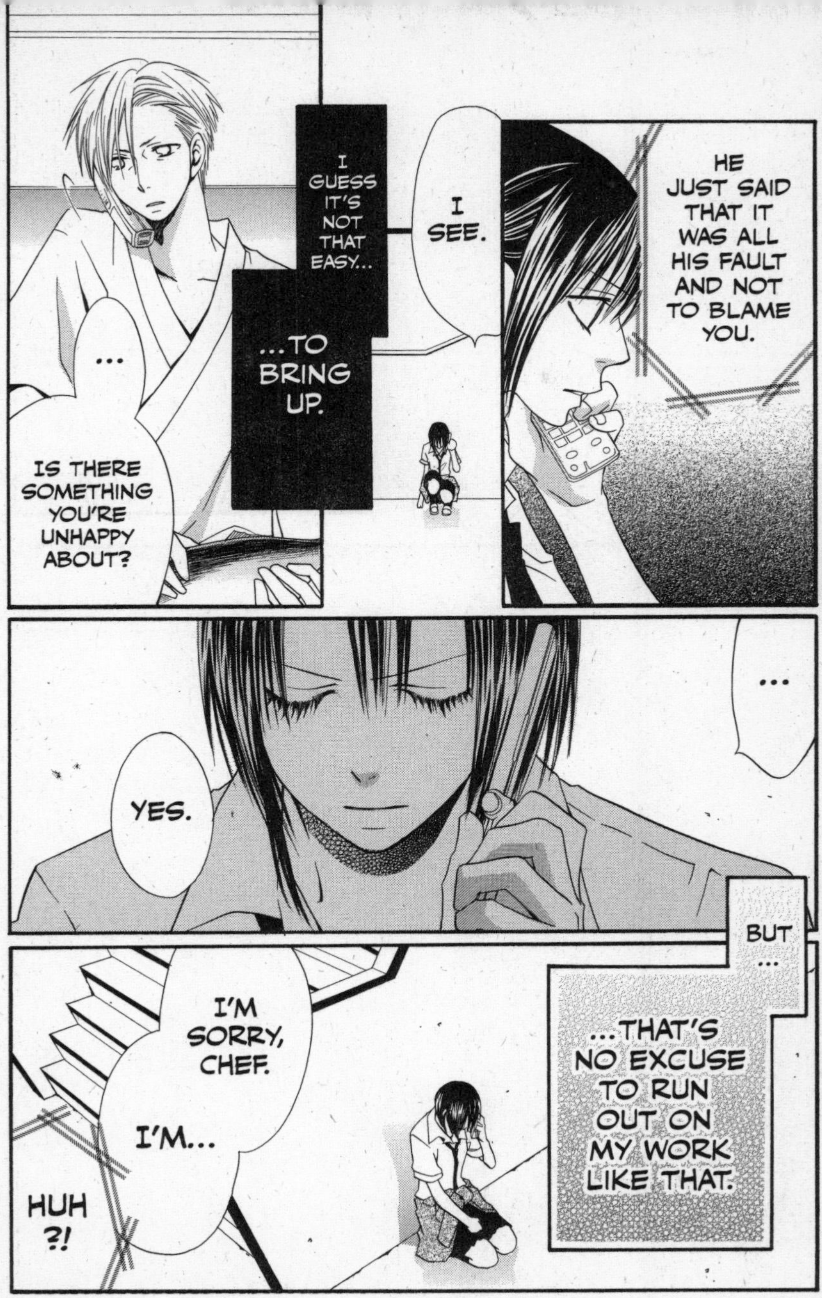
HE JUST SAID THAT IT WAS ALL HIS FAULT AND NOT TO BLAME YOU.
I SEE.
I GUESS IT'S NOT THAT EASY...
...TO BRING UP.
...
IS THERE SOMETHING YOU'RE UNHAPPY ABOUT?
...
YES.
BUT ...
...THAT'S NO EXCUSE TO RUN OUT ON MY WORK LIKE THAT.
I'M SORRY, CHEF.
I'M...
HUH ?!

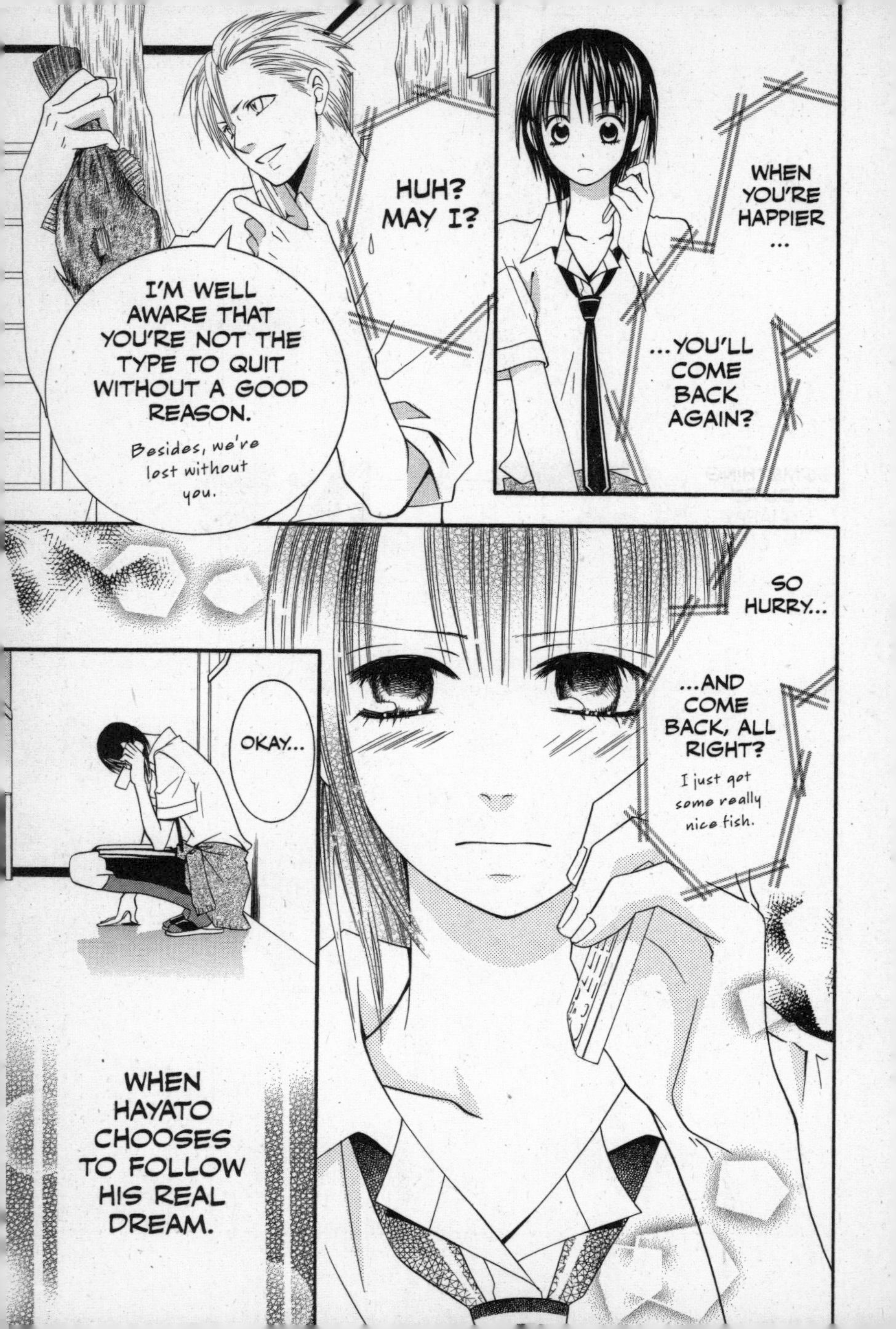
WHEN YOU'RE HAPPIER ...
...YOU'LL COME BACK AGAIN?
HUH? MAY I?
I'M WELL AWARE THAT YOU'RE NOT THE TYPE TO QUIT WITHOUT A GOOD REASON.
Besides, we're lost without you.
SO HURRY...
...AND COME BACK, ALL RIGHT?
I just got some really nice fish.
OKAY...
WHEN HAYATO CHOOSES TO FOLLOW HIS REAL DREAM.

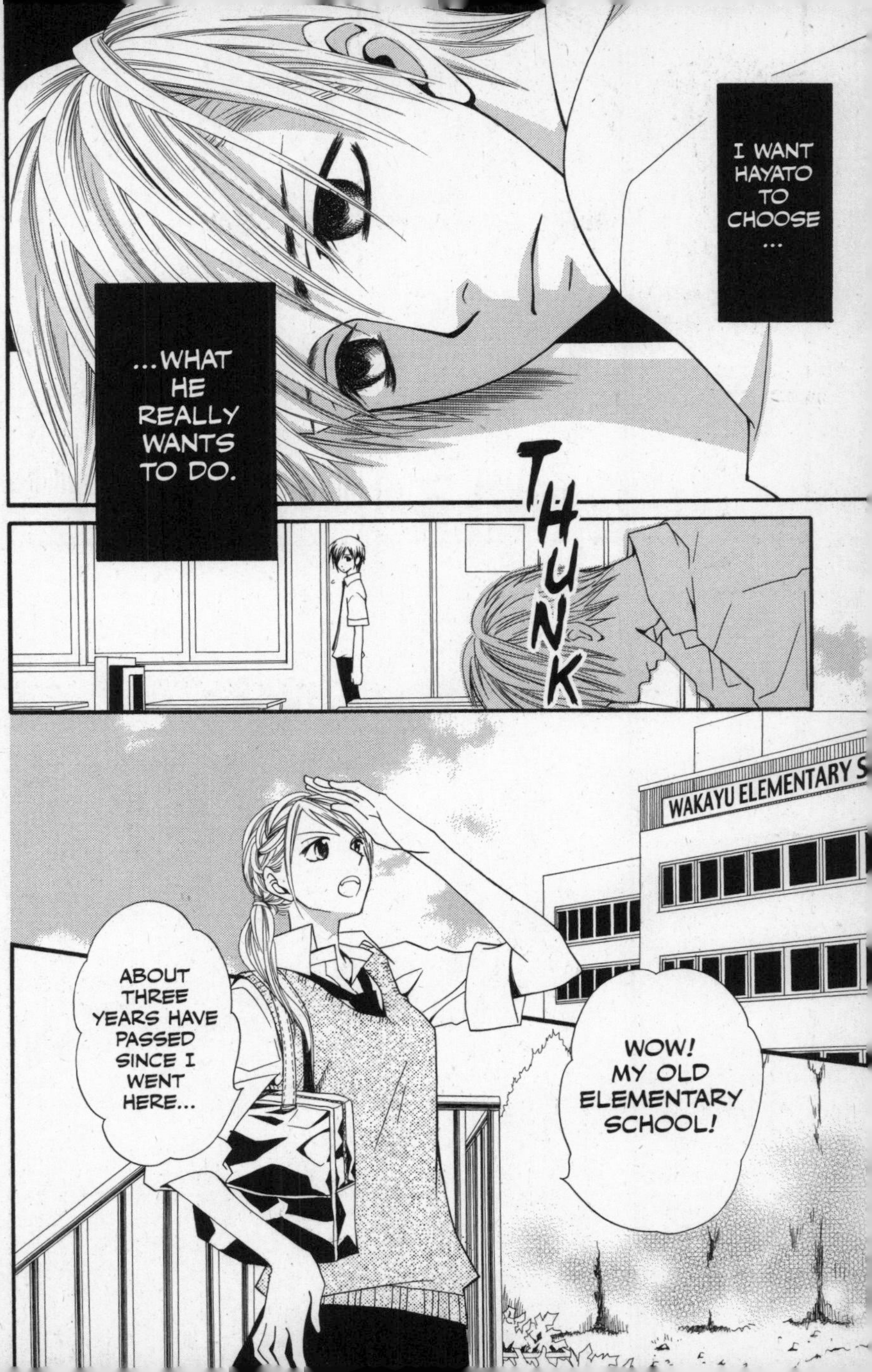
I WANT HAYATO TO CHOOSE ...
...WHAT HE REALLY WANTS TO DO.
THUNK
WAKAYU ELEMENTARY S
WOW! MY OLD ELEMENTARY SCHOOL!
ABOUT THREE YEARS HAVE PASSED SINCE I WENT HERE...

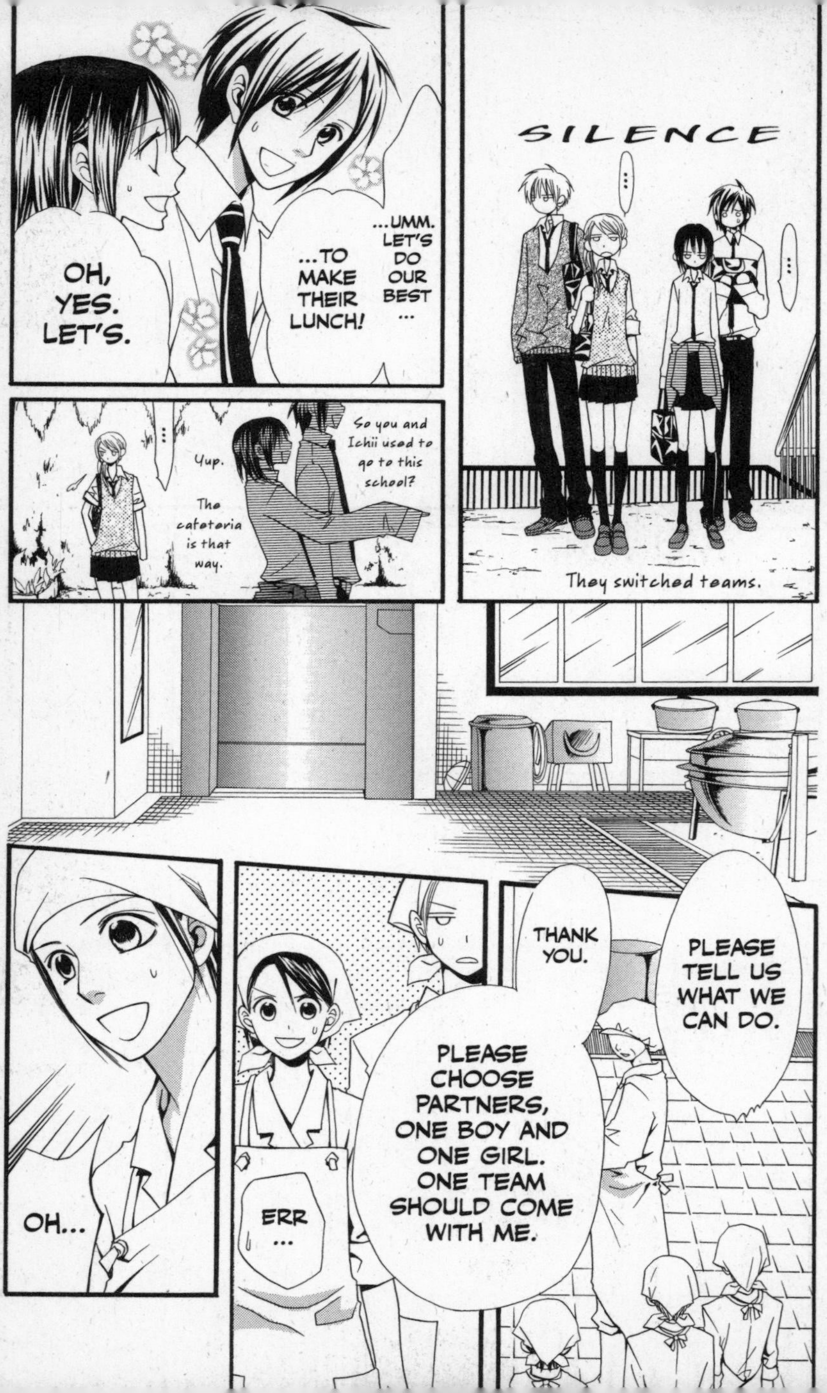
SILENCE
...
...
They switched teams.
...UMM. LET'S DO OUR BEST...
...TO MAKE THEIR LUNCH!
OH, YES. LET'S.
So you and Ichii used to go to this school?
Yup.
The cafeteria is that way.
...
PLEASE TELL US WHAT WE CAN DO.
THANK YOU.
PLEASE CHOOSE PARTNERS, ONE BOY AND ONE GIRL. ONE TEAM SHOULD COME WITH ME.
ERR...
OH...

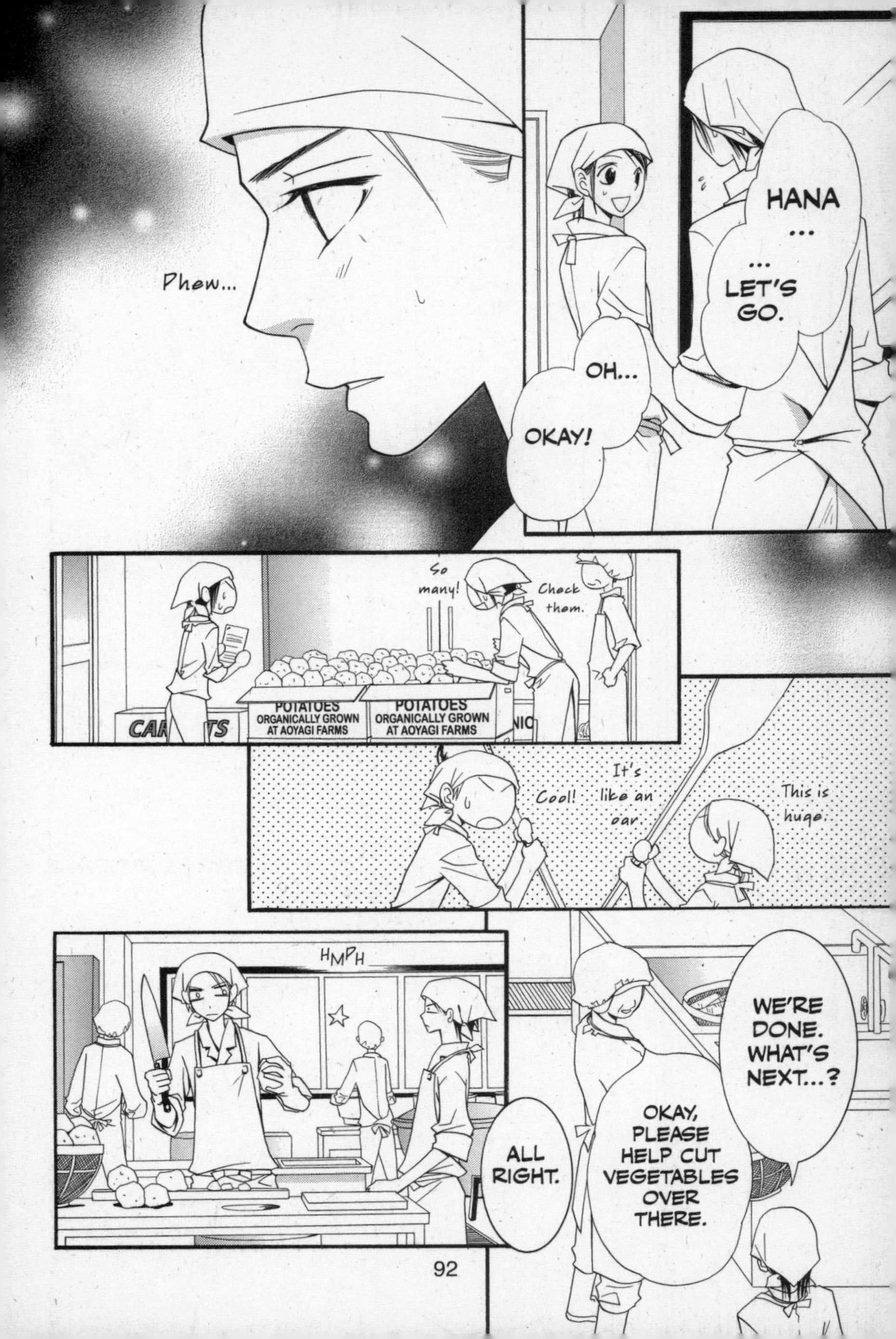
HANA ... ... LET'S GO.
OH... OKAY!
Phew...
Check them.
So many!
POTATOES ORGANICALLY GROWN AT AOYAGI FARMS
POTATOES ORGANICALLY GROWN AT AOYAGI FARMS
This is huge.
It's like an oar.
Cool!
WE'RE DONE. WHAT'S NEXT...?
OKAY, PLEASE HELP CUT VEGETABLES OVER THERE.
ALL RIGHT.
HMPH

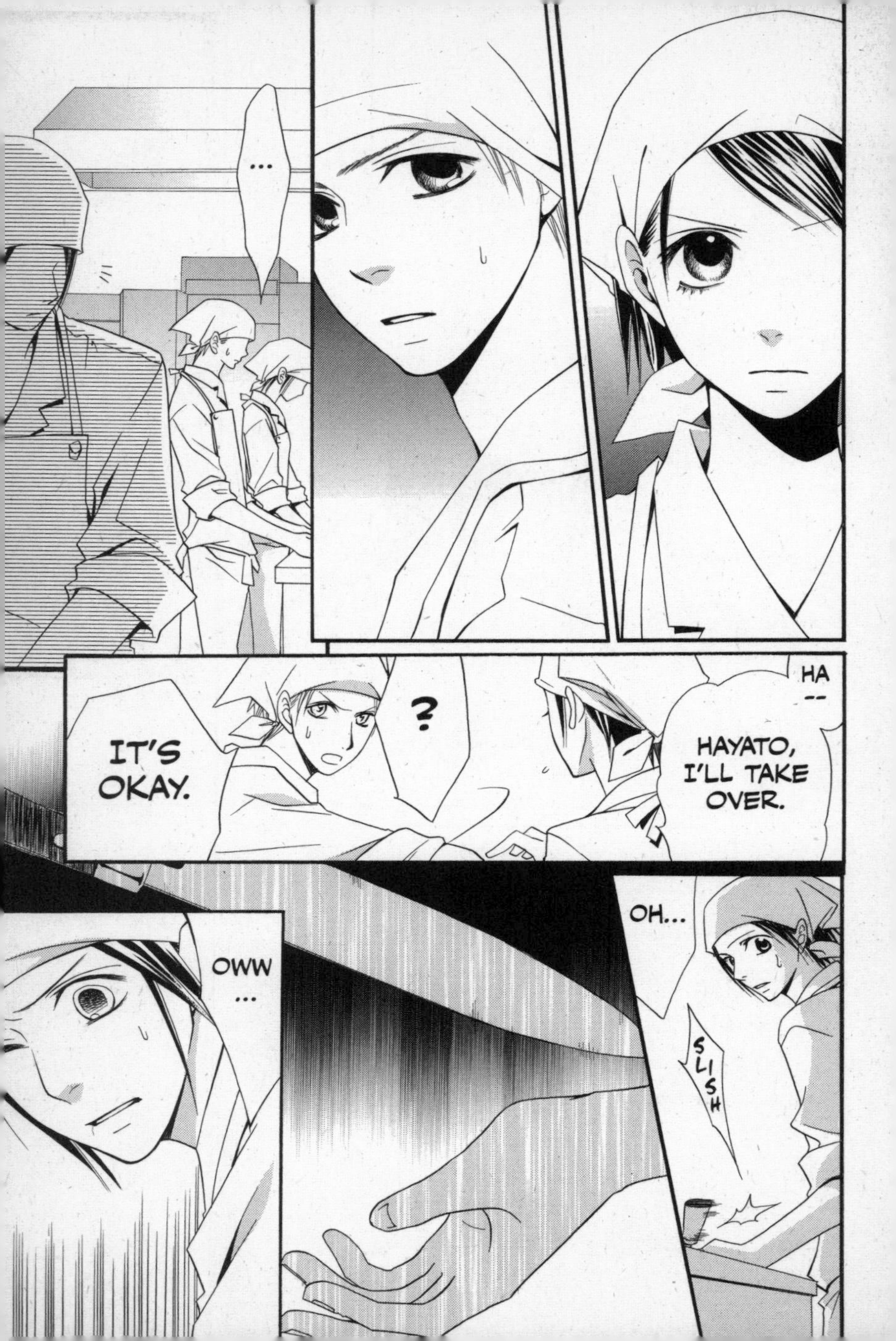
...
HA--
HAYATO, I'LL TAKE OVER.
?
IT'S OKAY.
OH...
SLISH
OWW...

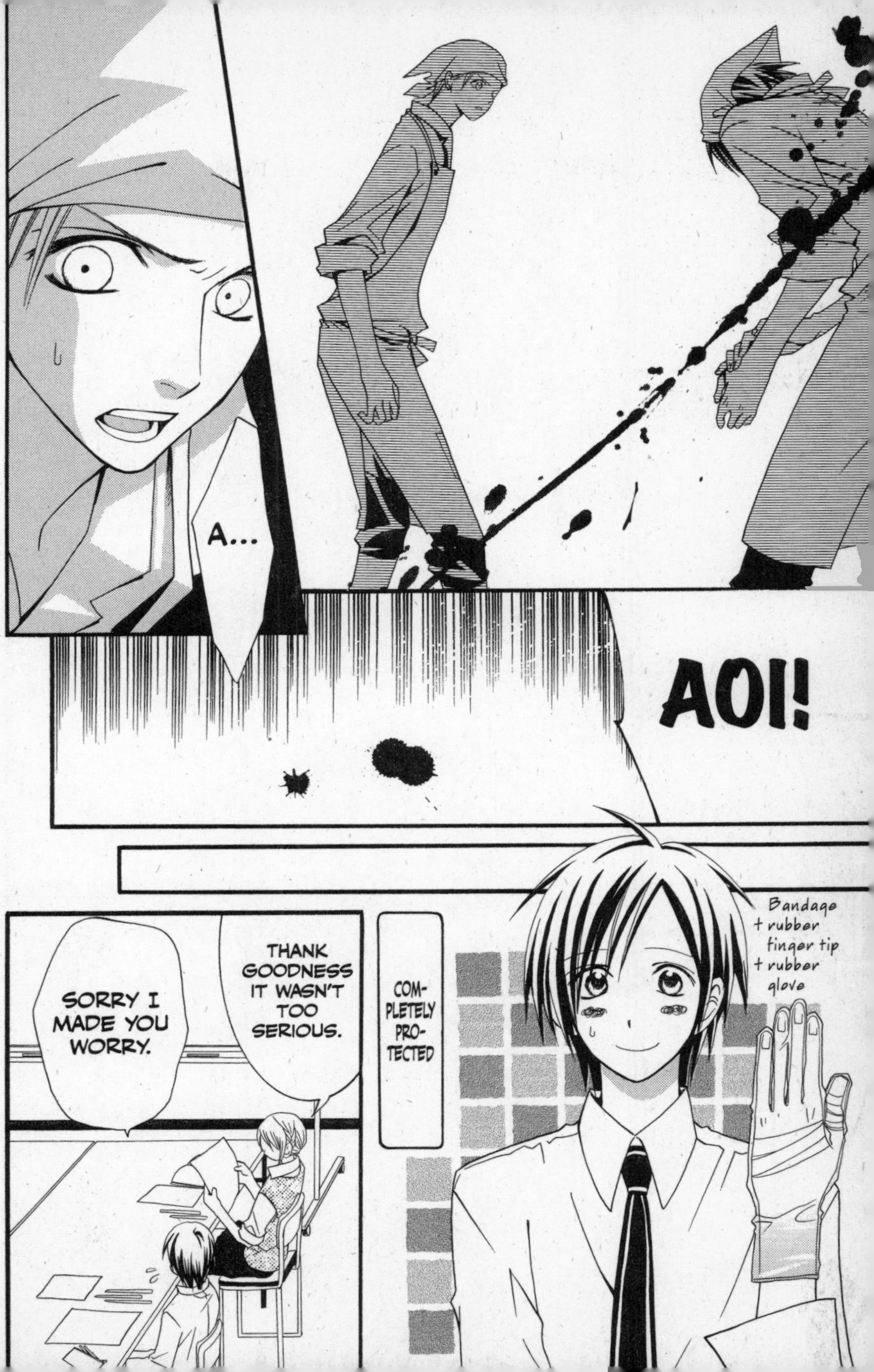
A...
AOI!
Bandage + rubber finger tip + rubber glove
COMPLETELY PROTECTED
THANK GOODNESS IT WASN'T TOO SERIOUS.
SORRY I MADE YOU WORRY.

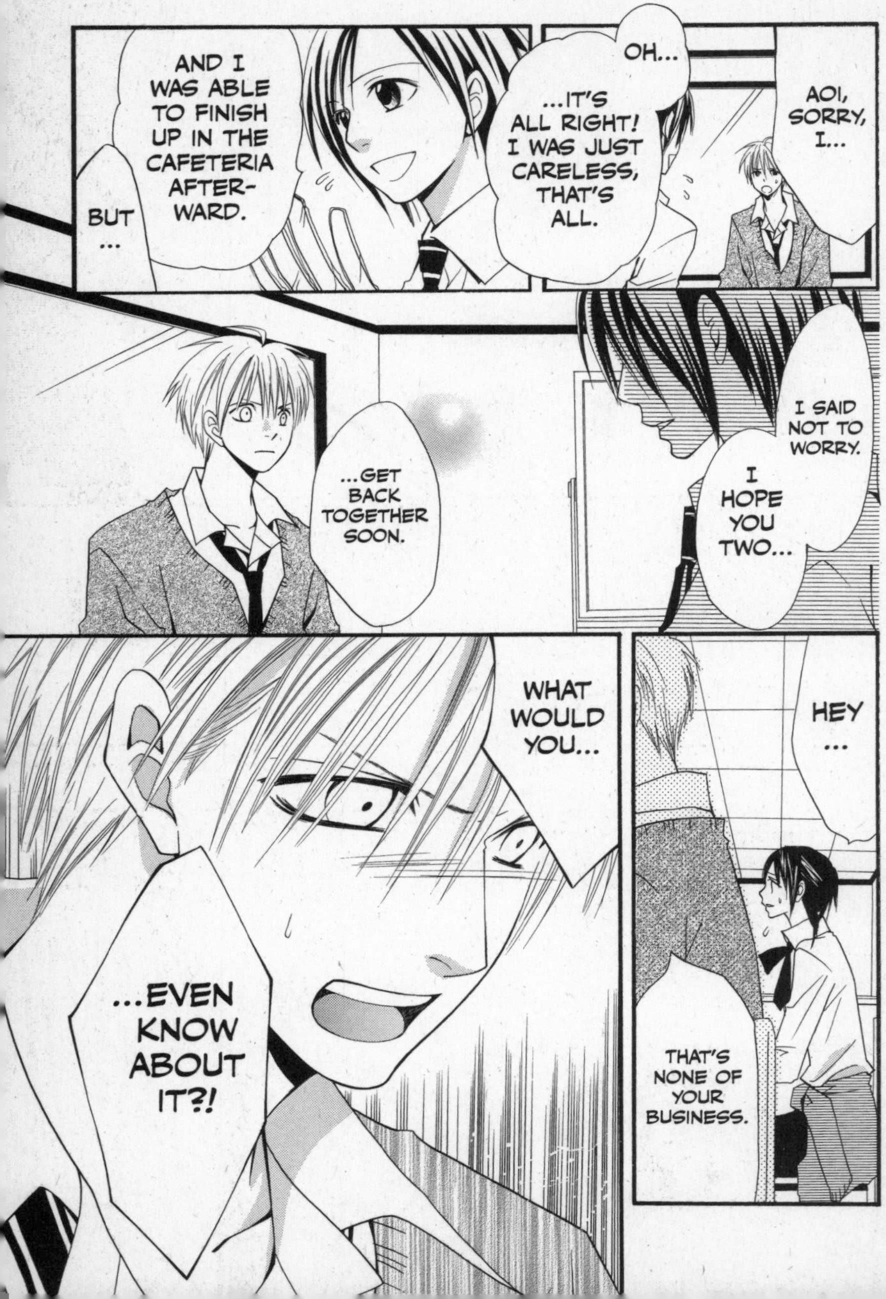
AOI, SORRY, I...
OH...
...IT'S ALL RIGHT! I WAS JUST CARELESS, THAT'S ALL.
AND I WAS ABLE TO FINISH UP IN THE CAFETERIA AFTER-WARD.
BUT ...
I SAID NOT TO WORRY.
I HOPE YOU TWO...
...GET BACK TOGETHER SOON.
HEY ...
THAT'S NONE OF YOUR BUSINESS.
WHAT WOULD YOU...
...EVEN KNOW ABOUT IT?!

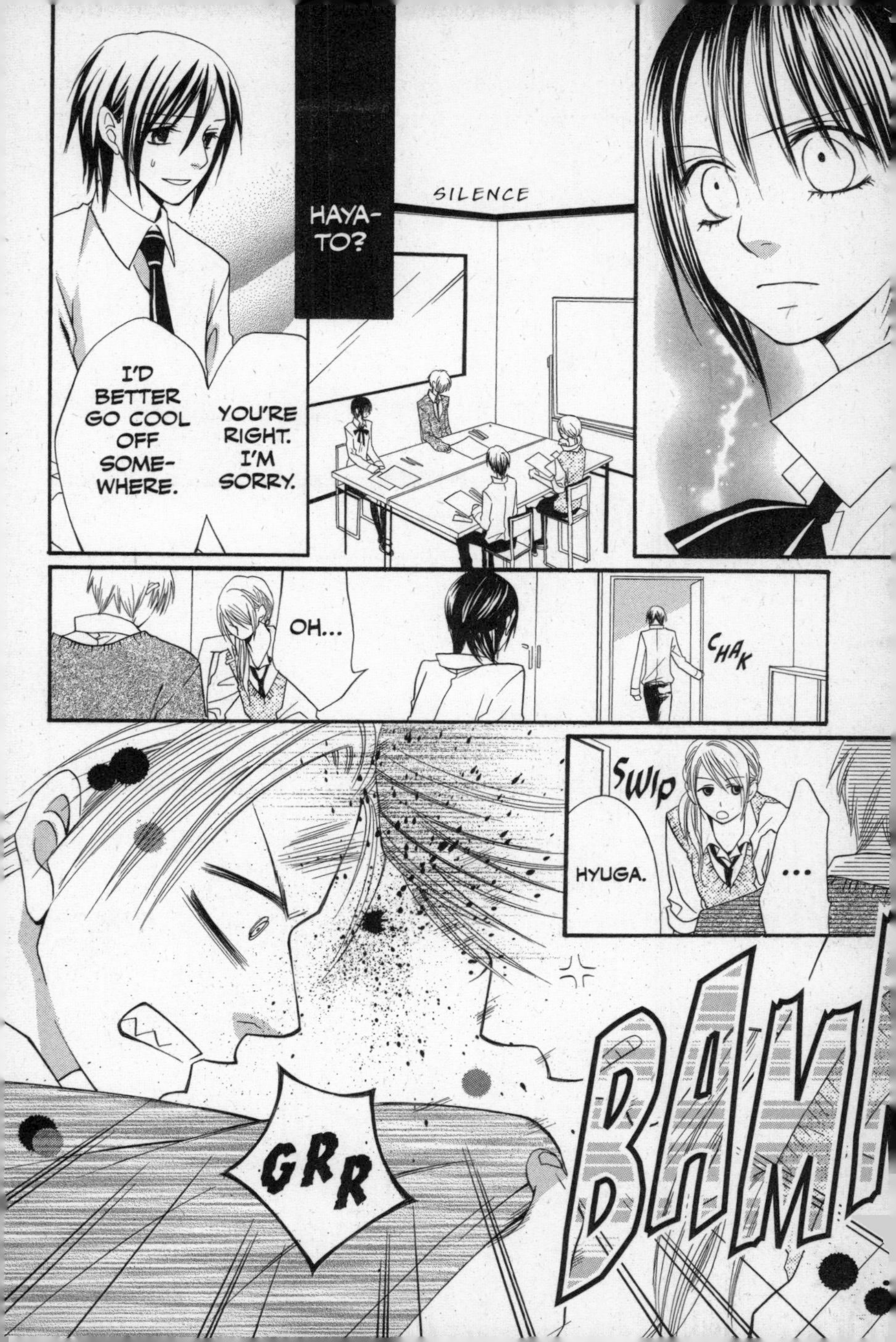
SILENCE
HAYA-TO?
YOU'RE RIGHT. I'M SORRY.
I'D BETTER GO COOL OFF SOME-WHERE.
CHAK
OH...
SWIP
...
HYUGA.
BAM
GRR

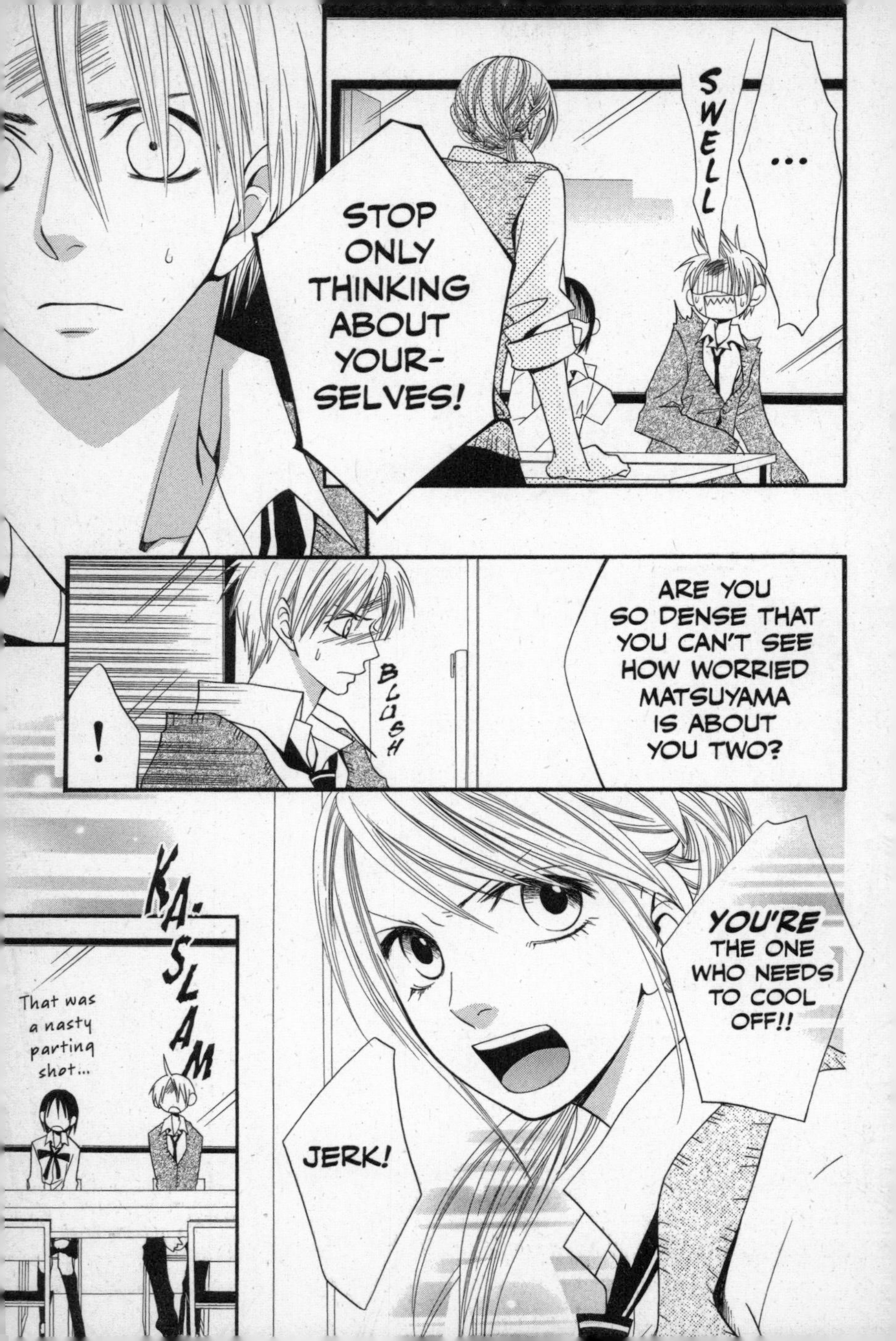
SWELL
...
STOP ONLY THINKING ABOUT YOUR-SELVES!
ARE YOU SO DENSE THAT YOU CAN'T SEE HOW WORRIED MATSUYAMA IS ABOUT YOU TWO?
BLUSH
!
YOU'RE THE ONE WHO NEEDS TO COOL OFF!!
JERK!
KA-SLAM
That was a nasty parting shot...

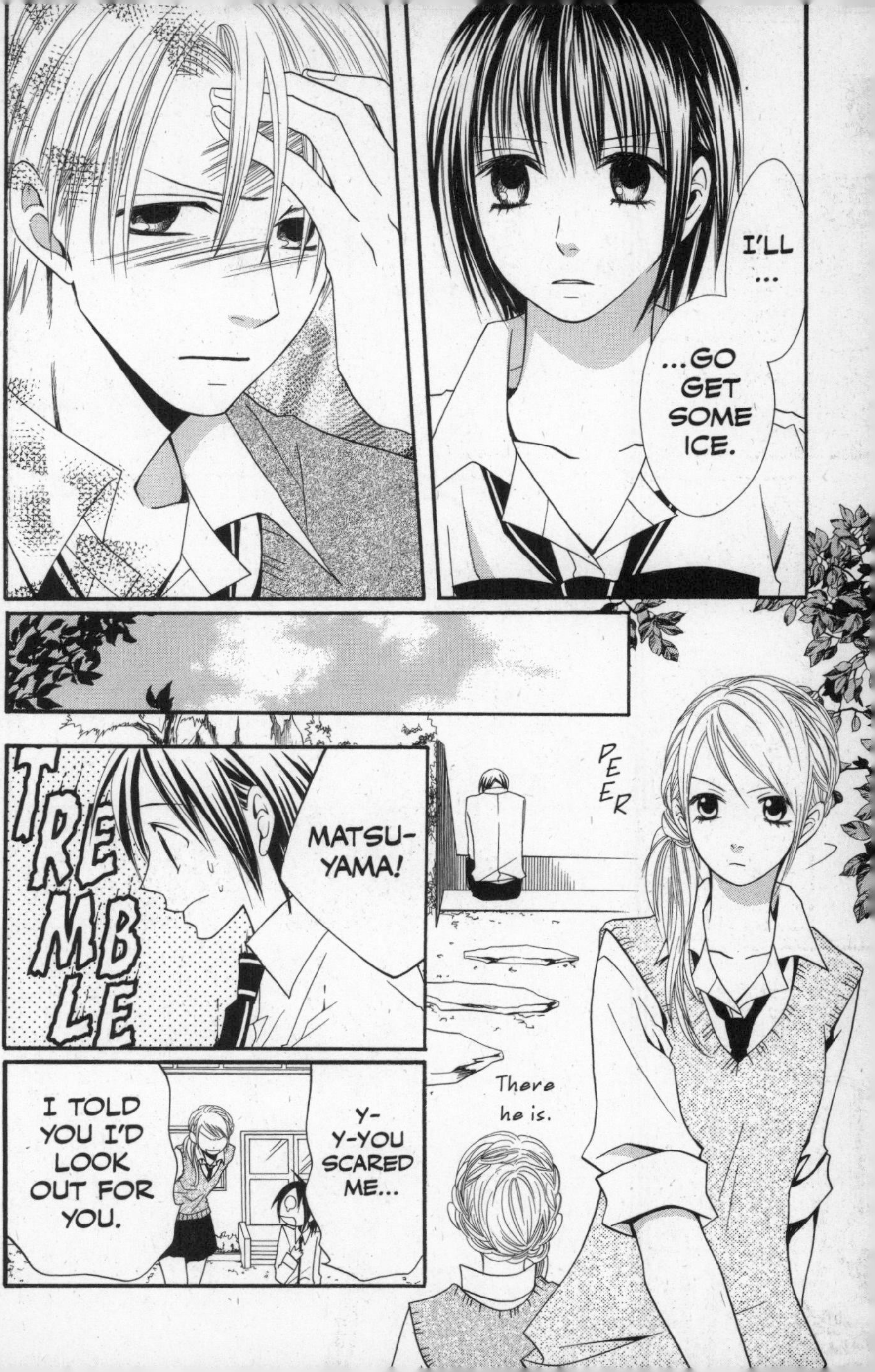
I'LL ...
...GO GET SOME ICE.
PEER
There he is.
TREMBLE
MATSU-YAMA!
Y-Y-YOU SCARED ME...
I TOLD YOU I'D LOOK OUT FOR YOU.

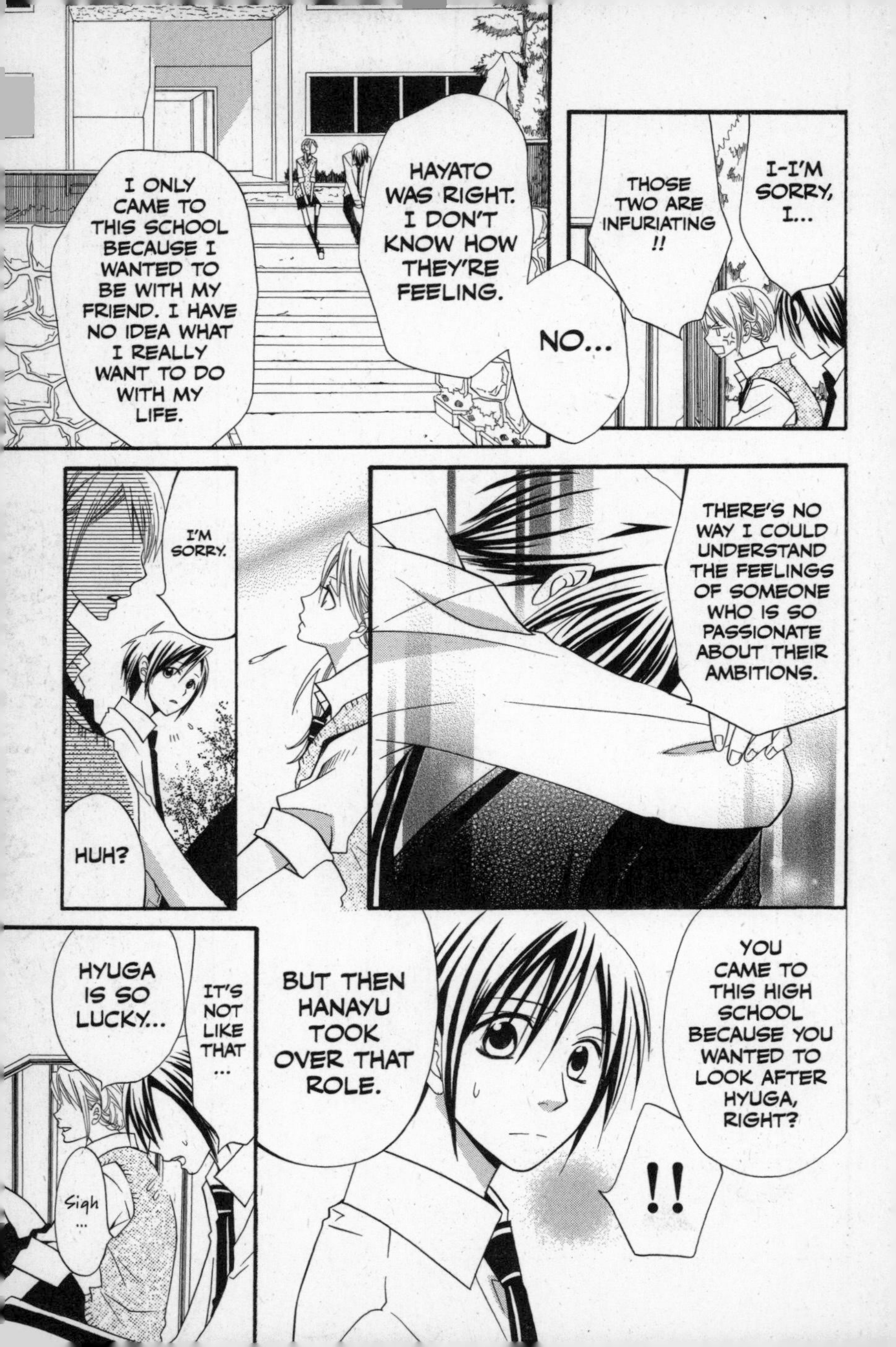
I-I'M SORRY, I...
THOSE TWO ARE INFURIATING !!
NO...
HAYATO WAS RIGHT. I DON'T KNOW HOW THEY'RE FEELING.
I ONLY CAME TO THIS SCHOOL BECAUSE I WANTED TO BE WITH MY FRIEND. I HAVE NO IDEA WHAT I REALLY WANT TO DO WITH MY LIFE.
THERE'S NO WAY I COULD UNDERSTAND THE FEELINGS OF SOMEONE WHO IS SO PASSIONATE ABOUT THEIR AMBITIONS.
I'M SORRY.
HUH?
YOU CAME TO THIS HIGH SCHOOL BECAUSE YOU WANTED TO LOOK AFTER HYUGA, RIGHT?
!!
BUT THEN HANAYU TOOK OVER THAT ROLE.
HYUGA IS SO LUCKY...
IT'S NOT LIKE THAT ...
Sigh ...

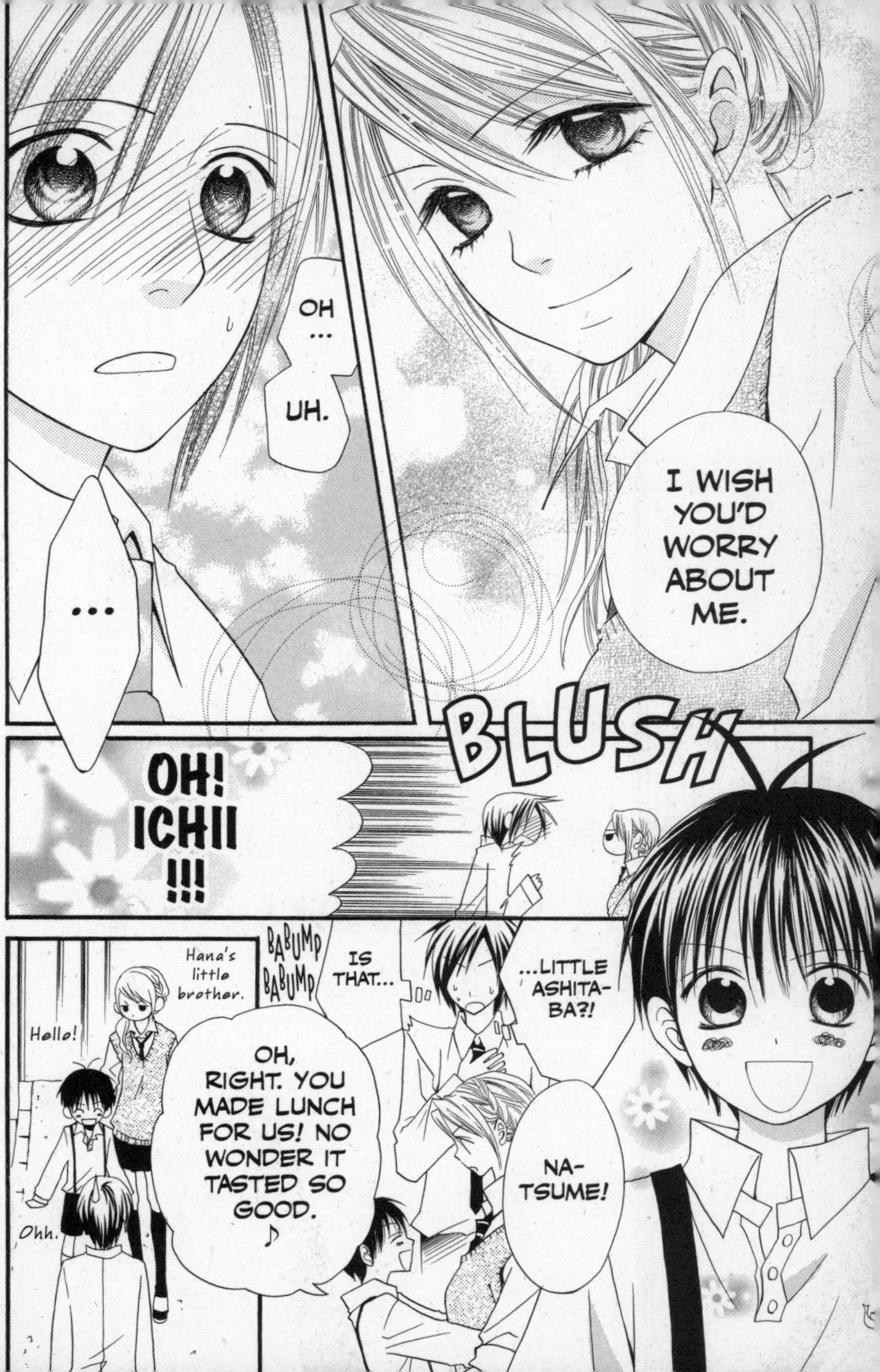
I WISH YOU'D WORRY ABOUT ME.
OH ... UH.
...
BLUSH
OH! ICHII !!!
NA-TSUME!
...LITTLE ASHITA-BA?!
IS THAT...
BABUMP BABUMP
OH, RIGHT. YOU MADE LUNCH FOR US! NO WONDER IT TASTED SO GOOD. ♪
Hana's little brother.
Hello!
Ohh.

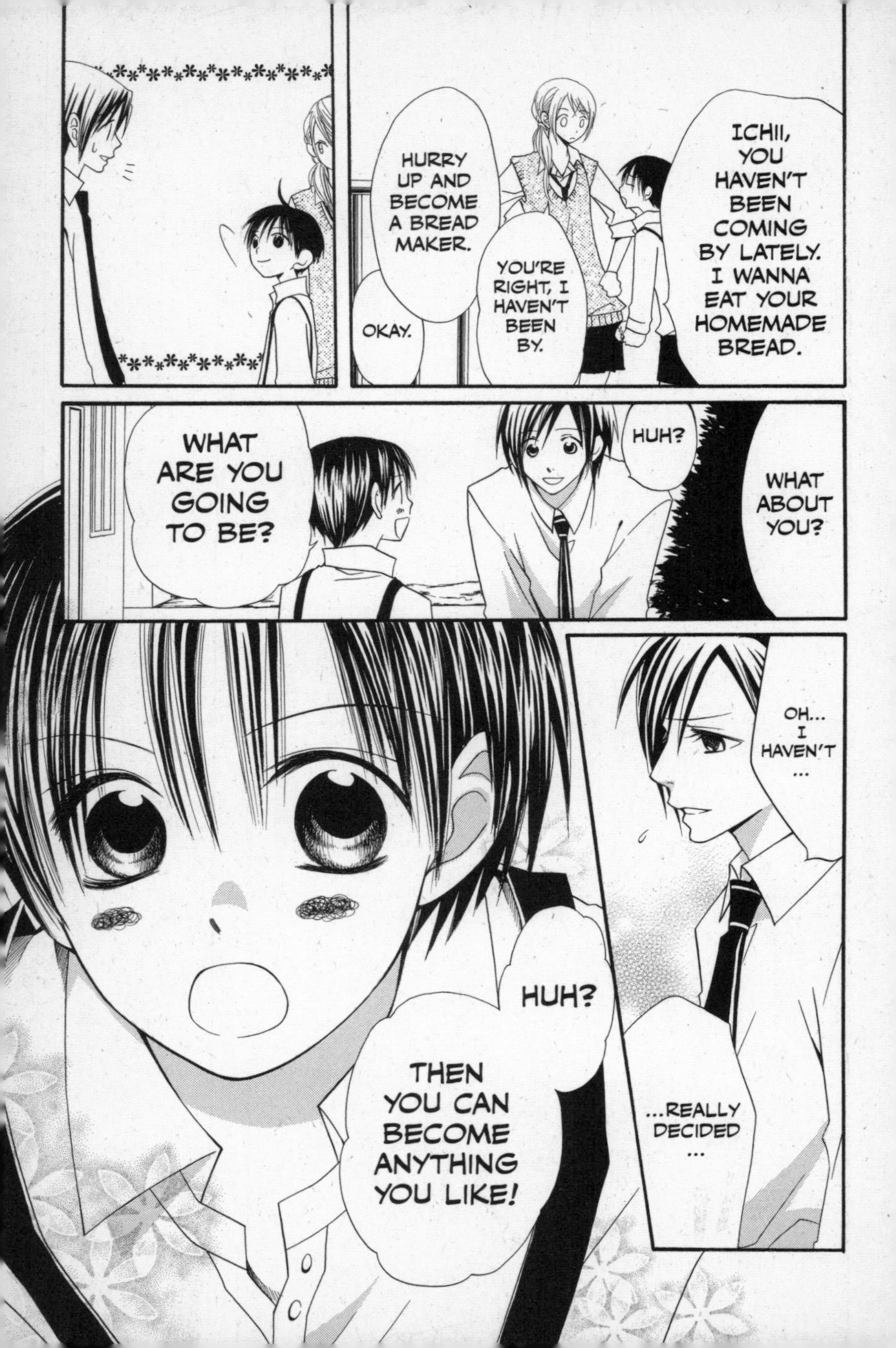
ICHII, YOU HAVEN'T BEEN COMING BY LATELY. I WANNA EAT YOUR HOMEMADE BREAD.
YOU'RE RIGHT, I HAVEN'T BEEN BY.
HURRY UP AND BECOME A BREAD MAKER.
OKAY.
WHAT ABOUT YOU?
HUH?
WHAT ARE YOU GOING TO BE?
OH... I HAVEN'T ...
...REALLY DECIDED ...
HUH?
THEN YOU CAN BECOME ANYTHING YOU LIKE!

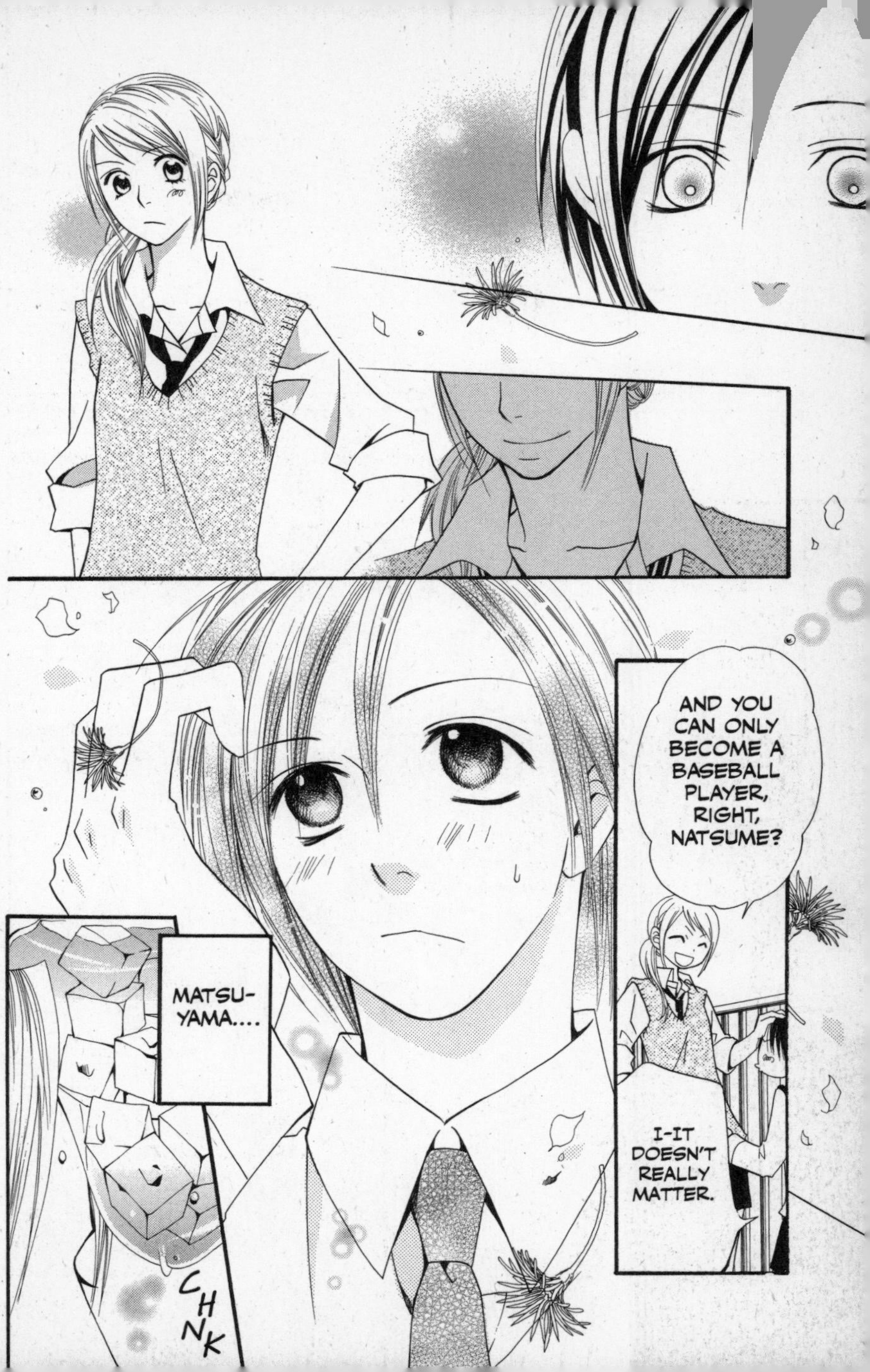
AND YOU CAN ONLY BECOME A BASEBALL PLAYER, RIGHT, NATSUME?
I-IT DOESN'T REALLY MATTER.
MATSU-YAMA....
CHNK

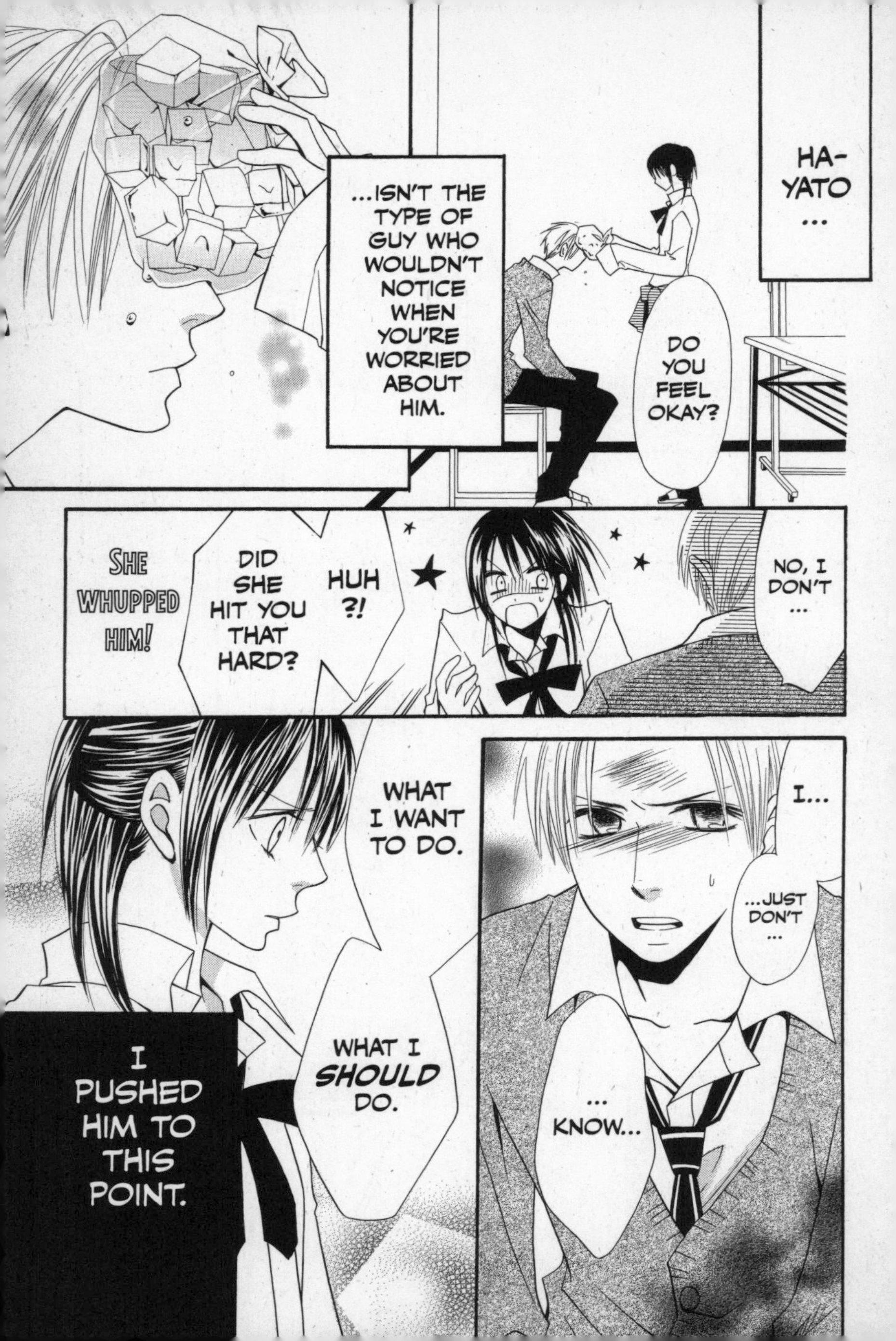
HA-YATO ...
...ISN'T THE TYPE OF GUY WHO WOULDN'T NOTICE WHEN YOU'RE WORRIED ABOUT HIM.
DO YOU FEEL OKAY?
NO, I DON'T ...
HUH ?!
DID SHE HIT YOU THAT HARD?
SHE WHUPPED HIM!
I...
...JUST DON'T ...
... KNOW...
WHAT I WANT TO DO.
WHAT I SHOULD DO.
I PUSHED HIM TO THIS POINT.

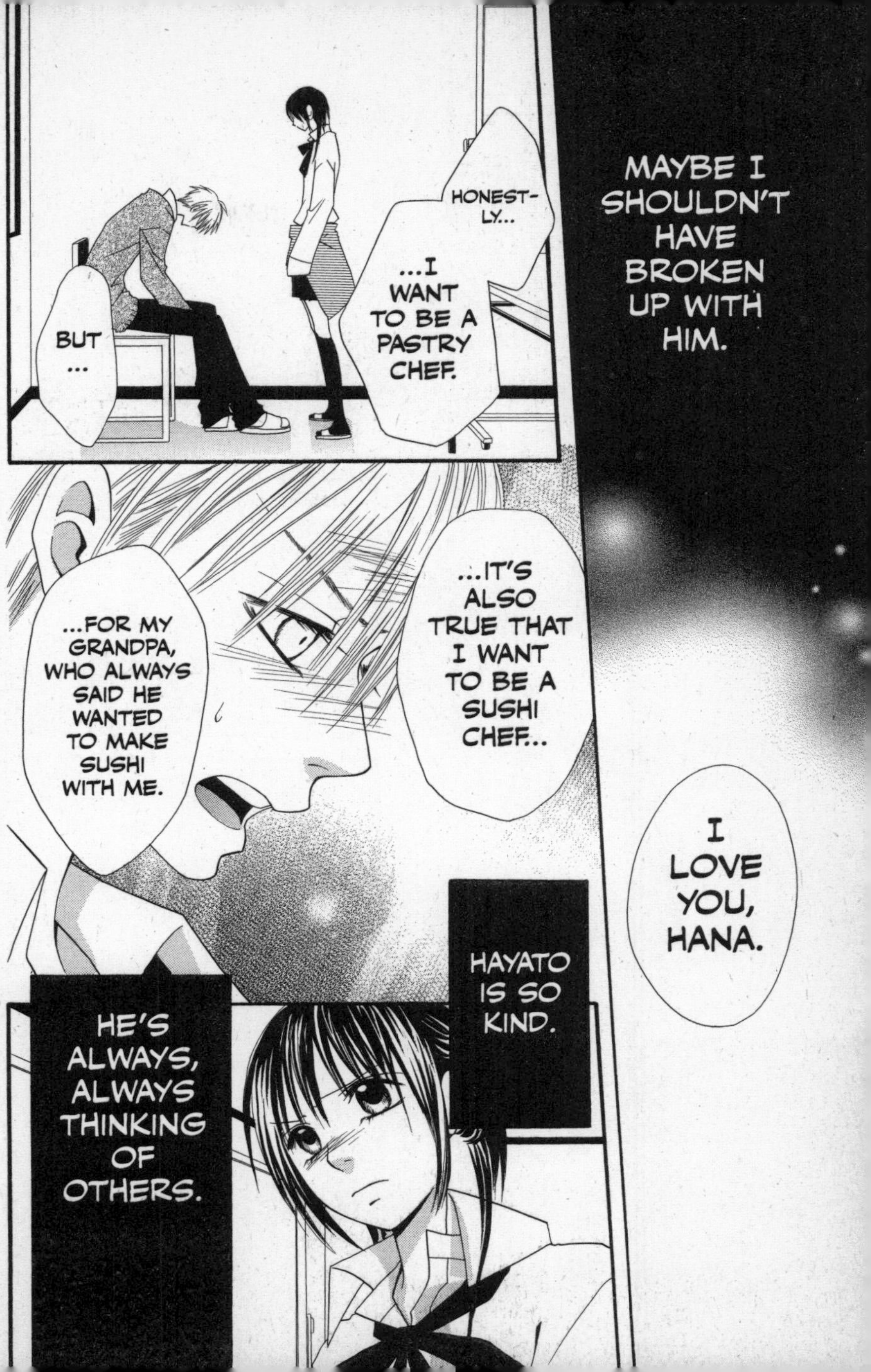
MAYBE I SHOULDN'T HAVE BROKEN UP WITH HIM.
I LOVE YOU, HANA.
HONEST-LY...
...I WANT TO BE A PASTRY CHEF.
BUT ...
...IT'S ALSO TRUE THAT I WANT TO BE A SUSHI CHEF...
...FOR MY GRANDPA, WHO ALWAYS SAID HE WANTED TO MAKE SUSHI WITH ME.
HAYATO IS SO KIND.
HE'S ALWAYS, ALWAYS THINKING OF OTHERS.

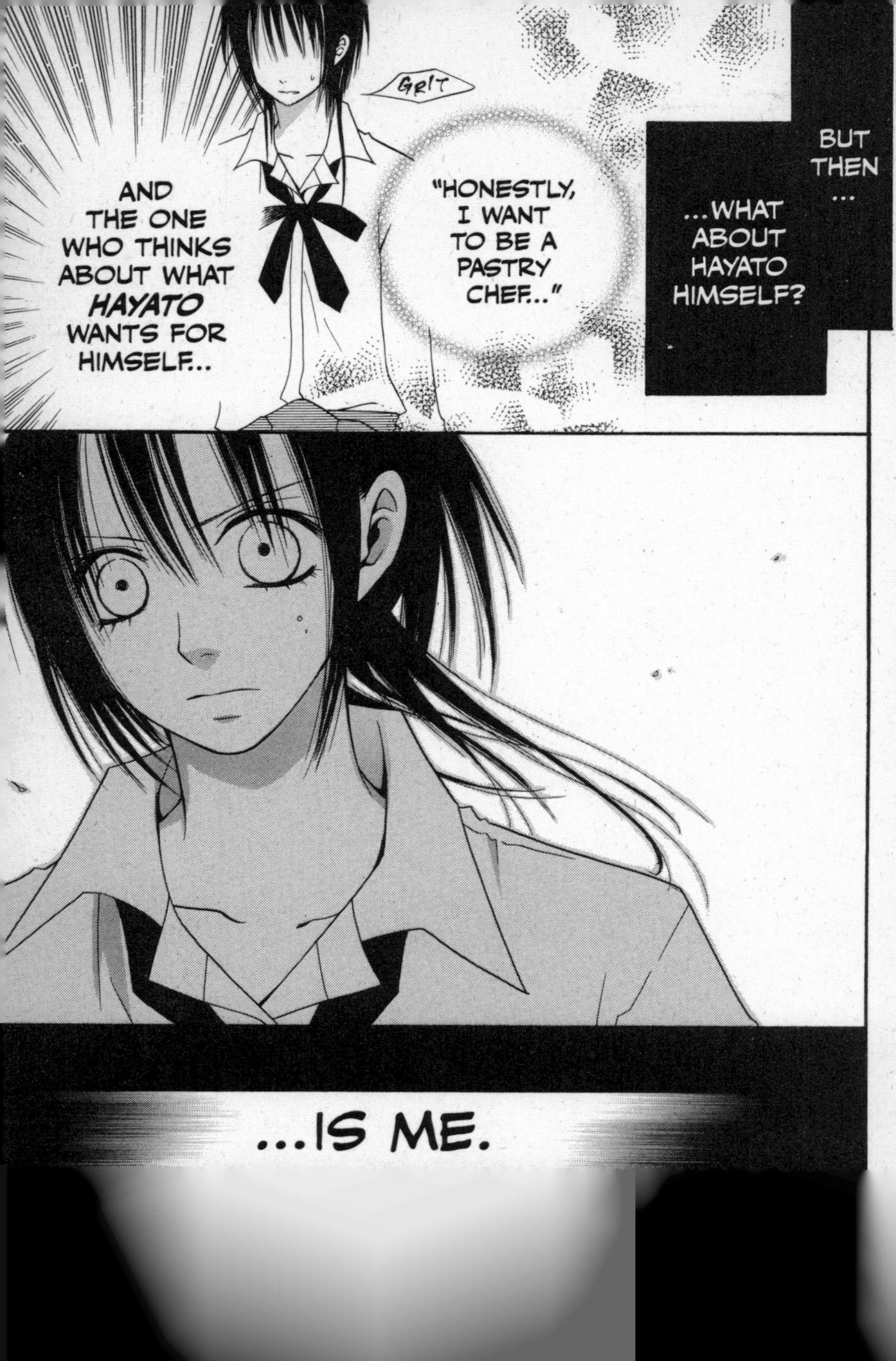
BUT THEN ...
...WHAT ABOUT HAYATO HIMSELF?
"HONESTLY, I WANT TO BE A PASTRY CHEF..."
GRIT
AND THE ONE WHO THINKS ABOUT WHAT *HAYATO* WANTS FOR HIMSELF...
...IS ME.

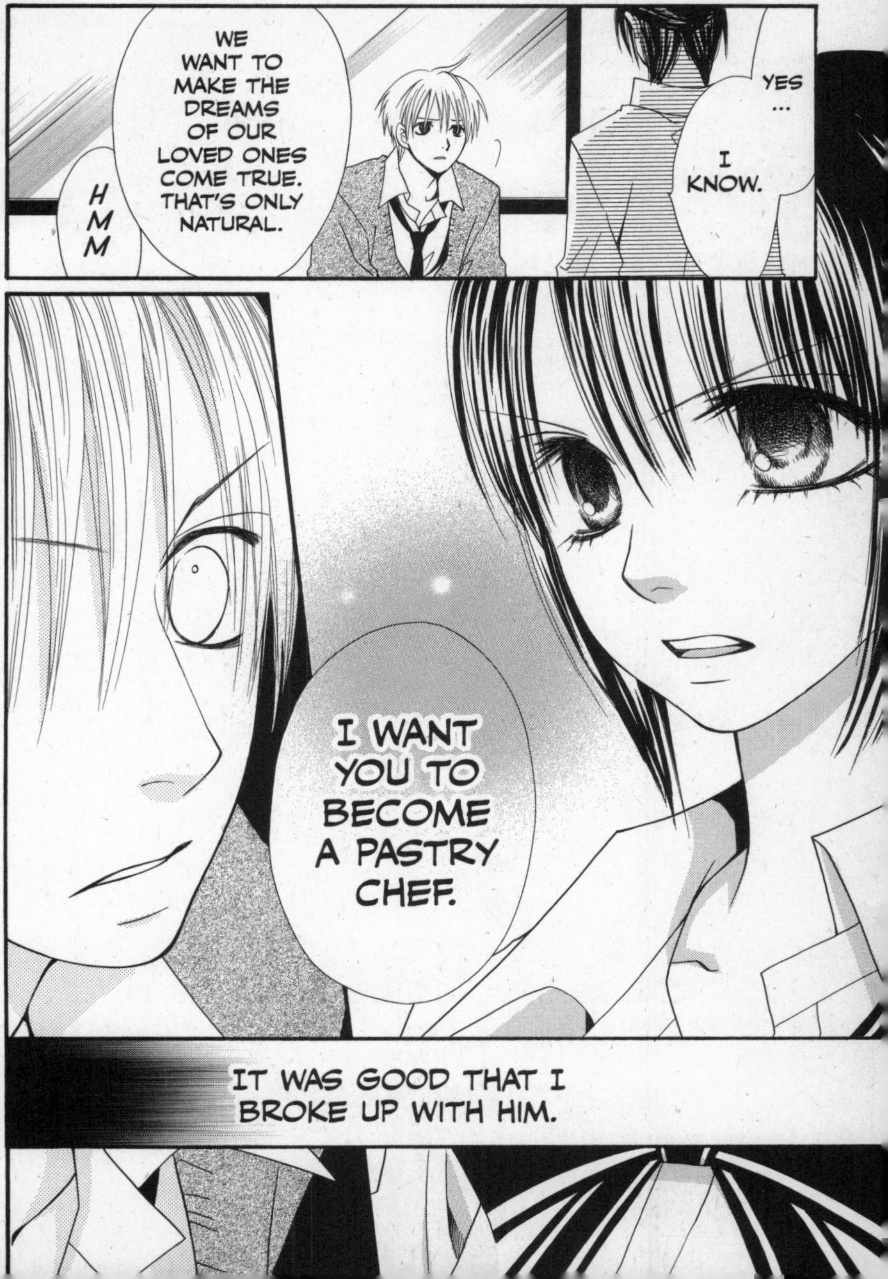
YES ... I KNOW.
WE WANT TO MAKE THE DREAMS OF OUR LOVED ONES COME TRUE. THAT'S ONLY NATURAL.
HMM
I WANT YOU TO BECOME A PASTRY CHEF.
IT WAS GOOD THAT I BROKE UP WITH HIM.

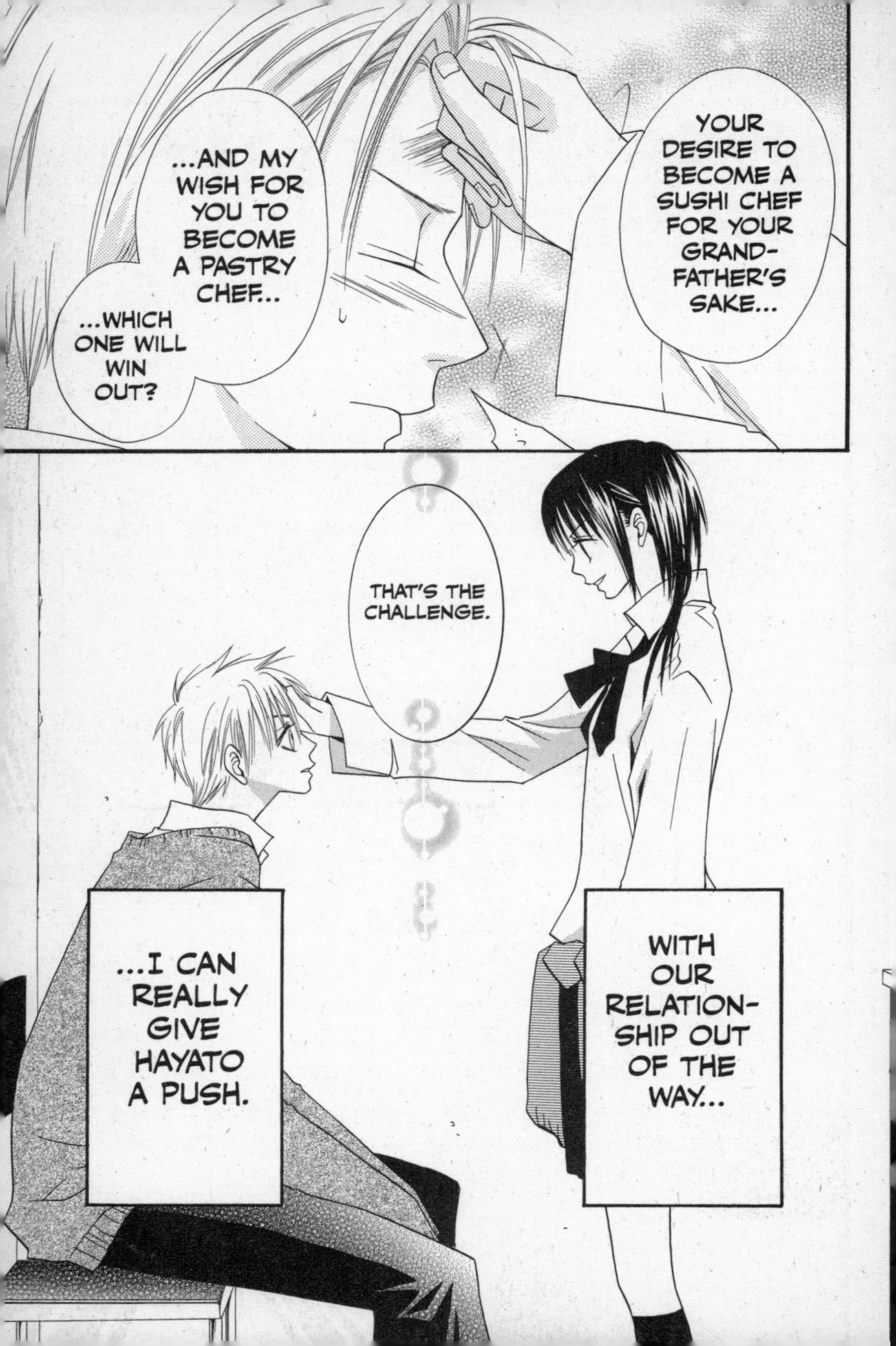
YOUR DESIRE TO BECOME A SUSHI CHEF FOR YOUR GRAND-FATHER'S SAKE...
...AND MY WISH FOR YOU TO BECOME A PASTRY CHEF...
...WHICH ONE WILL WIN OUT?
THAT'S THE CHALLENGE.
WITH OUR RELATION-SHIP OUT OF THE WAY...
...I CAN REALLY GIVE HAYATO A PUSH.

MIXED VEGETABLES Encyclopedia of Characters

REA MATSUZAKAI

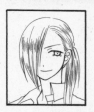

MATSUZAKA → MATSUZAKA BEEF
REA → RARE

I WAS HAVING TROUBLE FINDING A NAME WHEN MY KID SISTER SUGGESTED, "HOW ABOUT USING THE NAME OF A MEAT?" I CHOSE THE KANJI PHONETICALLY.

I DREW HER AS DEFINITELY A WOMAN AT FIRST, BUT SOMEONE ASKED ME, "MAN OR WOMAN?" AND I THOUGHT IT WOULD BE MORE FUN IF PEOPLE COULDN'T TELL. SOME READERS RECOGNIZED THAT SHE WAS A WOMAN FROM THE DRAWING, AND I'M VERY HAPPY ABOUT THAT. THE MODEL FOR REA WAS A TEACHER I HAD IN HIGH SCHOOL. SHE WAS VERY STRICT, BUT ALWAYS FAIR, AND I LOVED HER. SHE WAS ALWAYS SUPPORTIVE OF MY BECOMING A MANGA ARTIST.

SADLY, SHE PASSED AWAY WITHOUT HAVING A CHANCE TO READ ANY OF MY MANGA. THANK YOU SO MUCH, SENSEI.

ISAKI ISHINAGI

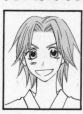

ISHINAGI/ISAKI → FISH

SAKI-SAN PARTS HIS HAIR IN THE MIDDLE, HE'S GOT DROOPY EYES, AND HE'S GREGARIOUS.

I CREATED THIS CHARACTER OUT OF NECESSITY, AND HE'S GROWN TO BE MUCH MORE THAN I EXPECTED.

IN *MV*, HE WAS A REFRESHING, EARNEST CHARACTER, AND I ENJOYED DRAWING HIM. YES, I LIKE HIM, I LIKE HIM A LOT. HEIGHT: 6'. HE'S THE TALLEST CHARACTER IN *MV*.

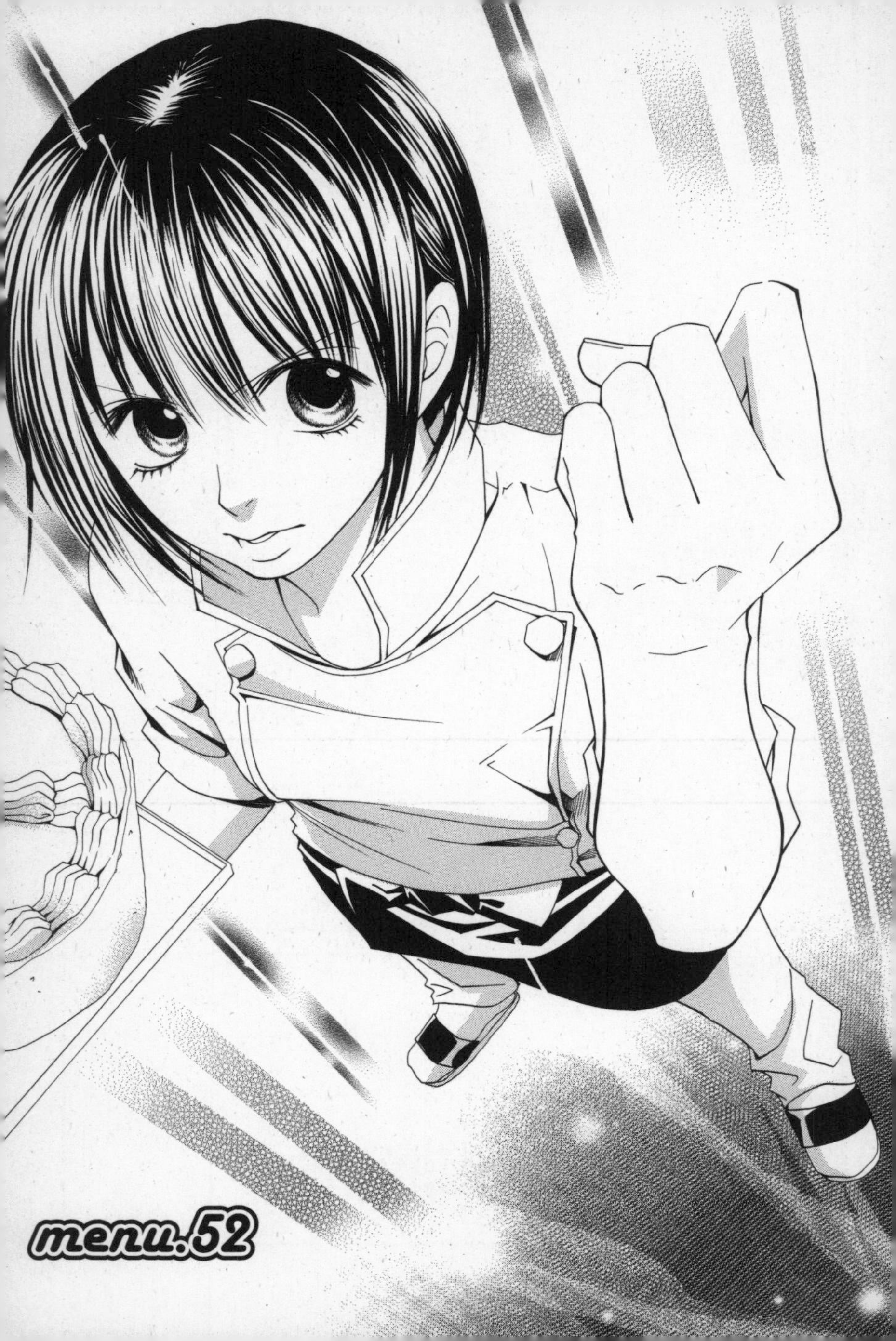
menu.52

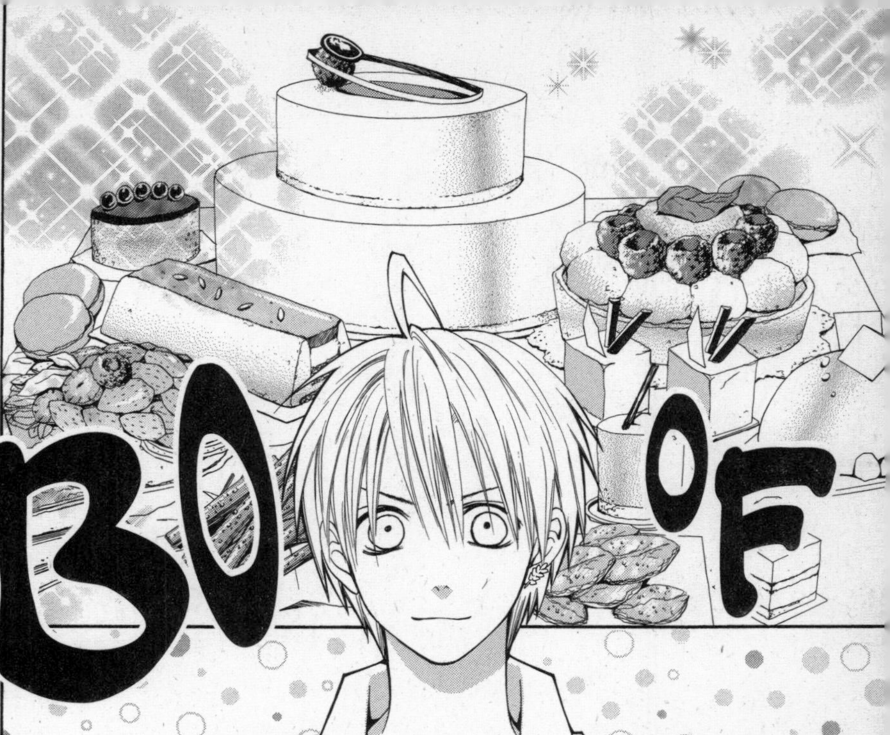
BO
OF

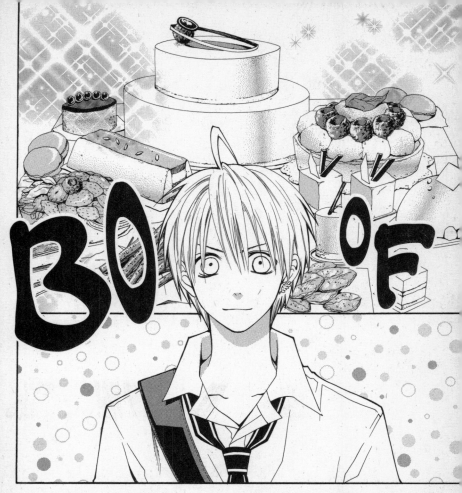

menu52

This cover is a counterpoint to the illustration for *MV*, Vol. 2, Menu 14.
Is this what people who are trying to emotionally support each other do?
Hana is going all out and it's quite fun.
Hayato's earring is a twig of wheat. It's been a while since I did something with his pierced ear.
Dad went to the convenience store to do his shopping. It seems both father and daughter like oshiruko.
Look for the scene where Hana is holding a can too!
The manager of my neighborhood convenience store let me take photos of his shop.
Thank you very much!

A friend of mine drew her version of Hana and...? (laugh)
We went to the river together the other day to swim.

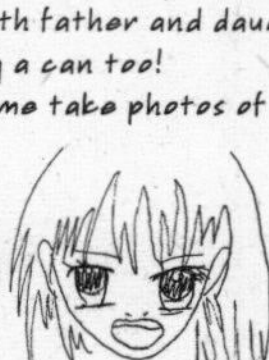

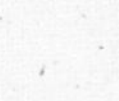

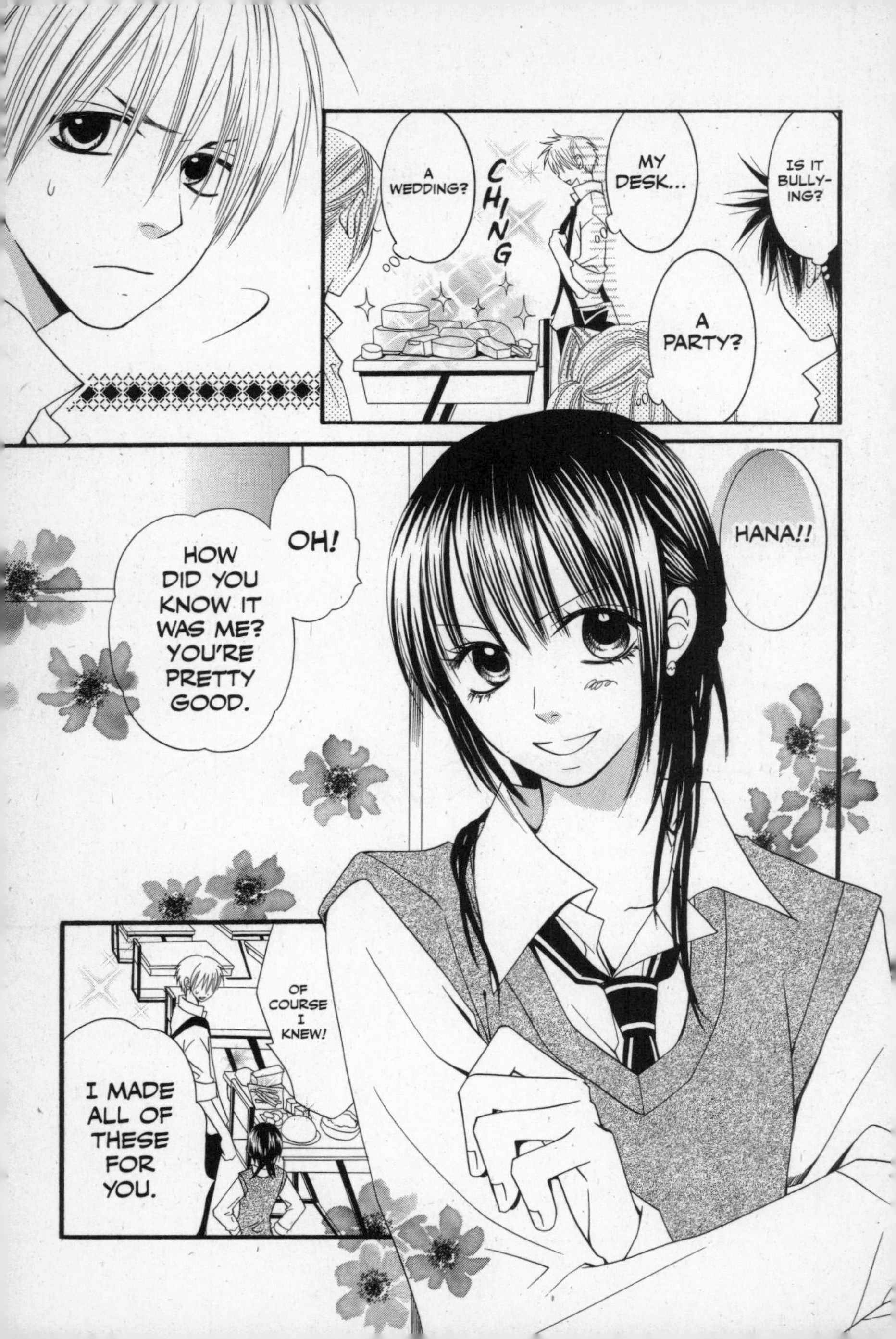

IS IT BULLY-ING?
MY DESK...
A PARTY?
A WEDDING?
CHING
HANA!!
OH!
HOW DID YOU KNOW IT WAS ME? YOU'RE PRETTY GOOD.
OF COURSE I KNEW!
I MADE ALL OF THESE FOR YOU.

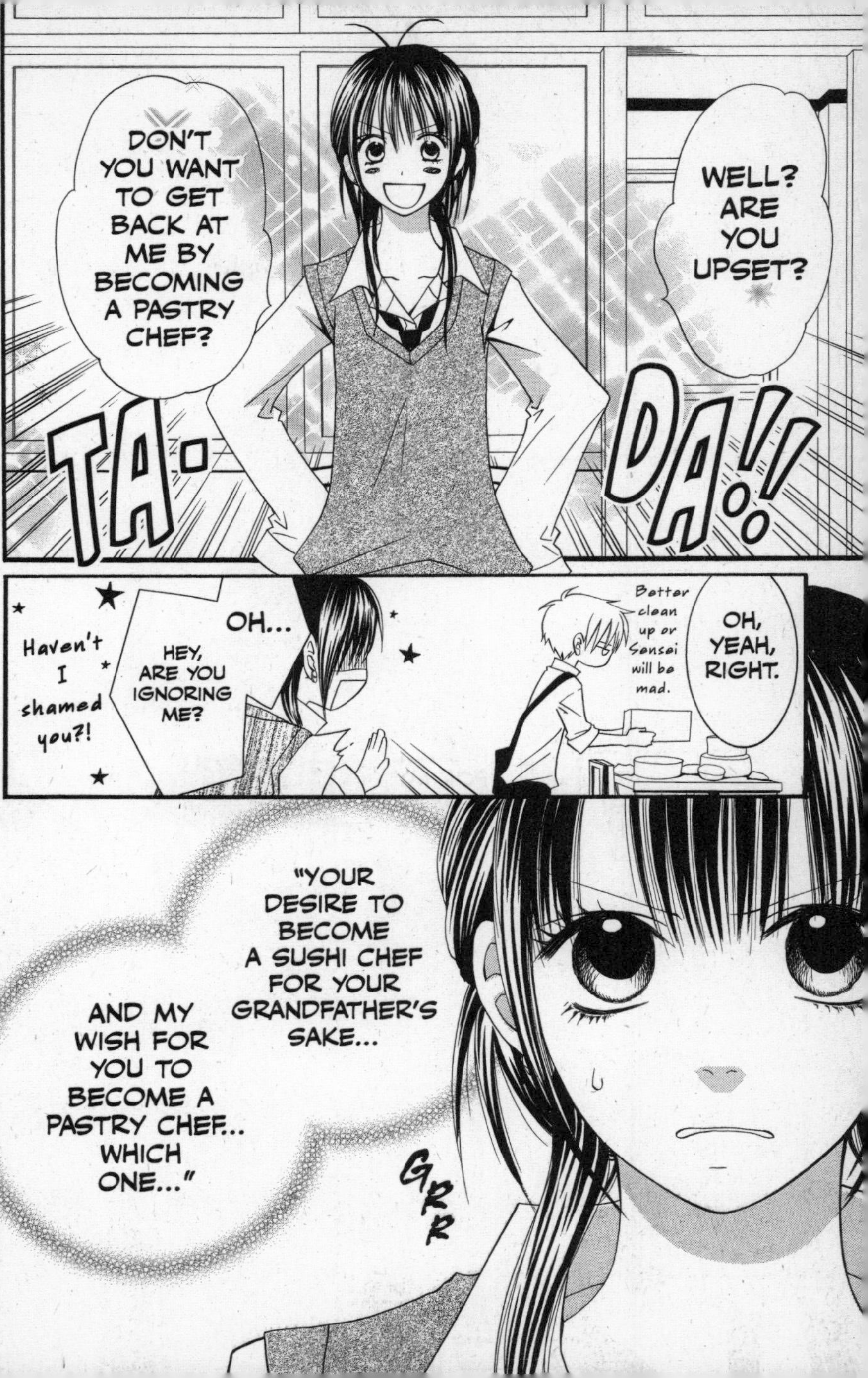
WELL? ARE YOU UPSET?
DON'T YOU WANT TO GET BACK AT ME BY BECOMING A PASTRY CHEF?
TA-DA!!
OH, YEAH, RIGHT.
Better clean up or Sensei will be mad.
OH...
HEY, ARE YOU IGNORING ME?
Haven't I shamed you?!
"YOUR DESIRE TO BECOME A SUSHI CHEF FOR YOUR GRANDFATHER'S SAKE...
AND MY WISH FOR YOU TO BECOME A PASTRY CHEF... WHICH ONE..."
GRR

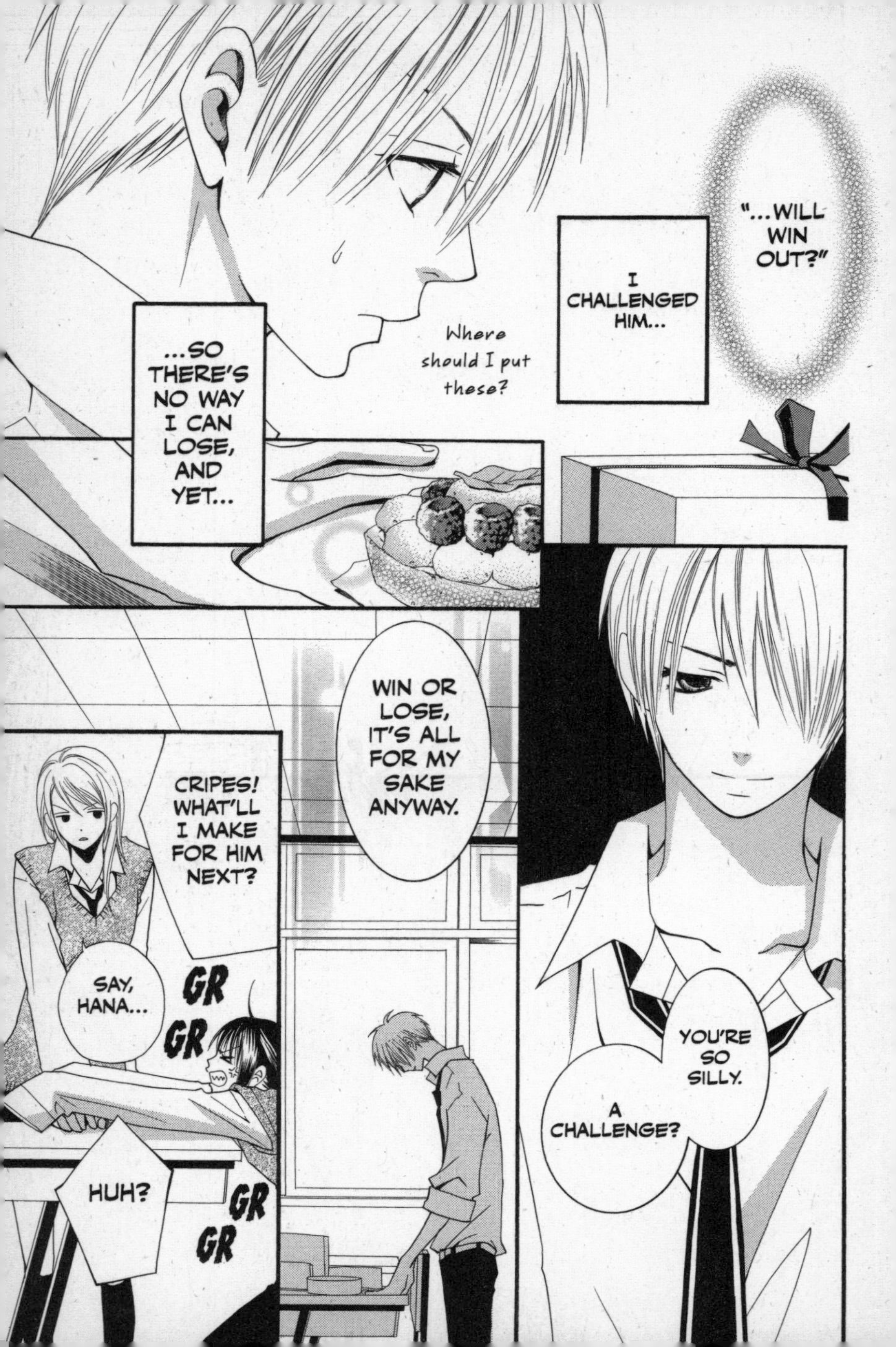
"...WILL WIN OUT?"
I CHALLENGED HIM...
Where should I put these?
...SO THERE'S NO WAY I CAN LOSE, AND YET...
YOU'RE SO SILLY.
A CHALLENGE?
WIN OR LOSE, IT'S ALL FOR MY SAKE ANYWAY.
CRIPES! WHAT'LL I MAKE FOR HIM NEXT?
SAY, HANA...
GR GR
HUH?
GR GR

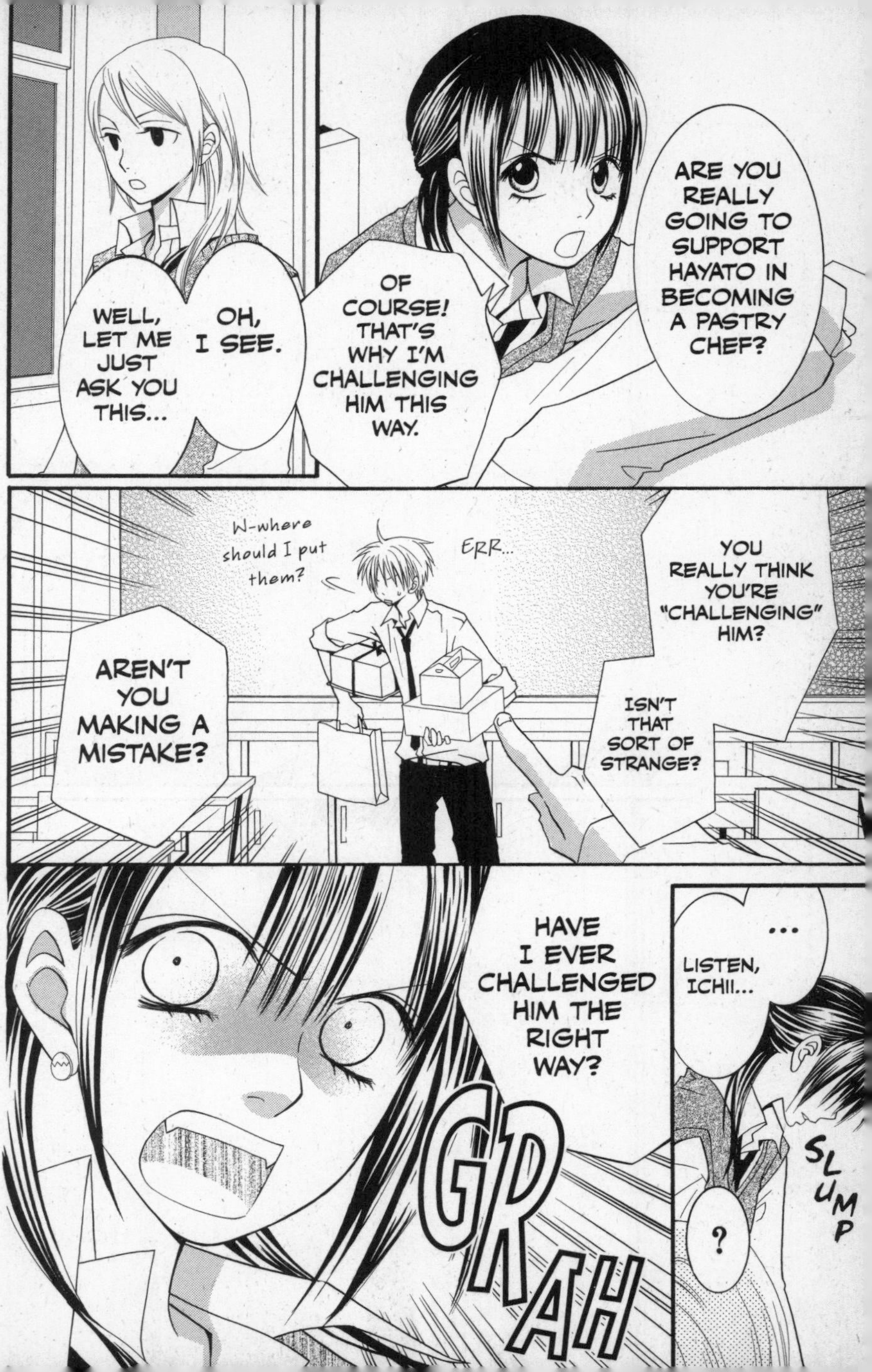
ARE YOU REALLY GOING TO SUPPORT HAYATO IN BECOMING A PASTRY CHEF?
OF COURSE! THAT'S WHY I'M CHALLENGING HIM THIS WAY.
OH, I SEE.
WELL, LET ME JUST ASK YOU THIS...
YOU REALLY THINK YOU'RE "CHALLENGING" HIM?
ISN'T THAT SORT OF STRANGE?
ERR...
W-where should I put them?
AREN'T YOU MAKING A MISTAKE?
...
LISTEN, ICHII...
SLUMP
?
HAVE I EVER CHALLENGED HIM THE RIGHT WAY?
GRAH

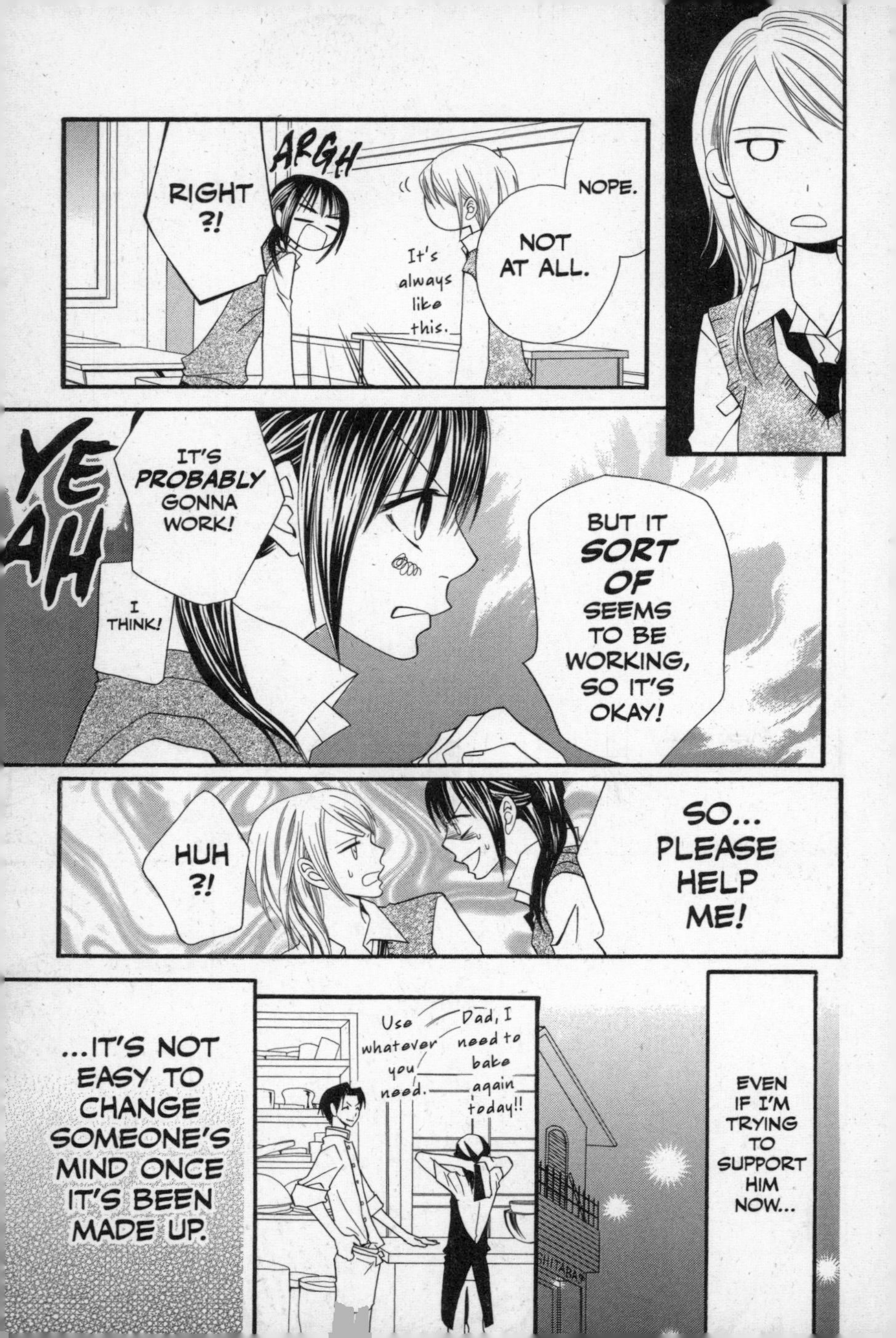
NOPE.
NOT AT ALL.
It's always like this.
ARGH
RIGHT?!
BUT IT SORT OF SEEMS TO BE WORKING, SO IT'S OKAY!
IT'S PROBABLY GONNA WORK!
I THINK!
YEAH
SO... PLEASE HELP ME!
HUH?!
EVEN IF I'M TRYING TO SUPPORT HIM NOW...
Dad, I need to bake again today!!
Use whatever you need.
...IT'S NOT EASY TO CHANGE SOMEONE'S MIND ONCE IT'S BEEN MADE UP.

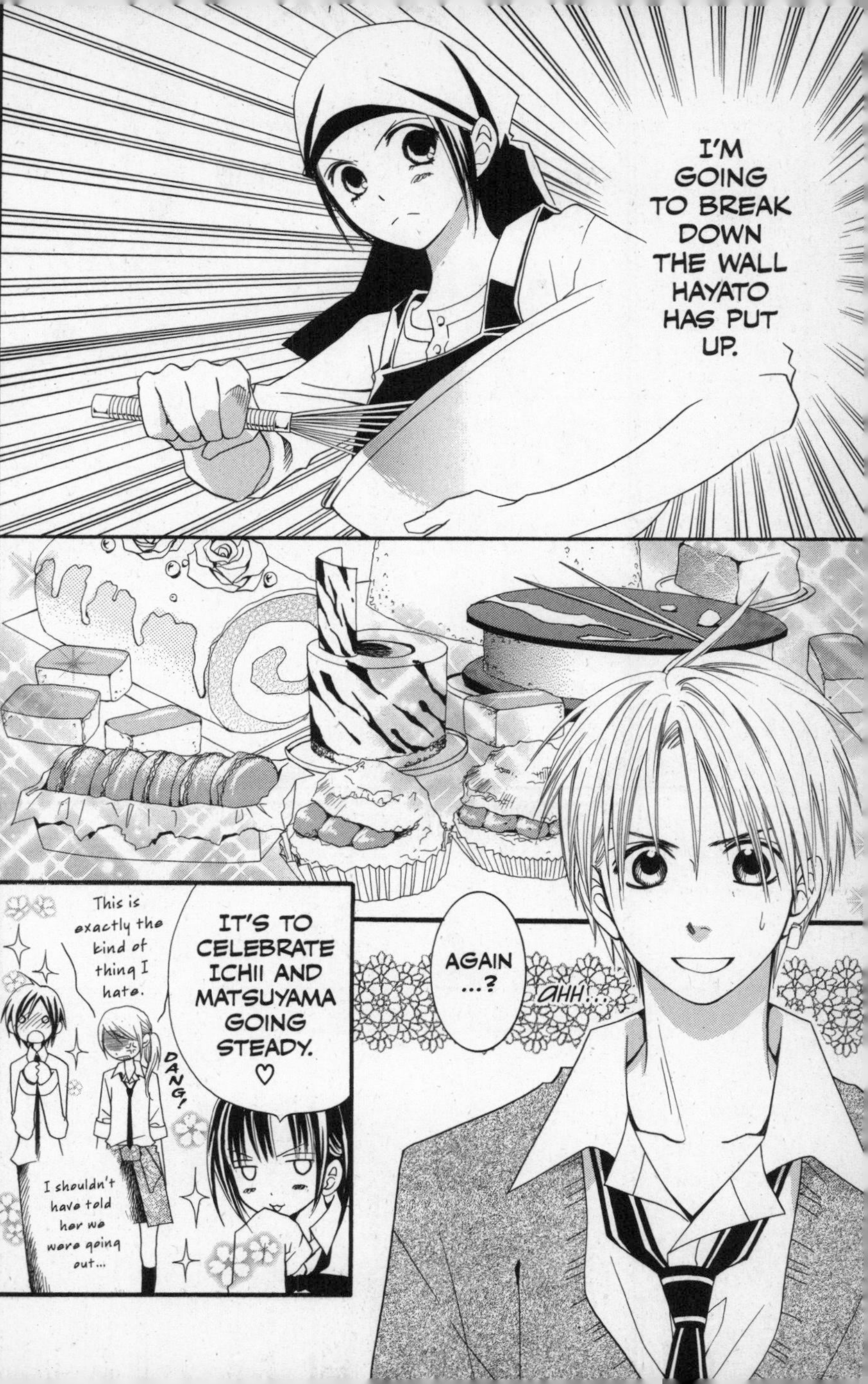
I'M GOING TO BREAK DOWN THE WALL HAYATO HAS PUT UP.
AGAIN ...?
AHH...
IT'S TO CELEBRATE ICHII AND MATSUYAMA GOING STEADY. ♡
This is exactly the kind of thing I hate.
DANG!
I shouldn't have told her we were going out...

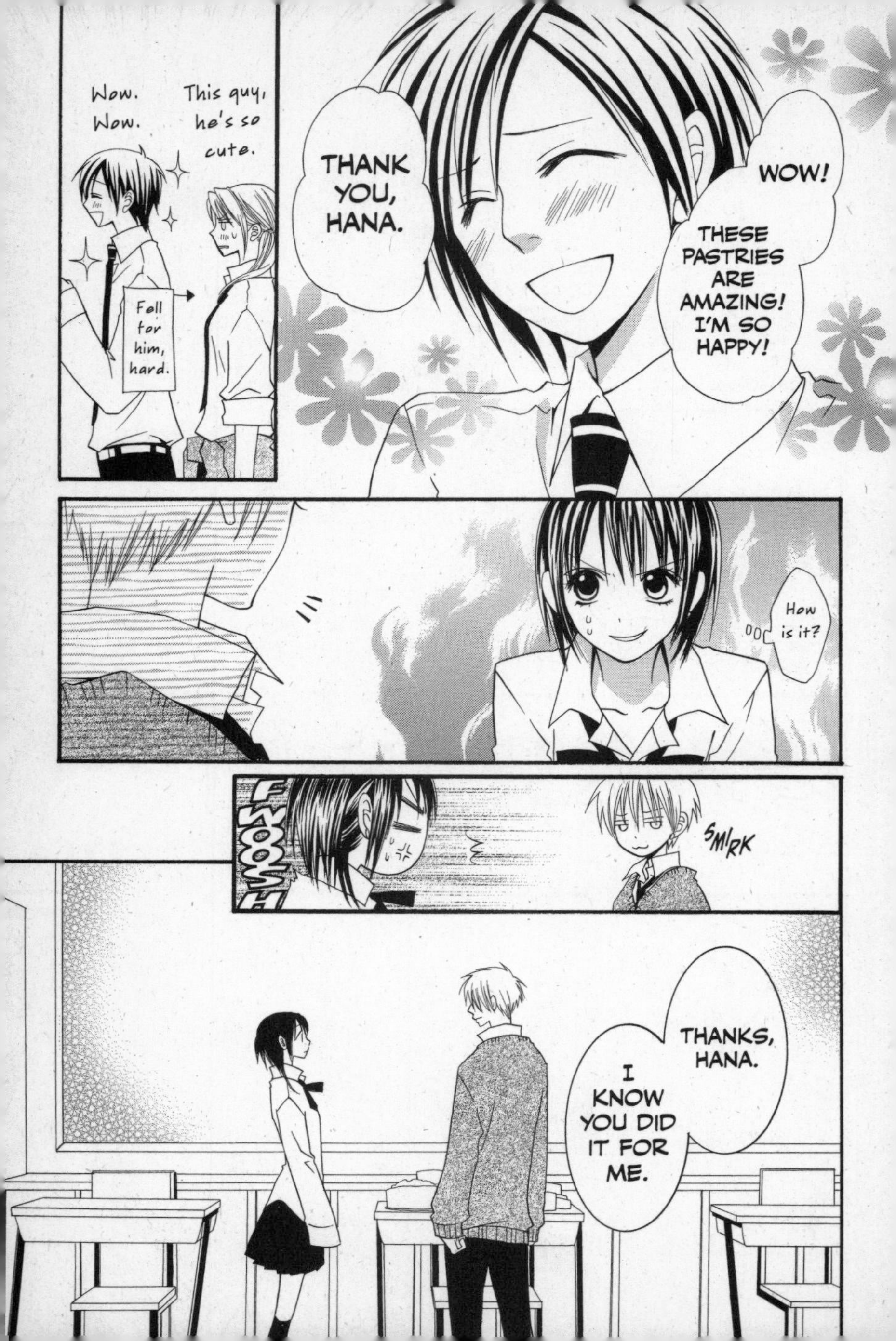
WOW!
THESE PASTRIES ARE AMAZING! I'M SO HAPPY!
THANK YOU, HANA.
This guy, he's so cute.
Wow. Wow.
Fell for him, hard.
How is it?
SMIRK
FWOOSH
THANKS, HANA.
I KNOW YOU DID IT FOR ME.

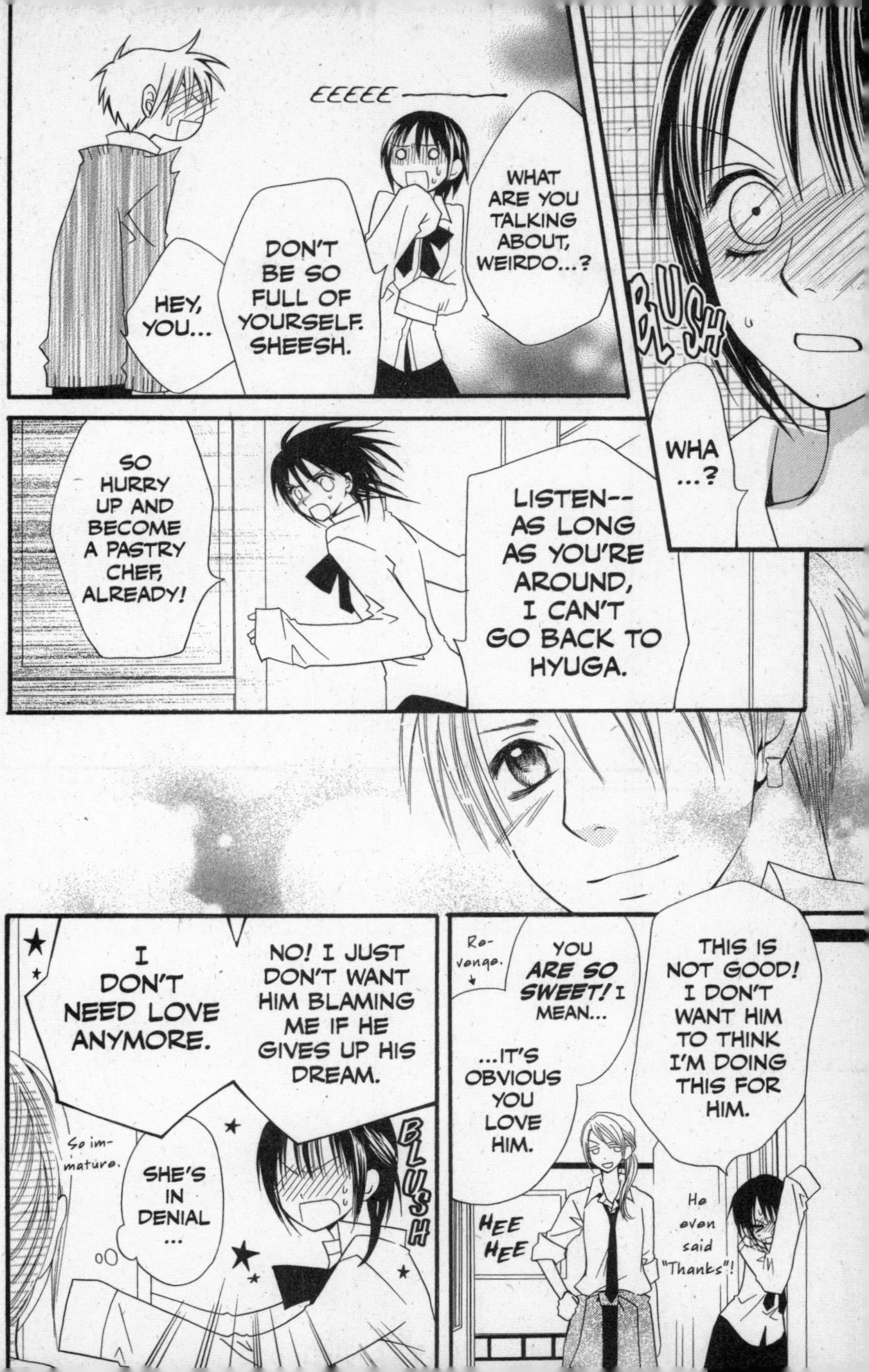

BLUSH
WHA ...?
EEEEE——
WHAT ARE YOU TALKING ABOUT, WEIRDO...?
DON'T BE SO FULL OF YOURSELF. SHEESH.
HEY, YOU...
LISTEN-- AS LONG AS YOU'RE AROUND, I CAN'T GO BACK TO HYUGA.
SO HURRY UP AND BECOME A PASTRY CHEF, ALREADY!
THIS IS NOT GOOD! I DON'T WANT HIM TO THINK I'M DOING THIS FOR HIM.
He even said "Thanks"!
YOU ARE SO SWEET! I MEAN...
Re-venge.
...IT'S OBVIOUS YOU LOVE HIM.
HEE HEE
NO! I JUST DON'T WANT HIM BLAMING ME IF HE GIVES UP HIS DREAM.
I DON'T NEED LOVE ANYMORE.
BLUSH
SHE'S IN DENIAL ...
So im-mature.

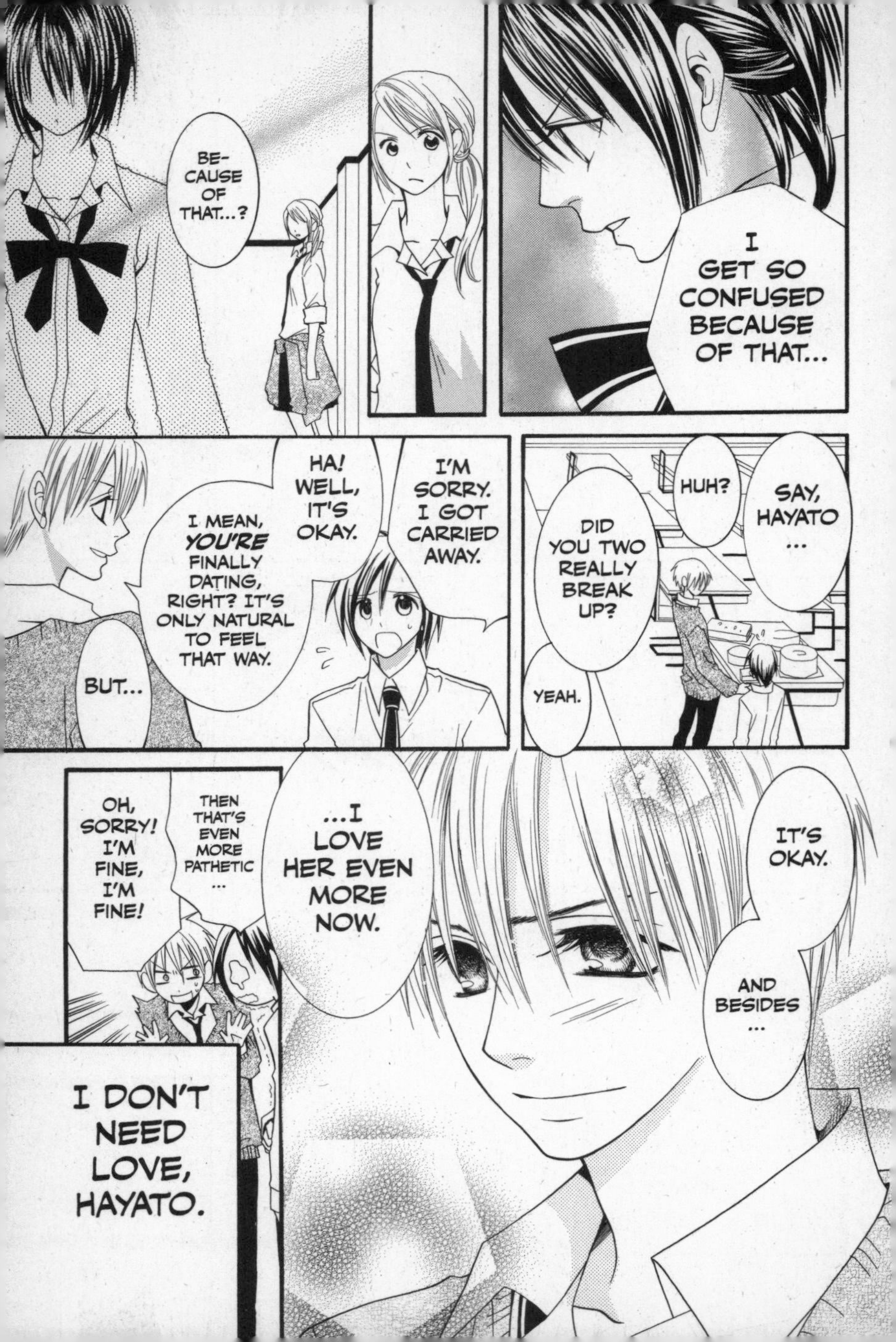
I GET SO CONFUSED BECAUSE OF THAT...
BE-CAUSE OF THAT...?
SAY, HAYATO ...
HUH?
DID YOU TWO REALLY BREAK UP?
YEAH.
I'M SORRY. I GOT CARRIED AWAY.
HA! WELL, IT'S OKAY.
I MEAN, *YOU'RE* FINALLY DATING, RIGHT? IT'S ONLY NATURAL TO FEEL THAT WAY.
BUT...
IT'S OKAY.
AND BESIDES ...
...I LOVE HER EVEN MORE NOW.
THEN THAT'S EVEN MORE PATHETIC ...
OH, SORRY! I'M FINE, I'M FINE!
I DON'T NEED LOVE, HAYATO.

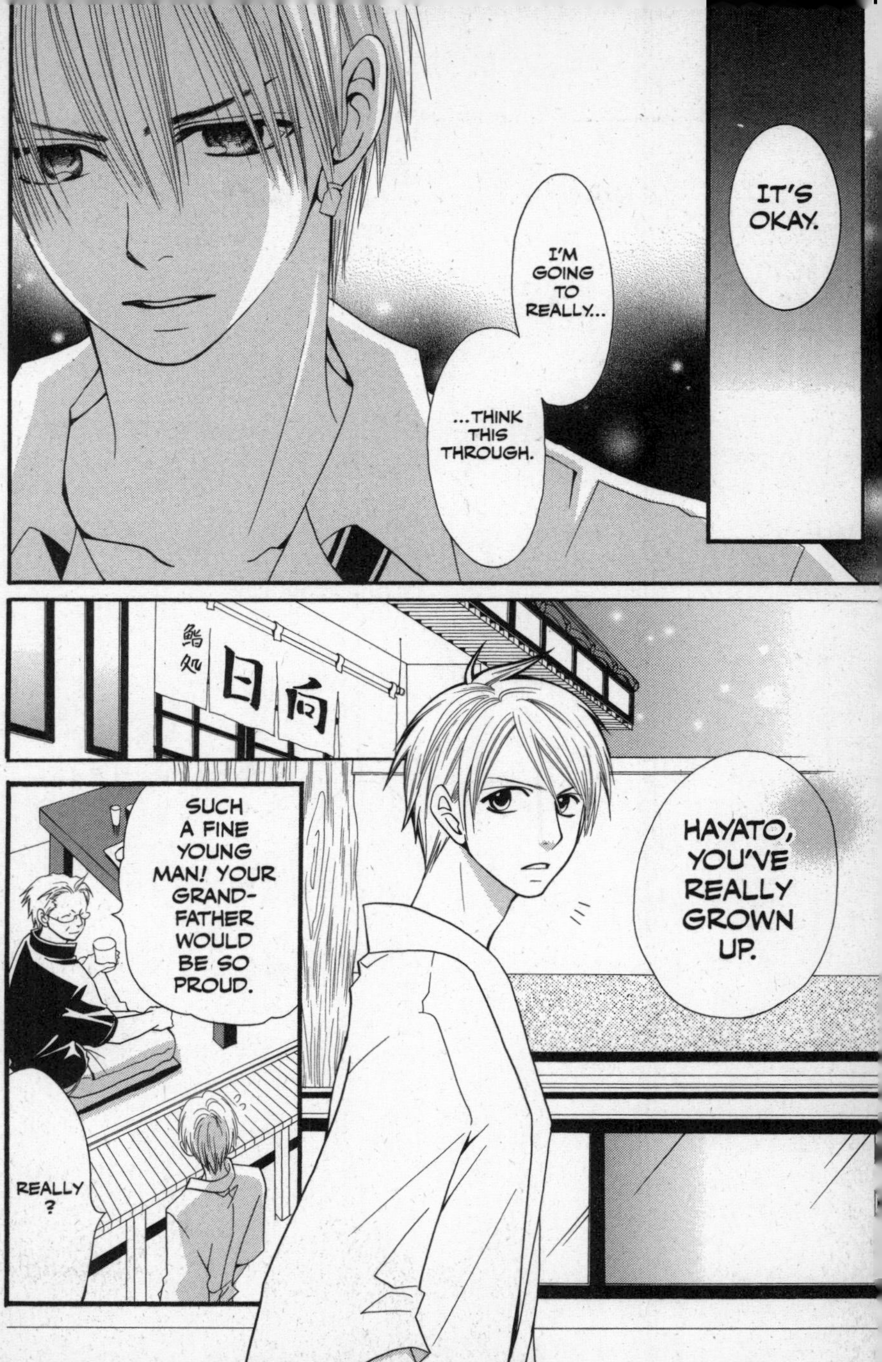
IT'S OKAY.
I'M GOING TO REALLY...
...THINK THIS THROUGH.
鮨処 日向
HAYATO, YOU'VE REALLY GROWN UP.
SUCH A FINE YOUNG MAN! YOUR GRAND-FATHER WOULD BE SO PROUD.
REALLY?

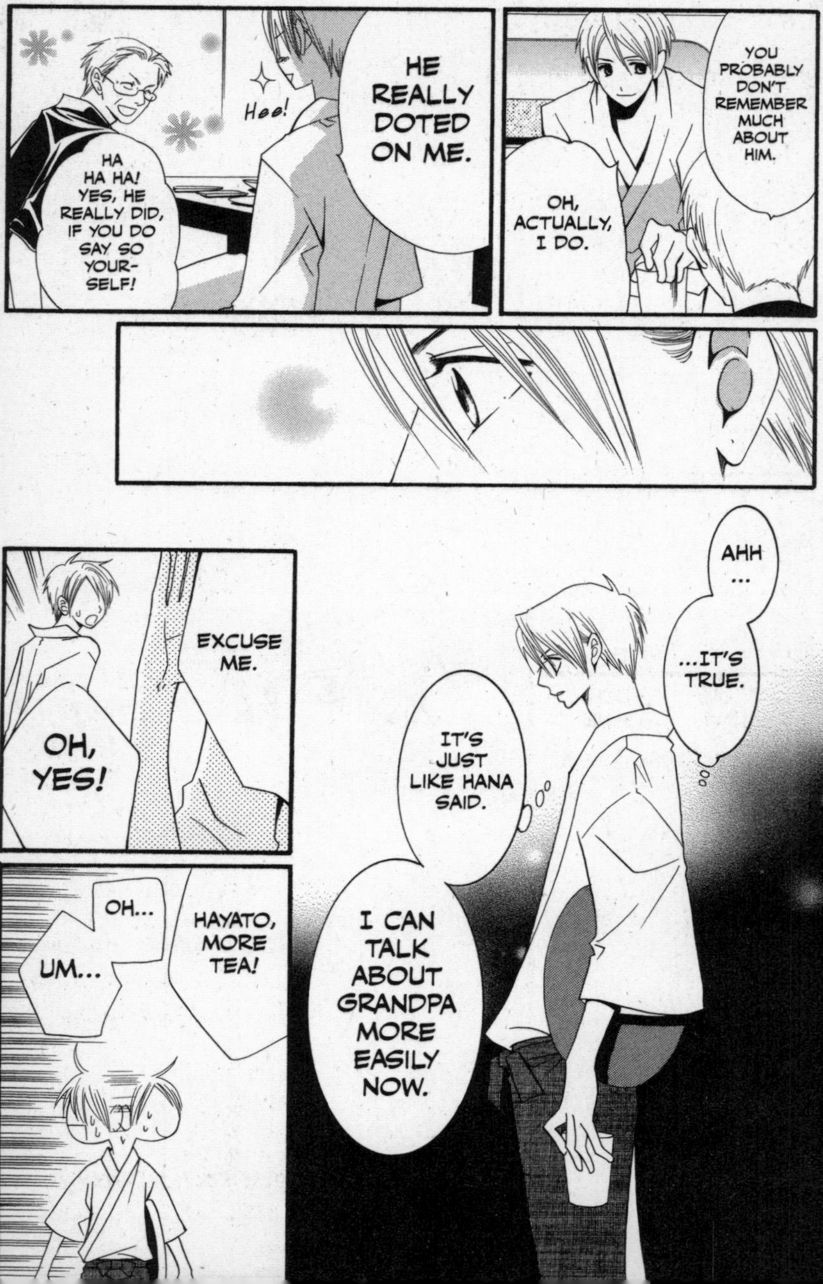
YOU PROBABLY DON'T REMEMBER MUCH ABOUT HIM.
OH, ACTUALLY, I DO.
HE REALLY DOTED ON ME.
Hee!
HA HA HA! YES, HE REALLY DID, IF YOU DO SAY SO YOUR-SELF!
AHH...
...IT'S TRUE.
IT'S JUST LIKE HANA SAID.
I CAN TALK ABOUT GRANDPA MORE EASILY NOW.
EXCUSE ME.
OH, YES!
HAYATO, MORE TEA!
OH...
UM...

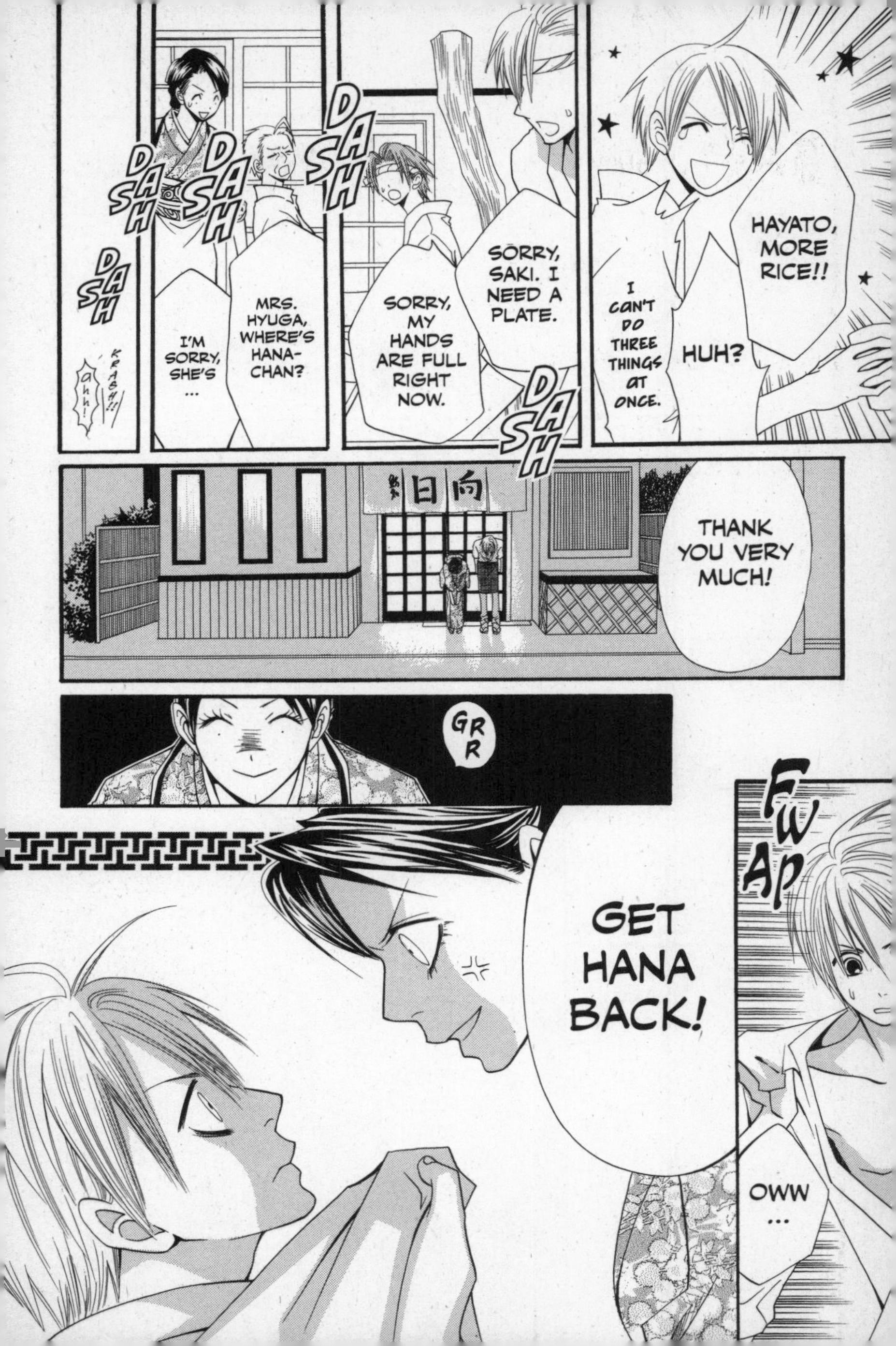
HAYATO, MORE RICE!!
HUH?
I CAN'T DO THREE THINGS AT ONCE.
SORRY, SAKI. I NEED A PLATE.
DASH
SORRY, MY HANDS ARE FULL RIGHT NOW.
DASH
MRS. HYUGA, WHERE'S HANA-CHAN?
I'M SORRY, SHE'S ...
DASH
DASH
DASH
KRASH!!
Ahh!
日向
THANK YOU VERY MUCH!
GRR
FWAP
OWW ...
GET HANA BACK!

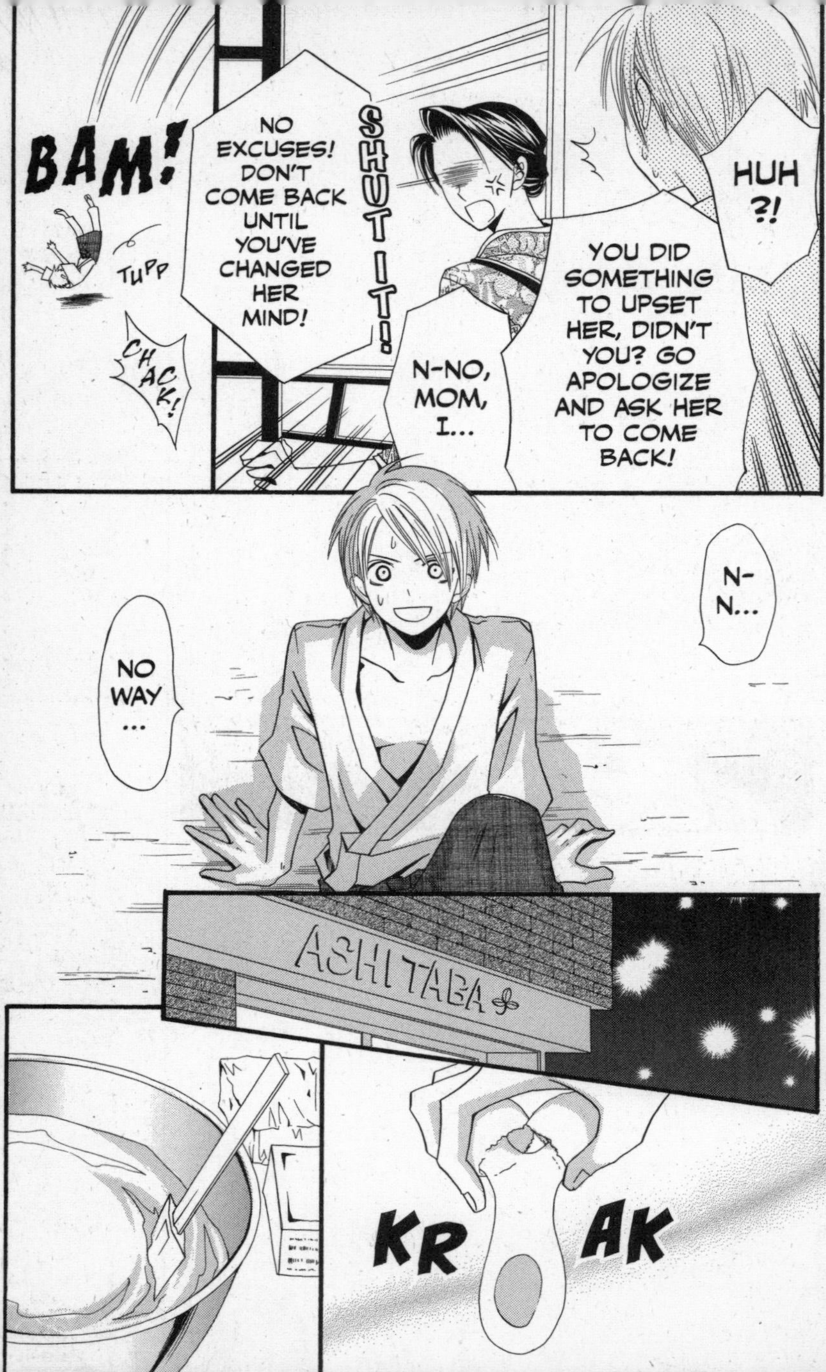
HUH ?!
YOU DID SOMETHING TO UPSET HER, DIDN'T YOU? GO APOLOGIZE AND ASK HER TO COME BACK!
N-NO, MOM, I...
SHUT IT!
NO EXCUSES! DON'T COME BACK UNTIL YOU'VE CHANGED HER MIND!
BAM!
TUPP
CHACK!
N-N...
NO WAY ...
ASHITABA
KR AK

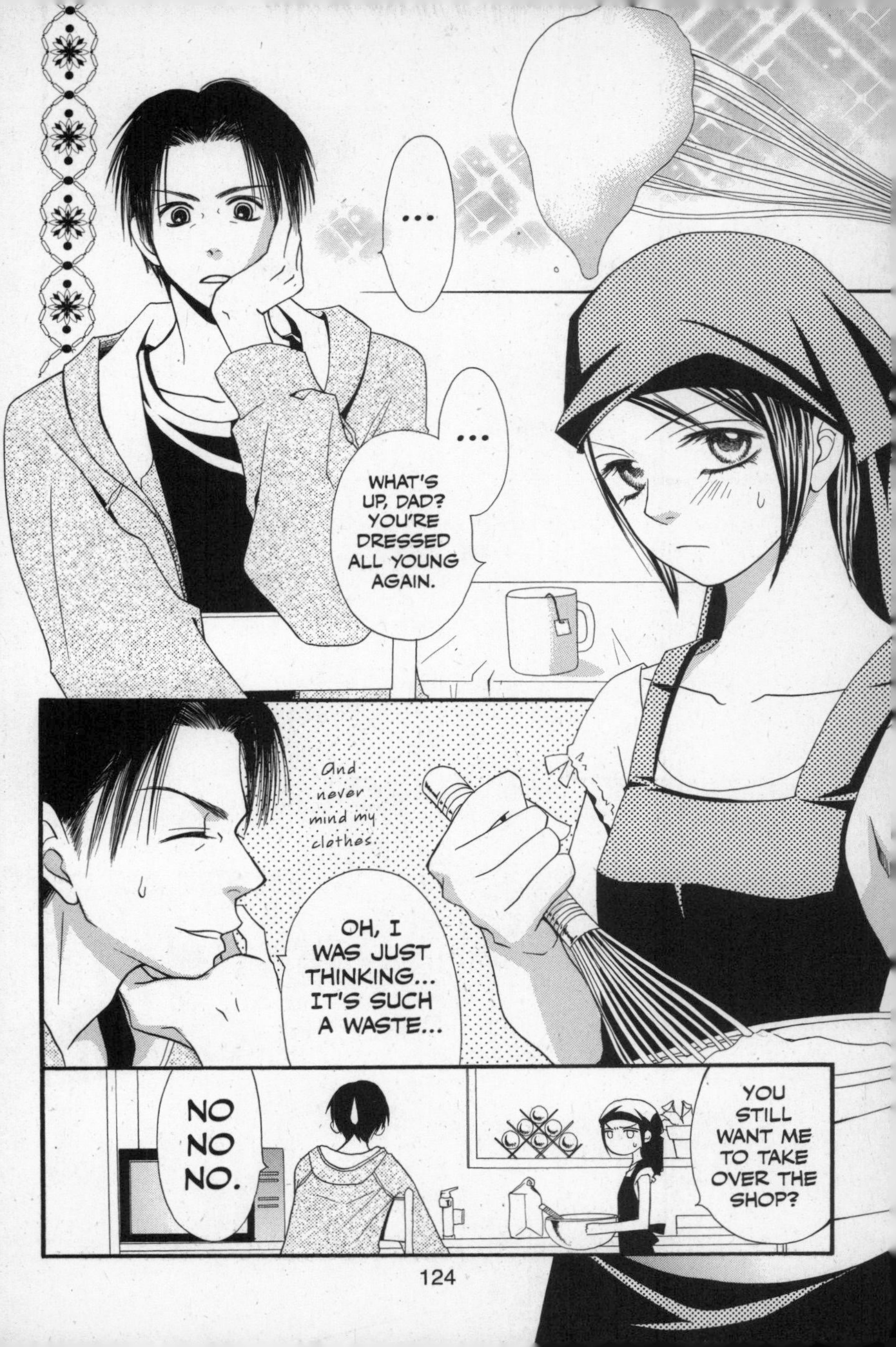
...
...
WHAT'S UP, DAD? YOU'RE DRESSED ALL YOUNG AGAIN.
OH, I WAS JUST THINKING... IT'S SUCH A WASTE...
And never mind my clothes.
YOU STILL WANT ME TO TAKE OVER THE SHOP?
NO NO NO.

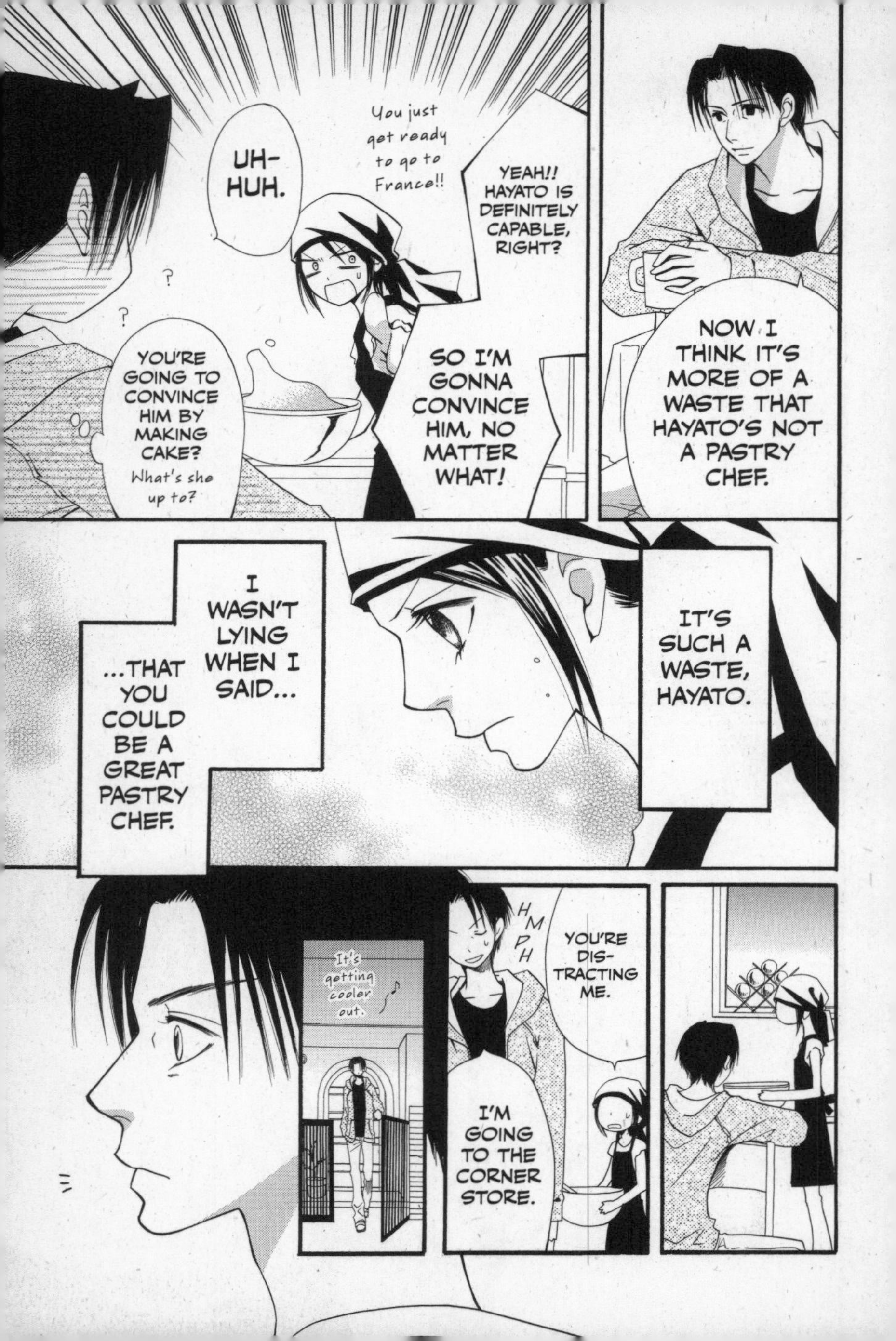
NOW I THINK IT'S MORE OF A WASTE THAT HAYATO'S NOT A PASTRY CHEF.
YEAH!! HAYATO IS DEFINITELY CAPABLE, RIGHT?
SO I'M GONNA CONVINCE HIM, NO MATTER WHAT!
You just get ready to go to France!!
UH-HUH.
YOU'RE GOING TO CONVINCE HIM BY MAKING CAKE?
What's she up to?
?
?
IT'S SUCH A WASTE, HAYATO.
I WASN'T LYING WHEN I SAID...
...THAT YOU COULD BE A GREAT PASTRY CHEF.
HMPH
YOU'RE DIS-TRACTING ME.
I'M GOING TO THE CORNER STORE.
It's getting cooler out.

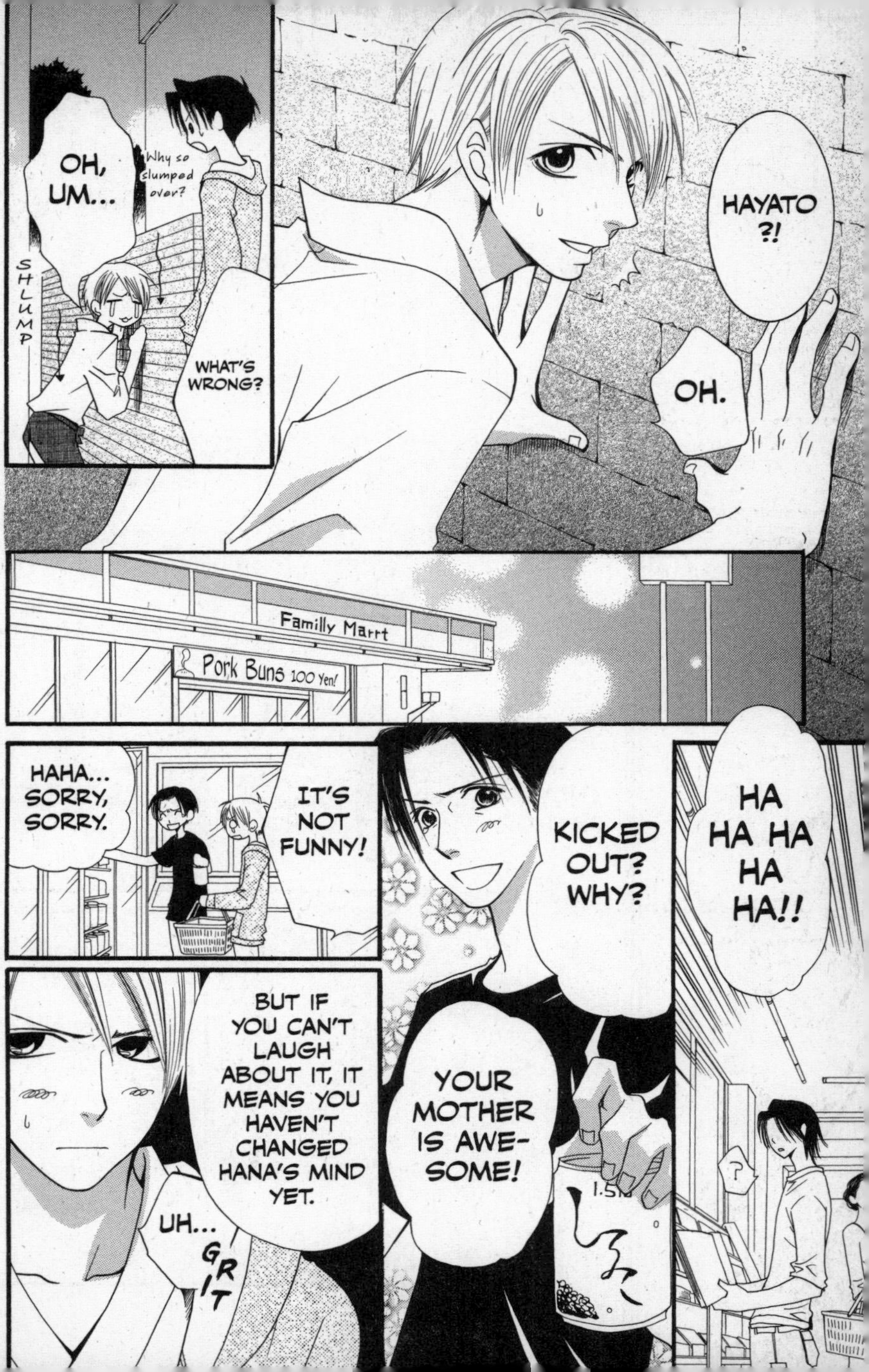
HAYATO ?!
OH.
Why so slumped over?
OH, UM...
SHLUMP
WHAT'S WRONG?
Familly Marrt
Pork Buns 100 Yen!
HA HA HA HA HA!!
KICKED OUT? WHY?
YOUR MOTHER IS AWE-SOME!
IT'S NOT FUNNY!
HAHA... SORRY, SORRY.
BUT IF YOU CAN'T LAUGH ABOUT IT, IT MEANS YOU HAVEN'T CHANGED HANA'S MIND YET.
UH...
GRIT

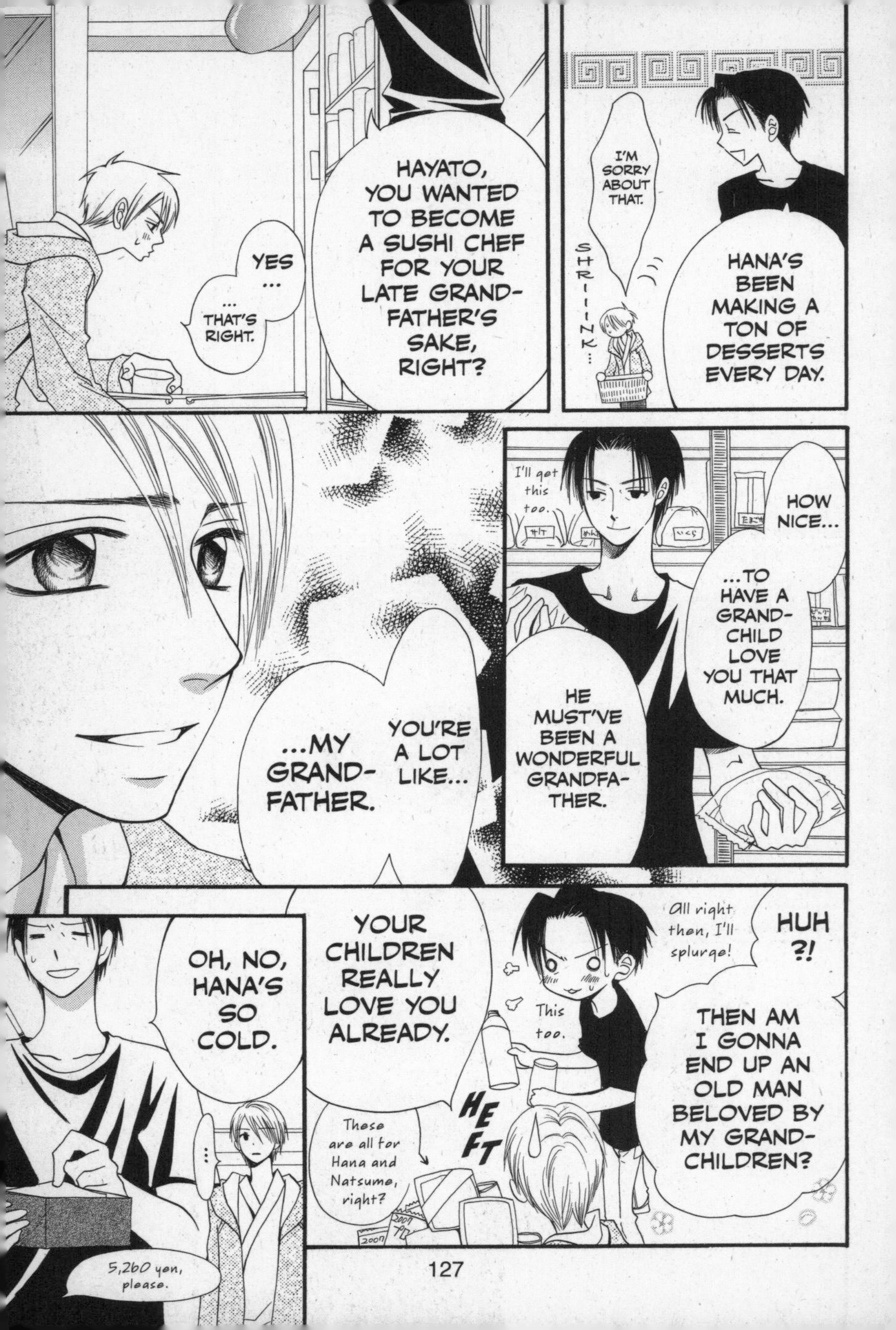
HANA'S BEEN MAKING A TON OF DESSERTS EVERY DAY.
I'M SORRY ABOUT THAT.
SHRIIINK...
HAYATO, YOU WANTED TO BECOME A SUSHI CHEF FOR YOUR LATE GRAND-FATHER'S SAKE, RIGHT?
YES ...
... THAT'S RIGHT.
HOW NICE...
...TO HAVE A GRAND-CHILD LOVE YOU THAT MUCH.
I'll get this too.
HE MUST'VE BEEN A WONDERFUL GRANDFA-THER.
YOU'RE A LOT LIKE...
...MY GRAND-FATHER.
HUH ?!
All right then, I'll splurge!
THEN AM I GONNA END UP AN OLD MAN BELOVED BY MY GRAND-CHILDREN?
This too.
HEFT
These are all for Hana and Natsume, right?
YOUR CHILDREN REALLY LOVE YOU ALREADY.
OH, NO, HANA'S SO COLD.
...
5,260 yen, please.

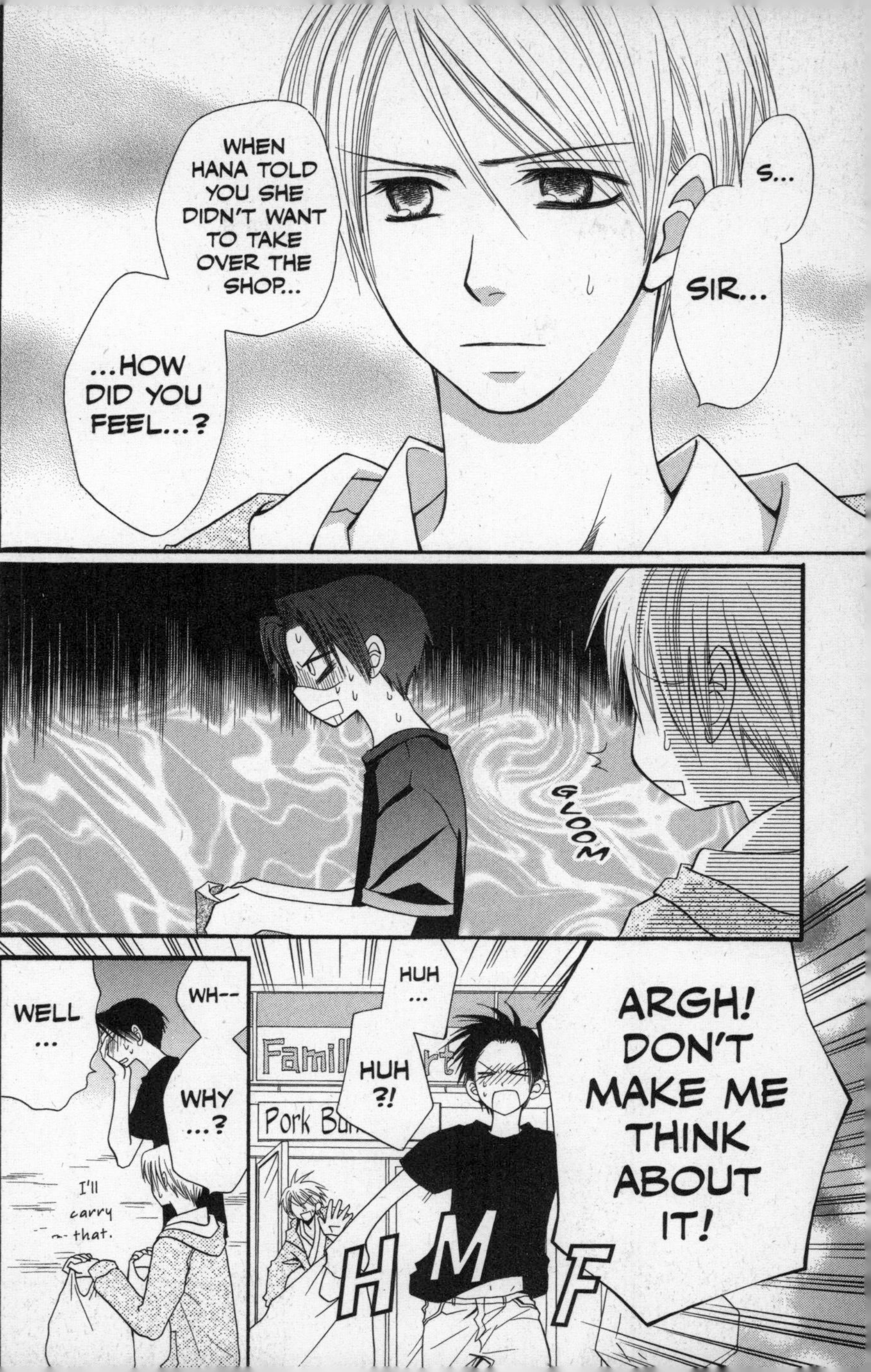
S...
SIR...
WHEN HANA TOLD YOU SHE DIDN'T WANT TO TAKE OVER THE SHOP...
...HOW DID YOU FEEL...?
GLOOM
ARGH! DON'T MAKE ME THINK ABOUT IT!
HUH...
HUH?!
HMF
WH--
WHY...?
WELL...
I'll carry that.

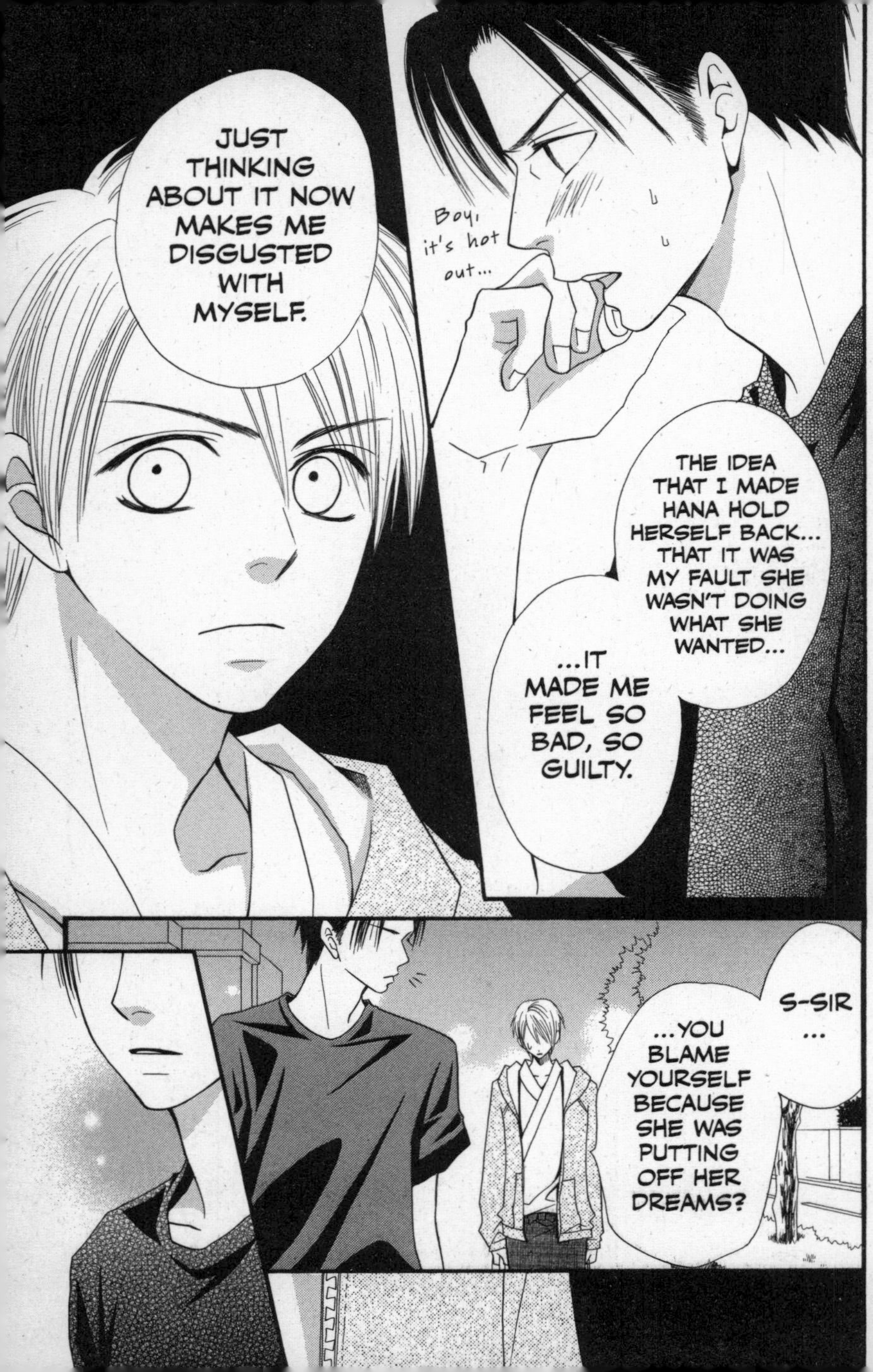
Boy, it's hot out...
THE IDEA THAT I MADE HANA HOLD HERSELF BACK... THAT IT WAS MY FAULT SHE WASN'T DOING WHAT SHE WANTED...
...IT MADE ME FEEL SO BAD, SO GUILTY.
JUST THINKING ABOUT IT NOW MAKES ME DISGUSTED WITH MYSELF.
S-SIR ...
...YOU BLAME YOURSELF BECAUSE SHE WAS PUTTING OFF HER DREAMS?

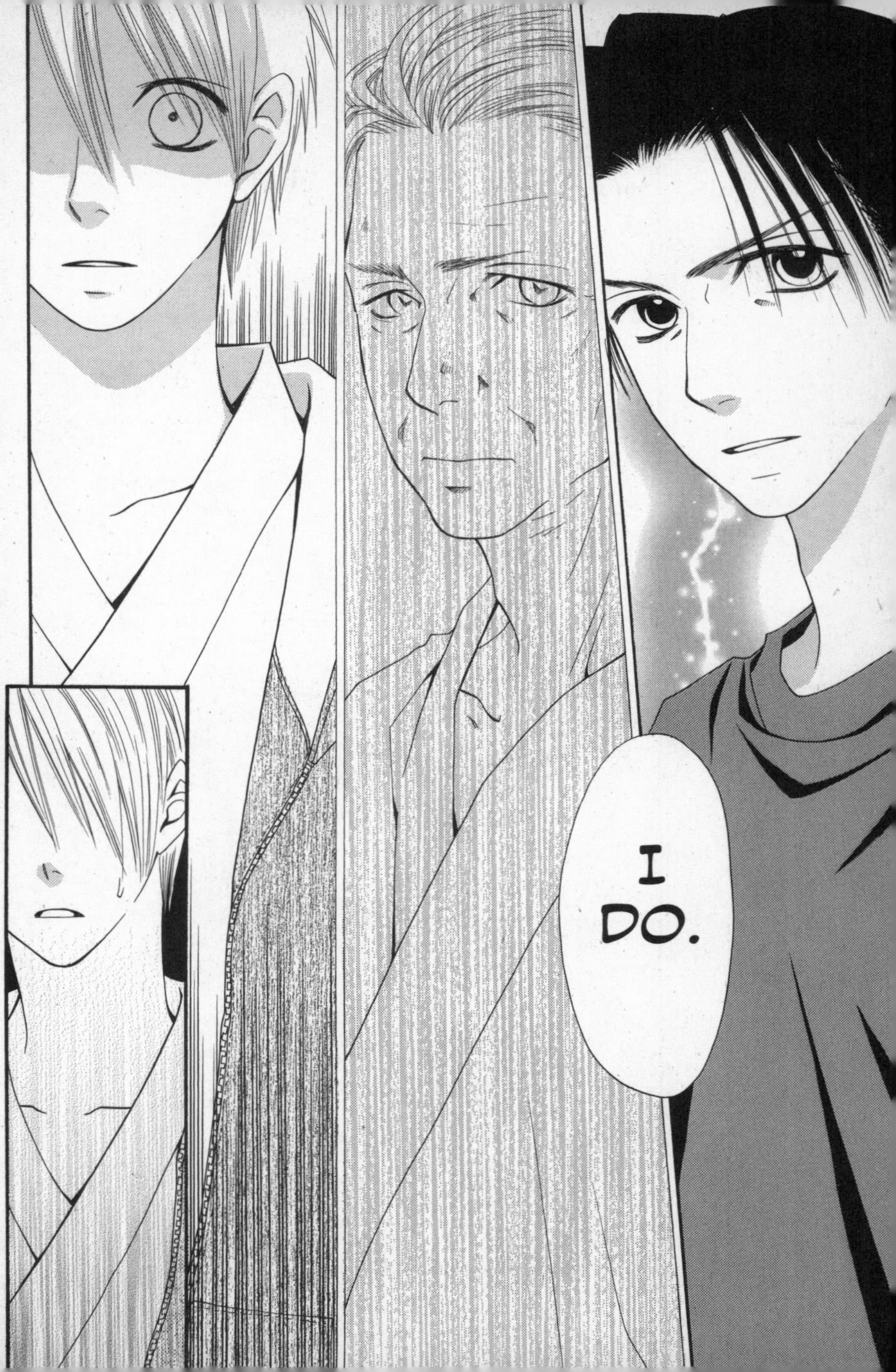
I DO.

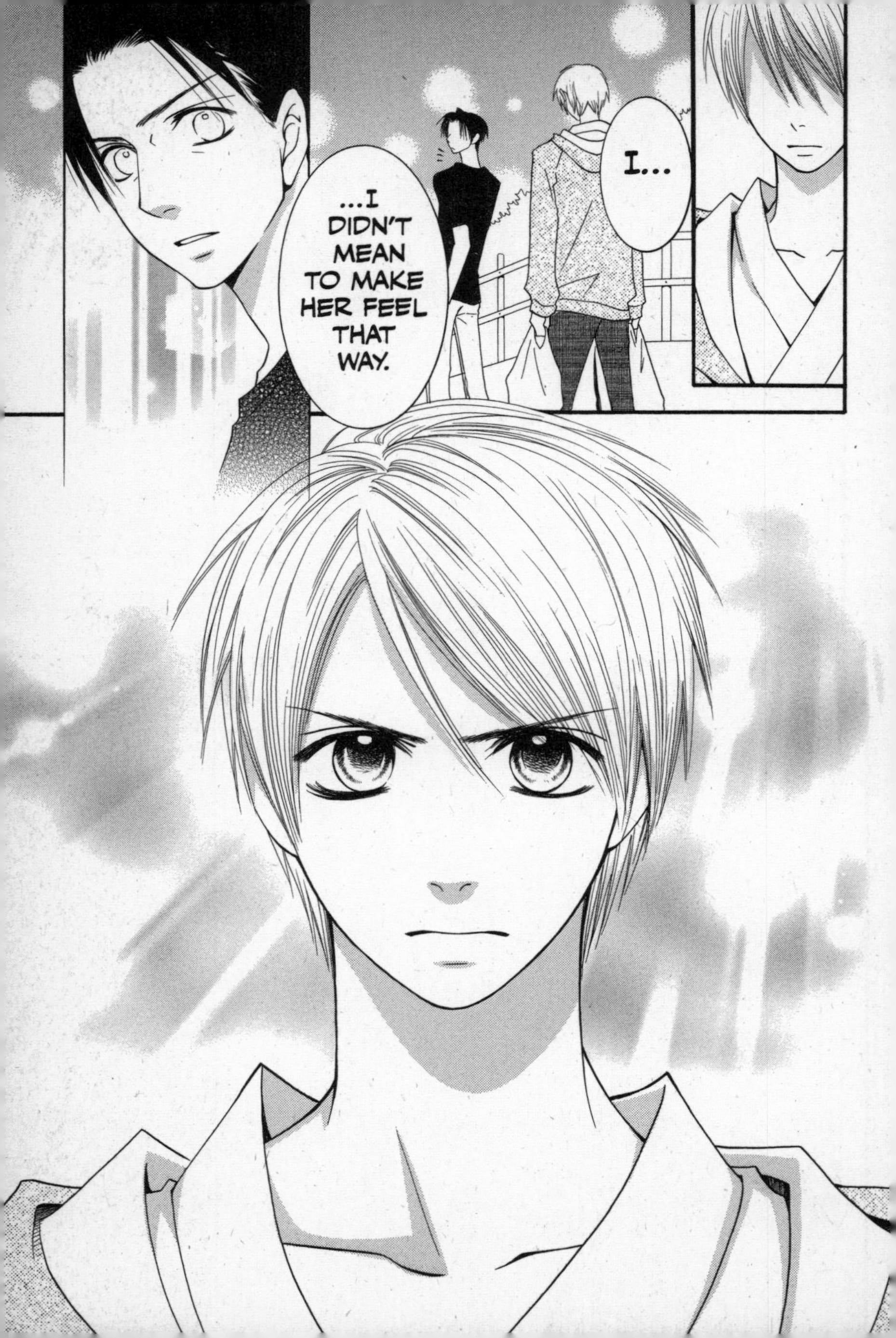
I...
...I DIDN'T MEAN TO MAKE HER FEEL THAT WAY.

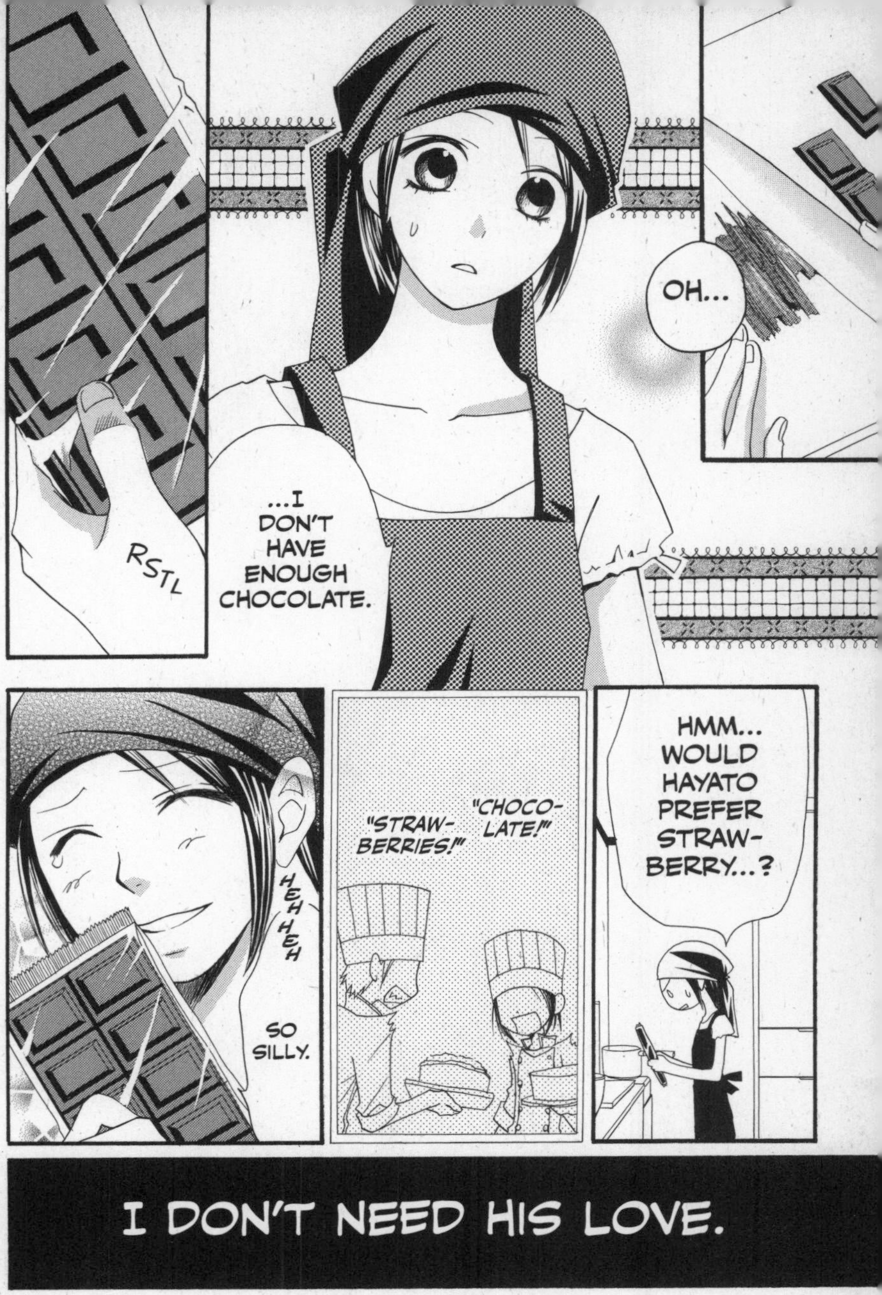
OH...
...I DON'T HAVE ENOUGH CHOCOLATE.
RSTL
HMM... WOULD HAYATO PREFER STRAW-BERRY...?
"CHOCO-LATE!"
"STRAW-BERRIES!"
HEH HEH
SO SILLY.
I DON'T NEED HIS LOVE.

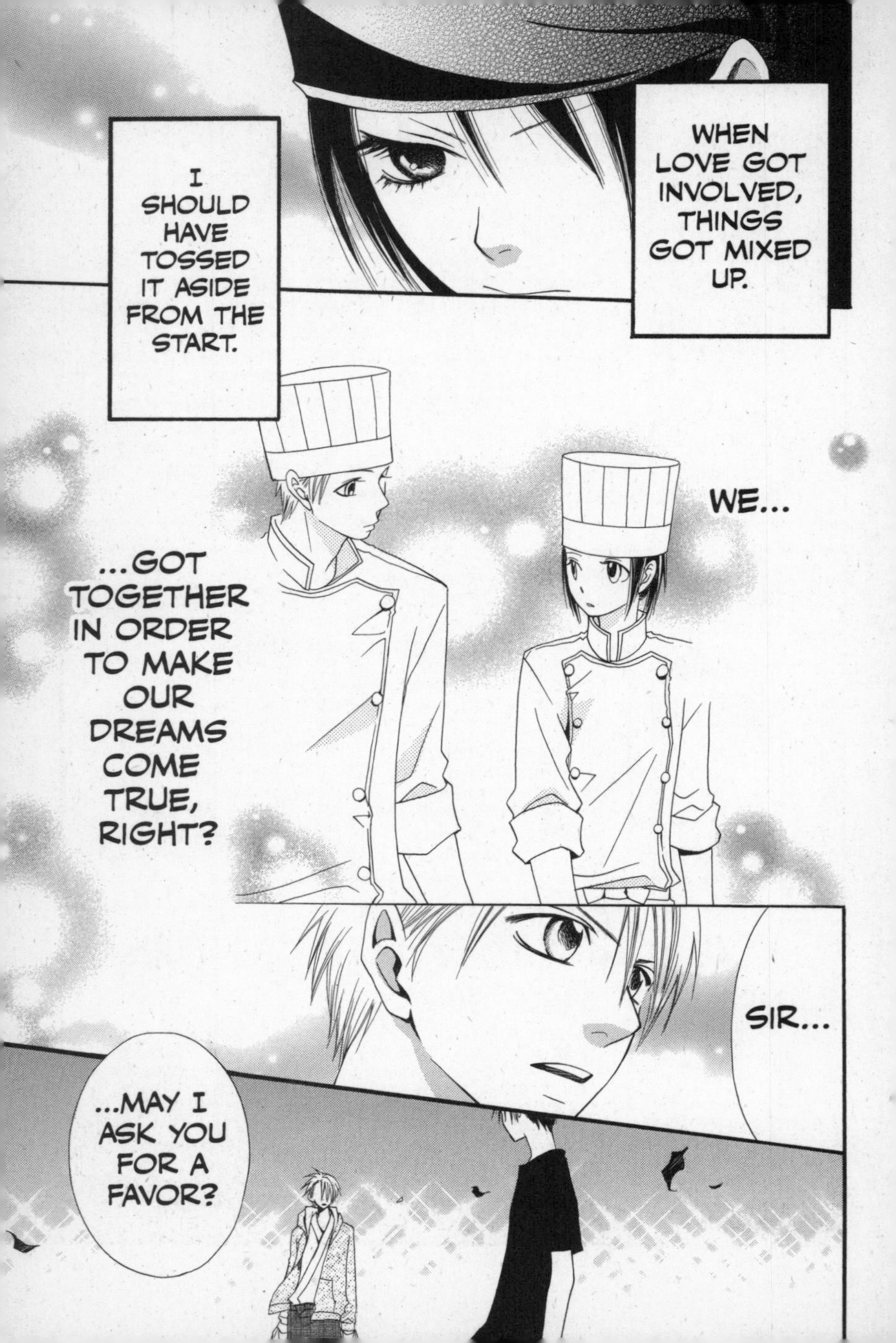
WHEN LOVE GOT INVOLVED, THINGS GOT MIXED UP.
I SHOULD HAVE TOSSED IT ASIDE FROM THE START.
WE...
...GOT TOGETHER IN ORDER TO MAKE OUR DREAMS COME TRUE, RIGHT?
SIR...
...MAY I ASK YOU FOR A FAVOR?

MIXED VEGETABLES Encyclopedia of Characters

KAN ASHITABA

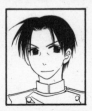

HANA'S MOTHER'S MAIDEN NAME IS "TACHIBANA," SO I CAME UP WITH THE NAME KAN FOR HIM. YOU WOULDN'T THINK IT AT FIRST, BUT IN ACTUALITY, HE'S AN AMAZING PATISSIER. HE CAUSED HIS FATHER A LOT OF HEADACHES. PEOPLE HAVE ASKED ME, "WHO'S YOUR FAVORITE CHARACTER?" AND I HAD A HARD TIME CHOOSING. BUT AFTER FURTHER THOUGHT, I NOW FEEL THAT HANA'S DAD WAS THE CHARACTER I COULD DEVELOP THE MOST.

NATSUME ASHITABA

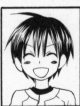

NATSUME → JUST NATSUME!

I STARTED CREATING HIM AS A VERY NICE, INNOCENT BOY FOR WHOM A PERSON MIGHT BE WILLING TO GIVE UP THEIR DREAMS.
I MADE NATSUME WANT TO BECOME A PRO BASEBALL PLAYER SIMPLY BECAUSE I LOVE BASEBALL. SORRY. ☆
IN MENU 51, WHEN HE HUGS ICHII, I REALIZED THAT HE'S REALLY STRONG. HE CALLS ICHII "CHII" BECAUSE WHEN HE WAS LITTLE, HE WAS UNABLE TO PRONOUNCE ICHII.

YUZU ASHITABA (FORMERLY TACHIBANA)

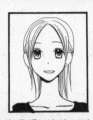

YUZU → POMELO

SHE HAS ONE OF THE SAME KANJI IN HER NAME AS HER DAUGHTER. (HANAYU AND YUZU) SHE'S NOT VERY GOOD AT COOKING AND DOES THINGS AT HER OWN PACE. BUT I THINK KAN-SAN, WHO TENDS TO EXCEL IN AREAS SHE DOESN'T, PROVIDES A GOOD BALANCE FOR HER.
SHE HAS A BEAUTIFUL FIGURE. BUT SHE'S FLAT CHESTED. RIGHT NOW, NATSUME AND HANA BOTH RESEMBLE THEIR MOTHER. BUT AS THEY GROW OLDER, HANA WILL START TO TAKE ON HER FATHER'S LOOKS WHILE NATSUME WILL CONTINUE TO LOOK LIKE HIS MOTHER.

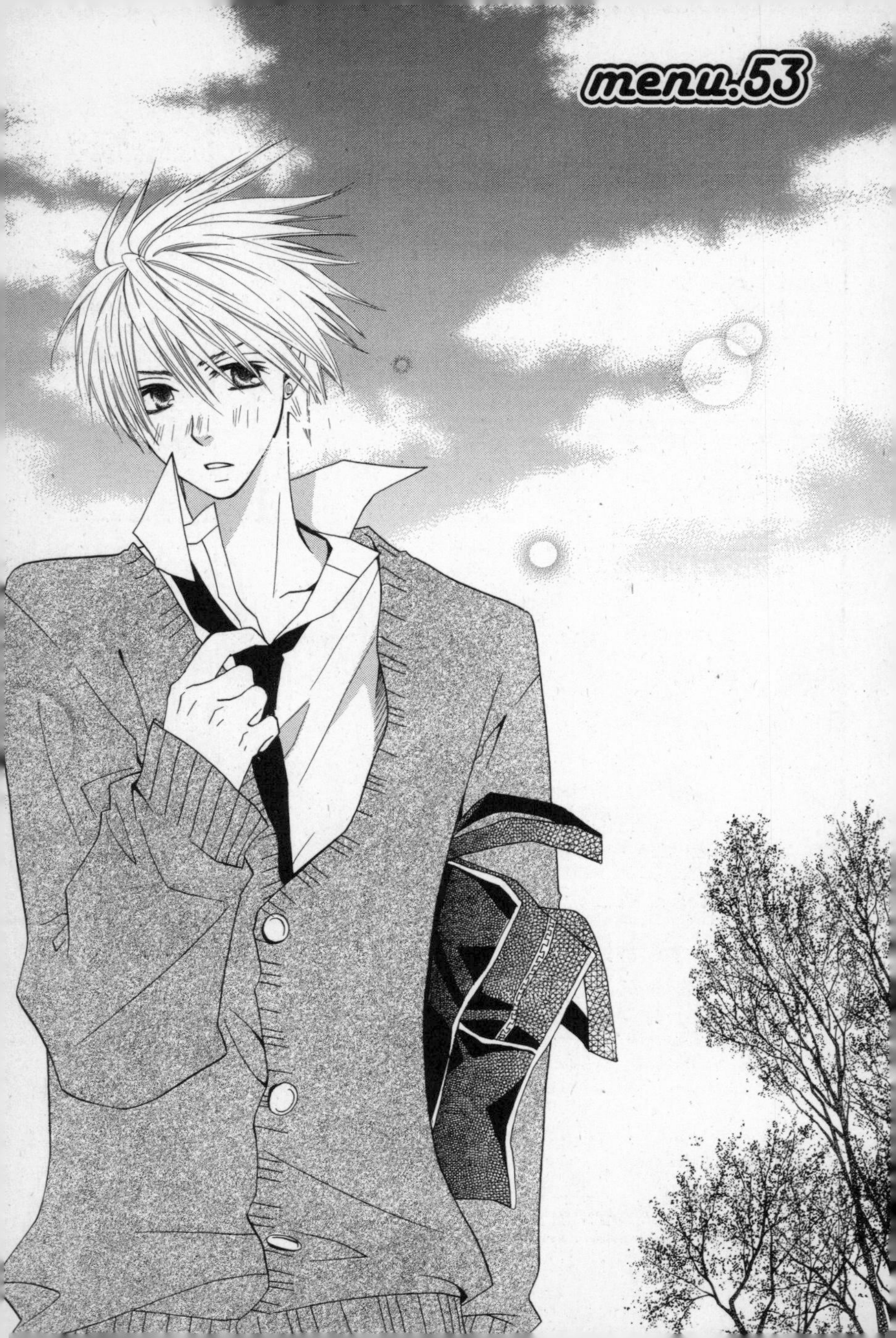
menu.53

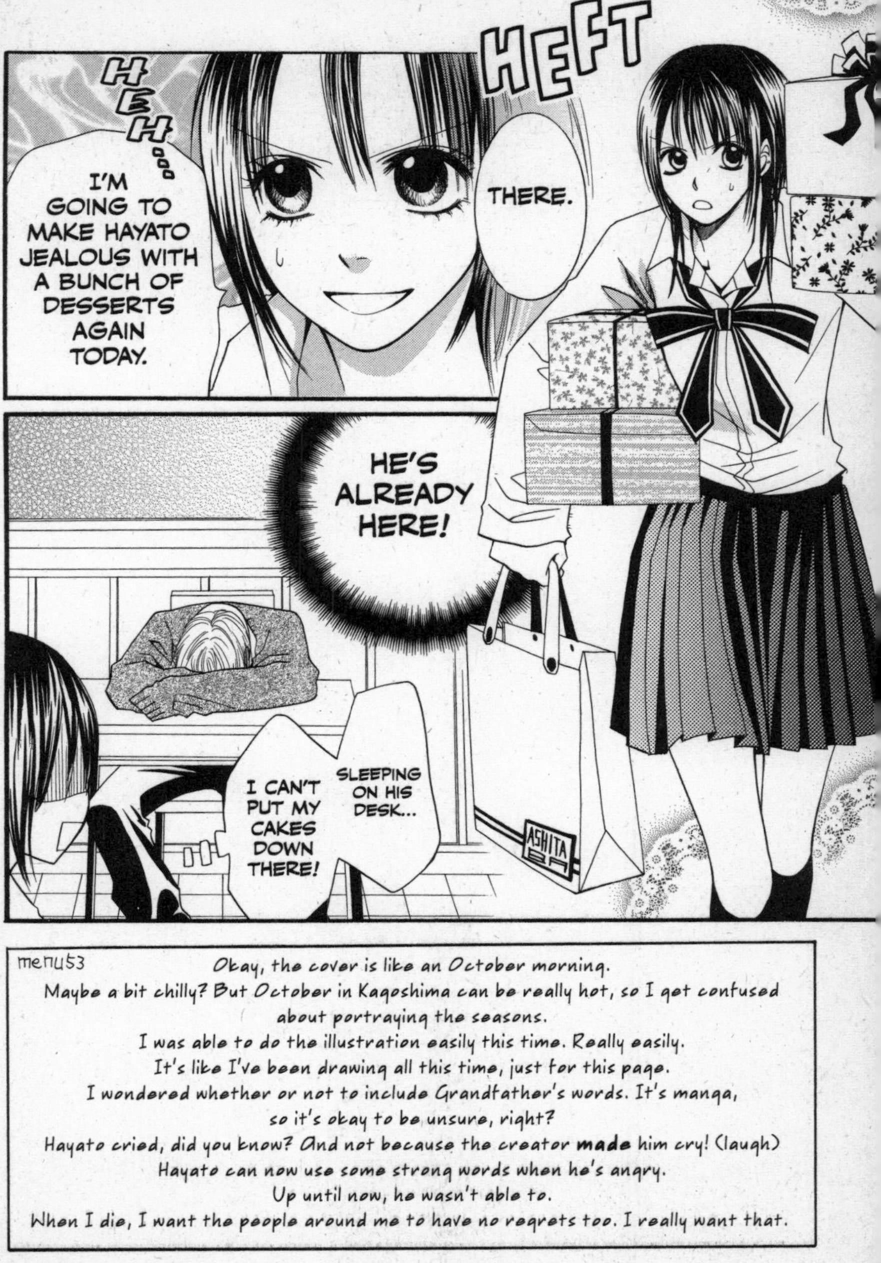
HEFT
THERE.
HEH...
I'M GOING TO MAKE HAYATO JEALOUS WITH A BUNCH OF DESSERTS AGAIN TODAY.
HE'S ALREADY HERE!
ASHITA BA
SLEEPING ON HIS DESK...
I CAN'T PUT MY CAKES DOWN THERE!

menu53

Okay, the cover is like an October morning.
Maybe a bit chilly? But October in Kagoshima can be really hot, so I get confused about portraying the seasons.
I was able to do the illustration easily this time. Really easily.
It's like I've been drawing all this time, just for this page.
I wondered whether or not to include Grandfather's words. It's manga, so it's okay to be unsure, right?
Hayato cried, did you know? And not because the creator **made** him cry! (laugh)
Hayato can now use some strong words when he's angry.
Up until now, he wasn't able to.
When I die, I want the people around me to have no regrets too. I really want that.

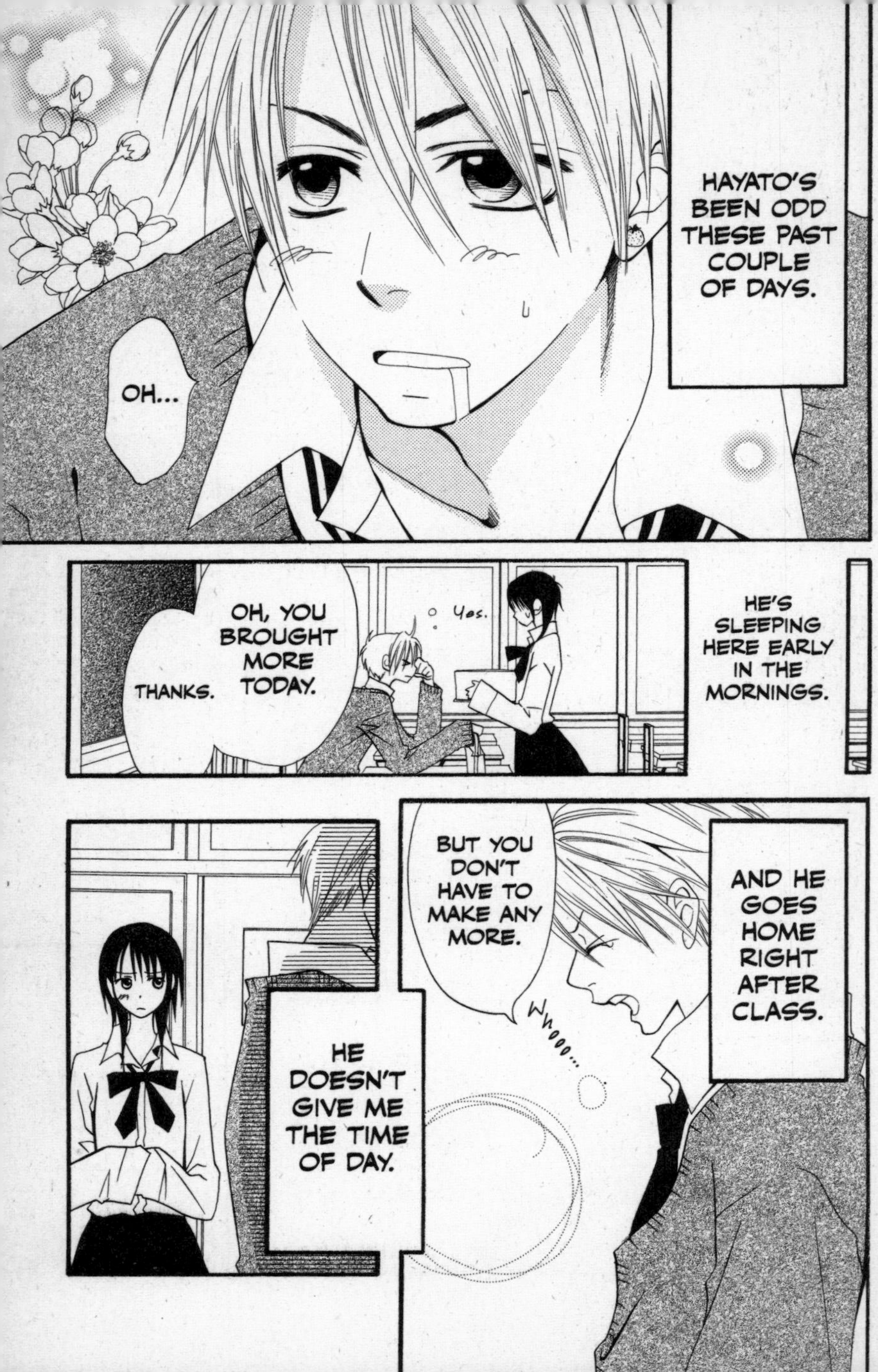
HAYATO'S BEEN ODD THESE PAST COUPLE OF DAYS.
OH...
HE'S SLEEPING HERE EARLY IN THE MORNINGS.
Yes.
OH, YOU BROUGHT MORE TODAY.
THANKS.
AND HE GOES HOME RIGHT AFTER CLASS.
BUT YOU DON'T HAVE TO MAKE ANY MORE.
Whooo...
HE DOESN'T GIVE ME THE TIME OF DAY.

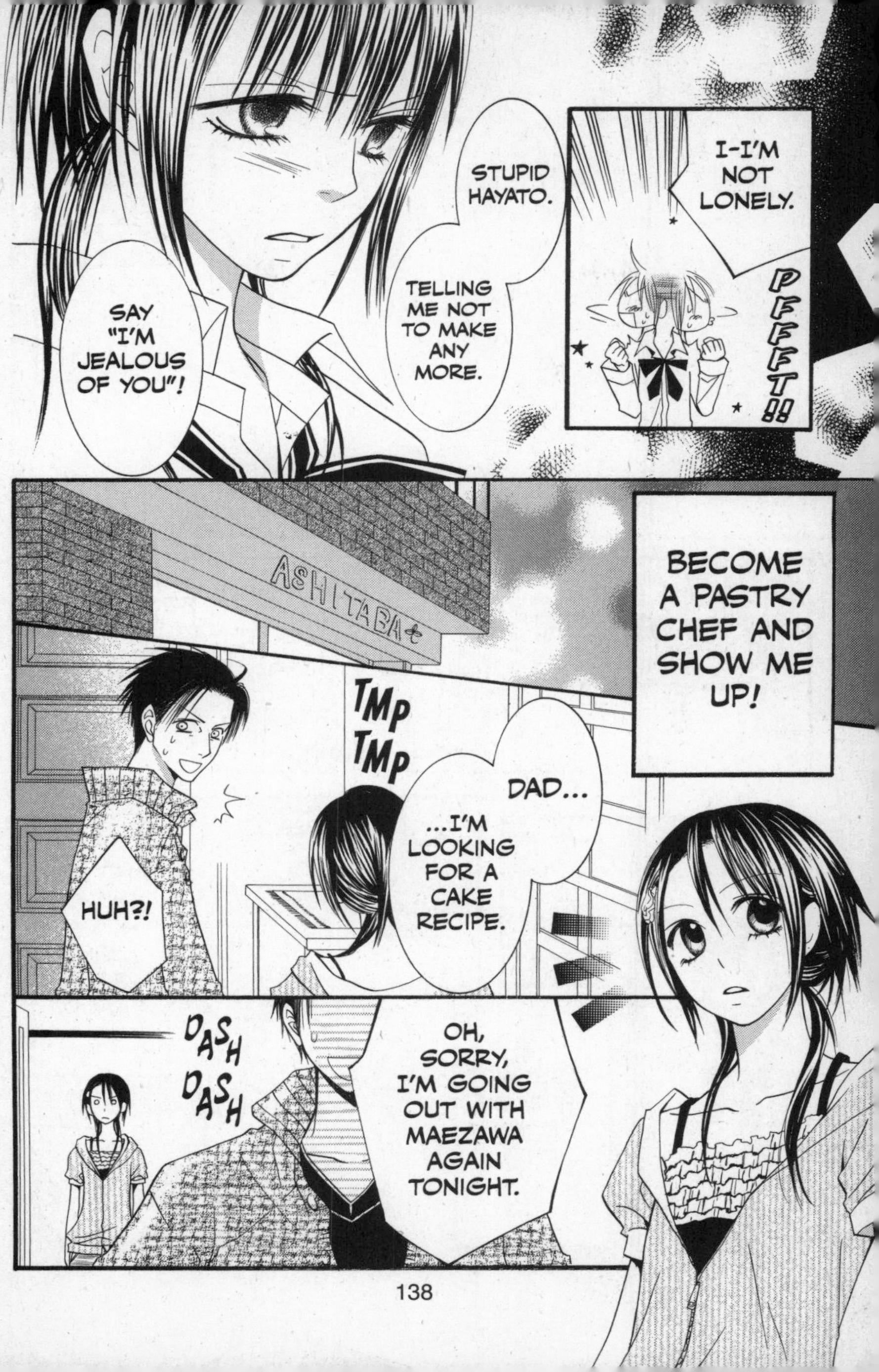
I-I'M NOT LONELY.
PFFFT!!
STUPID HAYATO.
TELLING ME NOT TO MAKE ANY MORE.
SAY "I'M JEALOUS OF YOU"!
BECOME A PASTRY CHEF AND SHOW ME UP!
ASHITABA
DAD...
...I'M LOOKING FOR A CAKE RECIPE.
TMP TMP
HUH?!
OH, SORRY, I'M GOING OUT WITH MAEZAWA AGAIN TONIGHT.
DASH DASH

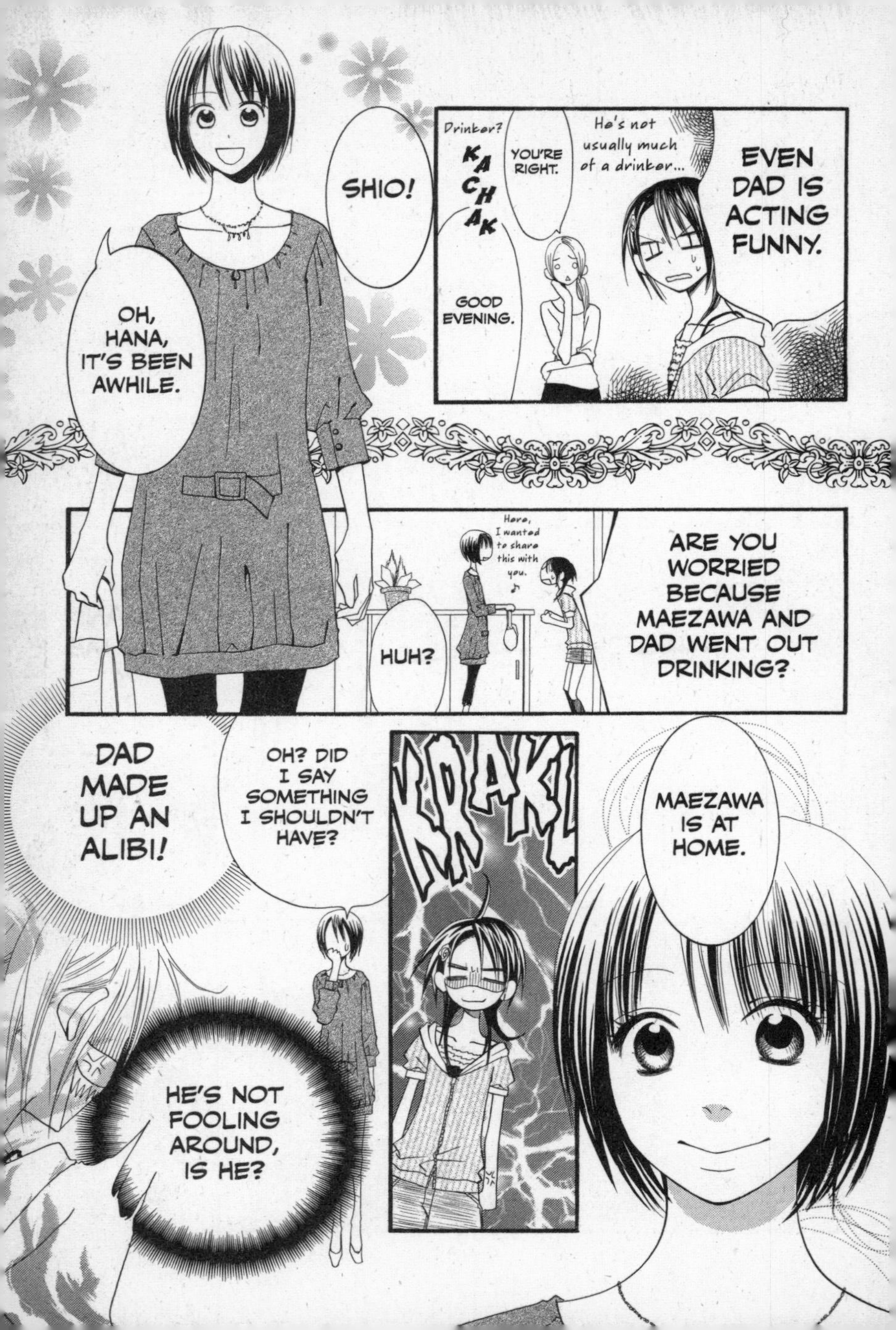
EVEN DAD IS ACTING FUNNY.
He's not usually much of a drinker...
YOU'RE RIGHT.
Drinker?
KACHAK
GOOD EVENING.
SHIO!
OH, HANA, IT'S BEEN AWHILE.
ARE YOU WORRIED BECAUSE MAEZAWA AND DAD WENT OUT DRINKING?
Here, I wanted to share this with you. ♪
HUH?
MAEZAWA IS AT HOME.
KRAK!
OH? DID I SAY SOMETHING I SHOULDN'T HAVE?
DAD MADE UP AN ALIBI!
HE'S NOT FOOLING AROUND, IS HE?

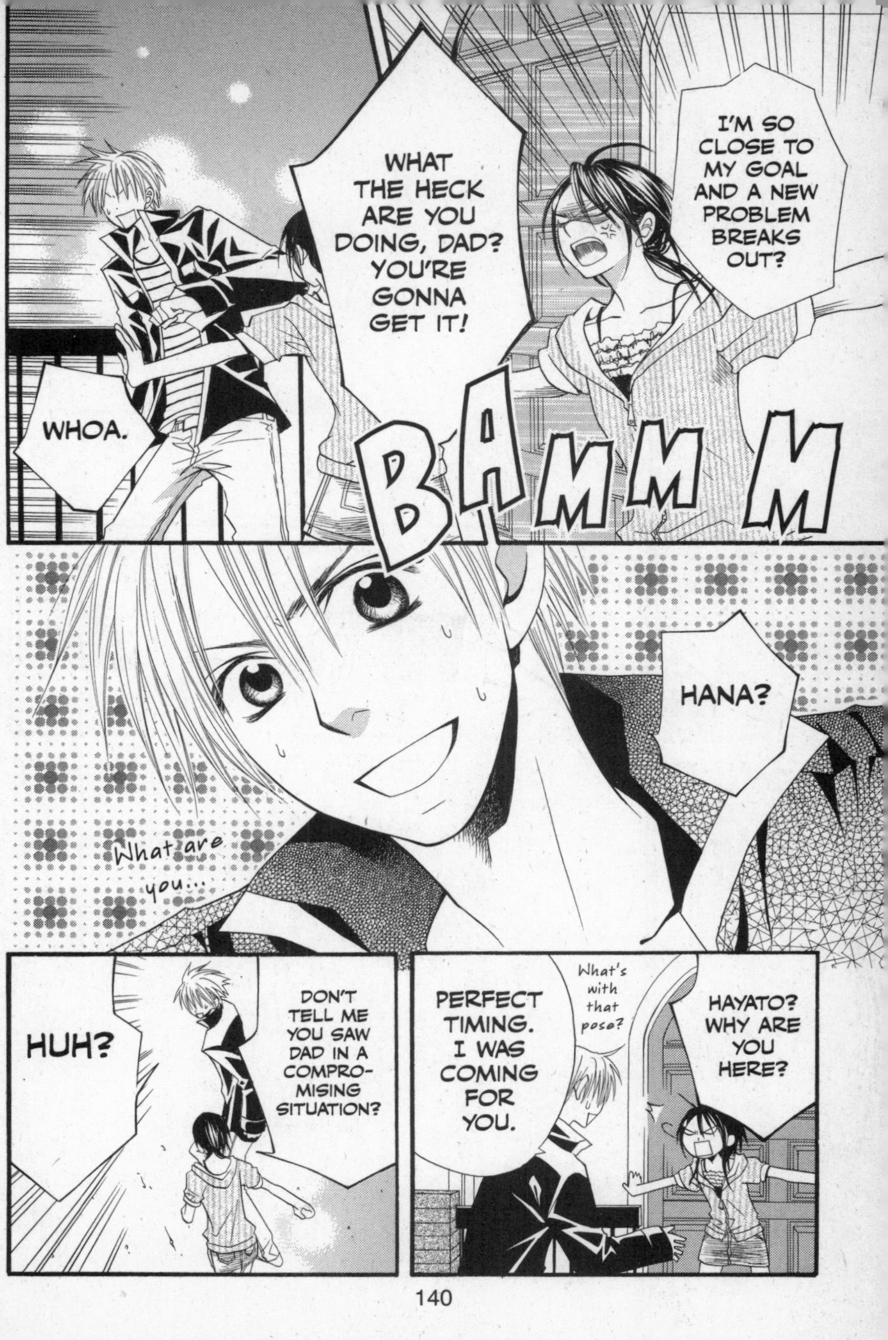
I'M SO CLOSE TO MY GOAL AND A NEW PROBLEM BREAKS OUT?
WHAT THE HECK ARE YOU DOING, DAD? YOU'RE GONNA GET IT!
WHOA.
BAMMM M
HANA?
What are you...
HAYATO? WHY ARE YOU HERE?
What's with that pose?
PERFECT TIMING. I WAS COMING FOR YOU.
DON'T TELL ME YOU SAW DAD IN A COMPRO-MISING SITUATION?
HUH?

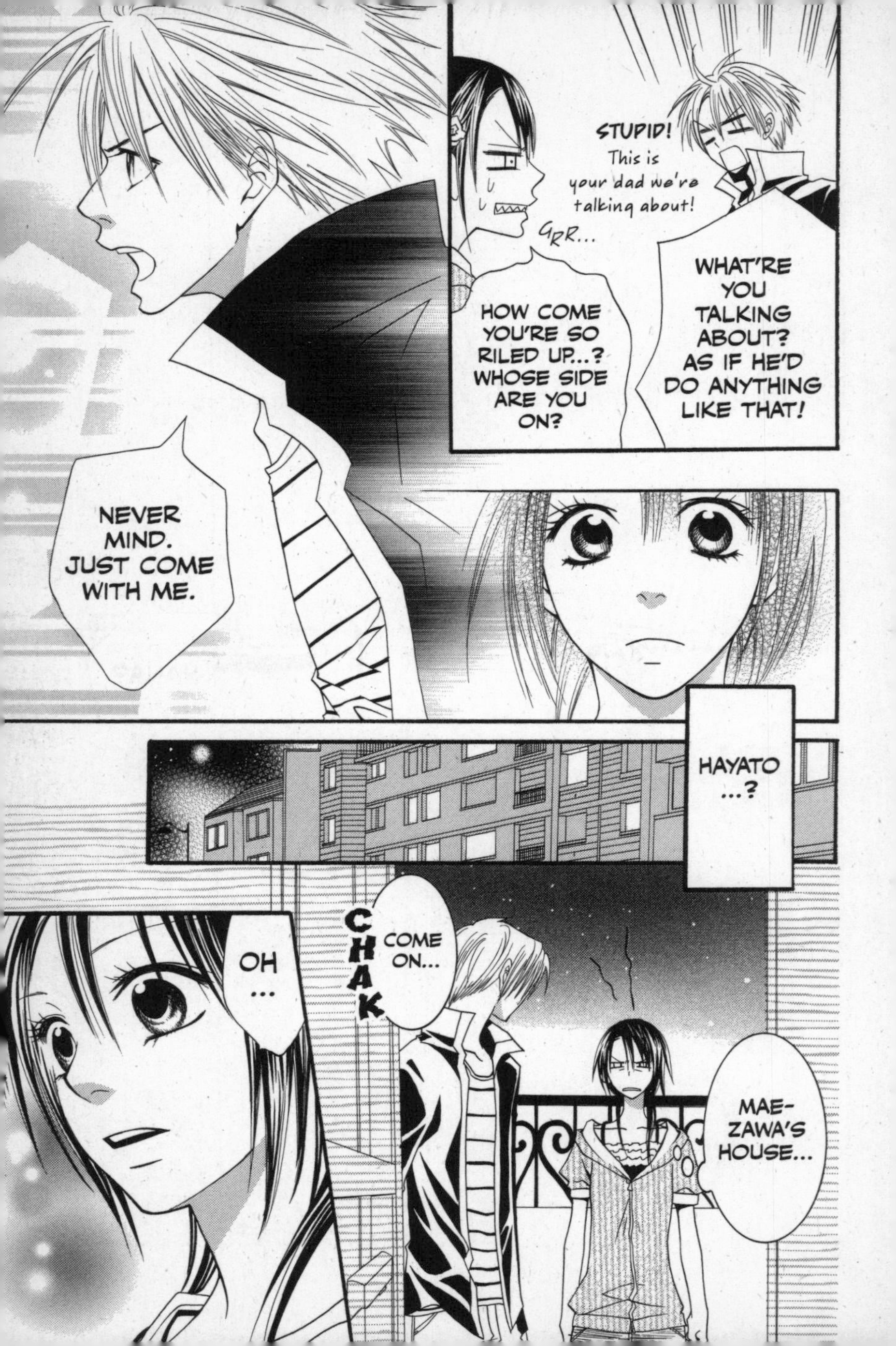
STUPID! This is your dad we're talking about!
GRR...
WHAT'RE YOU TALKING ABOUT? AS IF HE'D DO ANYTHING LIKE THAT!
HOW COME YOU'RE SO RILED UP...? WHOSE SIDE ARE YOU ON?
NEVER MIND. JUST COME WITH ME.
HAYATO ...?
MAE-ZAWA'S HOUSE...
COME ON...
CHAK
OH ...

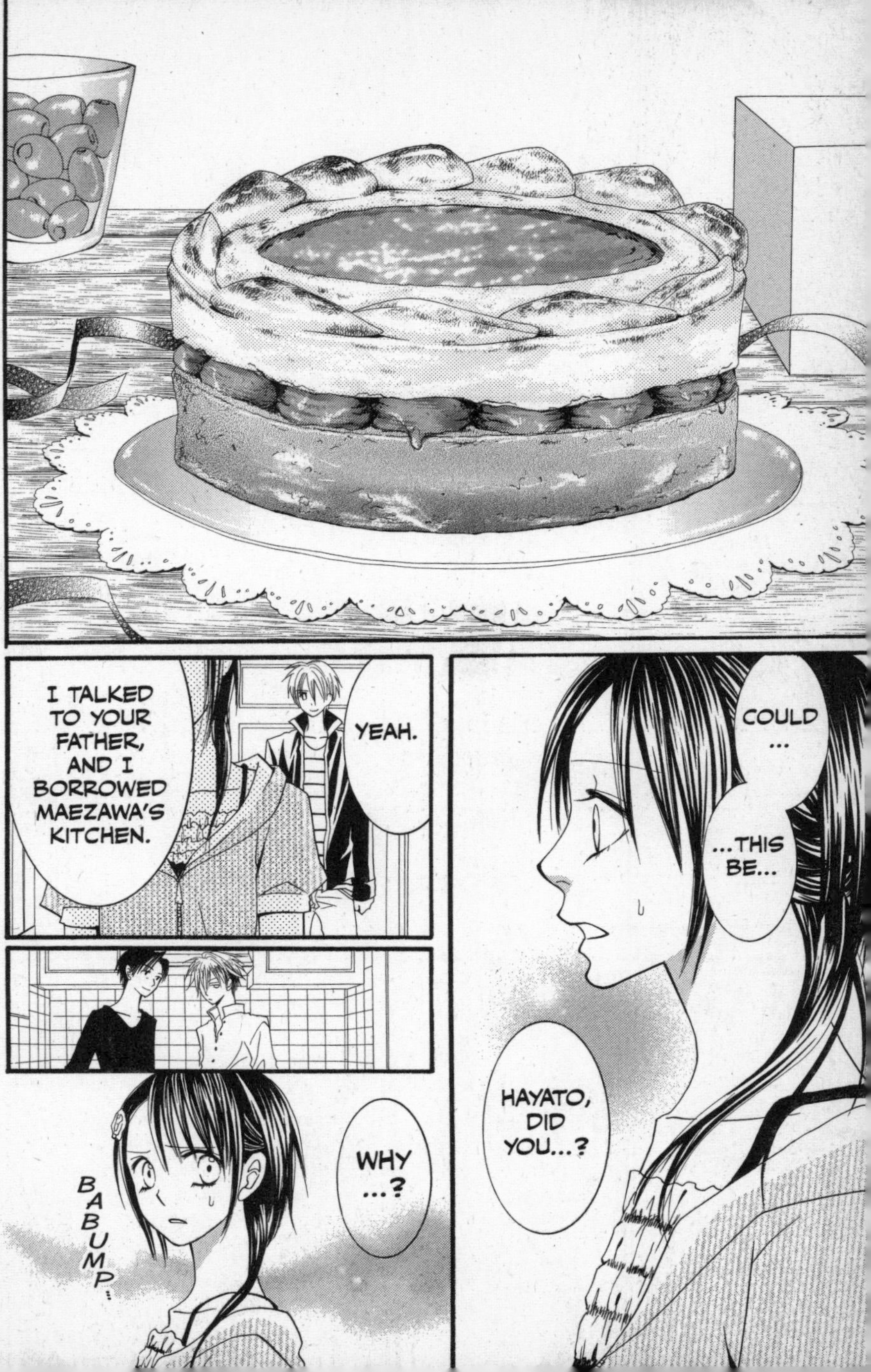
COULD ...
...THIS BE...
HAYATO, DID YOU...?
YEAH.
I TALKED TO YOUR FATHER, AND I BORROWED MAEZAWA'S KITCHEN.
WHY ...?
BABUMP..

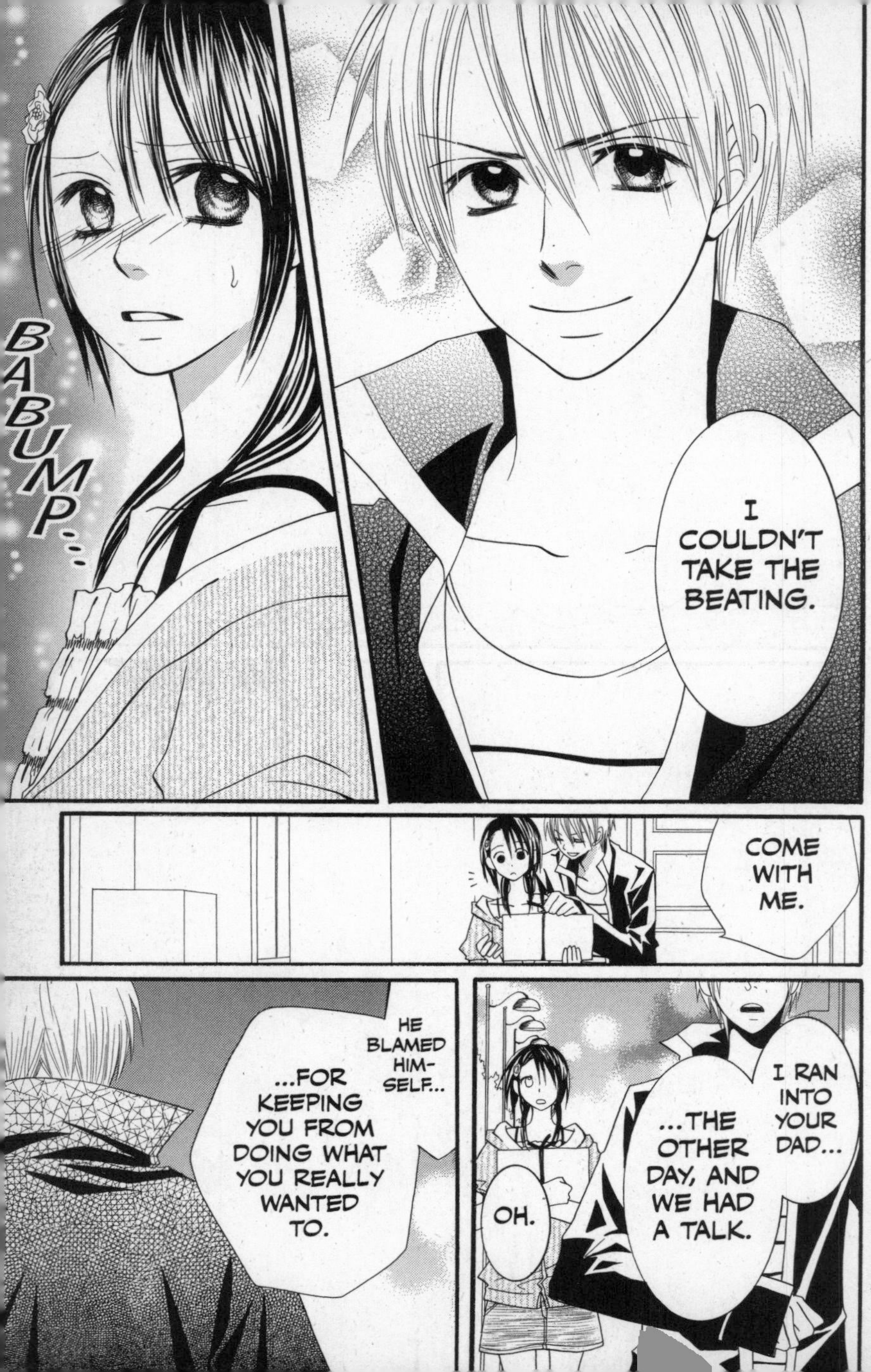
I COULDN'T TAKE THE BEATING.
BABUMP...
COME WITH ME.
I RAN INTO YOUR DAD...
...THE OTHER DAY, AND WE HAD A TALK.
OH.
HE BLAMED HIMSELF...
...FOR KEEPING YOU FROM DOING WHAT YOU REALLY WANTED TO.

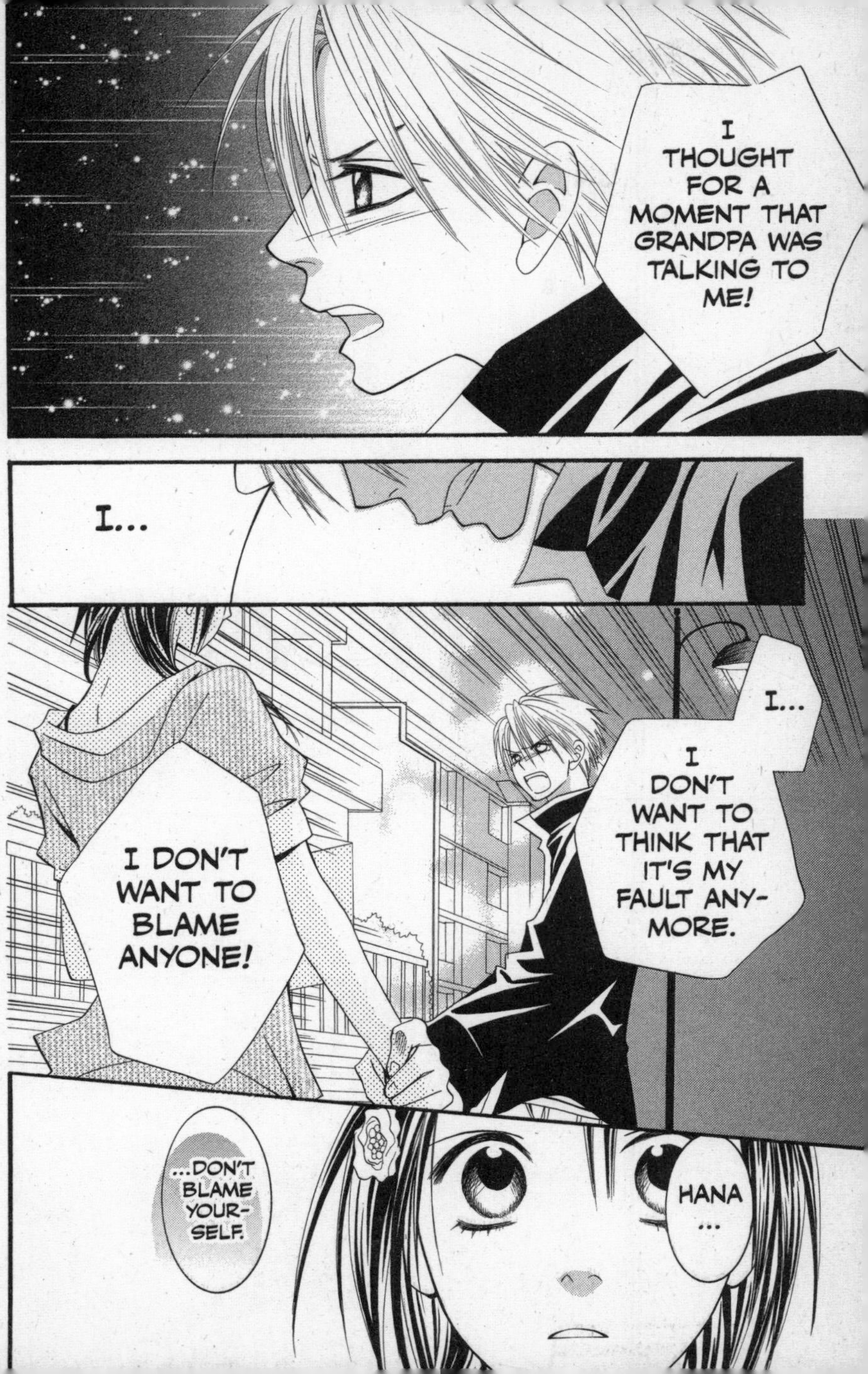
I THOUGHT FOR A MOMENT THAT GRANDPA WAS TALKING TO ME!
I...
I...
I DON'T WANT TO THINK THAT IT'S MY FAULT ANYMORE.
I DON'T WANT TO BLAME ANYONE!
HANA...
...DON'T BLAME YOURSELF.

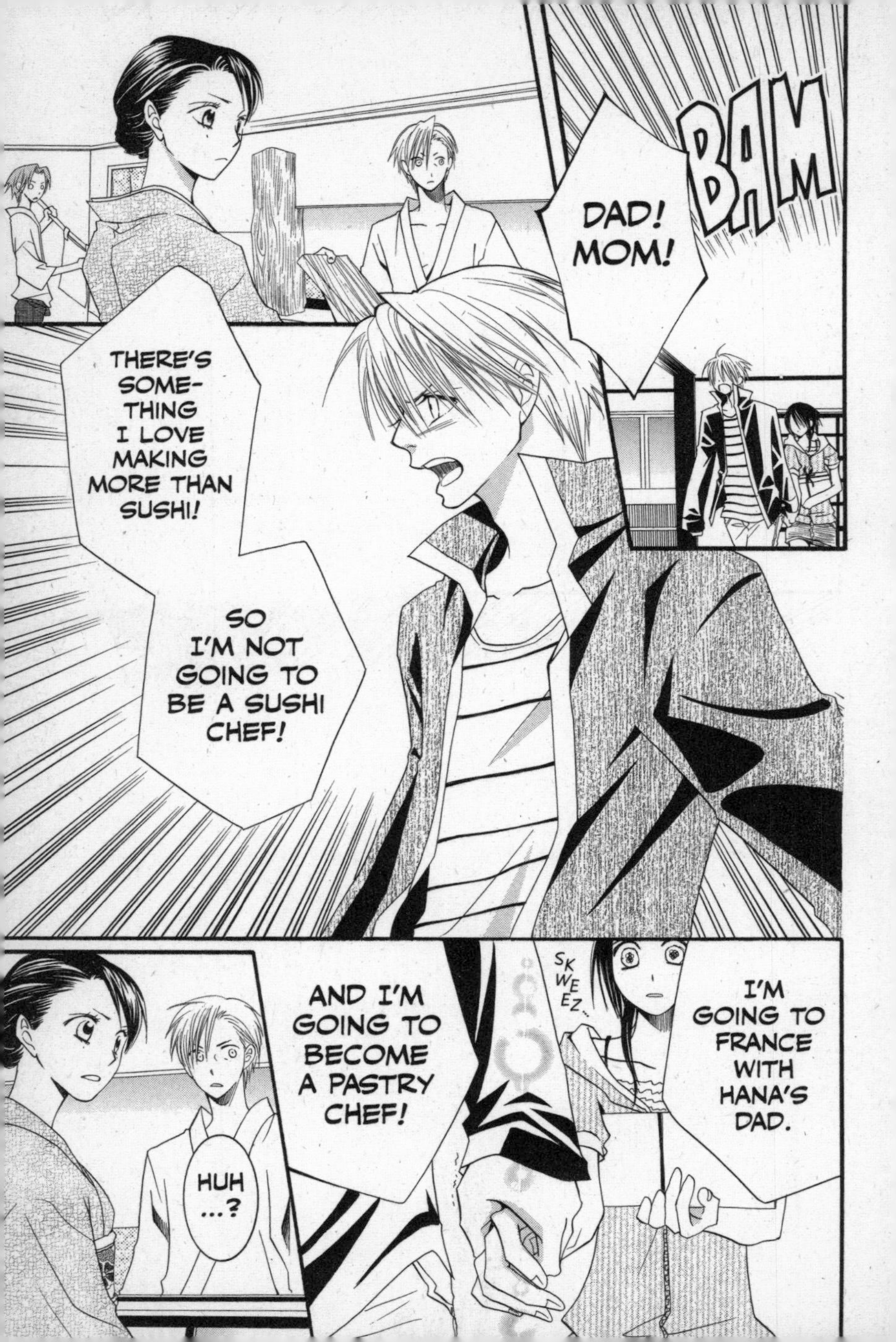
BAM
DAD! MOM!
THERE'S SOME-THING I LOVE MAKING MORE THAN SUSHI!
SO I'M NOT GOING TO BE A SUSHI CHEF!
I'M GOING TO FRANCE WITH HANA'S DAD.
SKWEEZ...
AND I'M GOING TO BECOME A PASTRY CHEF!
HUH ...?

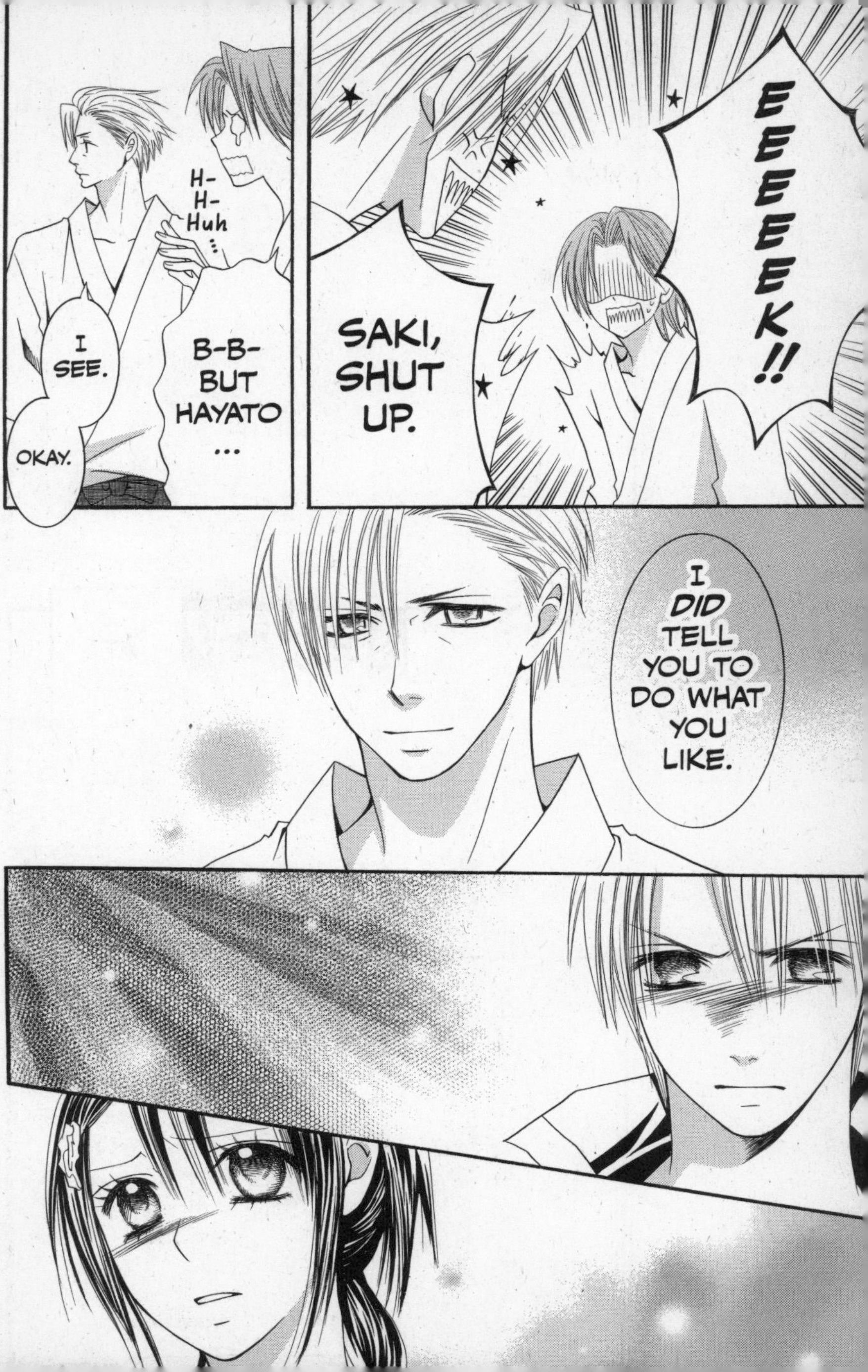
EEEEEEK!!
SAKI, SHUT UP.
H-H-Huh...
B-B-BUT HAYATO...
I SEE.
OKAY.
I *DID* TELL YOU TO DO WHAT YOU LIKE.

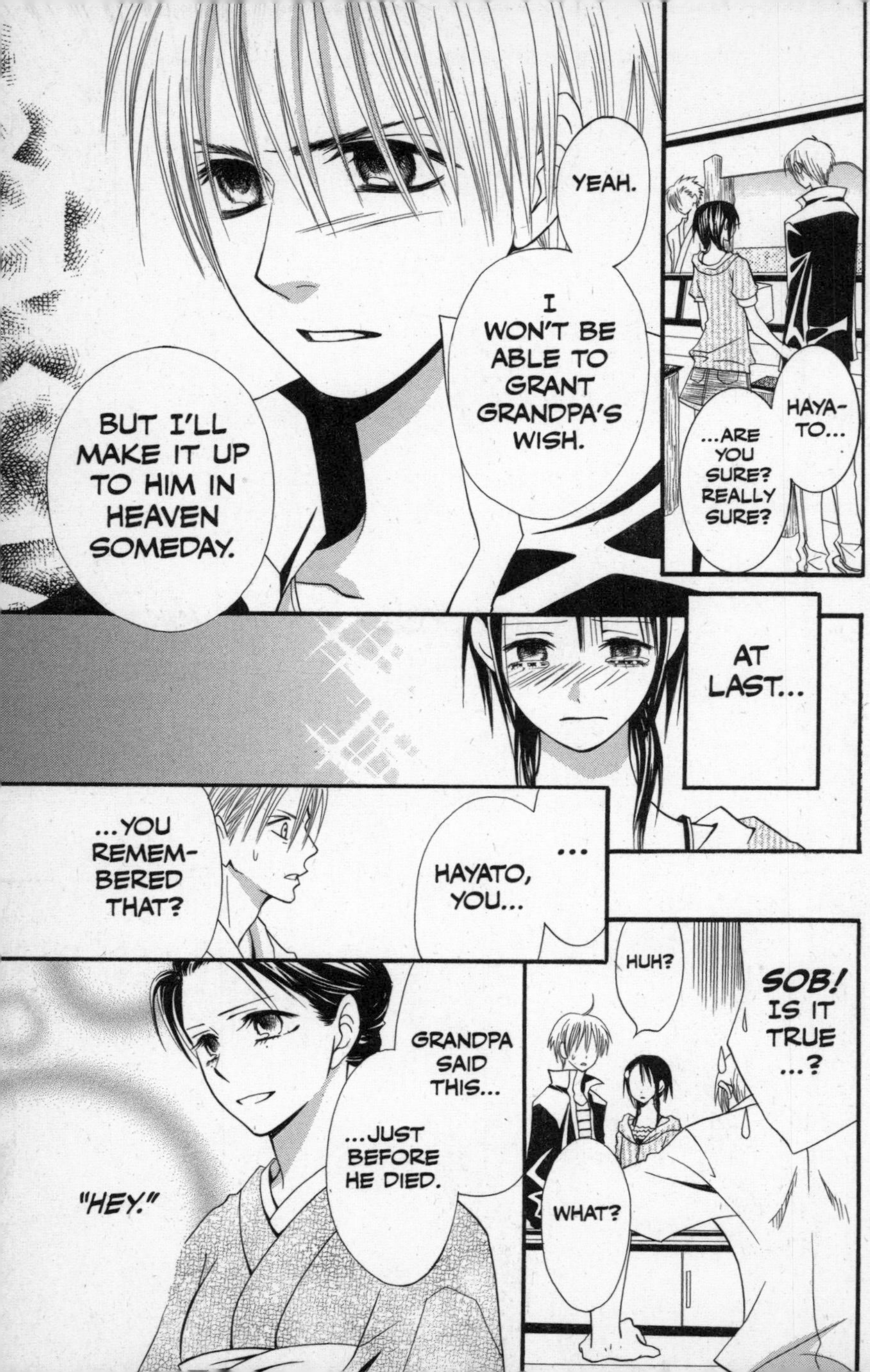
HAYATO...
...ARE YOU SURE? REALLY SURE?
YEAH.
I WON'T BE ABLE TO GRANT GRANDPA'S WISH.
BUT I'LL MAKE IT UP TO HIM IN HEAVEN SOMEDAY.
AT LAST...
...
HAYATO, YOU...
...YOU REMEMBERED THAT?
SOB! IS IT TRUE...?
HUH?
WHAT?
GRANDPA SAID THIS...
...JUST BEFORE HE DIED.
"HEY."

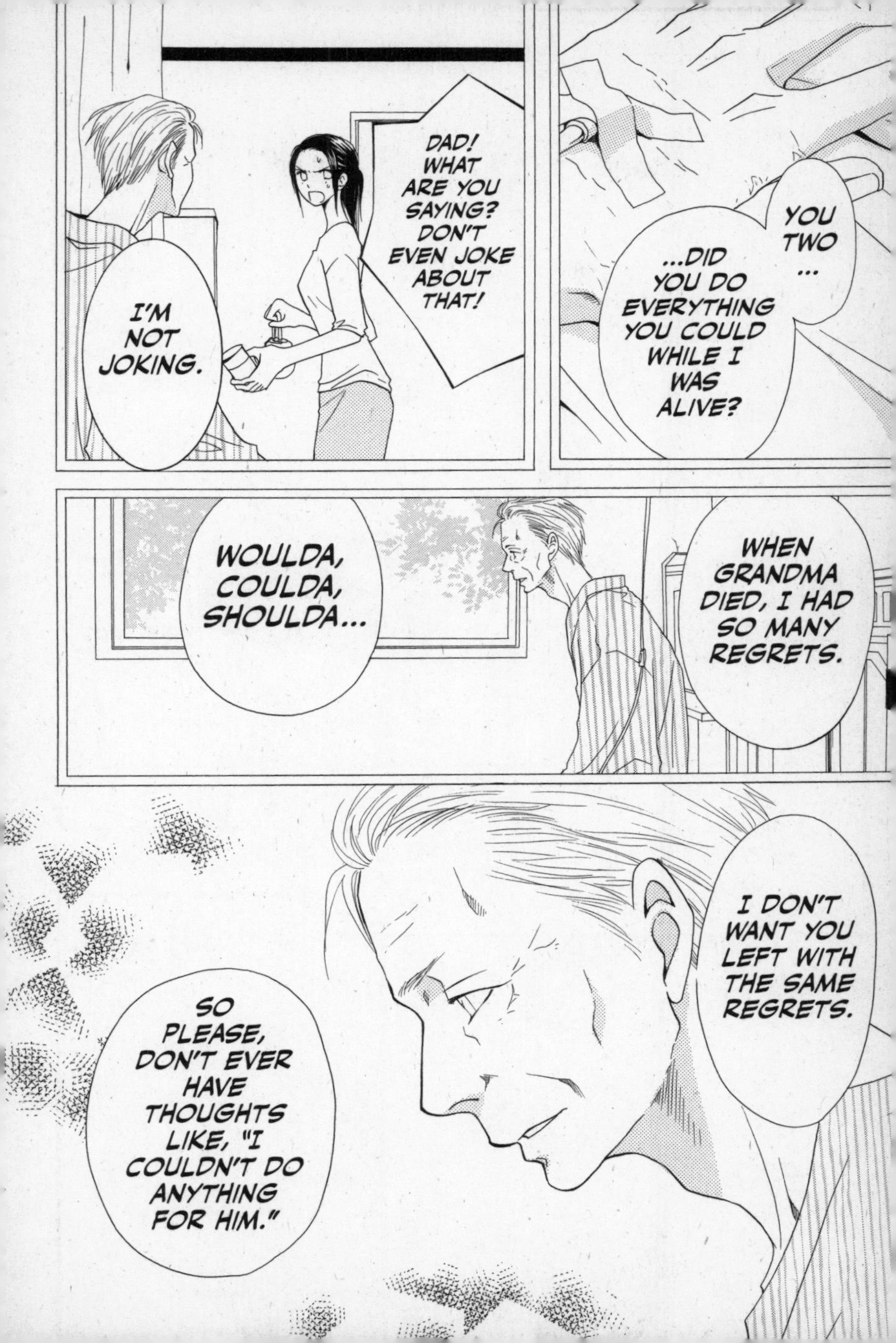
YOU TWO ...
...DID YOU DO EVERYTHING YOU COULD WHILE I WAS ALIVE?
DAD! WHAT ARE YOU SAYING? DON'T EVEN JOKE ABOUT THAT!
I'M NOT JOKING.
WHEN GRANDMA DIED, I HAD SO MANY REGRETS.
WOULDA, COULDA, SHOULDA...
I DON'T WANT YOU LEFT WITH THE SAME REGRETS.
SO PLEASE, DON'T EVER HAVE THOUGHTS LIKE, "I COULDN'T DO ANYTHING FOR HIM."

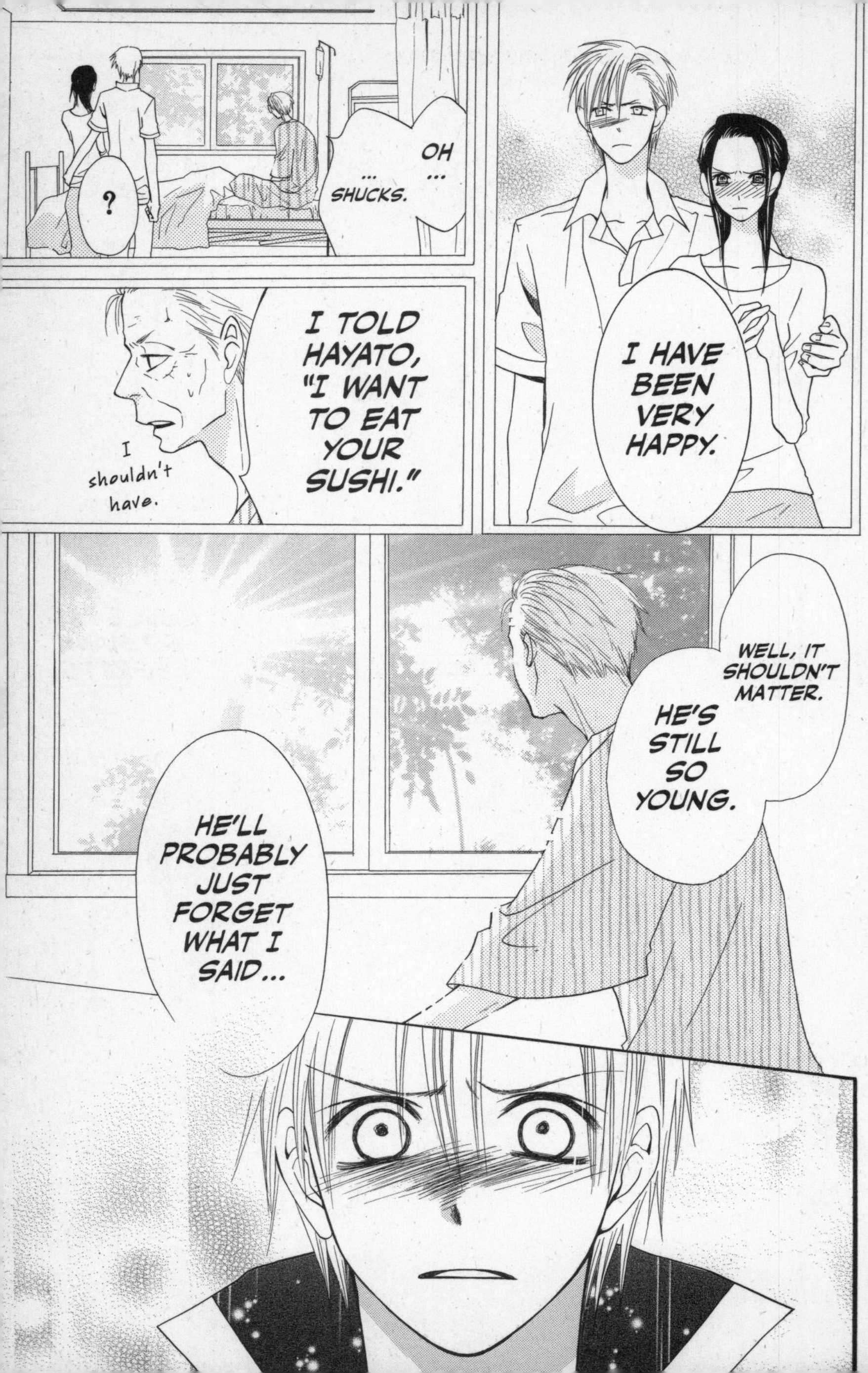
I HAVE BEEN VERY HAPPY.
OH ... ... SHUCKS.
?
I TOLD HAYATO, "I WANT TO EAT YOUR SUSHI."
I shouldn't have.
WELL, IT SHOULDN'T MATTER.
HE'S STILL SO YOUNG.
HE'LL PROBABLY JUST FORGET WHAT I SAID...

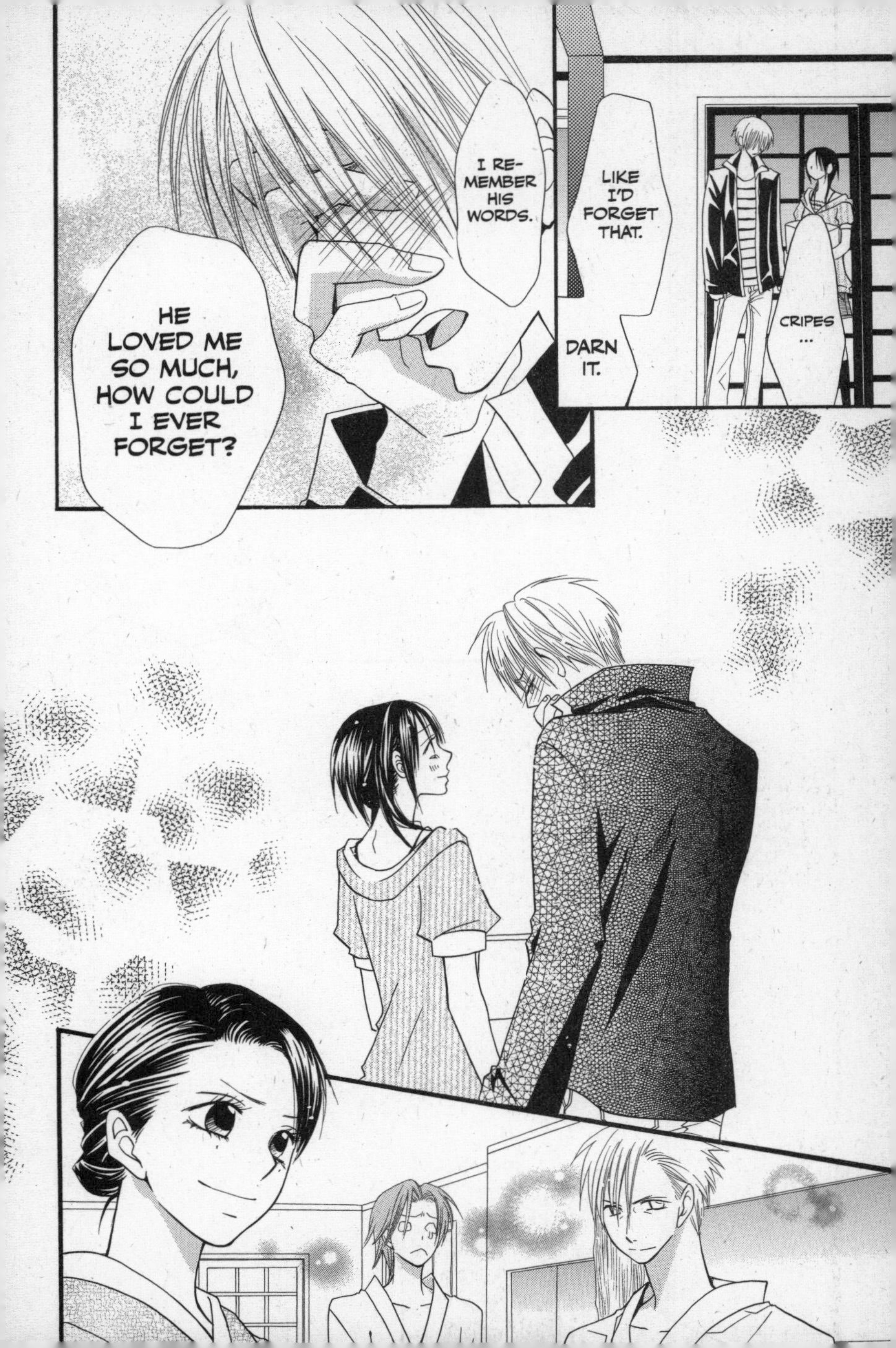
LIKE I'D FORGET THAT.
CRIPES...
DARN IT.
I RE-MEMBER HIS WORDS.
HE LOVED ME SO MUCH, HOW COULD I EVER FORGET?

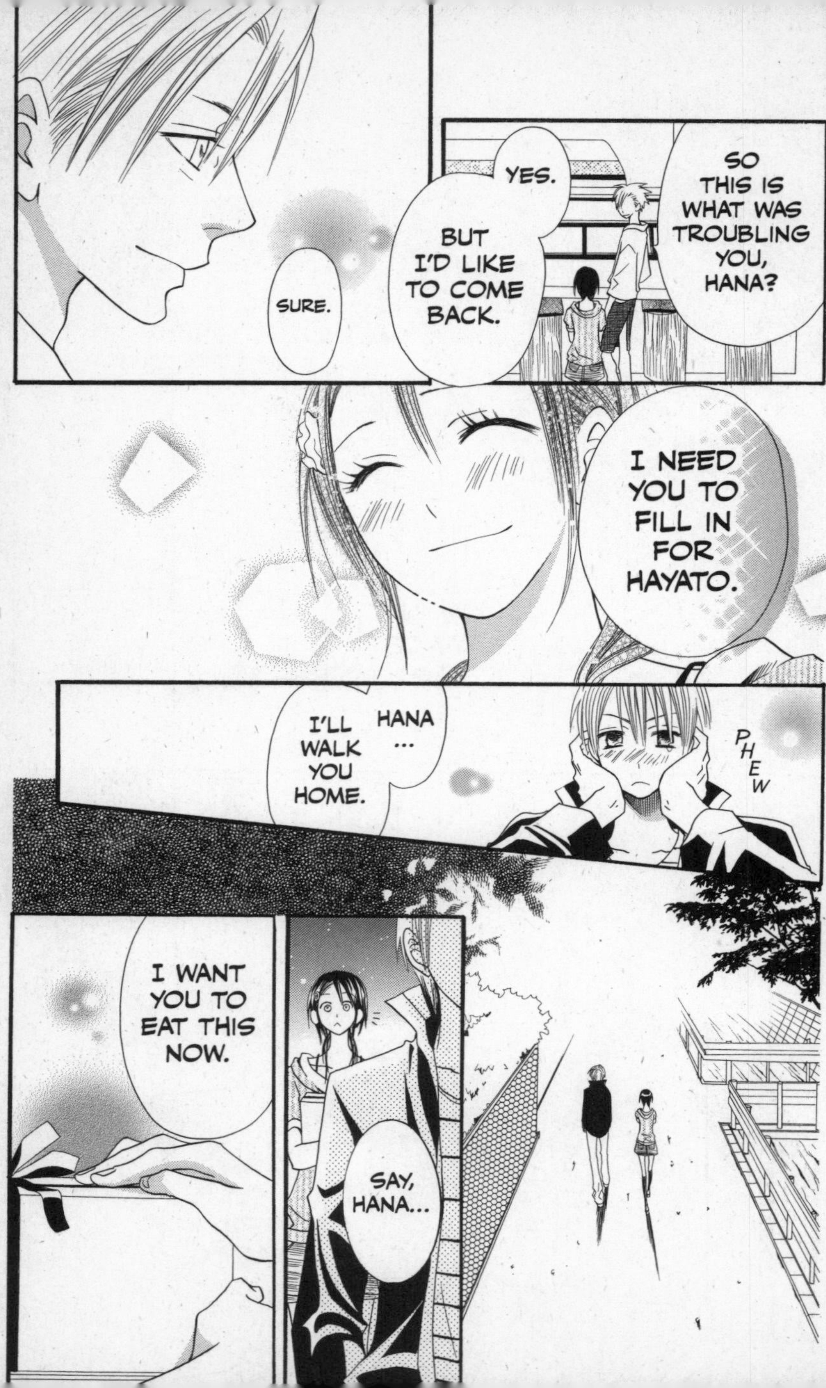
SO THIS IS WHAT WAS TROUBLING YOU, HANA?
YES.
BUT I'D LIKE TO COME BACK.
SURE.
I NEED YOU TO FILL IN FOR HAYATO.
PHEW
HANA ...
I'LL WALK YOU HOME.
SAY, HANA...
I WANT YOU TO EAT THIS NOW.

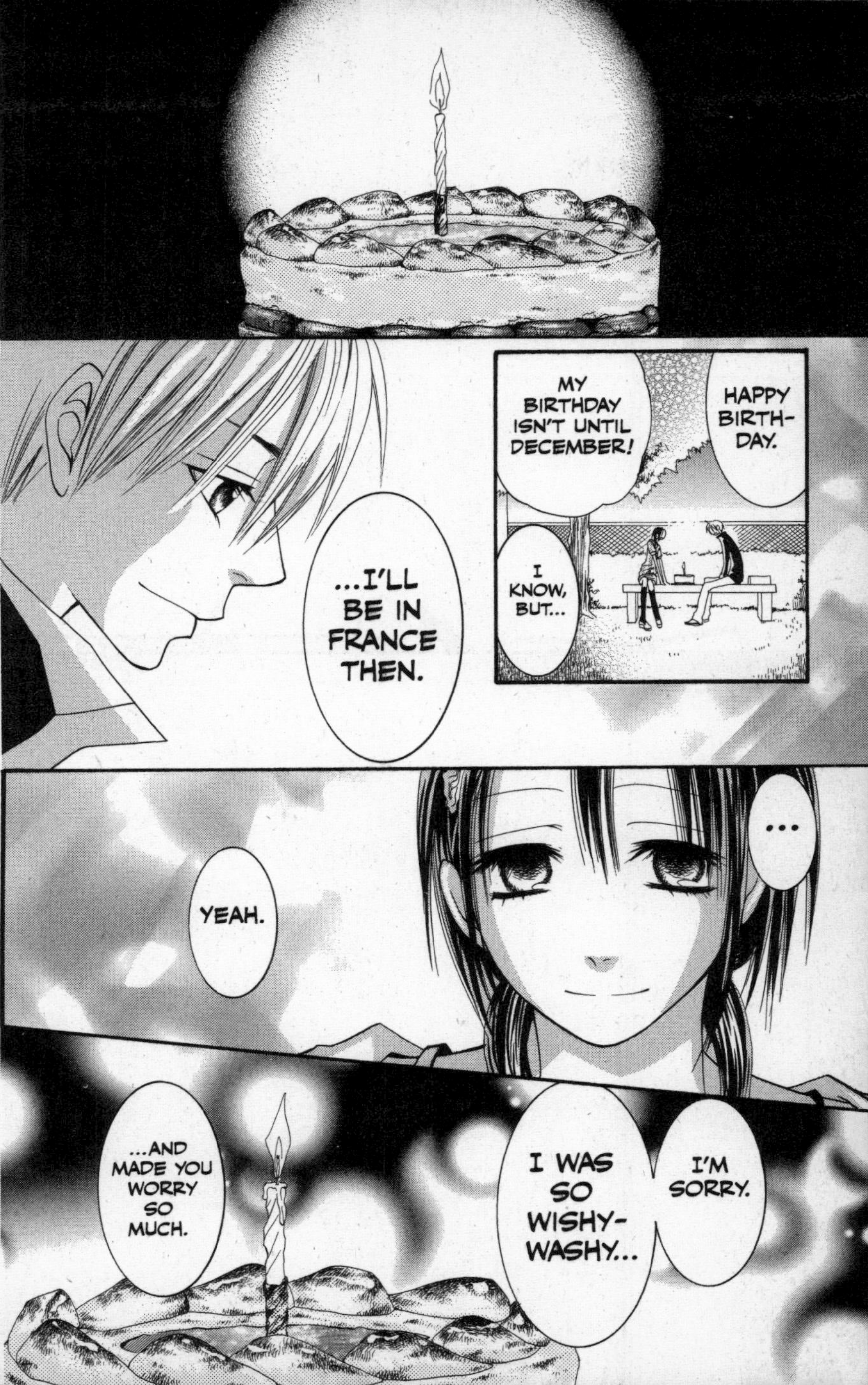
HAPPY BIRTH-DAY.
MY BIRTHDAY ISN'T UNTIL DECEMBER!
I KNOW, BUT...
...I'LL BE IN FRANCE THEN.
...
YEAH.
I'M SORRY.
I WAS SO WISHY-WASHY...
...AND MADE YOU WORRY SO MUCH.

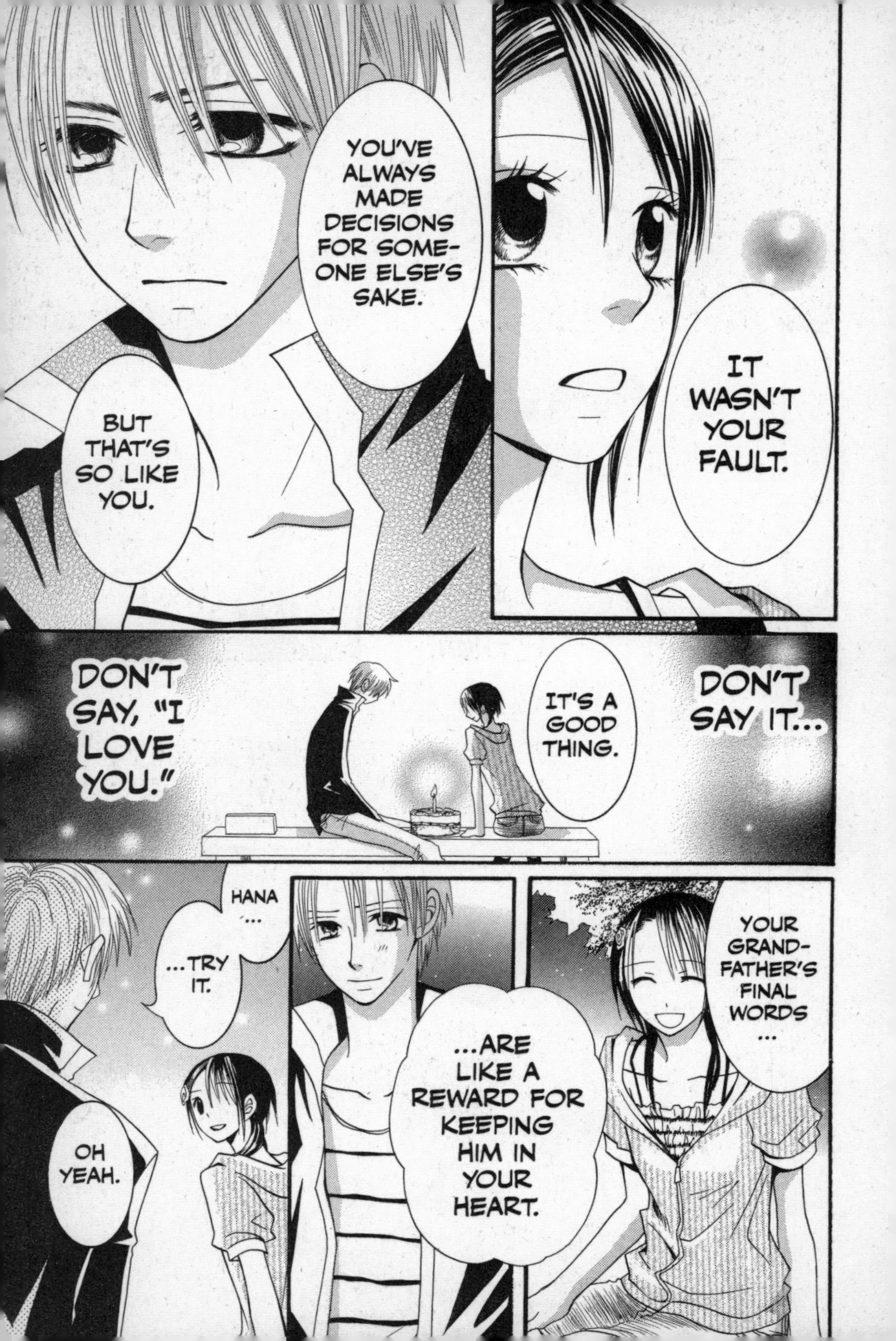
IT WASN'T YOUR FAULT.
YOU'VE ALWAYS MADE DECISIONS FOR SOME-ONE ELSE'S SAKE.
BUT THAT'S SO LIKE YOU.
DON'T SAY IT...
IT'S A GOOD THING.
DON'T SAY, "I LOVE YOU."
YOUR GRAND-FATHER'S FINAL WORDS ...
...ARE LIKE A REWARD FOR KEEPING HIM IN YOUR HEART.
HANA...
...TRY IT.
OH YEAH.

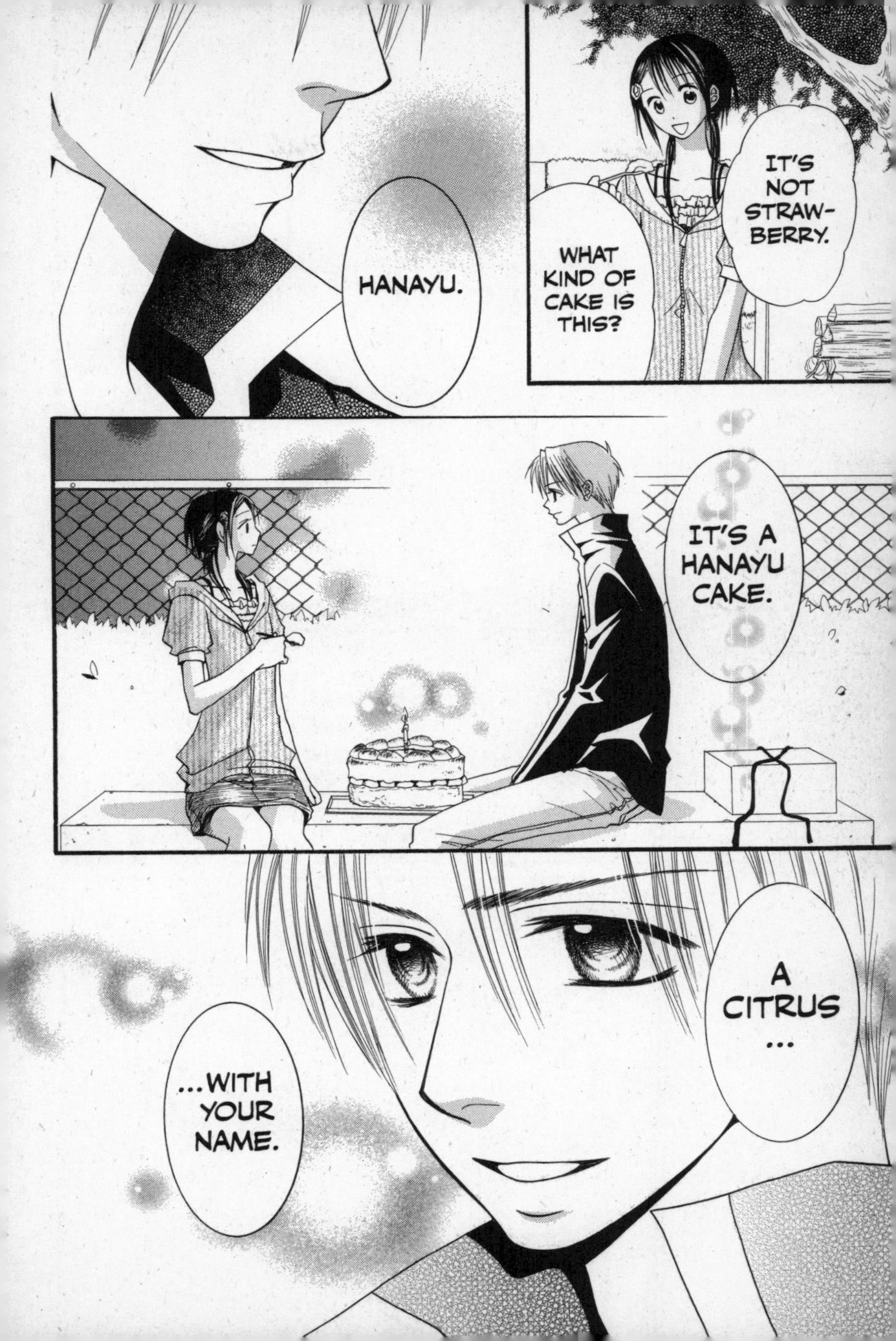
IT'S NOT STRAWBERRY.
WHAT KIND OF CAKE IS THIS?
HANAYU.
IT'S A HANAYU CAKE.
A CITRUS...
...WITH YOUR NAME.

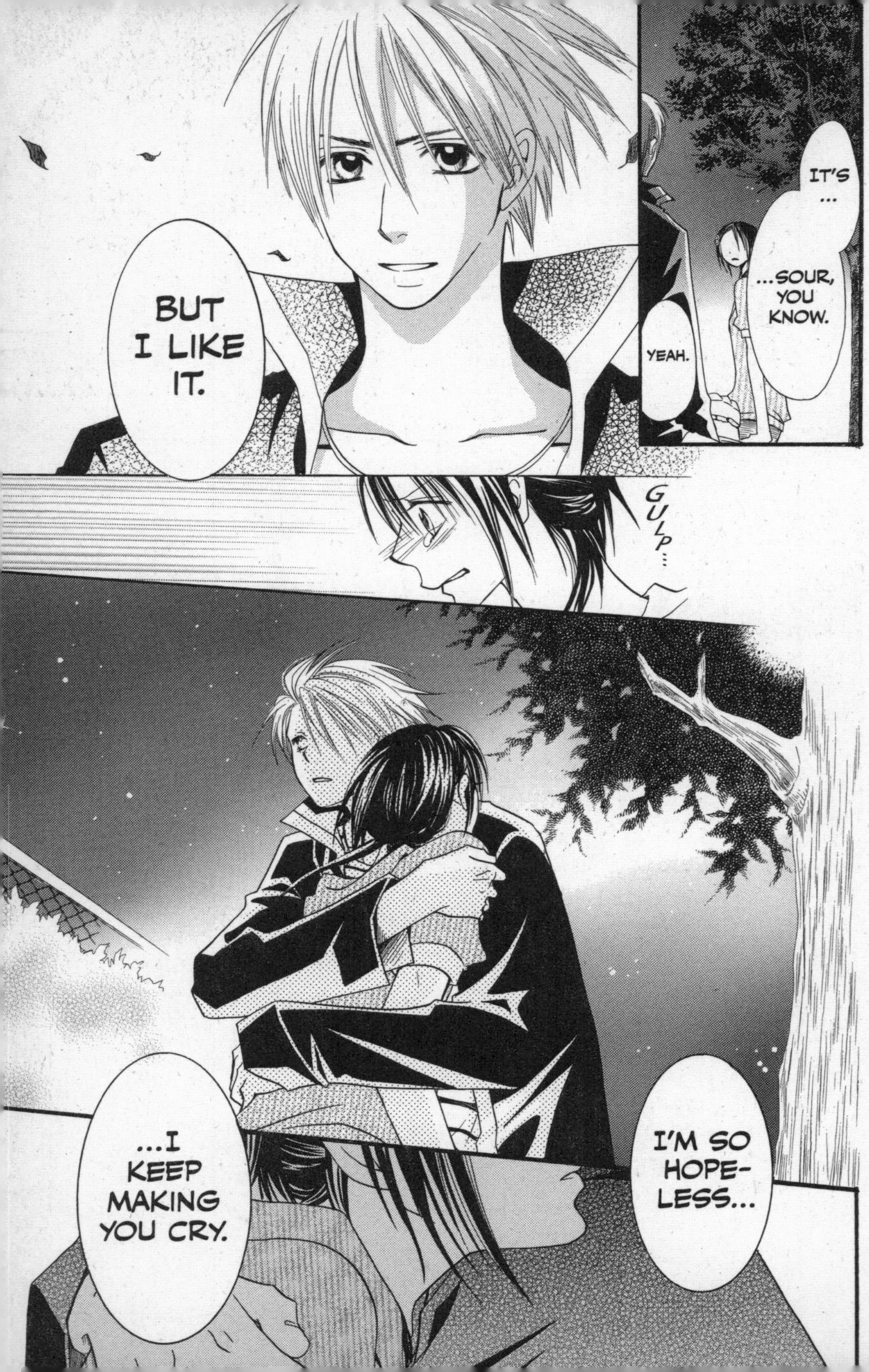
IT'S ...
...SOUR, YOU KNOW.
YEAH.
BUT I LIKE IT.
GULP...
I'M SO HOPELESS...
...I KEEP MAKING YOU CRY.

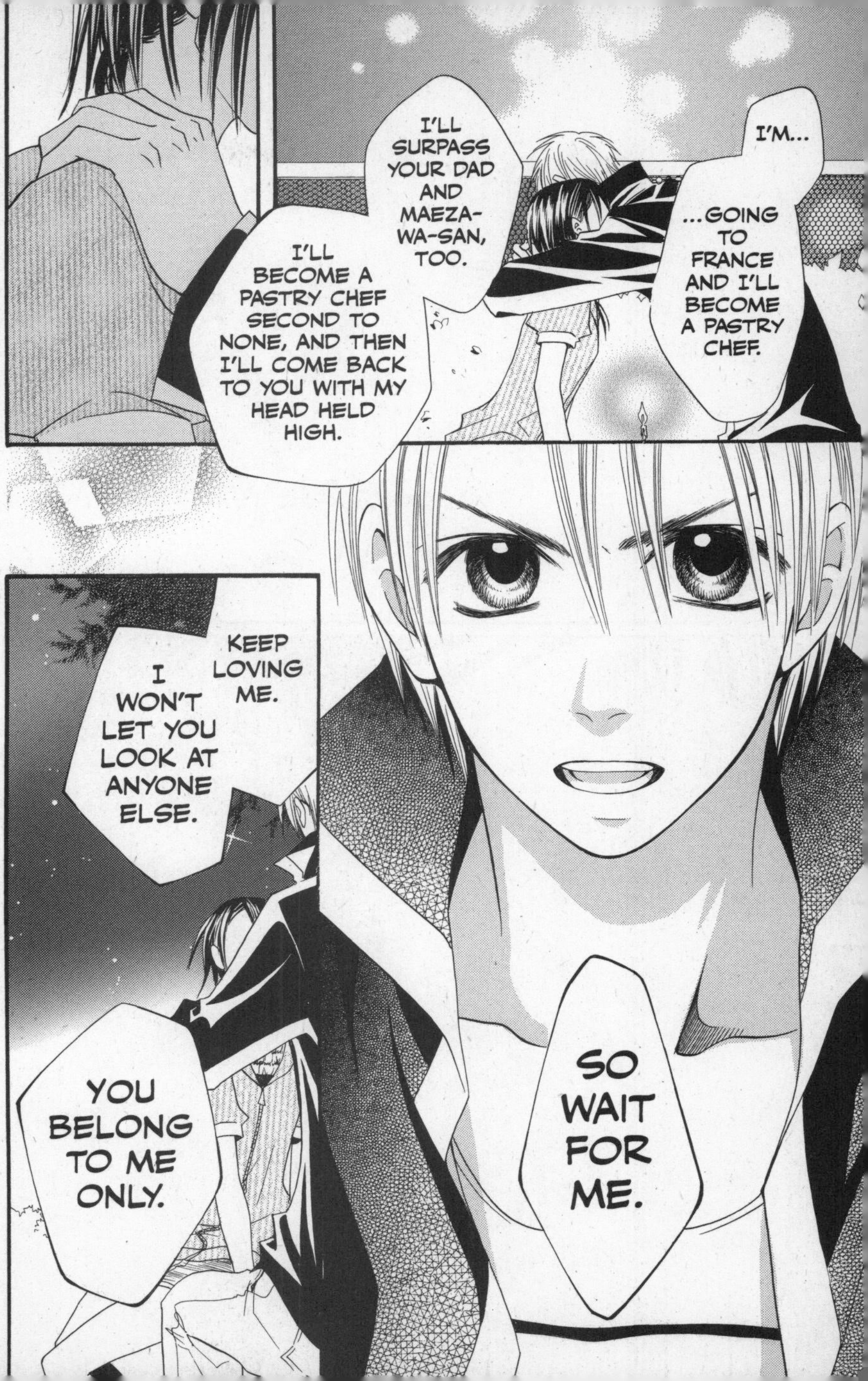
I'M...
...GOING TO FRANCE AND I'LL BECOME A PASTRY CHEF.
I'LL SURPASS YOUR DAD AND MAEZA-WA-SAN, TOO.
I'LL BECOME A PASTRY CHEF SECOND TO NONE, AND THEN I'LL COME BACK TO YOU WITH MY HEAD HELD HIGH.
SO WAIT FOR ME.
KEEP LOVING ME.
I WON'T LET YOU LOOK AT ANYONE ELSE.
YOU BELONG TO ME ONLY.

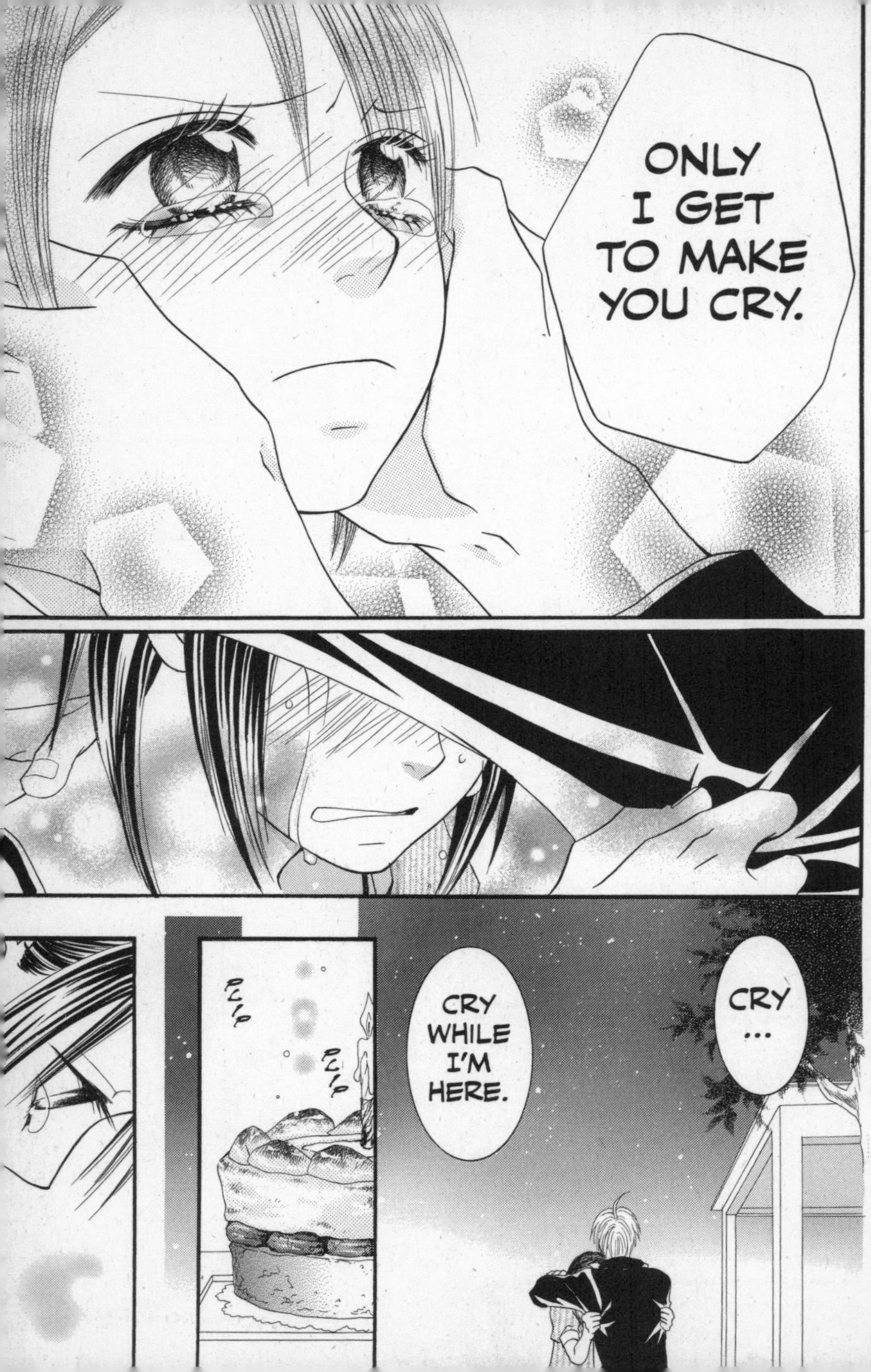
ONLY I GET TO MAKE YOU CRY.
CRY ...
CRY WHILE I'M HERE.

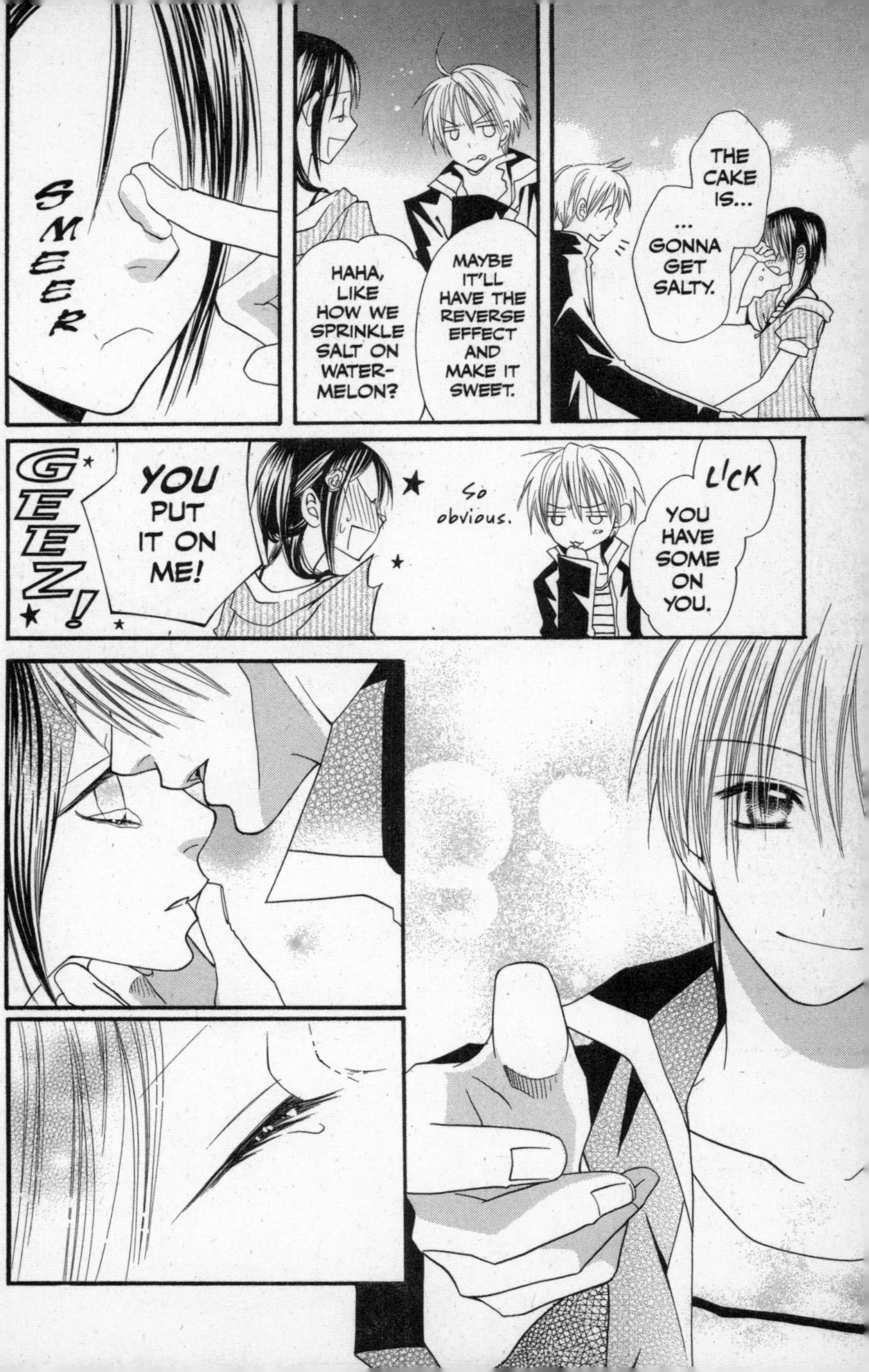
THE CAKE IS...
... GONNA GET SALTY.
MAYBE IT'LL HAVE THE REVERSE EFFECT AND MAKE IT SWEET.
HAHA, LIKE HOW WE SPRINKLE SALT ON WATER-MELON?
SMEER
LICK
YOU HAVE SOME ON YOU.
So obvious.
YOU PUT IT ON ME!
GEEZ!

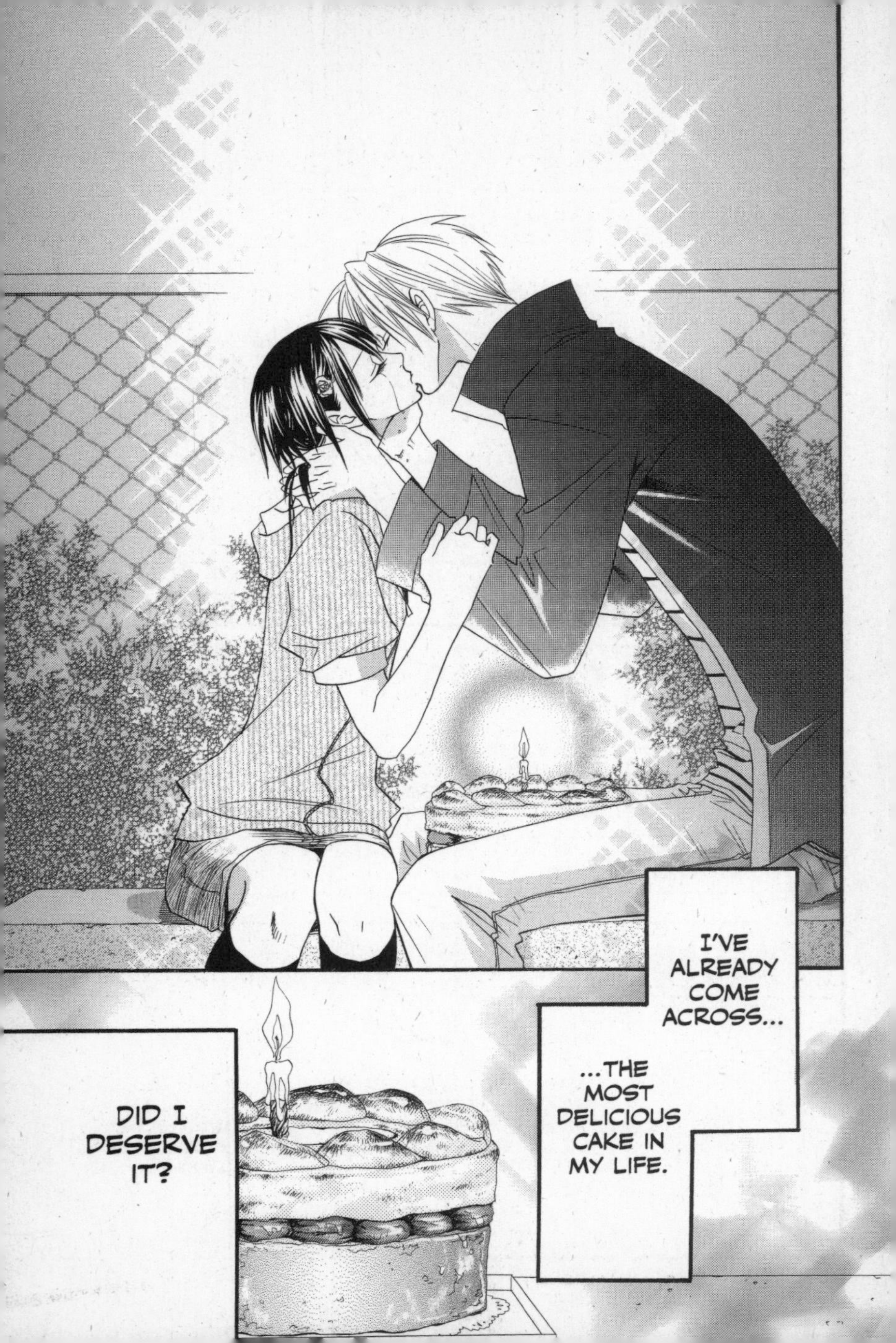
I'VE ALREADY COME ACROSS...
...THE MOST DELICIOUS CAKE IN MY LIFE.
DID I DESERVE IT?

MIXED VEGETABLES Encyclopedia of Characters

YAKUMO HYUGA

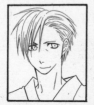

YAKUMO → I THINK IT'S A KIND OF APPLE...

REALLY, FOOD NAMES THAT CAN BE USED FOR MEN ARE RARE. IN THE FIRST CHAPTER, I REALLY DIDN'T HAVE PLANS FOR THE CHARACTER WHO WOULD BE HAYATO'S FATHER. I GUESS THAT'S HOW MANGA IS DEVELOPED! THE TAMAGOYAKI AT HYUGA IS AN IDEA I GOT FROM THE SUSHI SHOP THAT HAS THE TAMA-GOYAKI I LOVE, AND THERE'S NO RECIPE FOR IT. THE CHEF IS 5'11".
I THINK HAYATO HAD GROWN JUST AS TALL BY THE LAST VOLUME.

KARIN HYUGA

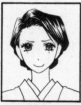

KARIN → AS IN THE THROAT LOZENGES

I JUST DECIDED ON HER NAME! I MEAN THE MISSUS IS THE MISSUS! SHE LOOKS SERIOUS, WITH DARK EYES, MOLES BENEATH HER EYES--WHICH LOOK LIKE TEARS--SHORT, PROMINENT EYEBROWS AND, AS MY EDITOR PUT IT, "A SEXY FACE." SHE HAS A BIG BUST. SHE'S OLDER THAN CHEF. THE REASON THAT SAKI APPEARED FIRST IN THE MANGA WAS SO THE ISSUE OF HAYATO'S DREAM WASN'T CLOUDED BY THE APPEARANCE OF THE MOTHER.

KOUSUI HYUGA

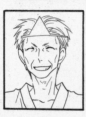

KOUSUI → PEAR

HAYATO'S BELOVED GRANDFATHER. HE LOOKS LIKE THE CHEF GROWN OLD. I'M NOT GOOD AT DRAWING OLDER MEN, SO OKAMOTO AND THE MANAGER OF THE LIONS ALL LOOK ALIKE. "GRANDPA" HAS BEEN INFLUENCED BY MY OWN EXPERIENCES. HANA'S DAD HAS A DIFFERENT INFLUENCE.

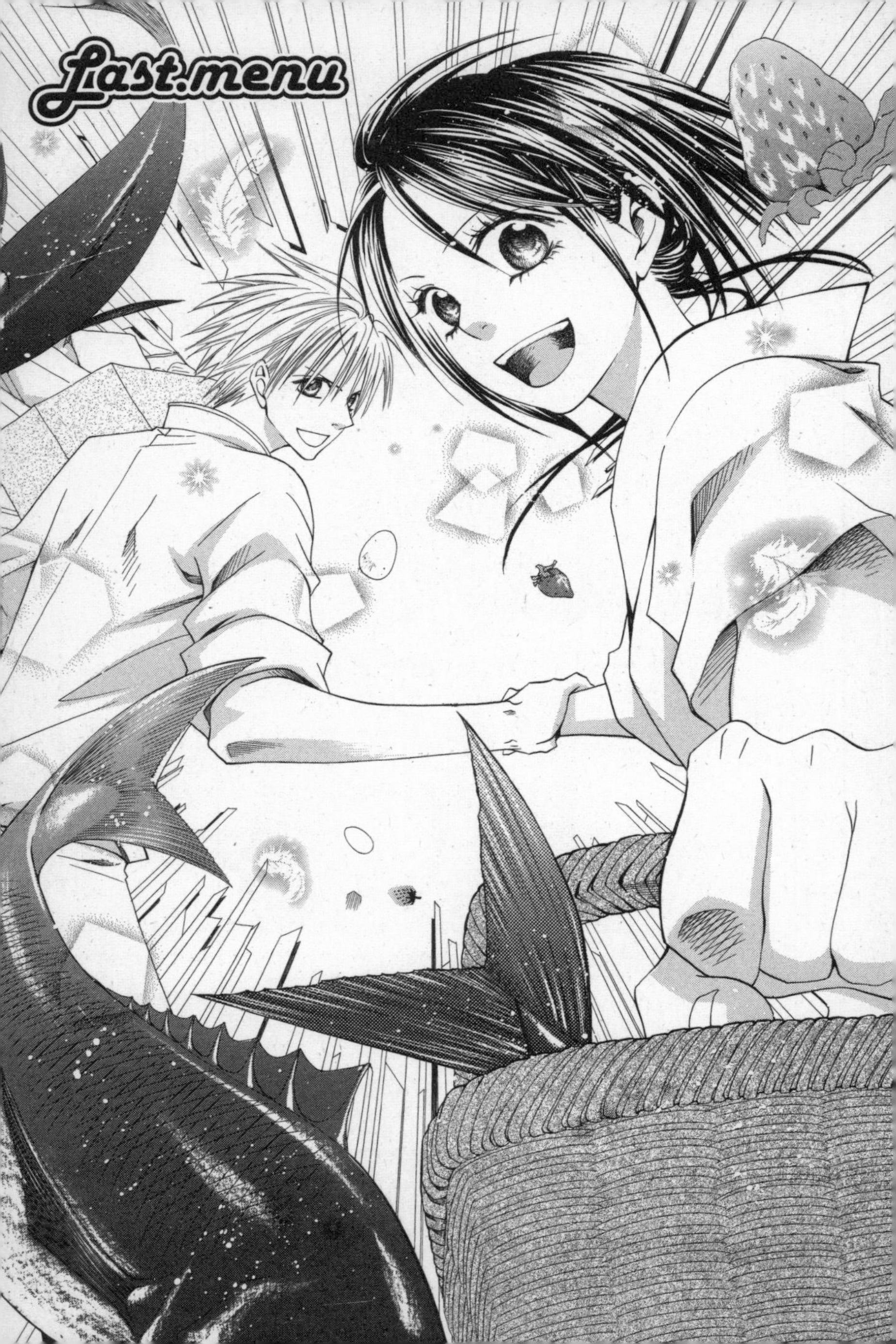
Last.menu

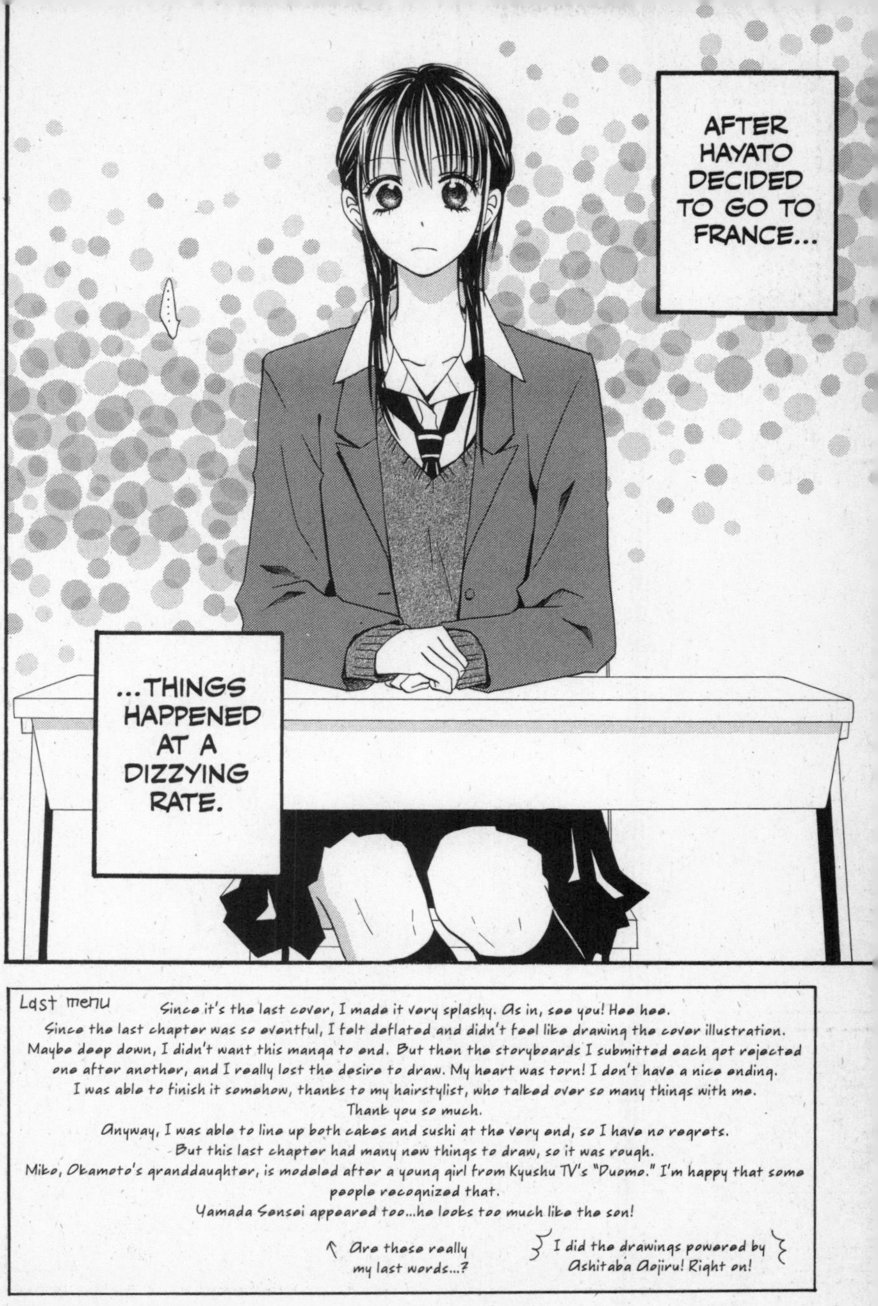
AFTER HAYATO DECIDED TO GO TO FRANCE...
...THINGS HAPPENED AT A DIZZYING RATE.

Last menu

Since it's the last cover, I made it very splashy. As in, see you! Hee hee.
Since the last chapter was so eventful, I felt deflated and didn't feel like drawing the cover illustration.
Maybe deep down, I didn't want this manga to end. But then the storyboards I submitted each got rejected one after another, and I really lost the desire to draw. My heart was torn! I don't have a nice ending.
I was able to finish it somehow, thanks to my hairstylist, who talked over so many things with me.
Thank you so much.
Anyway, I was able to line up both cakes and sushi at the very end, so I have no regrets.
But this last chapter had many new things to draw, so it was rough.
Miko, Okamoto's granddaughter, is modeled after a young girl from Kyushu TV's "Duomo." I'm happy that some people recognized that.
Yamada Sensei appeared too...he looks too much like the son!

↑ Are these really my last words...?

I did the drawings powered by Ashitaba Aojiru! Right on!

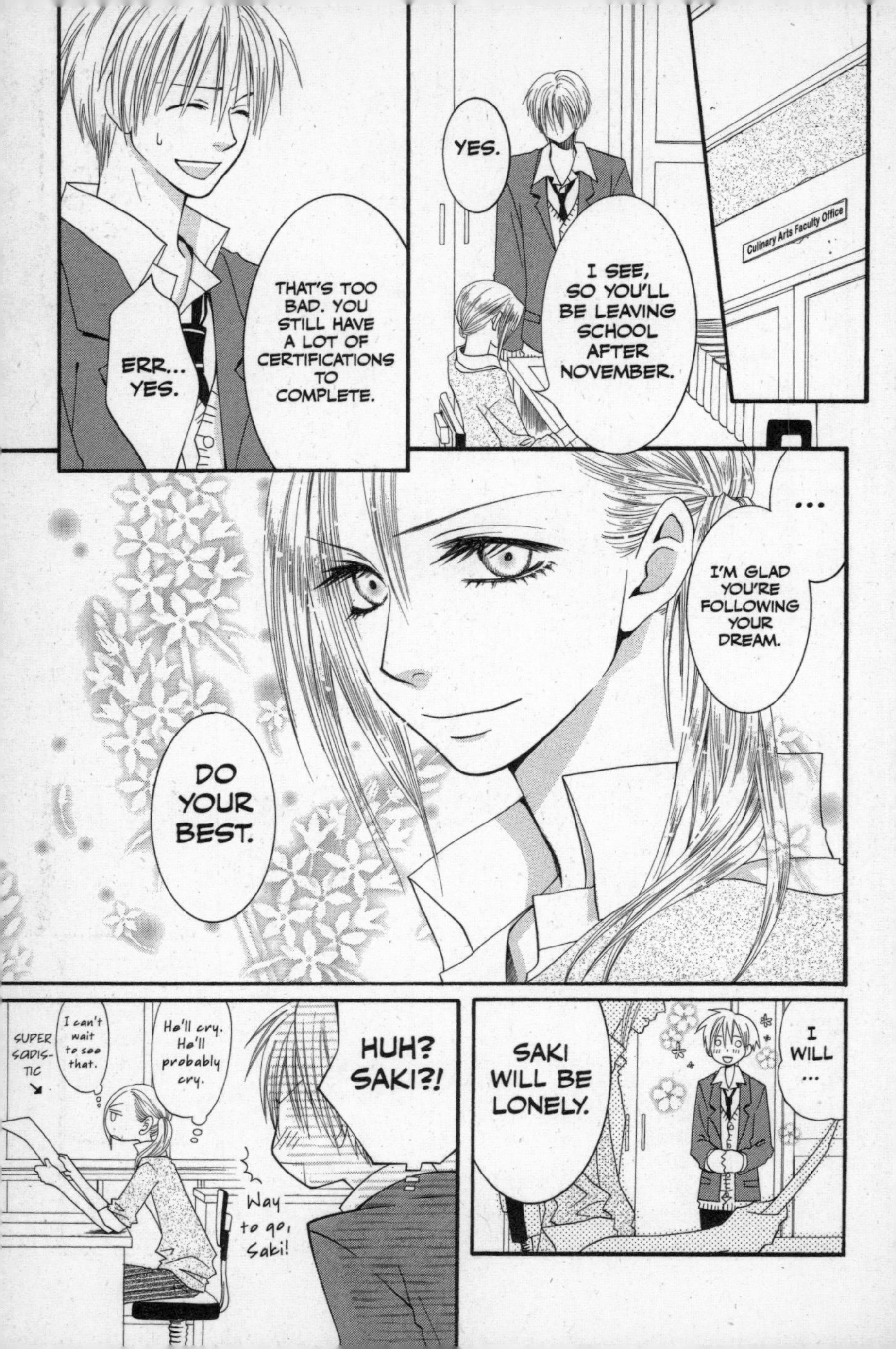
Culinary Arts Faculty Office
I SEE, SO YOU'LL BE LEAVING SCHOOL AFTER NOVEMBER.
YES.
THAT'S TOO BAD. YOU STILL HAVE A LOT OF CERTIFICATIONS TO COMPLETE.
ERR... YES.
...
I'M GLAD YOU'RE FOLLOWING YOUR DREAM.
DO YOUR BEST.
I WILL ...
SAKI WILL BE LONELY.
HUH? SAKI?!
He'll cry. He'll probably cry.
I can't wait to see that.
SUPER SADIS-TIC
Way to go, Saki!

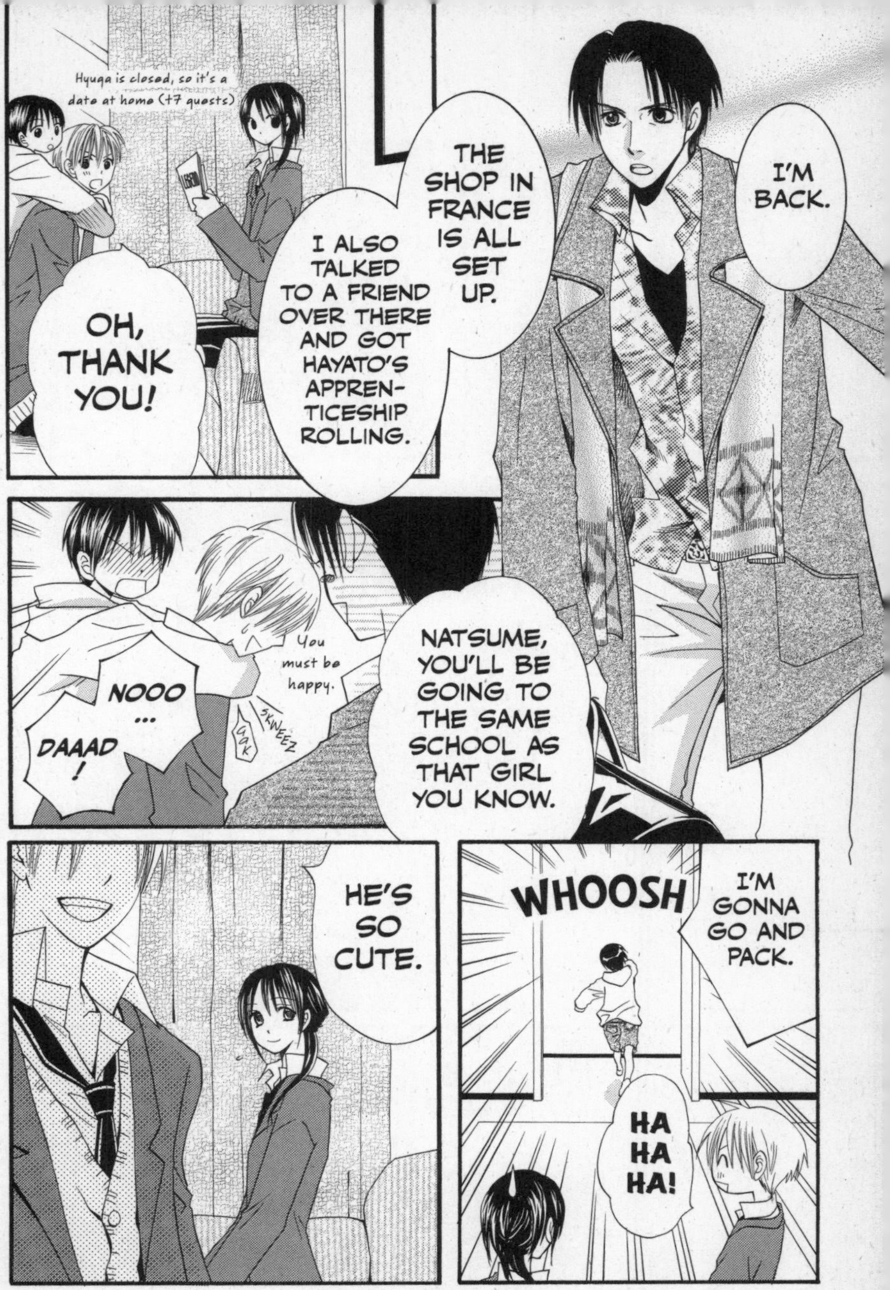
I'M BACK.
THE SHOP IN FRANCE IS ALL SET UP.
I ALSO TALKED TO A FRIEND OVER THERE AND GOT HAYATO'S APPREN-TICESHIP ROLLING.
NATSUME, YOU'LL BE GOING TO THE SAME SCHOOL AS THAT GIRL YOU KNOW.
Hyuga is closed, so it's a date at home (+7 guests)
OH, THANK YOU!
NOOO... DAAAD!
You must be happy.
SKWEEZ
GAK
I'M GONNA GO AND PACK.
WHOOSH
HA HA HA!
HE'S SO CUTE.

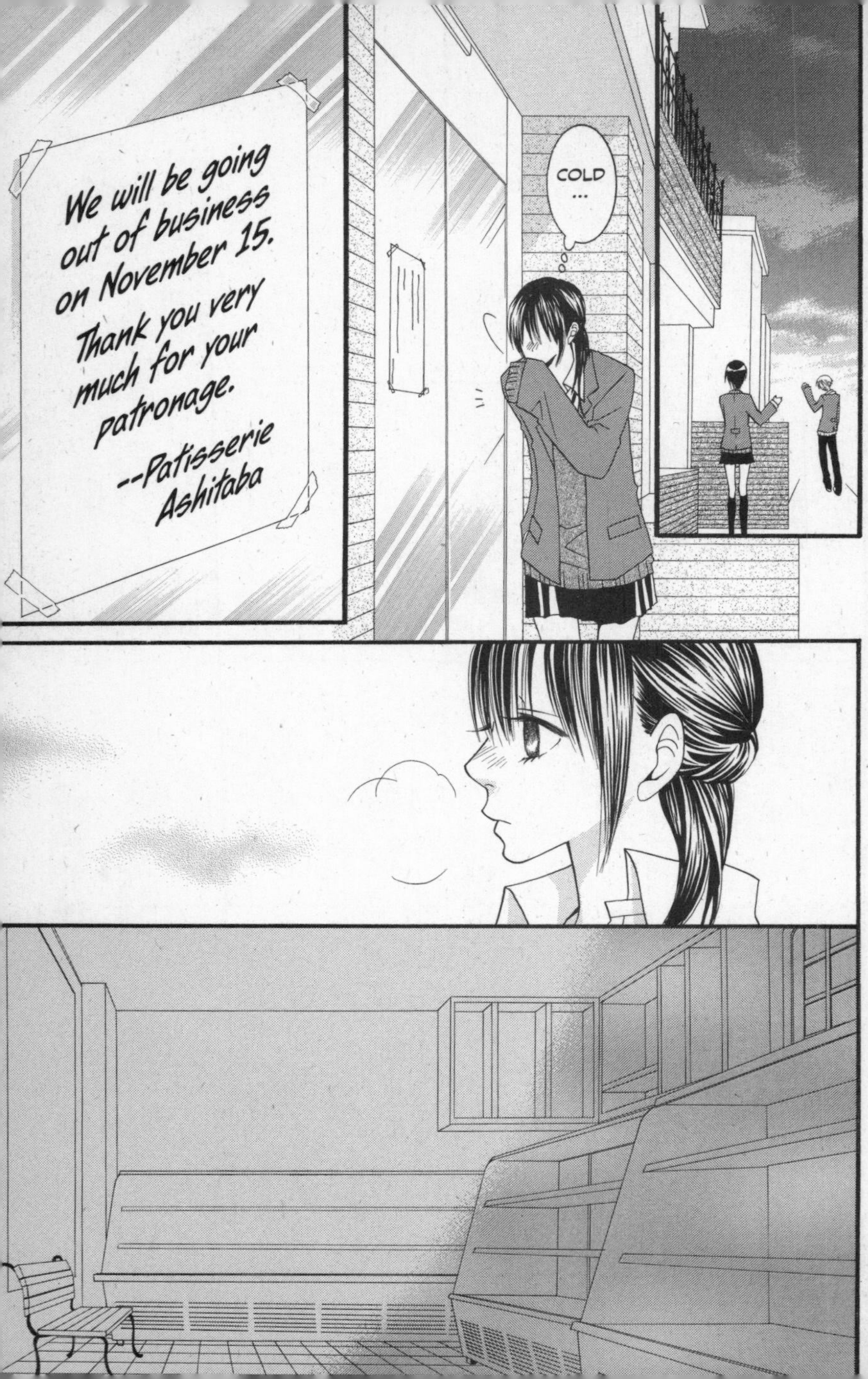
COLD ...
We will be going out of business on November 15. Thank you very much for your patronage. --Patisserie Ashitaba

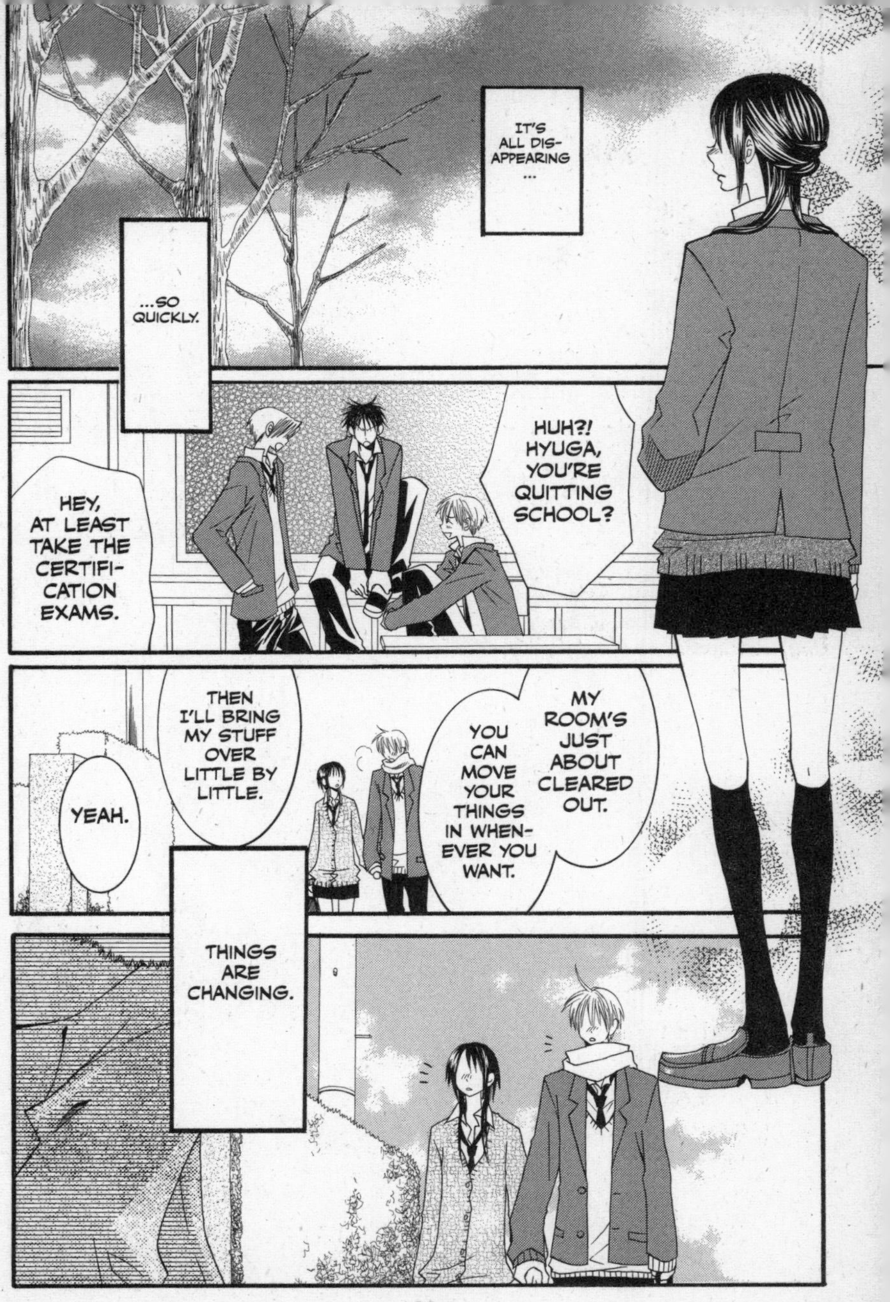
IT'S ALL DIS-APPEARING ...
...SO QUICKLY.
HUH?! HYUGA, YOU'RE QUITTING SCHOOL?
HEY, AT LEAST TAKE THE CERTIFI-CATION EXAMS.
MY ROOM'S JUST ABOUT CLEARED OUT.
YOU CAN MOVE YOUR THINGS IN WHEN-EVER YOU WANT.
THEN I'LL BRING MY STUFF OVER LITTLE BY LITTLE.
YEAH.
THINGS ARE CHANGING.

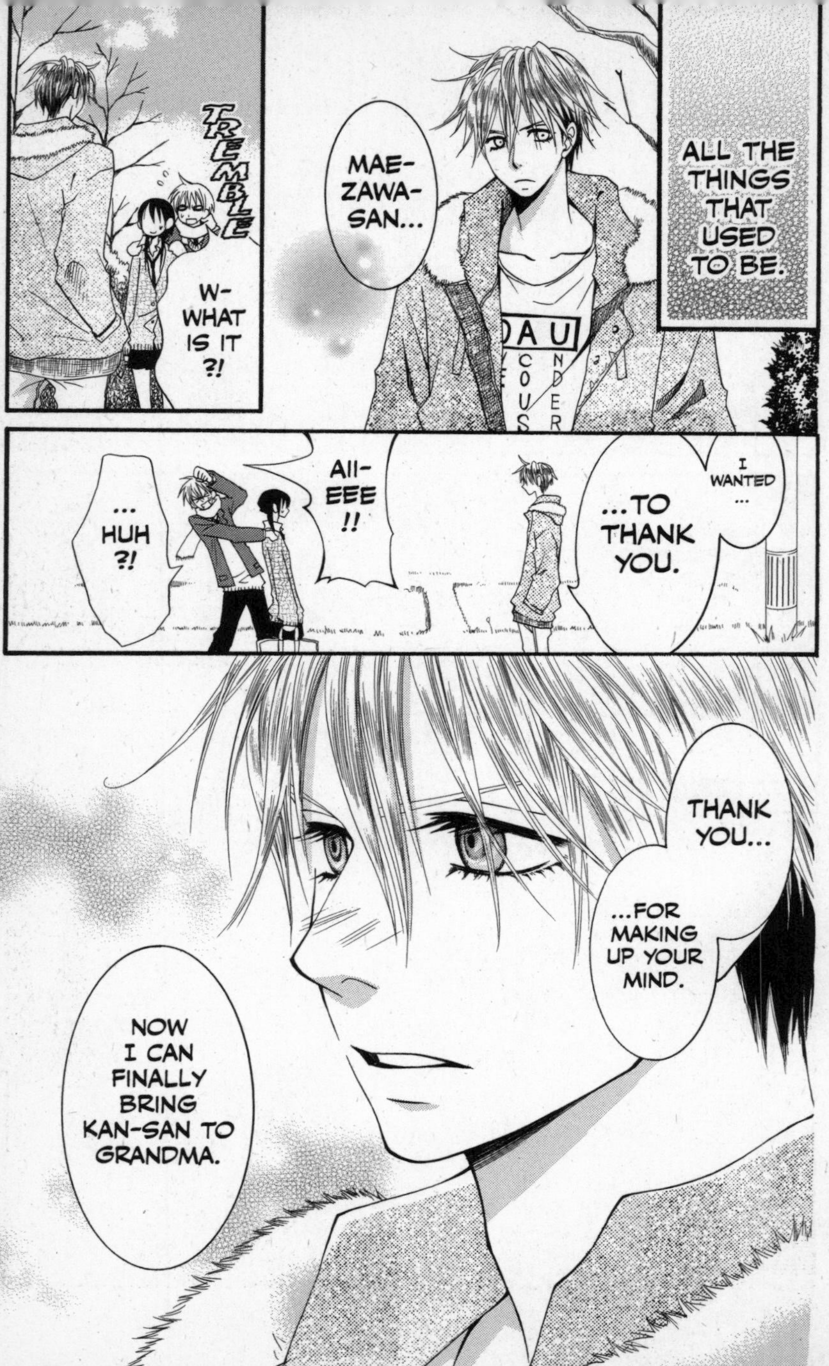
ALL THE THINGS THAT USED TO BE.
MAE-ZAWA-SAN...
TREMBLE
W-WHAT IS IT ?!
I WANTED ...
...TO THANK YOU.
AII-EEE !!
... HUH ?!
THANK YOU...
...FOR MAKING UP YOUR MIND.
NOW I CAN FINALLY BRING KAN-SAN TO GRANDMA.

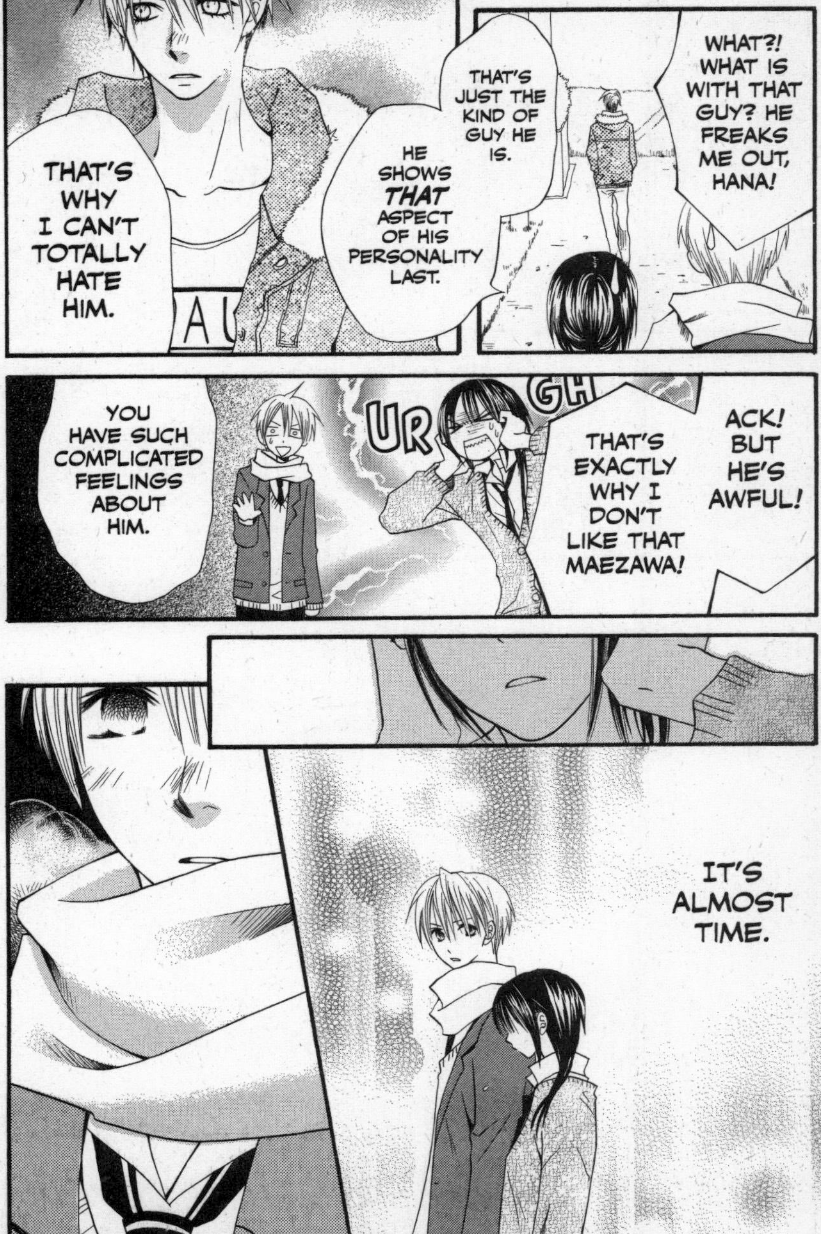
WHAT?! WHAT IS WITH THAT GUY? HE FREAKS ME OUT, HANA!
THAT'S JUST THE KIND OF GUY HE IS.
HE SHOWS *THAT* ASPECT OF HIS PERSONALITY LAST.
THAT'S WHY I CAN'T TOTALLY HATE HIM.
ACK! BUT HE'S AWFUL!
THAT'S EXACTLY WHY I DON'T LIKE THAT MAEZAWA!
URGH
YOU HAVE SUCH COMPLICATED FEELINGS ABOUT HIM.
IT'S ALMOST TIME.

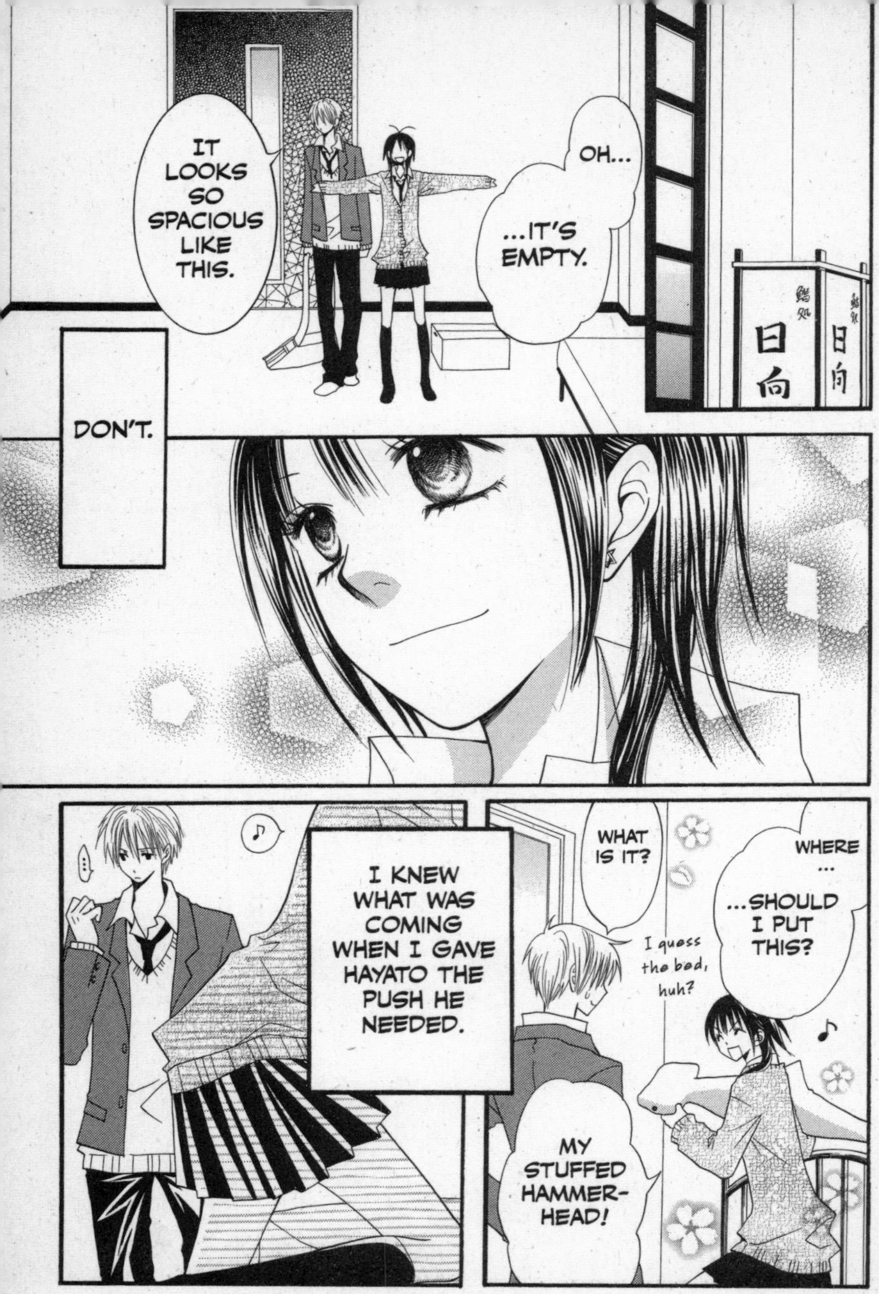
OH...
...IT'S EMPTY.
日向
日向
IT LOOKS SO SPACIOUS LIKE THIS.
DON'T.
WHERE ...
...SHOULD I PUT THIS?
WHAT IS IT?
MY STUFFED HAMMER-HEAD!
I guess the bed, huh?
♪
I KNEW WHAT WAS COMING WHEN I GAVE HAYATO THE PUSH HE NEEDED.
♪
...

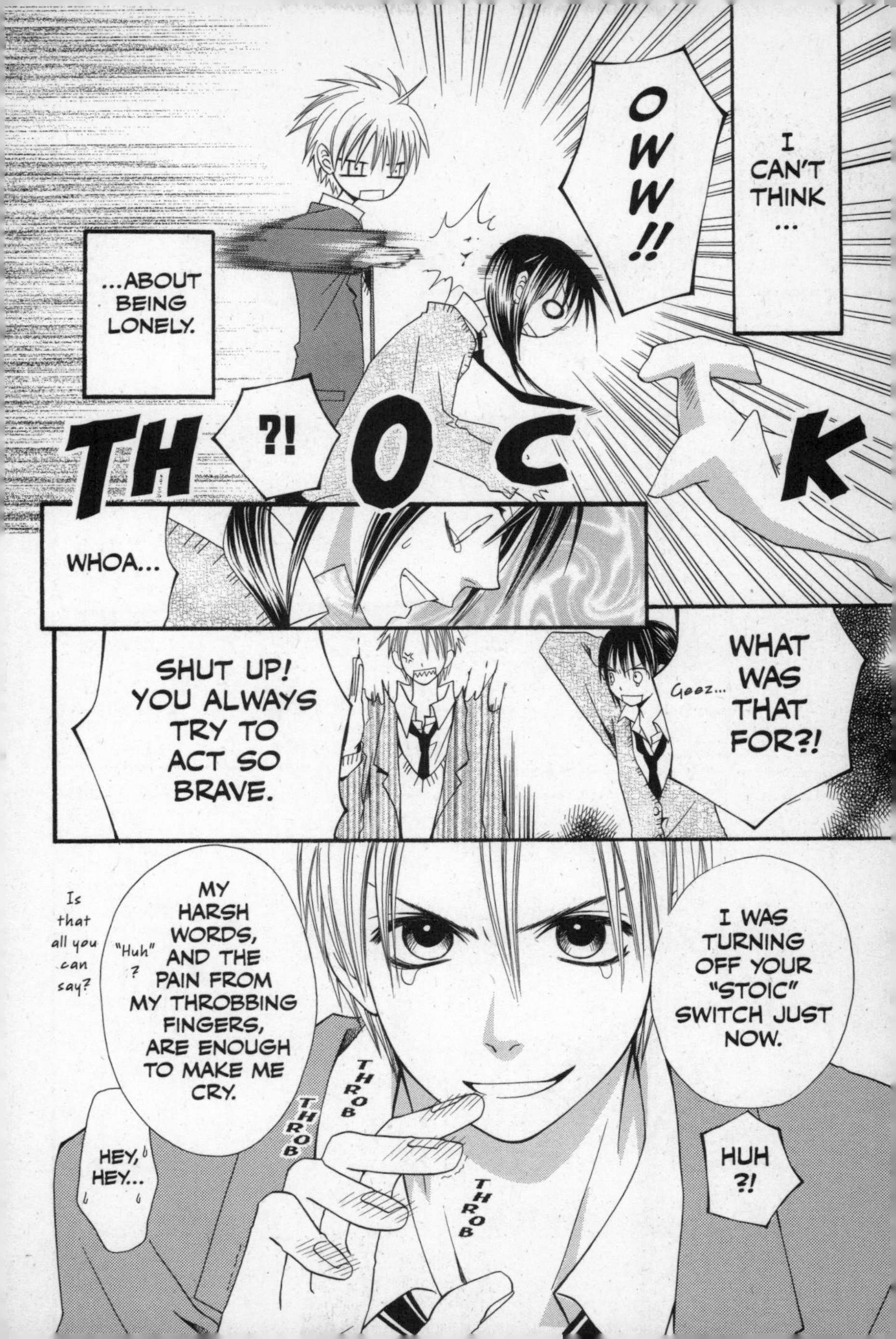
I CAN'T THINK ...
OWW!!
...ABOUT BEING LONELY.
?!
THOCK
WHOA...
WHAT WAS THAT FOR?!
Geez...
SHUT UP! YOU ALWAYS TRY TO ACT SO BRAVE.
I WAS TURNING OFF YOUR "STOIC" SWITCH JUST NOW.
HUH ?!
THROB THROB THROB
MY HARSH WORDS, AND THE PAIN FROM MY THROBBING FINGERS, ARE ENOUGH TO MAKE ME CRY.
"Huh" ?
Is that all you can say?
HEY, HEY...

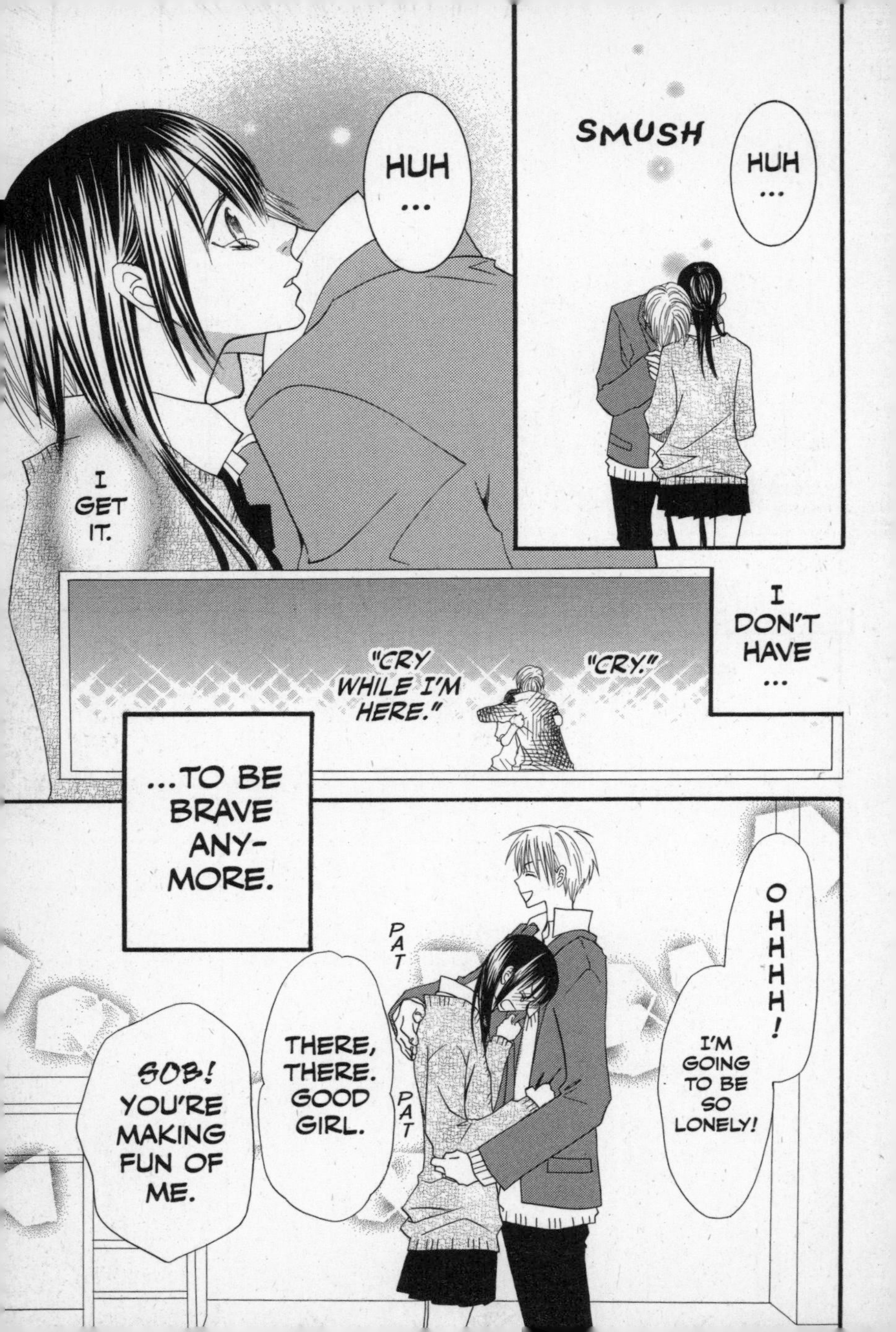
SMUSH
HUH ...
HUH ...
I GET IT.
I DON'T HAVE ...
"CRY."
"CRY WHILE I'M HERE."
...TO BE BRAVE ANYMORE.
OHHHH!
I'M GOING TO BE SO LONELY!
PAT
PAT
THERE, THERE. GOOD GIRL.
SOB! YOU'RE MAKING FUN OF ME.

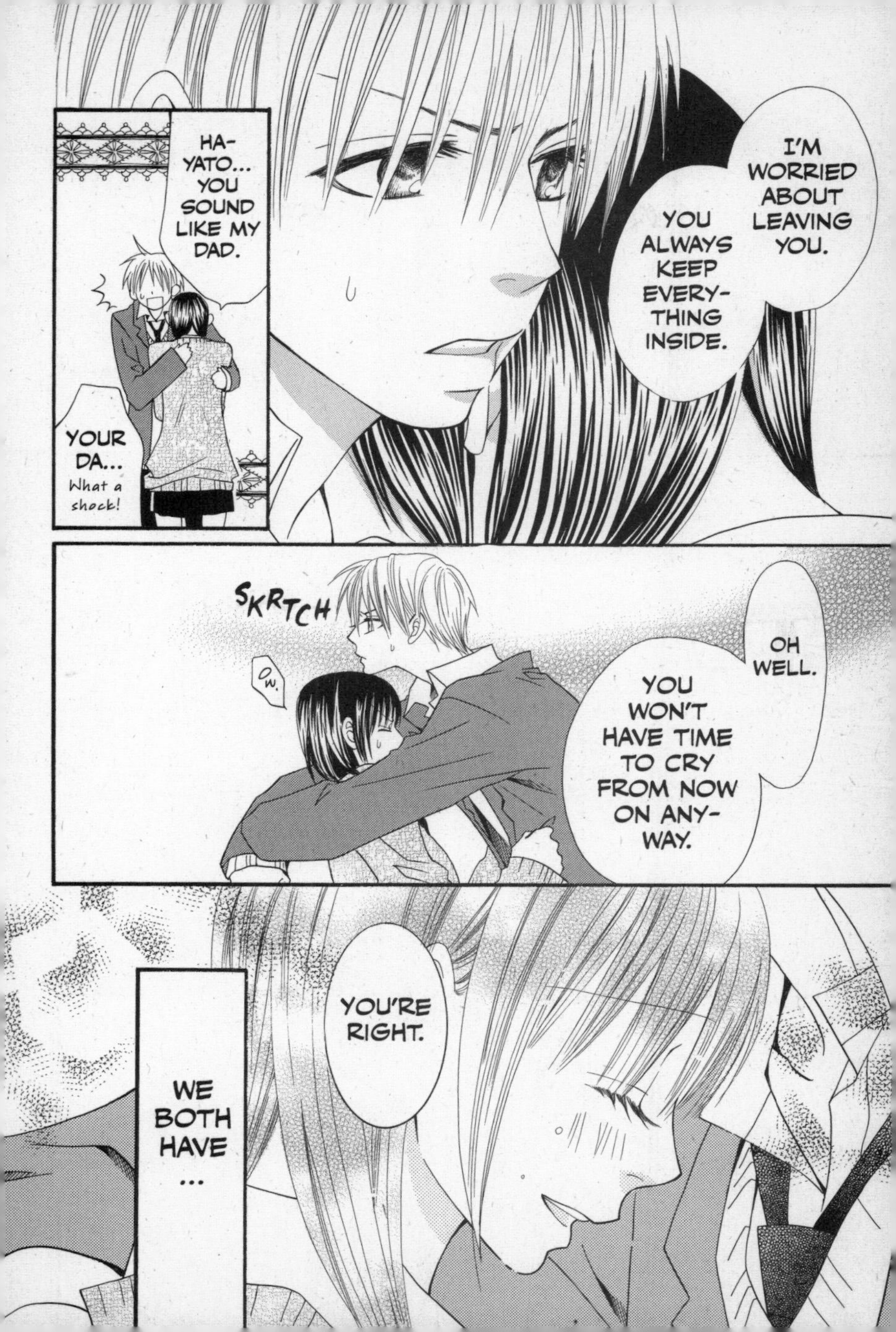
I'M WORRIED ABOUT LEAVING YOU.
YOU ALWAYS KEEP EVERY-THING INSIDE.
HA-YATO... YOU SOUND LIKE MY DAD.
YOUR DA... What a shock!
OH WELL.
YOU WON'T HAVE TIME TO CRY FROM NOW ON ANY-WAY.
SKRTCH
Ow.
YOU'RE RIGHT.
WE BOTH HAVE ...

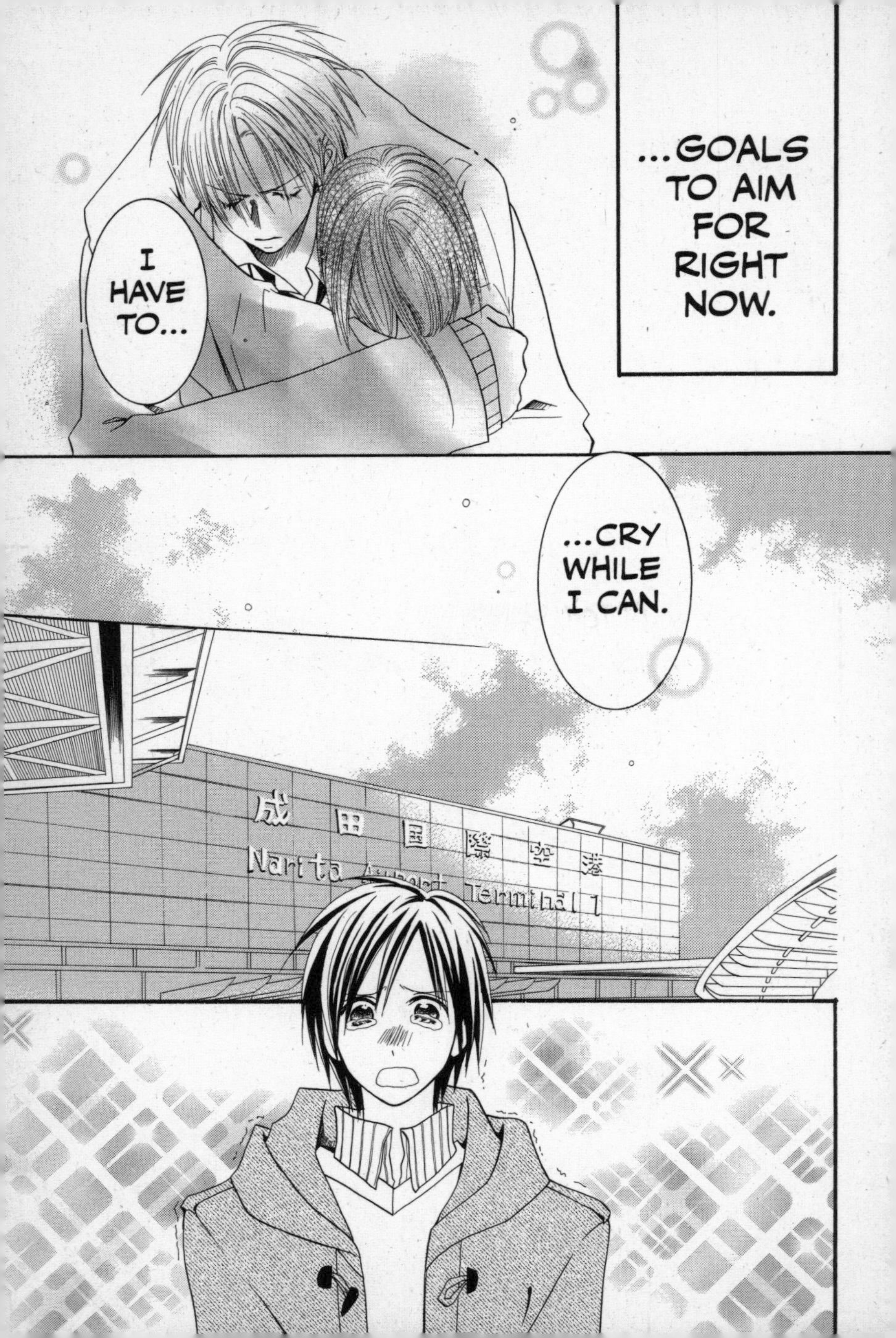
...GOALS TO AIM FOR RIGHT NOW.
I HAVE TO...
...CRY WHILE I CAN.
成田国際空港

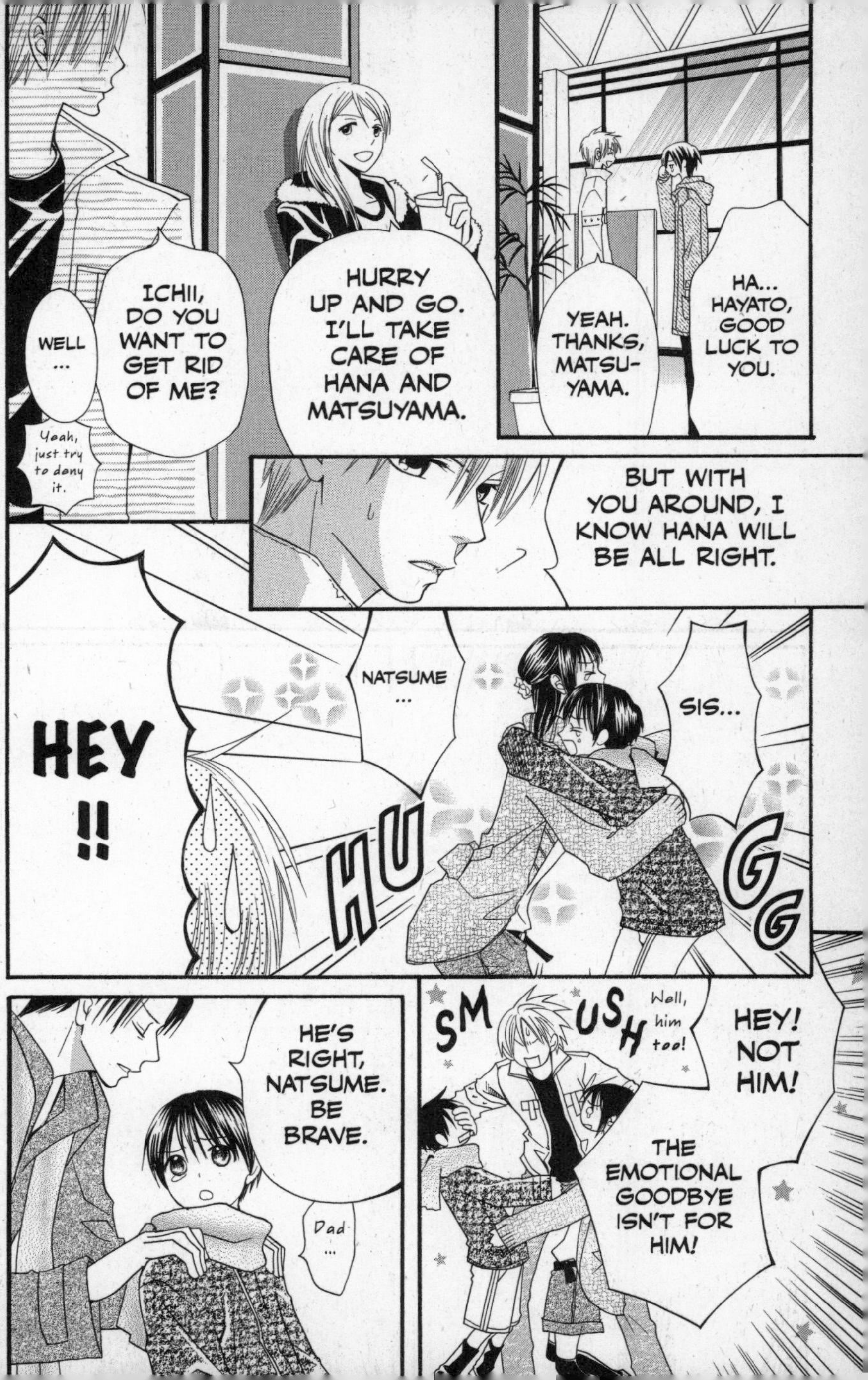
HA... HAYATO, GOOD LUCK TO YOU.
YEAH. THANKS, MATSUYAMA.
HURRY UP AND GO. I'LL TAKE CARE OF HANA AND MATSUYAMA.
ICHII, DO YOU WANT TO GET RID OF ME?
WELL ...
Yeah, just try to deny it.
BUT WITH YOU AROUND, I KNOW HANA WILL BE ALL RIGHT.
SIS...
NATSUME ...
HUGG
HEY !!
HEY! NOT HIM!
Well, him too!
SMUSH
THE EMOTIONAL GOODBYE ISN'T FOR HIM!
HE'S RIGHT, NATSUME. BE BRAVE.
Dad ...

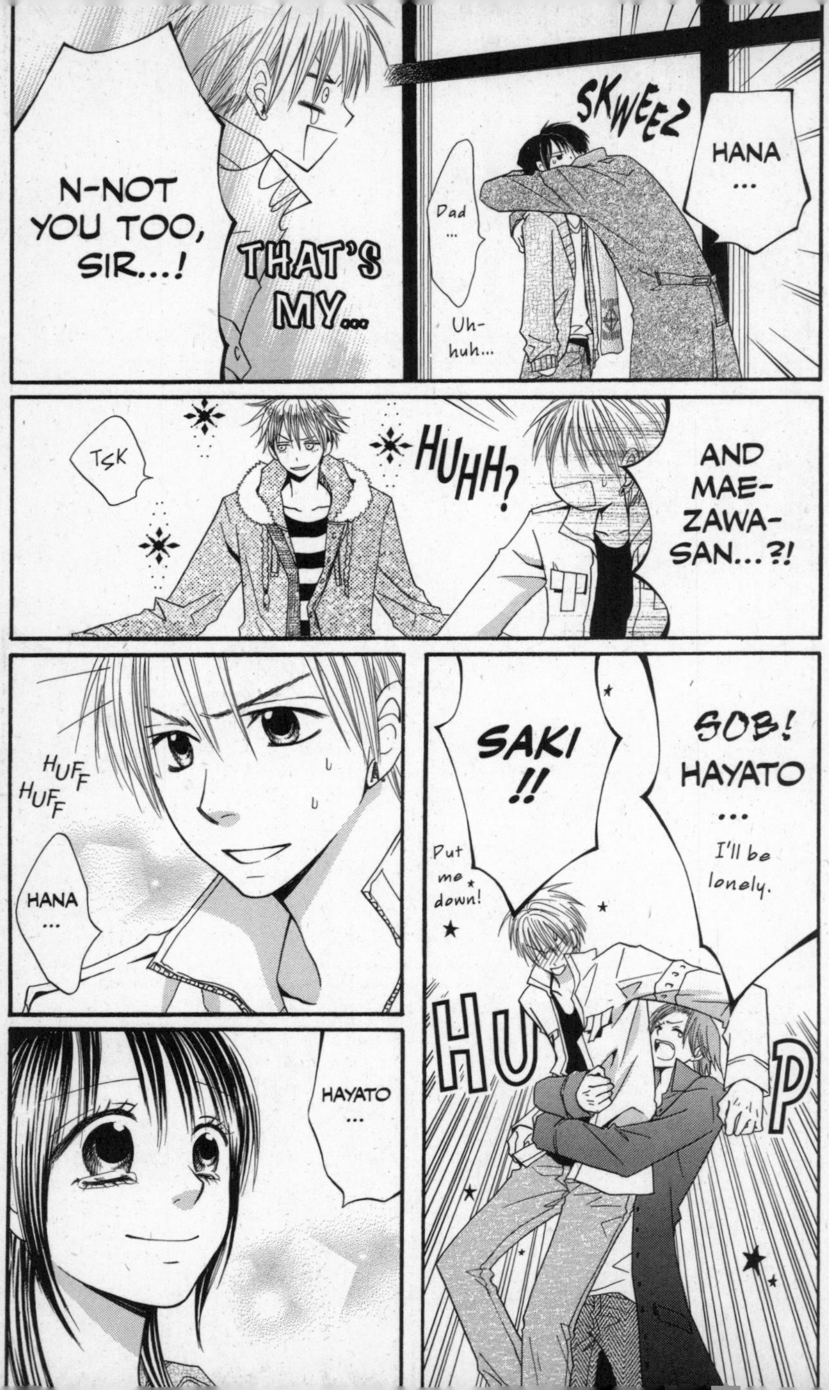
SKWEEZ
HANA ...
Dad ...
Uh-huh...
N-NOT YOU TOO, SIR...!
THAT'S MY...
AND MAE-ZAWA-SAN...?!
HUHH?
TSK
SOB! HAYATO ... I'll be lonely.
SAKI !!
Put me down!
HUP
HUFF HUFF
HANA ...
HAYATO ...

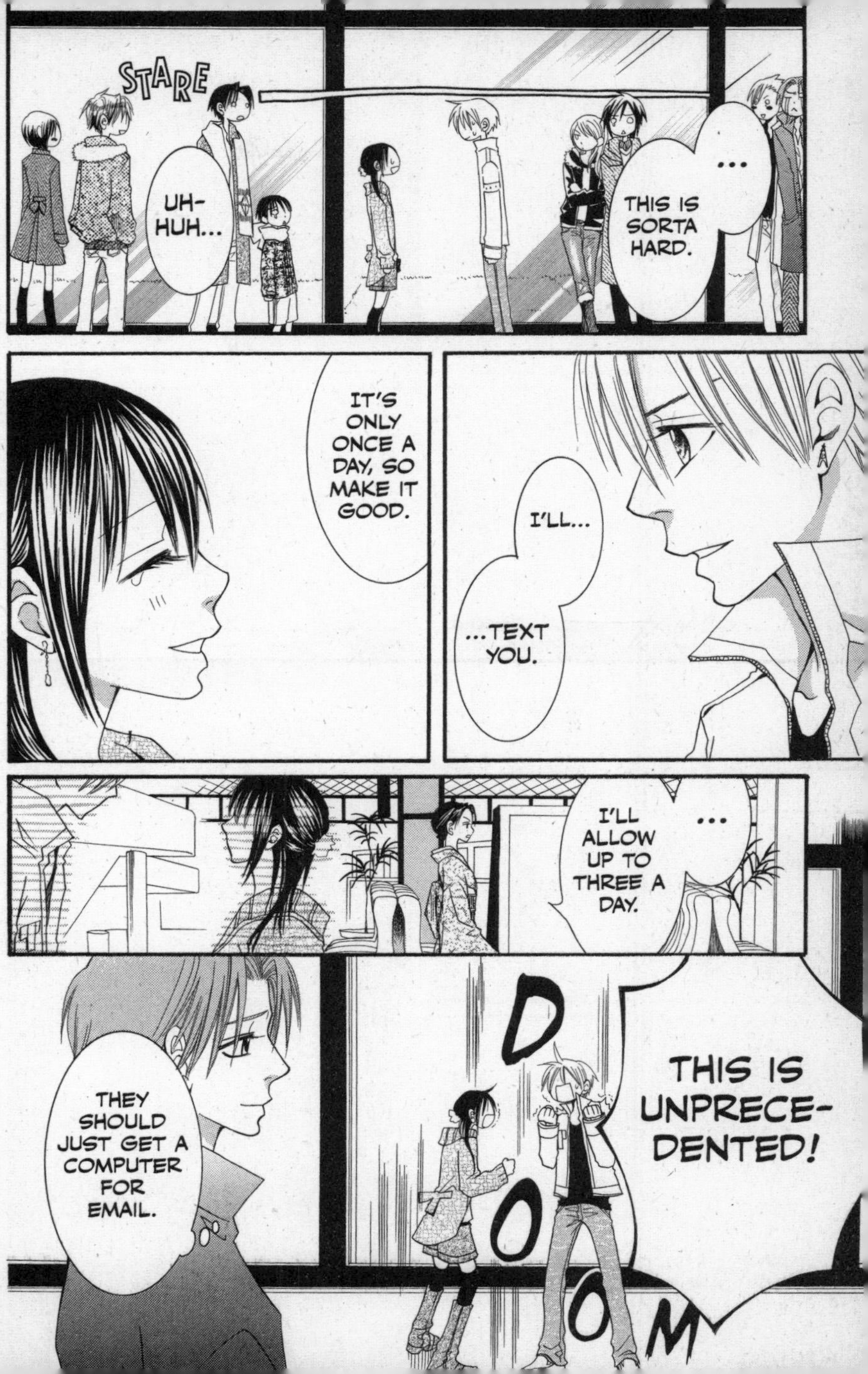
...
THIS IS SORTA HARD.
STARE
UH-HUH...
I'LL...
...TEXT YOU.
IT'S ONLY ONCE A DAY, SO MAKE IT GOOD.
...
I'LL ALLOW UP TO THREE A DAY.
DOOM
THIS IS UNPRECE-DENTED!
THEY SHOULD JUST GET A COMPUTER FOR EMAIL.

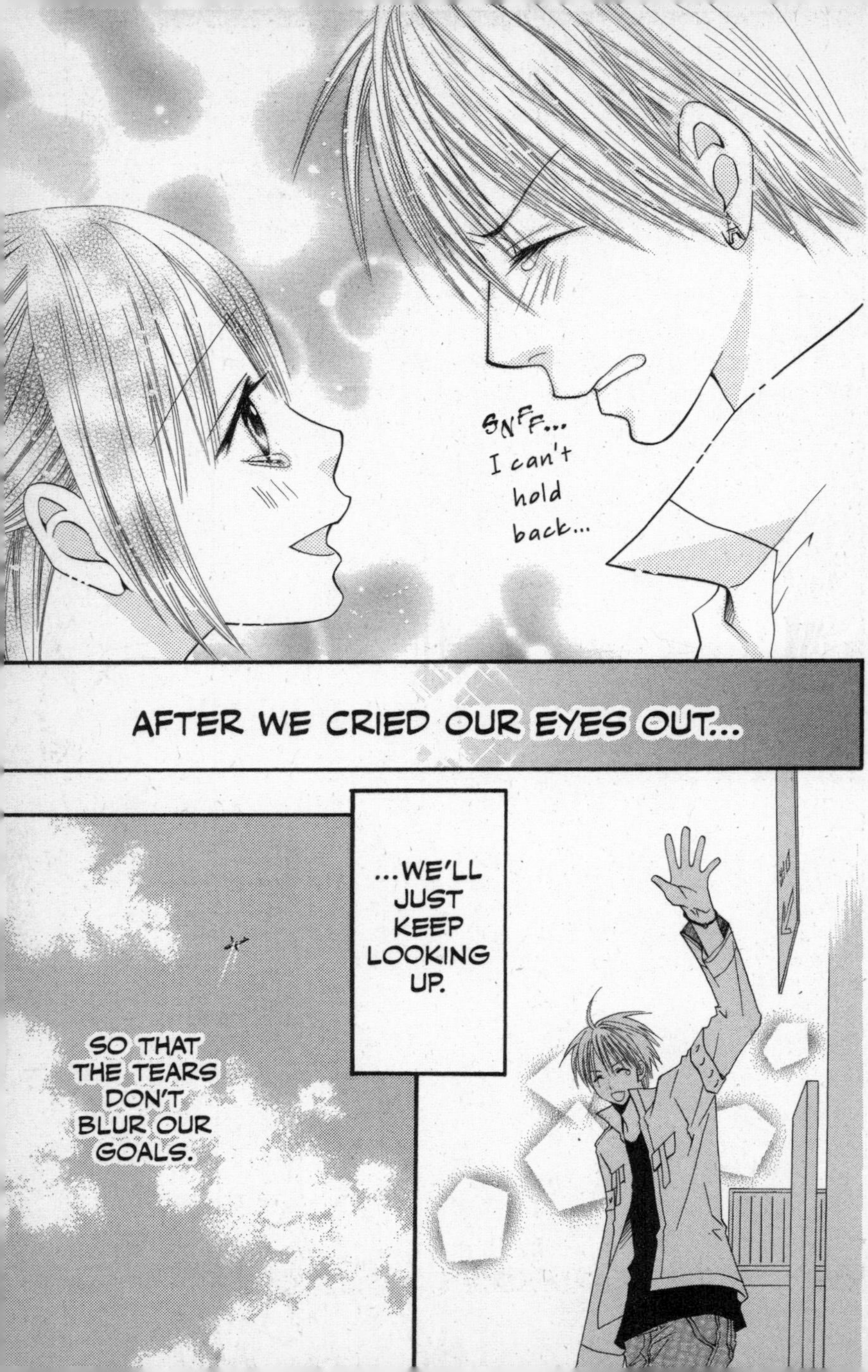
SNFF... I can't hold back...
AFTER WE CRIED OUR EYES OUT...
...WE'LL JUST KEEP LOOKING UP.
SO THAT THE TEARS DON'T BLUR OUR GOALS.

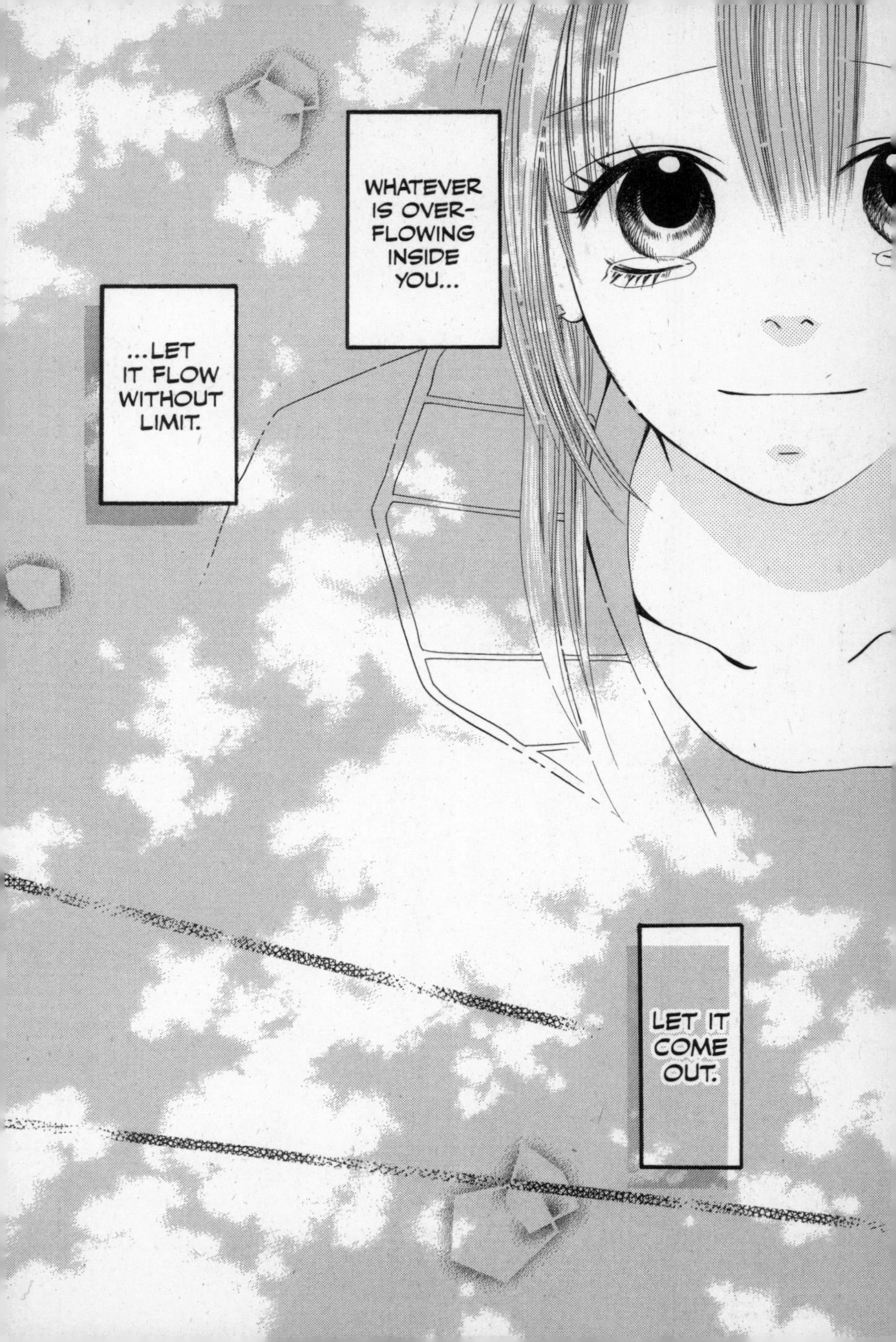
WHATEVER IS OVER-FLOWING INSIDE YOU...
...LET IT FLOW WITHOUT LIMIT.
LET IT COME OUT.

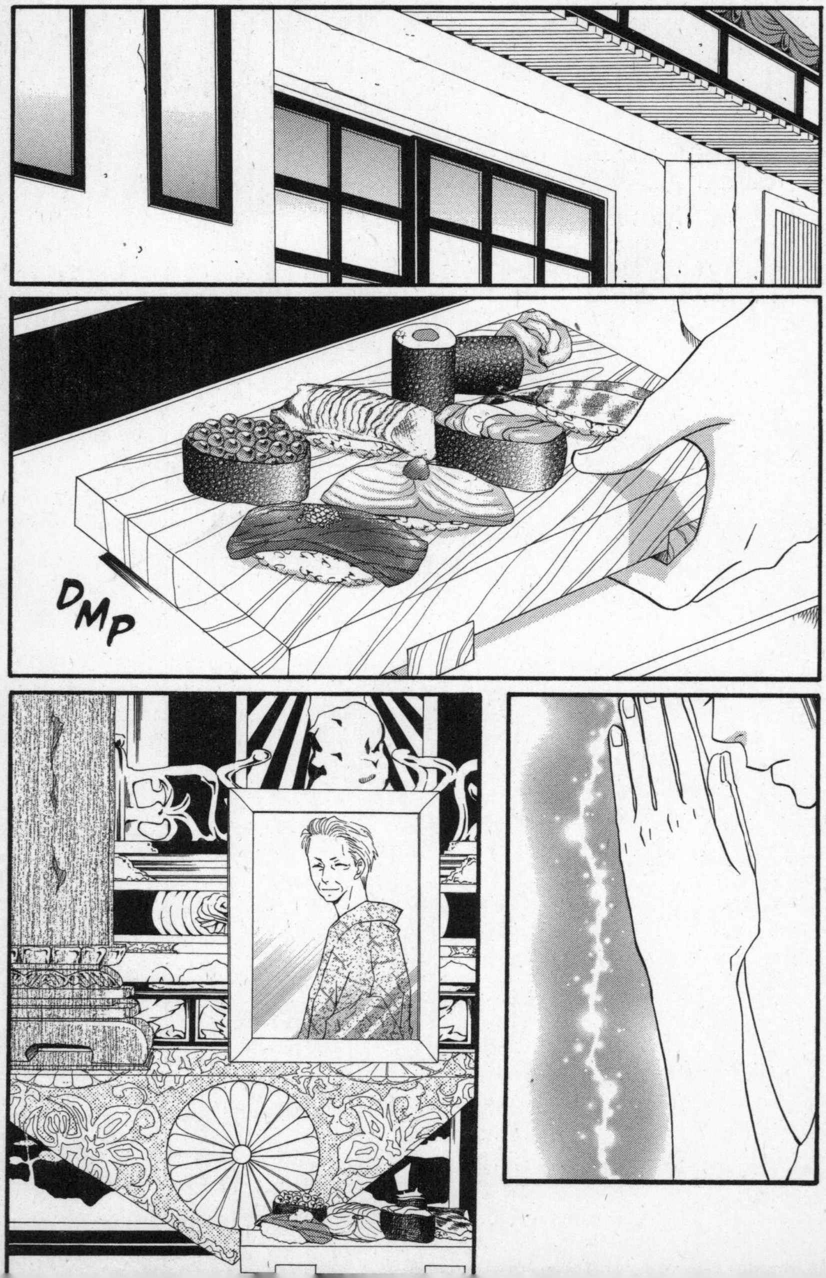
DMP

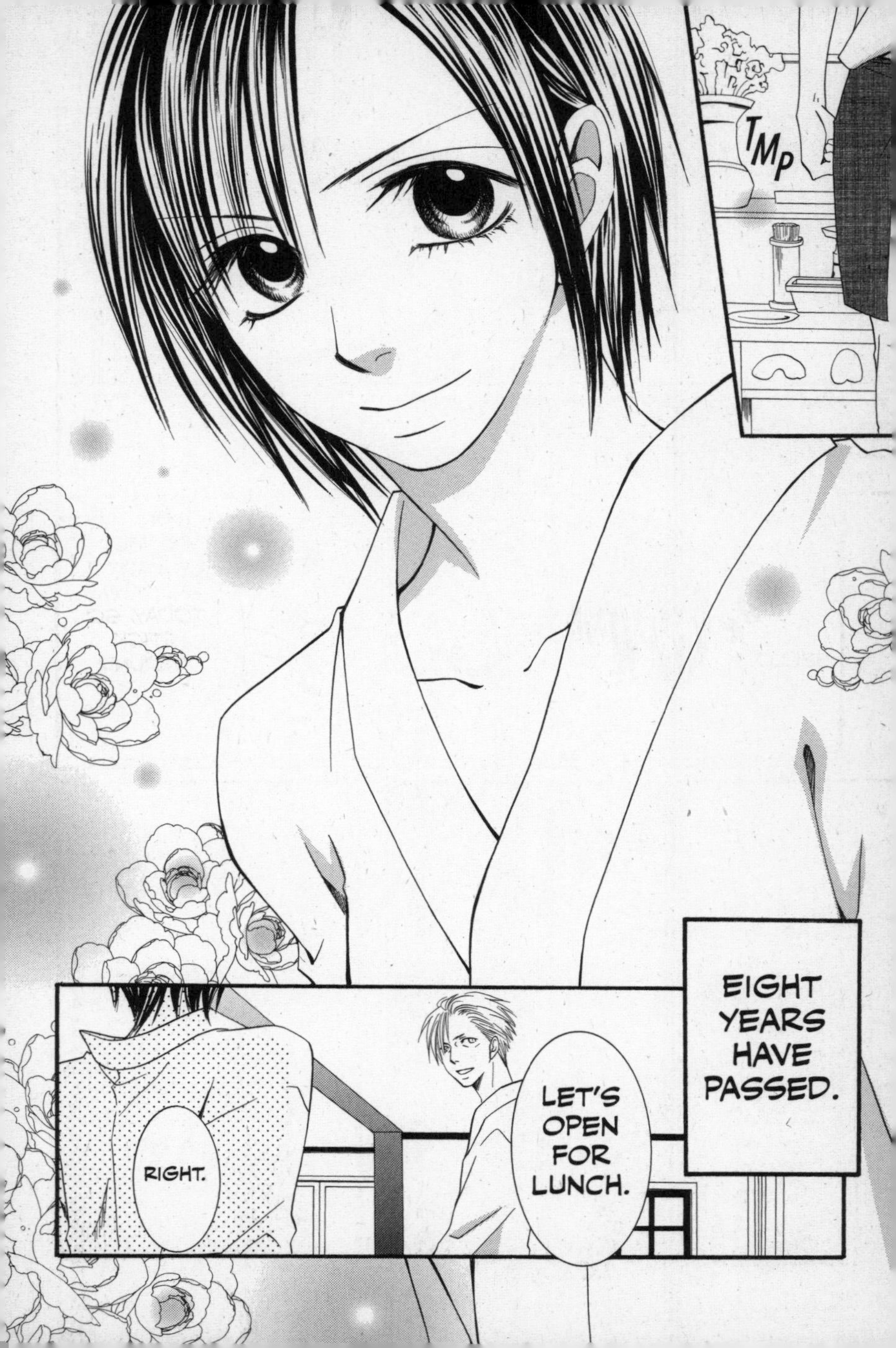
TMP
EIGHT YEARS HAVE PASSED.
LET'S OPEN FOR LUNCH.
RIGHT.

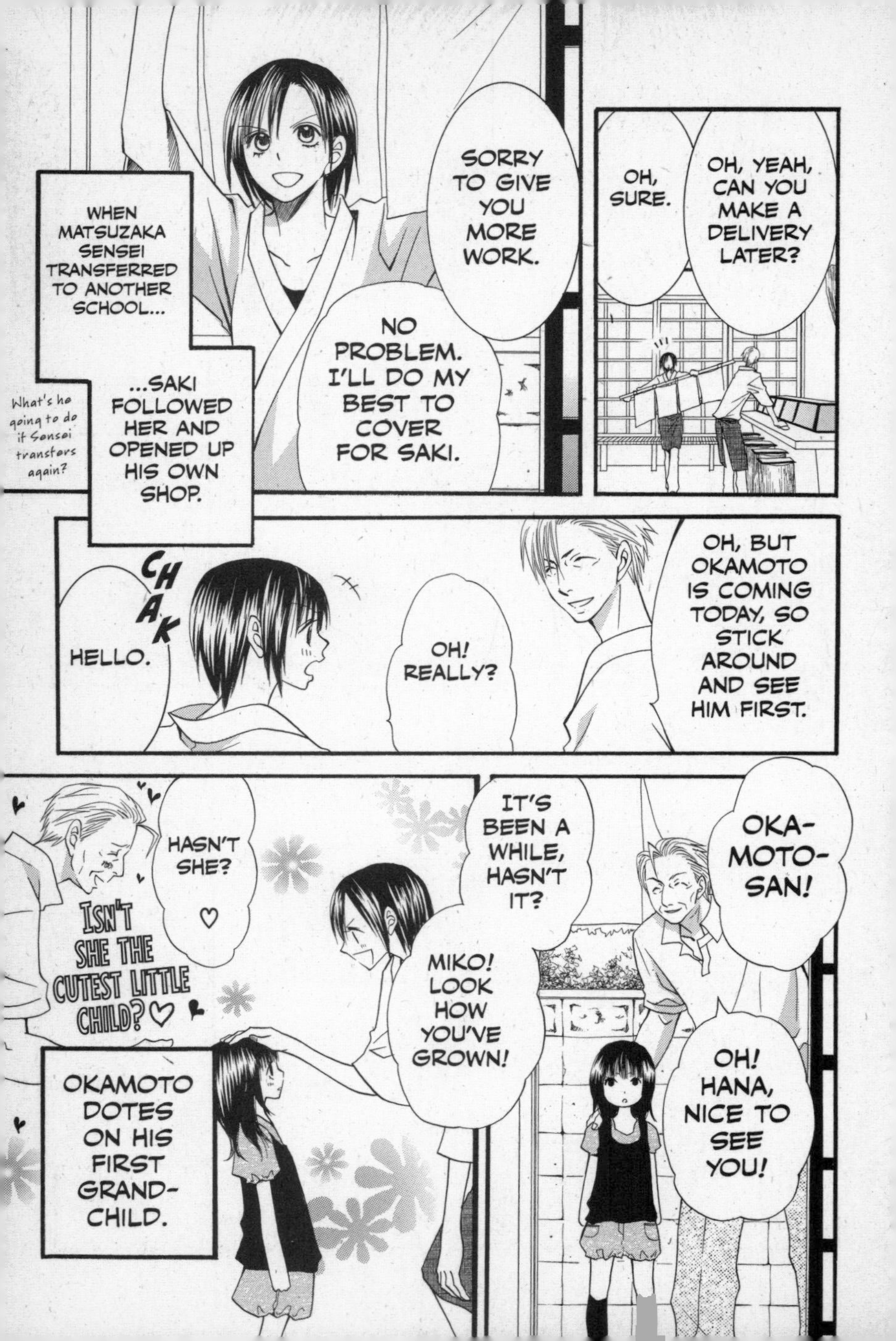
OH, YEAH, CAN YOU MAKE A DELIVERY LATER?
OH, SURE.
SORRY TO GIVE YOU MORE WORK.
WHEN MATSUZAKA SENSEI TRANSFERRED TO ANOTHER SCHOOL...
NO PROBLEM. I'LL DO MY BEST TO COVER FOR SAKI.
...SAKI FOLLOWED HER AND OPENED UP HIS OWN SHOP.
What's he going to do if Sensei transfers again?
OH, BUT OKAMOTO IS COMING TODAY, SO STICK AROUND AND SEE HIM FIRST.
OH! REALLY?
CHAK
HELLO.
OKA-MOTO-SAN!
IT'S BEEN A WHILE, HASN'T IT?
OH! HANA, NICE TO SEE YOU!
MIKO! LOOK HOW YOU'VE GROWN!
HASN'T SHE? ♡
ISN'T SHE THE CUTEST LITTLE CHILD? ♡
OKAMOTO DOTES ON HIS FIRST GRAND-CHILD.

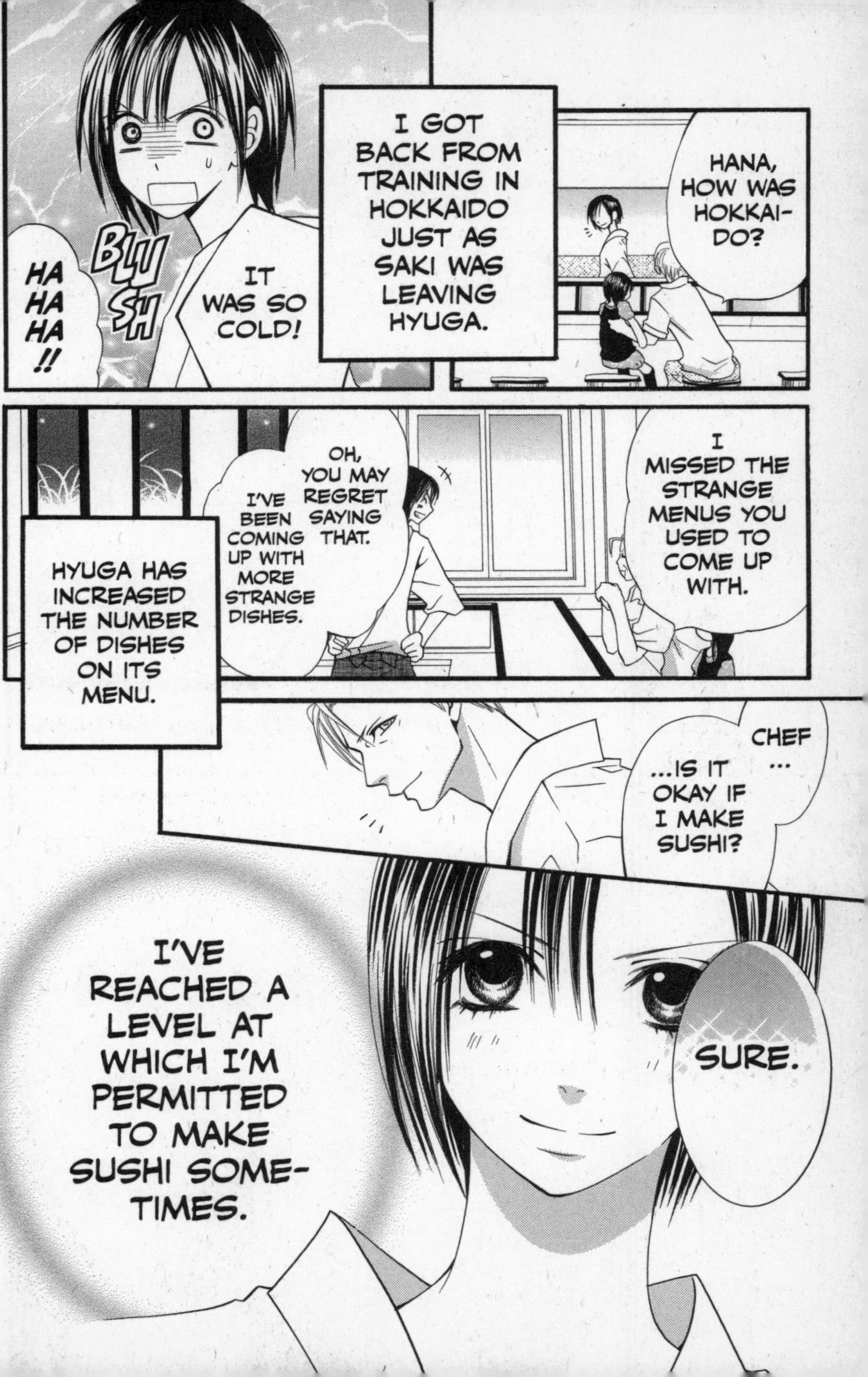
HANA, HOW WAS HOKKAIDO?
I GOT BACK FROM TRAINING IN HOKKAIDO JUST AS SAKI WAS LEAVING HYUGA.
IT WAS SO COLD!
BLUSH
HA HA HA!!
I MISSED THE STRANGE MENUS YOU USED TO COME UP WITH.
OH, YOU MAY REGRET SAYING THAT.
I'VE BEEN COMING UP WITH MORE STRANGE DISHES.
HYUGA HAS INCREASED THE NUMBER OF DISHES ON ITS MENU.
CHEF ...
...IS IT OKAY IF I MAKE SUSHI?
SURE.
I'VE REACHED A LEVEL AT WHICH I'M PERMITTED TO MAKE SUSHI SOMETIMES.

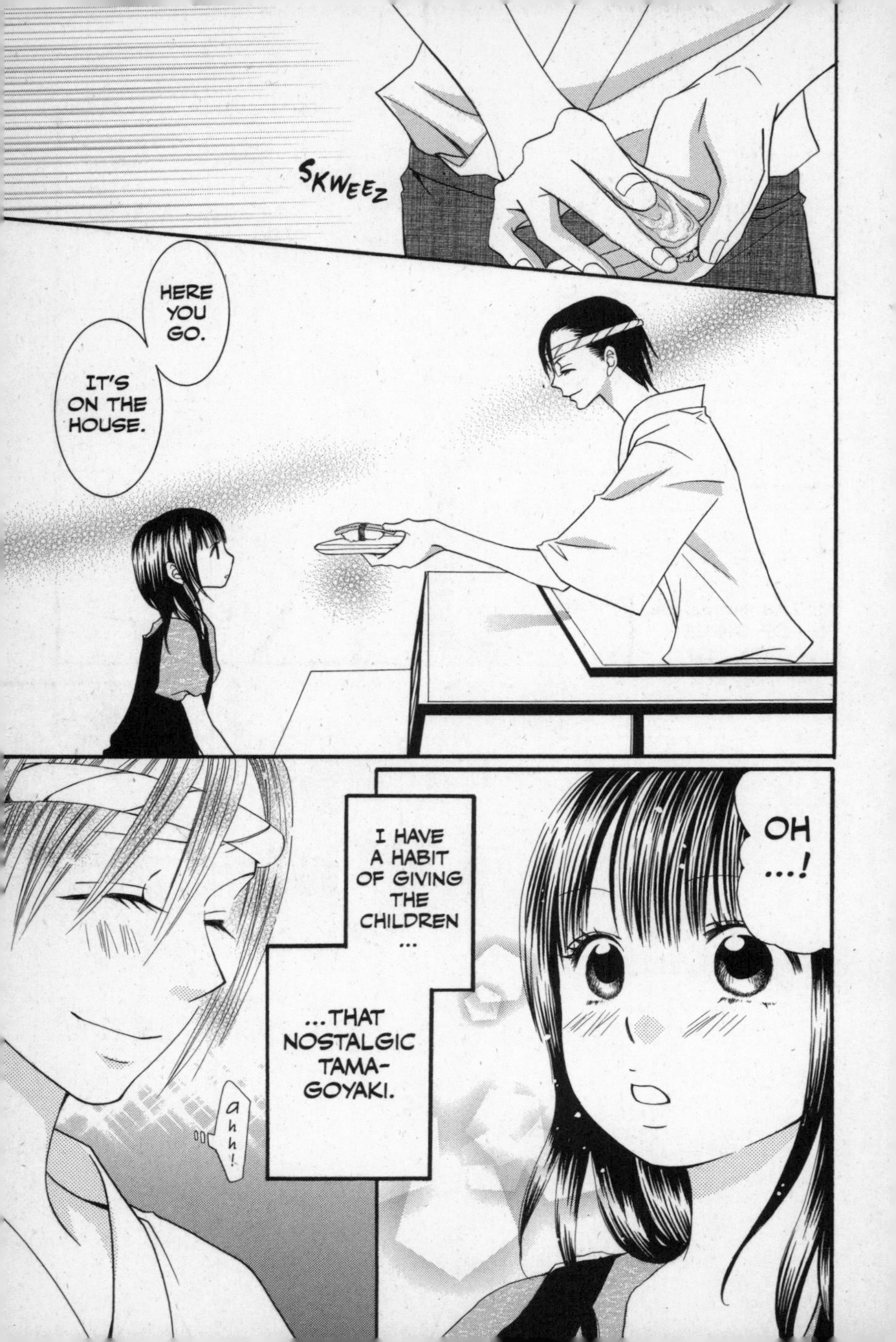
SKWEEZ
HERE YOU GO.
IT'S ON THE HOUSE.
OH ...!
I HAVE A HABIT OF GIVING THE CHILDREN ...
...THAT NOSTALGIC TAMA-GOYAKI.
ahh!

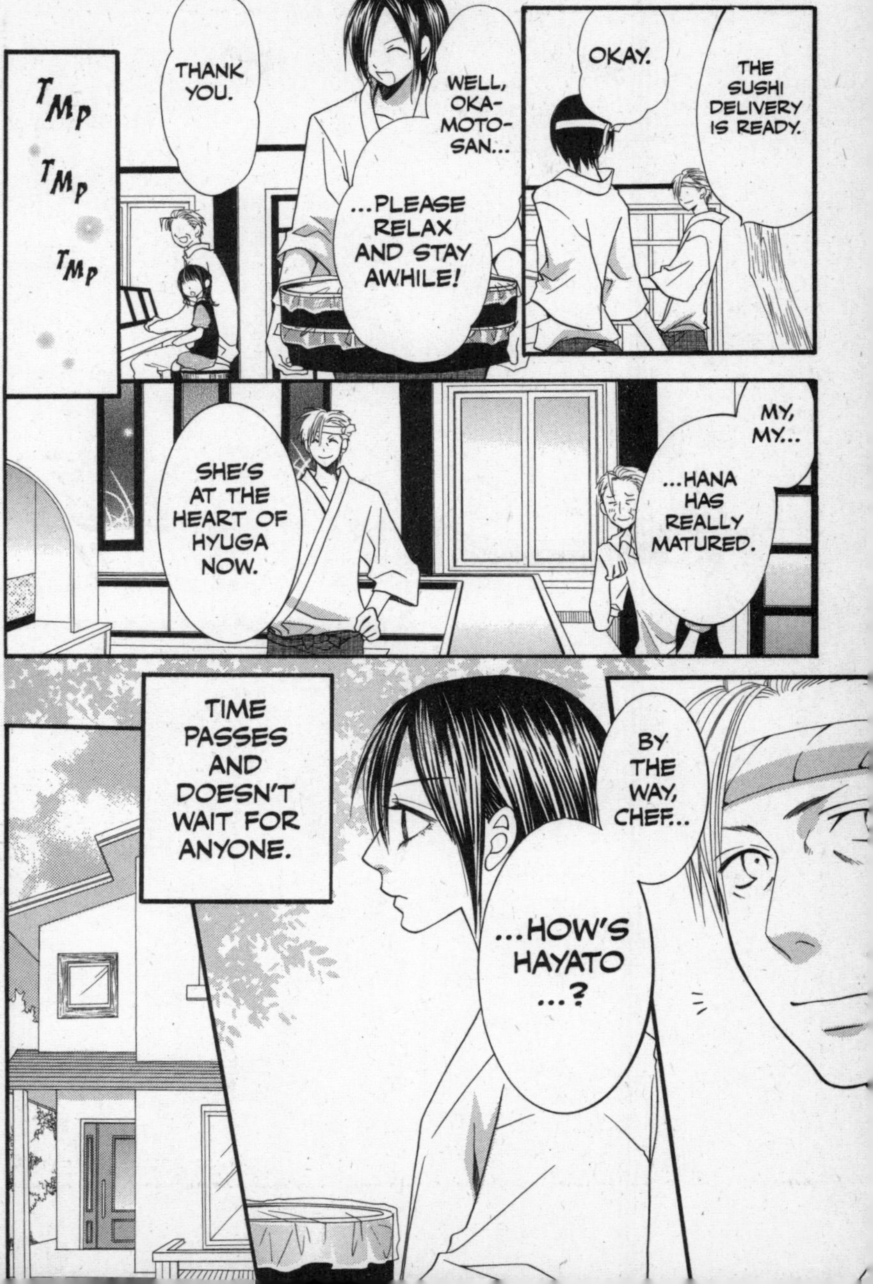
THE SUSHI DELIVERY IS READY.
OKAY.
WELL, OKA-MOTO-SAN...
...PLEASE RELAX AND STAY AWHILE!
THANK YOU.
TMP
TMP
TMP
MY, MY...
...HANA HAS REALLY MATURED.
SHE'S AT THE HEART OF HYUGA NOW.
BY THE WAY, CHEF...
...HOW'S HAYATO ...?
TIME PASSES AND DOESN'T WAIT FOR ANYONE.

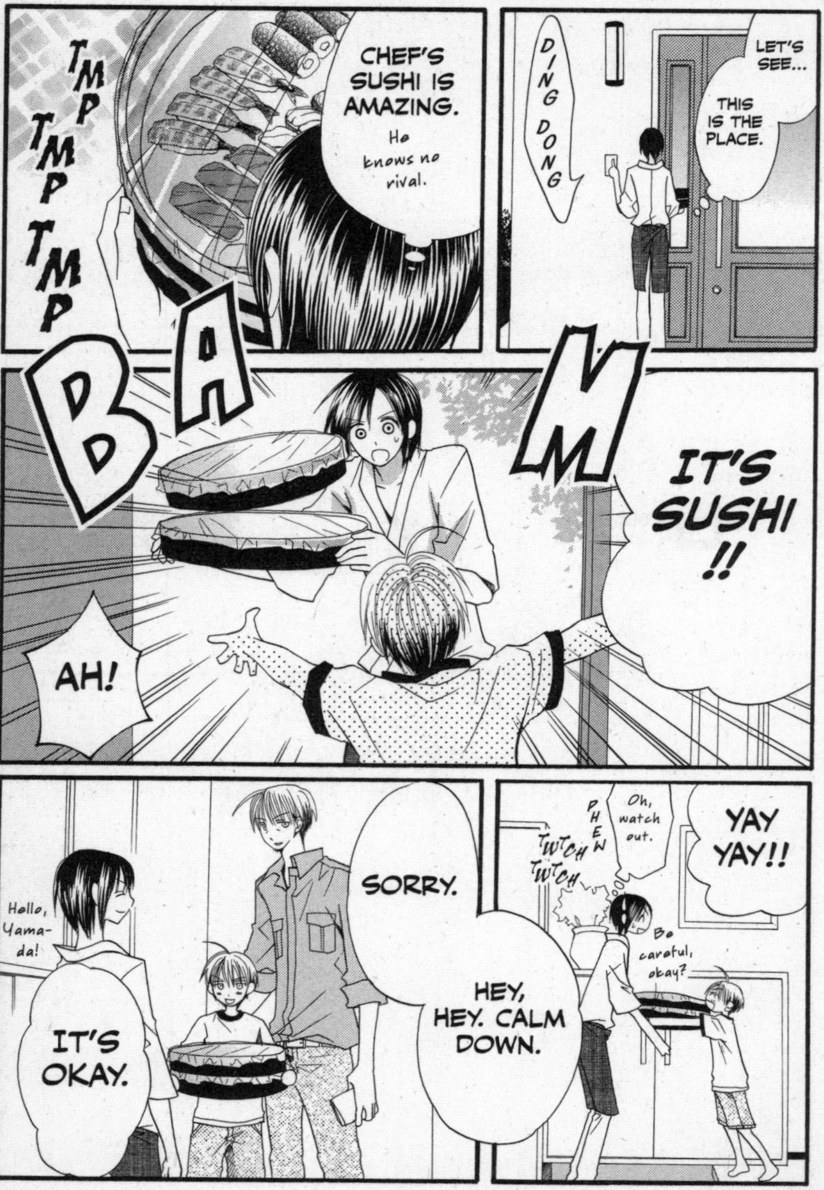
DING DONG
LET'S SEE...
THIS IS THE PLACE.
TMP TMP TMP TMP
CHEF'S SUSHI IS AMAZING.
He knows no rival.
BAM
IT'S SUSHI!!
AH!
YAY YAY!!
Oh, watch out.
PHEW
TWITCH TWITCH
Be careful, okay?
SORRY.
HEY, HEY. CALM DOWN.
Hello, Yamada!
IT'S OKAY.

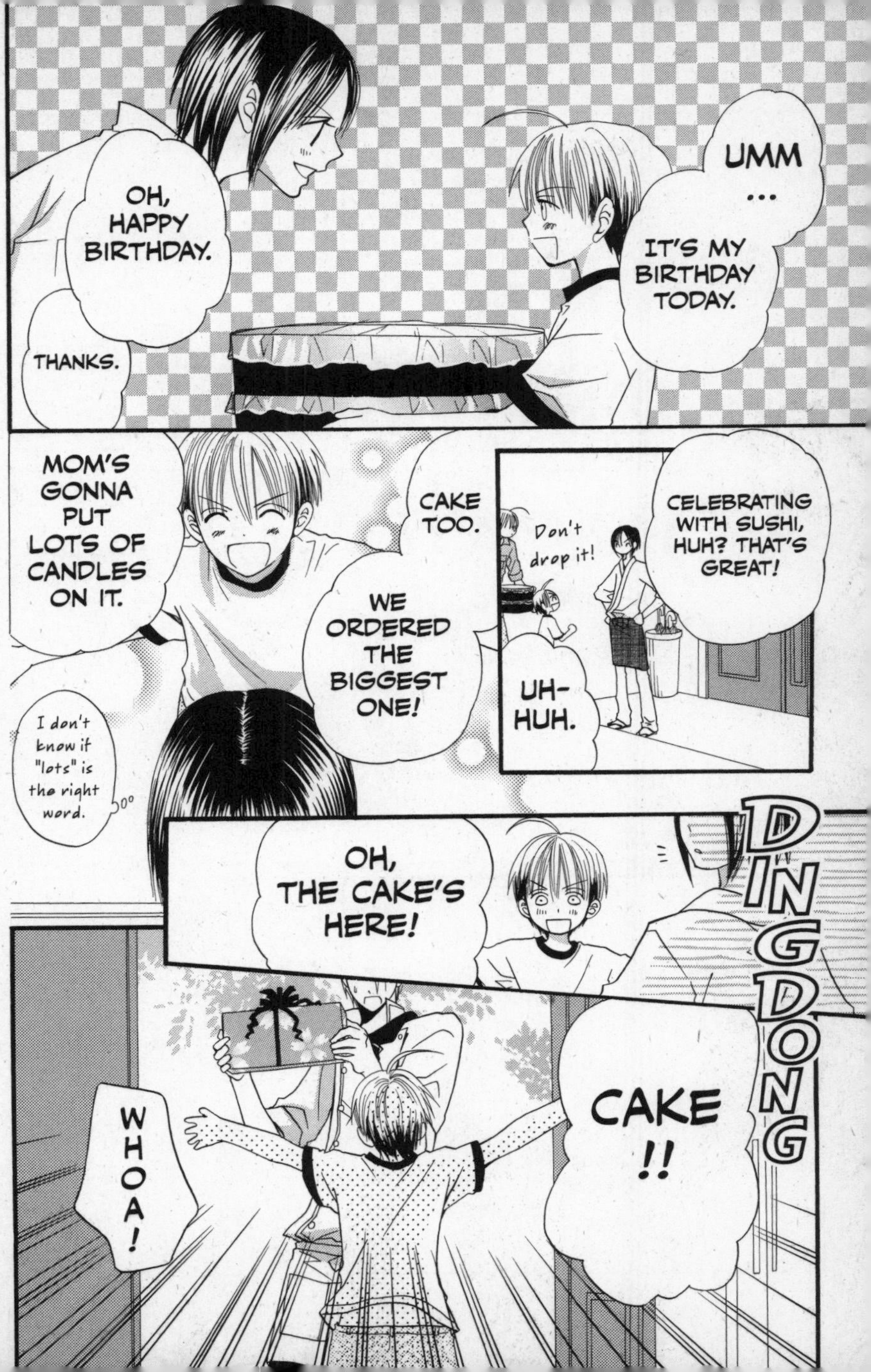
UMM ...
IT'S MY BIRTHDAY TODAY.
OH, HAPPY BIRTHDAY.
THANKS.
CELEBRATING WITH SUSHI, HUH? THAT'S GREAT!
Don't drop it!
UH-HUH.
CAKE TOO.
WE ORDERED THE BIGGEST ONE!
MOM'S GONNA PUT LOTS OF CANDLES ON IT.
I don't know if "lots" is the right word.
DING DONG
OH, THE CAKE'S HERE!
CAKE !!
WHOA!

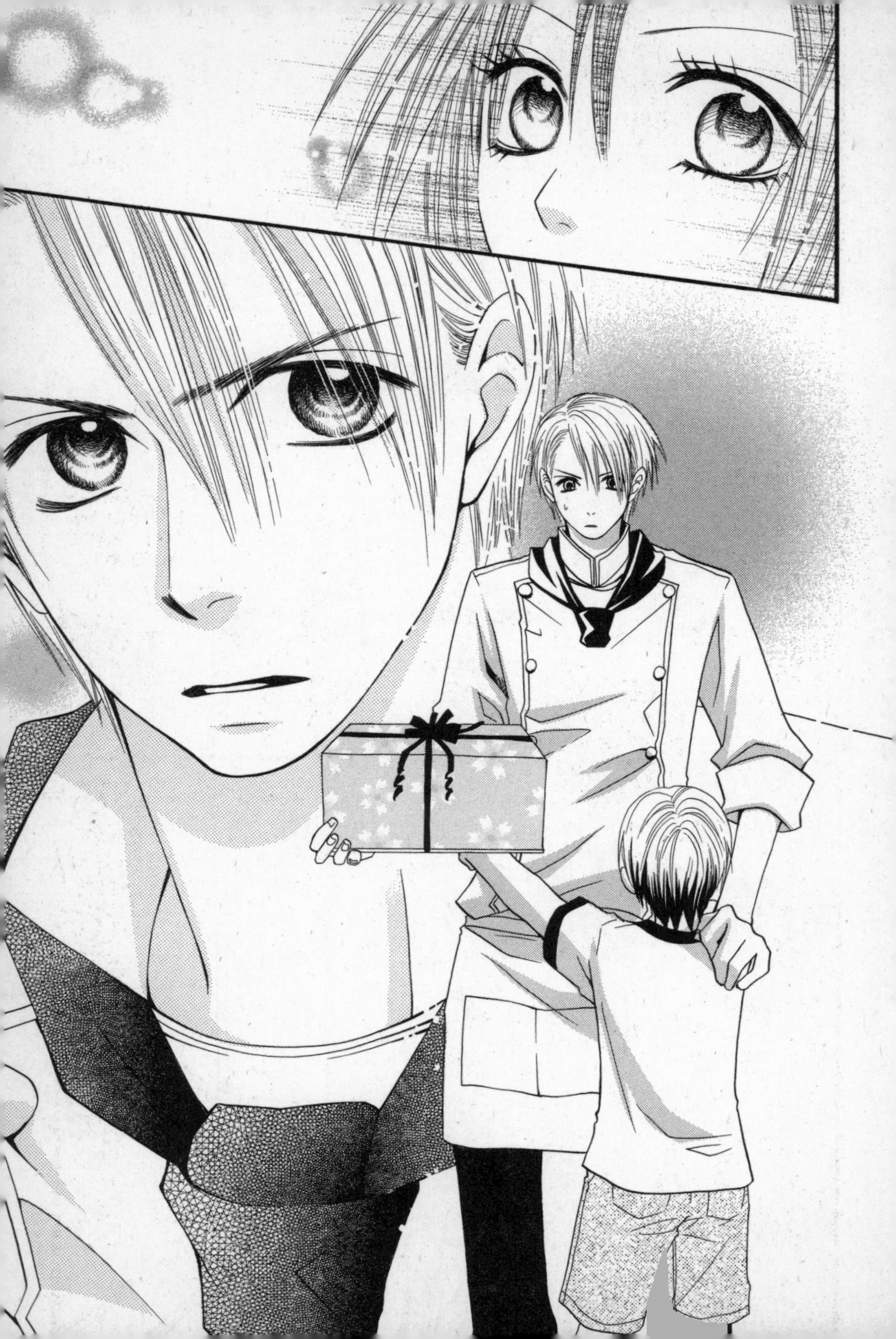

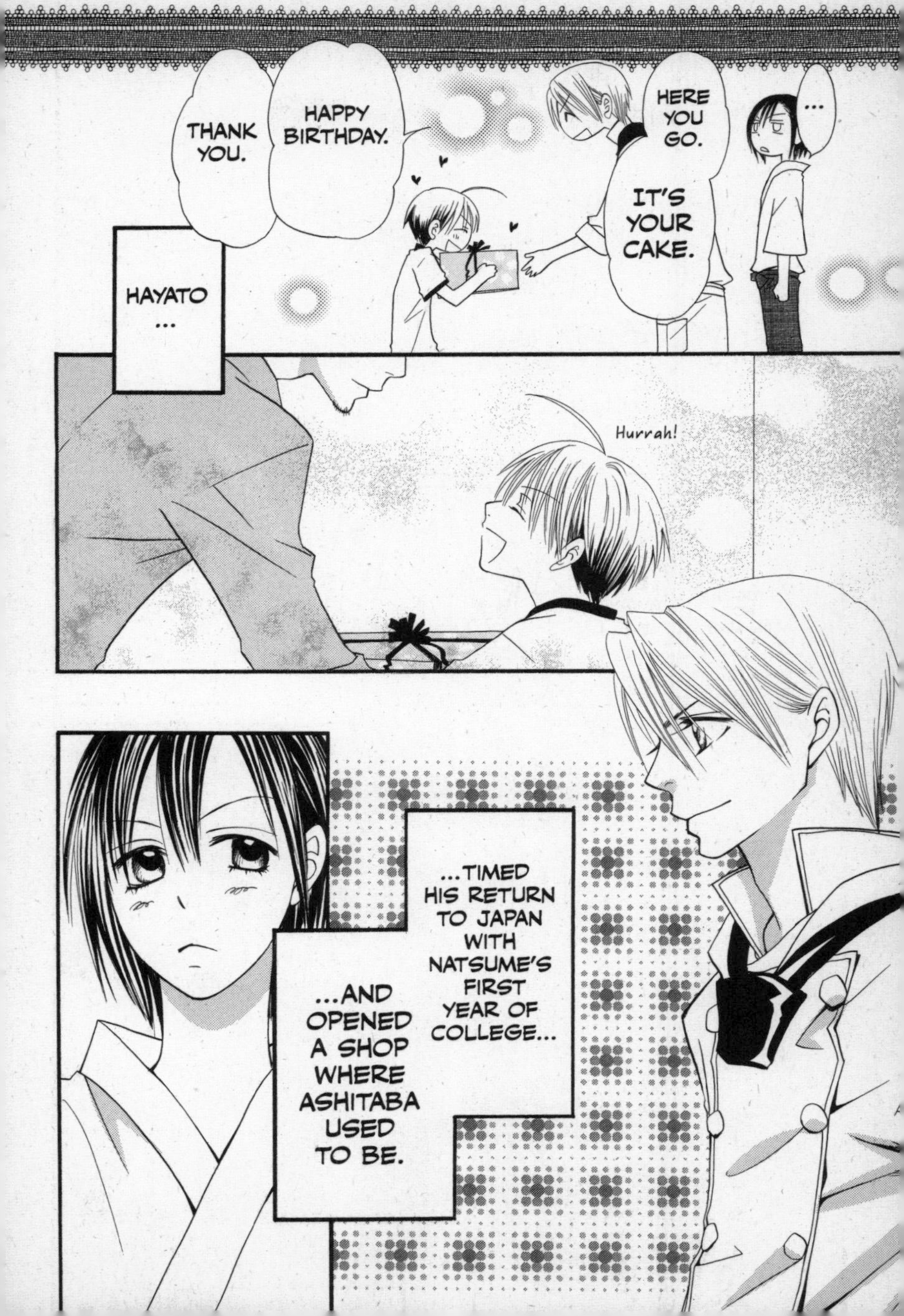
...
HERE YOU GO.
IT'S YOUR CAKE.
HAPPY BIRTHDAY.
THANK YOU.
HAYATO ...
Hurrah!
...TIMED HIS RETURN TO JAPAN WITH NATSUME'S FIRST YEAR OF COLLEGE...
...AND OPENED A SHOP WHERE ASHITABA USED TO BE.

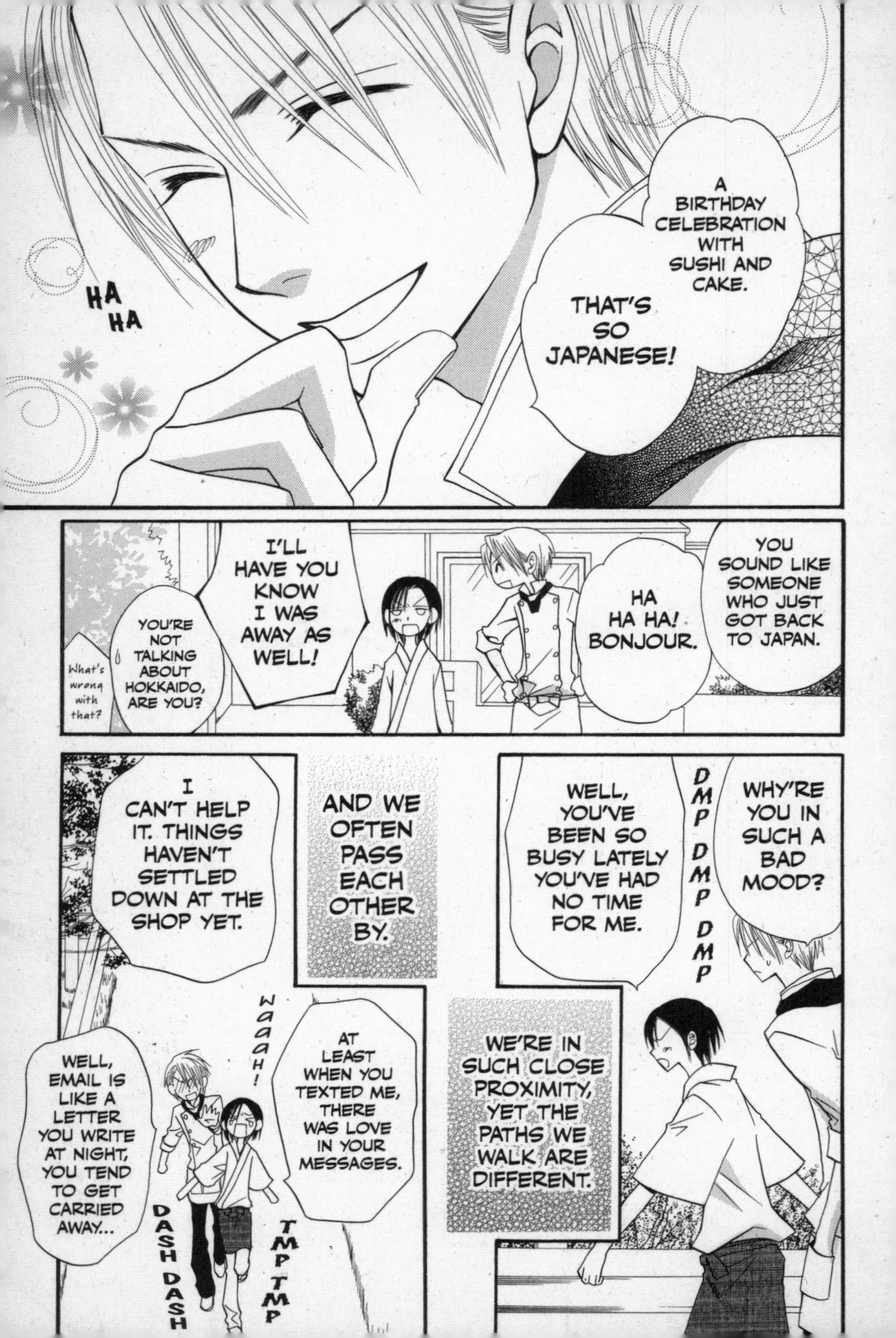
A BIRTHDAY CELEBRATION WITH SUSHI AND CAKE.
THAT'S SO JAPANESE!
HA HA
YOU SOUND LIKE SOMEONE WHO JUST GOT BACK TO JAPAN.
HA HA HA! BONJOUR.
I'LL HAVE YOU KNOW I WAS AWAY AS WELL!
YOU'RE NOT TALKING ABOUT HOKKAIDO, ARE YOU?
What's wrong with that?
WHY'RE YOU IN SUCH A BAD MOOD?
DMP DMP DMP DMP
WELL, YOU'VE BEEN SO BUSY LATELY YOU'VE HAD NO TIME FOR ME.
WE'RE IN SUCH CLOSE PROXIMITY, YET THE PATHS WE WALK ARE DIFFERENT.
AND WE OFTEN PASS EACH OTHER BY.
I CAN'T HELP IT. THINGS HAVEN'T SETTLED DOWN AT THE SHOP YET.
AT LEAST WHEN YOU TEXTED ME, THERE WAS LOVE IN YOUR MESSAGES.
Waaaah!
TMP TMP
WELL, EMAIL IS LIKE A LETTER YOU WRITE AT NIGHT, YOU TEND TO GET CARRIED AWAY...
DASH DASH

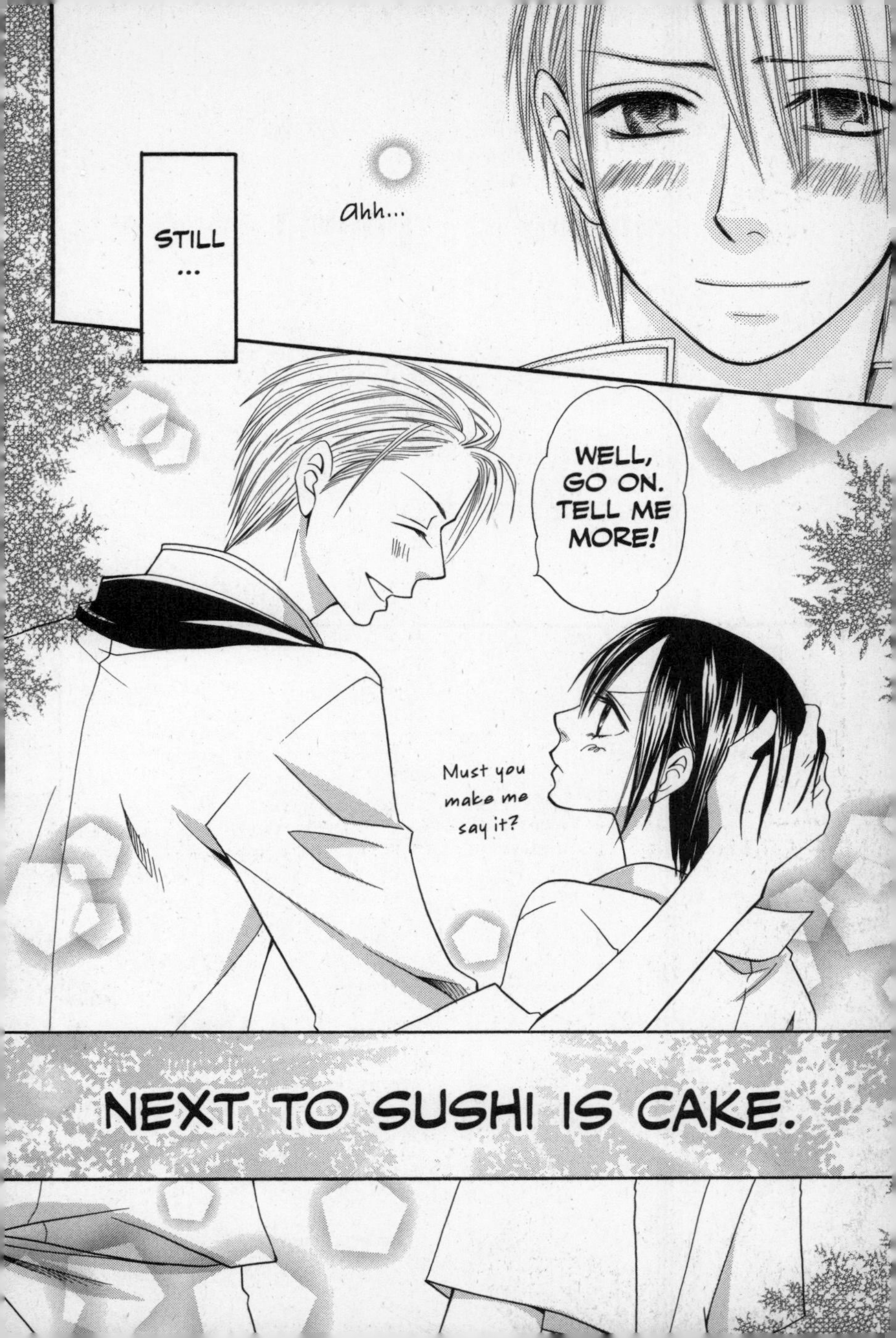
ahh...
STILL...
WELL, GO ON. TELL ME MORE!
Must you make me say it?
NEXT TO SUSHI IS CAKE.

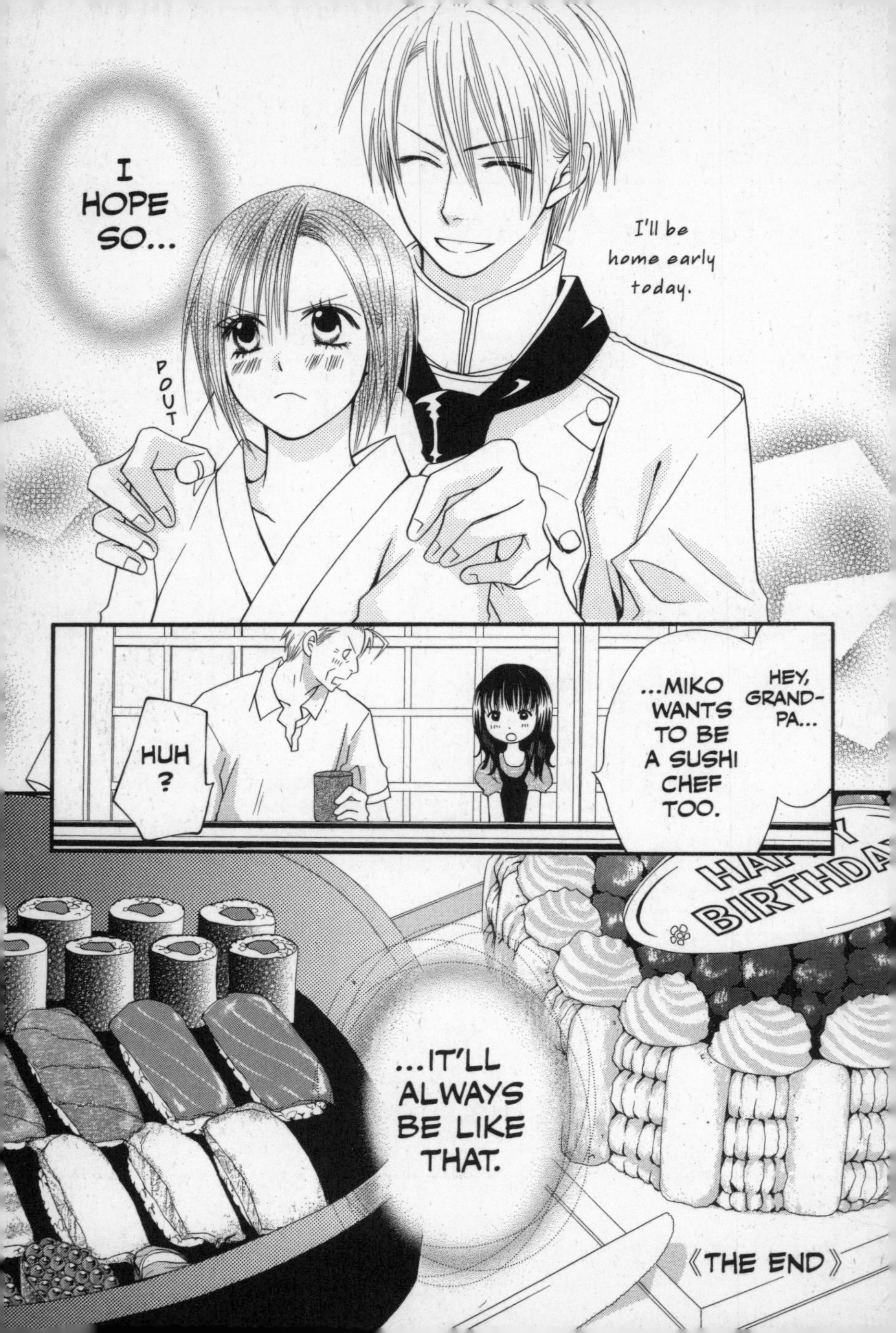
I'll be home early today.
I HOPE SO...
POUT
HEY, GRANDPA...
...MIKO WANTS TO BE A SUSHI CHEF TOO.
HUH?
...IT'LL ALWAYS BE LIKE THAT.
《THE END》

MIXED VEGETABLES Encyclopedia of Characters

KEIGO MAEZAWA

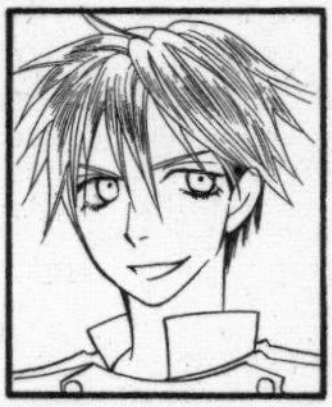

MAEZAWA → MAEZAWA BEEF

KEIGO MEANS "HONORIFIC LANGUAGE," AND SINCE I WAS TOLD TO USE POLITE SPEECH, I CHOSE KEIGO. ACTUALLY, MAEZAWA WAS NOT IN MY PLANS. A CHARACTER WHO MAKES HAYATO NERVOUS... THAT COULD'VE BEEN PLAYED BY ANYONE. (THAT'S WHY I CREATED THAT CLASSMATE WITH THE POINTY HAIR.)

HIS EYES ARE TINGED WITH GREEN, AND HE HAS THICK, CURLY EYELASHES AND BUSHY EYEBROWS. HE'S EXTREMELY VISUAL. WHEN MAEZAWA'S FIRST NAME HADN'T BEEN PICKED YET, I REFERRED TO HIM AS "MEDIUM MAEZAWA" AND THOUGHT "MEDIUM" SOUNDED SORT OF FOREIGN. BUT HE'S SO ATTRACTIVE THAT IT MADE SENSE TO ME... THE ARTIST WHO WORKS WITH VARIOUS MEDIUMS... ANYWAY, I WANTED TO CREATE SOMEONE WHO WOULD MAKE PEOPLE SAY, "HE'S SO AWFUL!" AND YOU EITHER LOVE HIM OR YOU HATE HIM. BUT IT WAS FUN DRAWING HIM.

SHIO MAEZAWA

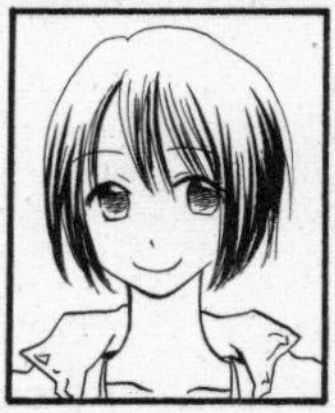

SHIO → SALT

GOOD MEAT TASTES BEST WITH A TOUCH OF SALT! MAEZAWA BEEF WITH SALT!

I MODELED HER AFTER SOMEONE, BUT THERE'S NO RESEMBLANCE. ANYWAY, SHE HAS A SMALL FACE; THAT'S HOW I PLANNED HER.

AS FOR HER PERSONALITY, I THOUGHT ABOUT WHO WOULD MARRY SOMEONE LIKE MAEZAWA AND CAME UP WITH HER.

ANIS-SAN

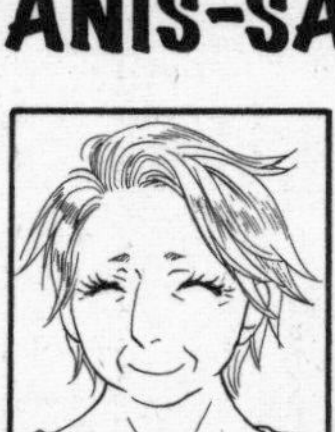

ANIS → THE SPICE ANISE

THE HAIRSTYLE AND HAIR TYPE IS JUST LIKE MAEZAWA'S. THE COLORING, TOO. THE IMAGE IS ONE OF A PLUMP FOREIGN WOMAN.

OKAMOTO FAMILY

THE EXCEPTION TO THE FOOD-NAMING RULE IS THE OKAMOTO FAMILY. I GOT THEIR NAMES FROM A LOCAL KYUSHU TELEVISION PROGRAM THAT I LOVE. IF YOU'RE NOT FROM KYUSHU, PLEASE CHECK IT OUT ON THE INTERNET.

IT'S CALLED "DUOMO." (DOO-MO)

...I hope I don't get scolded for that little advertisement!

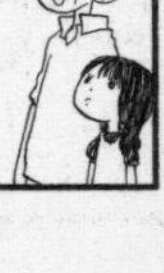

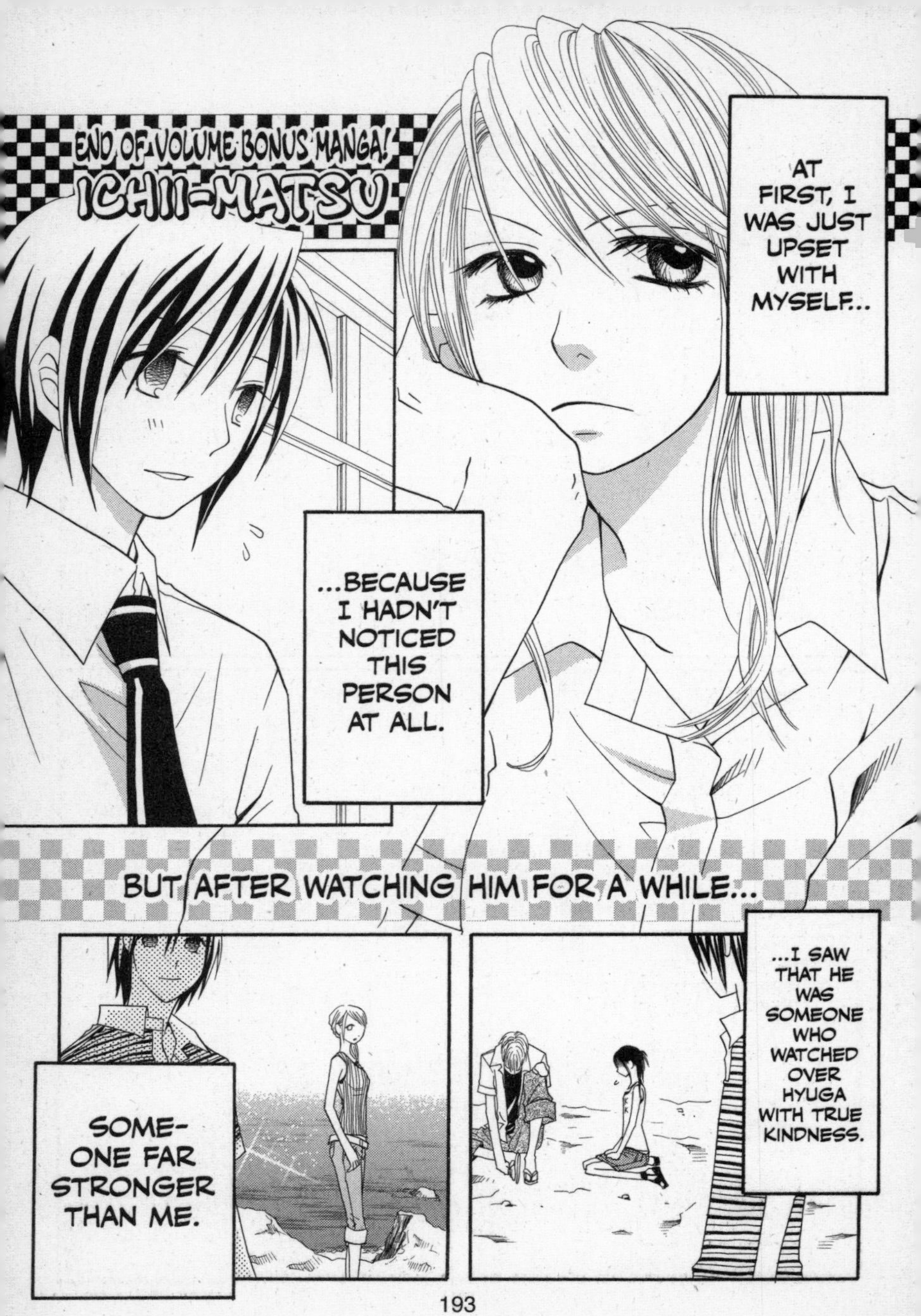
END OF VOLUME BONUS MANGA!
ICHII-MATSU
AT FIRST, I WAS JUST UPSET WITH MYSELF...
...BECAUSE I HADN'T NOTICED THIS PERSON AT ALL.
BUT AFTER WATCHING HIM FOR A WHILE...
...I SAW THAT HE WAS SOMEONE WHO WATCHED OVER HYUGA WITH TRUE KINDNESS.
SOME-ONE FAR STRONGER THAN ME.

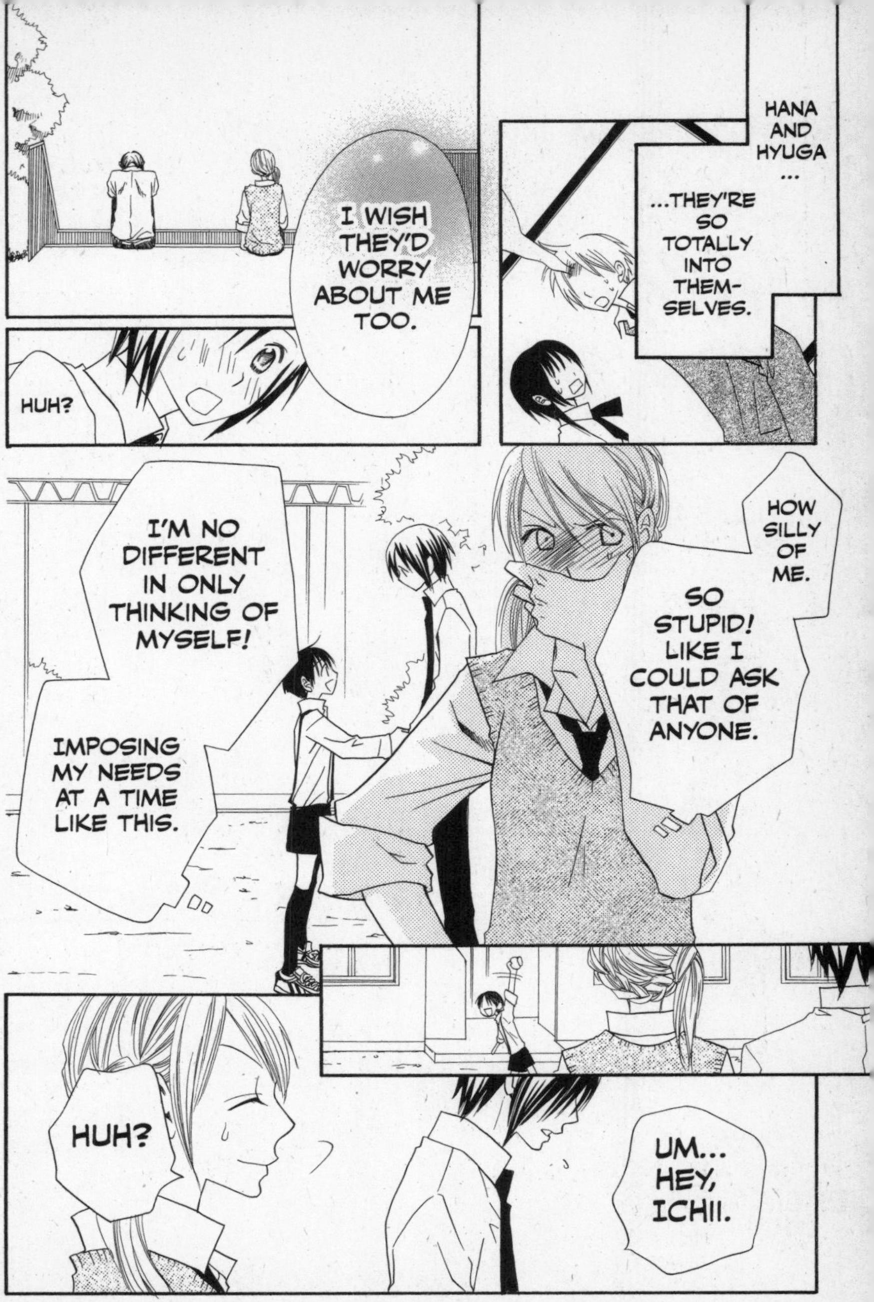
HANA AND HYUGA ...
...THEY'RE SO TOTALLY INTO THEM-SELVES.
I WISH THEY'D WORRY ABOUT ME TOO.
HUH?
HOW SILLY OF ME.
SO STUPID! LIKE I COULD ASK THAT OF ANYONE.
I'M NO DIFFERENT IN ONLY THINKING OF MYSELF!
IMPOSING MY NEEDS AT A TIME LIKE THIS.
UM... HEY, ICHII.
HUH?

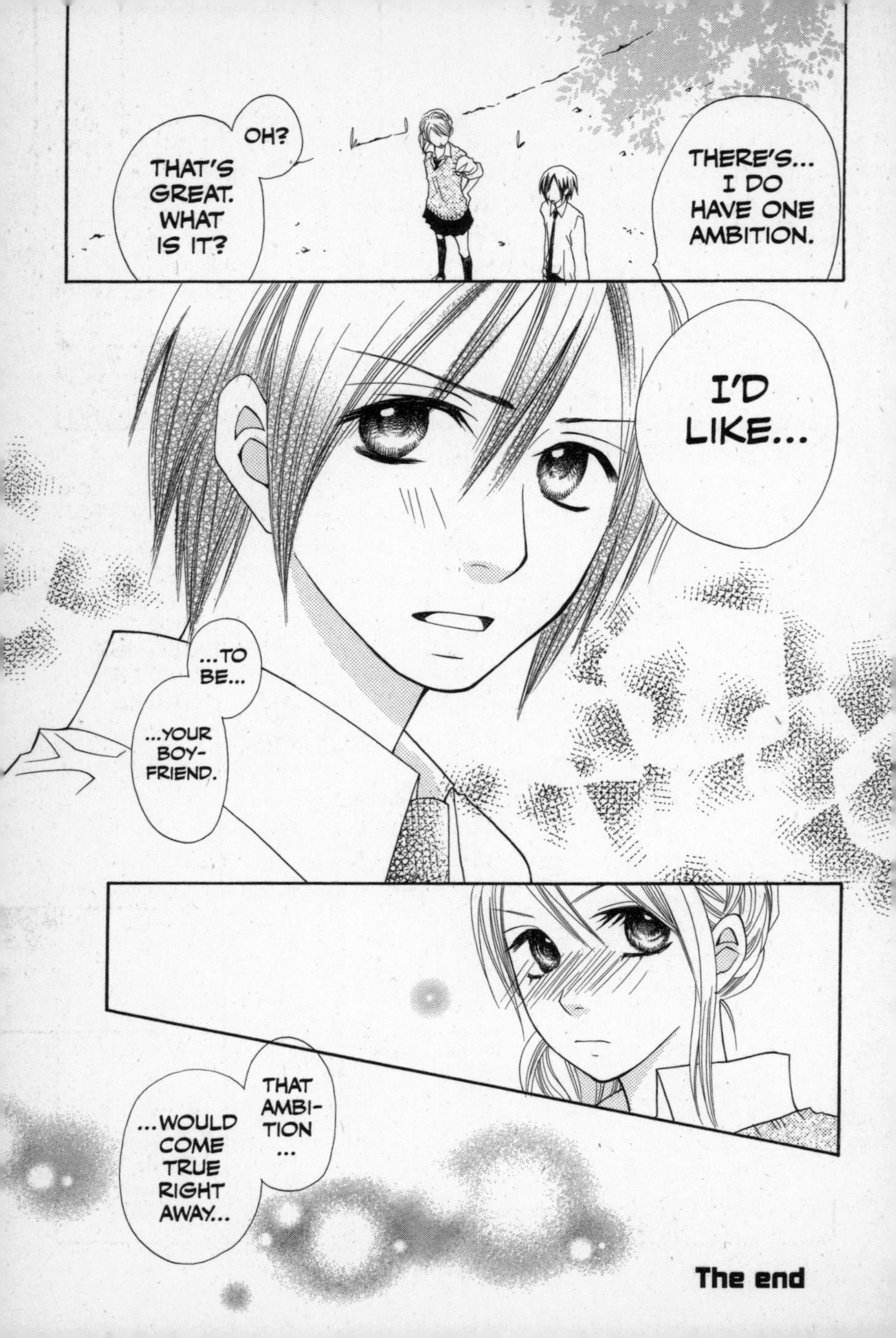
THERE'S... I DO HAVE ONE AMBITION.
OH? THAT'S GREAT. WHAT IS IT?
I'D LIKE...
...TO BE...
...YOUR BOY-FRIEND.
THAT AMBI-TION...
...WOULD COME TRUE RIGHT AWAY...
The end

This concludes **MV**.
Please forgive the scribble, but since this is the last volume,
I wanted to handwrite it. Please bear with me.

I started this series with the resolve to create two strong,
capable characters.
My last series was about baseball, and I realized that when there
are a lot of characters, the amount of drawing involved is so
extreme that many things get blurred over.
In the end, the number of characters I used this time increased,
but I think I was able to handle it, since I mainly focused on the
main two.
The last volume did follow up with all of the characters, but I really
was able to keep it to a minimum. This manga was really about the
two primary characters, and I think it worked. Though I'm still
learning...

Many wonderful things came out of doing **MV**. But at the same
time, there were also many rough patches. I mean, really, a lot!
So many that I lost the energy to watch baseball! And so (?) it
wasn't a feeling of "I'm so sad" that accompanied my completion
of this series, but "I'm glad I was able to finish it."
Still, although I don't feel exactly sad that **MV** is over, I feel very
sad that I'm not working on a manga now.
I'm sure I'll happily go through tough times again to create
another manga.
M...? Margaret...?
I'll be happy if you read my next manga too.

And finally, since I was able to make it this far, thanks to all of you
who read this manga. Yes, you!
Thank you so much.
I'm also grateful to everyone who was involved with this work.

--Ayumi Komura, August 2007

Side Dish—End Notes

For those who want to know a little more about the menu.

Page 28
Hanayu:
Hanayu's name references a type of yuzu citrus fruit.
Ashitaba:
A medicinal, celery-like plant that thrives in volcanic soil. Its name literally means "tomorrow leaf" and is purported to have an incredible amount of anti-oxidants.

Page 30, author notes:
Mt. Sakurajima
Volcano in Kyushu.

Page 54: Hayato uri
Known elsewhere as chayote, this summer squash has thick, prickly skin and firm flesh.

Page 69, panel 3:
Tamagoyaki
A Japanese omelet made by rolling several layers of cooked egg together. It can have either a soft or firm texture. Sushi restaurants are often judged by the quality of their tamagoyaki.

Page 82
Kaya no mi:
Japanese nutmeg from the Japanese *Torreya* evergreen tree.
Aoi:
When combined with the character *yama* (part of Aoi's last name), the two characters together can be read "wasabi," which is a spicy green paste made from Japanese horseradish root and often served with sushi.
Boku:
In Japanese, using *boku* as the equivalent of the English "me" can have a childish, innocent, or deferential nuance. Older males often use the alternatives *ore* or *watashi*.

Page 84, author notes:
S••bata Asuka
A fellow manga artist.

Page 108: Ishinagi/Isaki
Two kinds of Japanese fish.

Page 110, author notes:
Oshiruko
Sweet Japanese soup or porridge made from red beans (*azuki*).

Page 134
Kan/Tachibana:
Kan means "citrus" and *Tachibana* means "mandarin orange."
Natsume:
Jujube or Chinese date.

Page 160
Karin:
A fruit related to the quince that is often used to flavor Japanese throat lozenges.
Kosui:
An Asian pear that is crisp, juicy and very sweet with no trace of tartness. In Japanese, kosui means "good water."

Page 162, author notes:
Ashitaba Aojiru
A green health drink made from the medicinal ashitaba plant.

Page 192
Anise:
A flowering plant with a flavor similar to black licorice, fennel and tarragon.

Page 199, author notes:
Gochisosama deshita
This is said after eating to express appreciation for a meal. It is like saying, "Thank you, it was delicious."

This is the last volume of *MV*!
Many issues came up in the process, but I'm glad to have worked on this manga series.
Thank you very much. *Gochisosama deshita*!

-Ayumi Komura

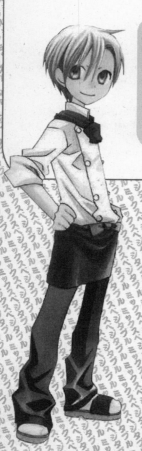

Ayumi Komura was born in Kagoshima Prefecture. Her favorite number is 22, and her hobbies include watching baseball. Her previous title is *Hybrid Berry*, about a high school girl who ends up posing as a boy on her school's baseball team.

MIXED VEGETABLES
VOL. 8
Shojo Beat Edition

STORY AND ART BY
AYUMI KOMURA

English Translation/JN Productions
English Adaptation/Stephanie V.W. Lucianovic
Touch-up Art & Lettering/Jim Keefe
Design/Yukiko Whitley
Editor/Megan Bates

VP, Production/Alvin Lu
VP, Sales & Product Marketing/Gonzalo Ferreyra
VP, Creative/Linda Espinosa
Publisher/Hyoe Narita

Printed in Canada

Published by VIZ Media, LLC
P.O. Box 77010
San Francisco, CA 94107

10 9 8 7 6 5 4 3 2 1
First printing, July 2010

www.viz.com   www.shojobeat.com

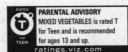